Operation Vengeance

Operation Vengeance

ALSO BY DAN HAMPTON

Nonfiction

Chasing the Demon

The Flight

The Hunter Killers

Lords of the Sky

Viper Pilot

Fiction

The Mercenary

Operation Vengeance

The Astonishing Aerial Ambush That Changed World War II

Dan Hampton

HARPER LARGE PRINT

An Imprint of HarperCollins*Publishers*

Maps by Nick Springer/Springer Cartographics LLC

HarperCollins books may be purchased for educational, business, or sales promotional use. For information, please e-mail the Special Markets Department at SPsales@harpercollins.com.

FIRST HARPER LARGE PRINT EDITION

ISBN: 978-0-06-300020-9

Library of Congress Cataloging-in-Publication Data is available upon request.

20 21 22 23 24   LSC   10 9 8 7 6 5 4 3 2 1

Contents

Part Two

Part Three

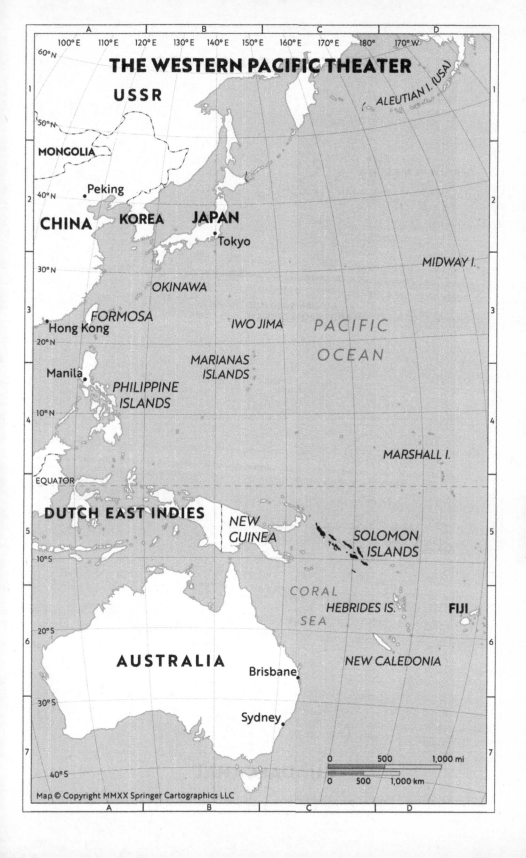

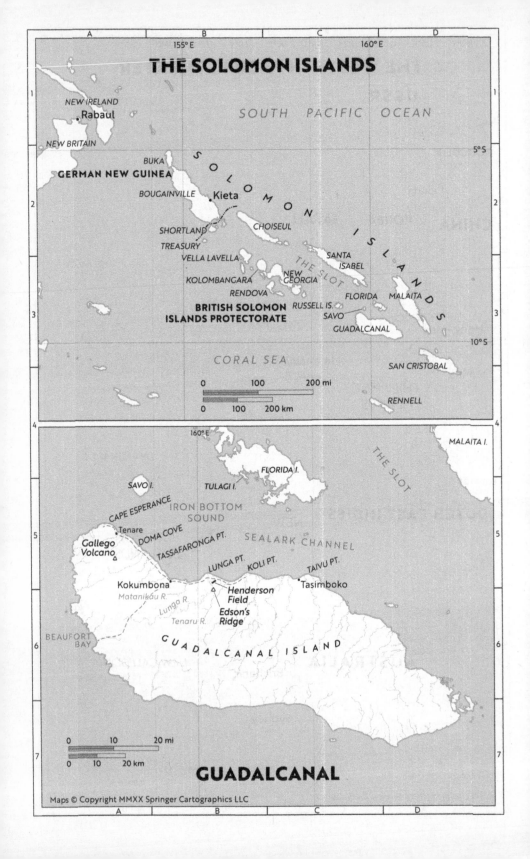

THE SOLOMON ISLANDS

SOUTH PACIFIC OCEAN

NEW IRELAND
Rabaul

NEW BRITAIN

BUKA
GERMAN NEW GUINEA

BOUGAINVILLE   Kieta

SOLOMON ISLANDS

SHORTLAND   CHOISEUL
TREASURY
VELLA LAVELLA   SANTA
                                      ISABEL
KOLOMBANGARA   NEW
                              GEORGIA
RENDOVA   FLORIDA   MALAITA
BRITISH SOLOMON   RUSSELL IS.
ISLANDS PROTECTORATE   SAVO
                                  GUADALCANAL

THE SLOT

CORAL SEA   SAN CRISTOBAL

RENNELL

0   100   200 mi

0   100   200 km

GUADALCANAL

MALAITA I.

SAVO I.   FLORIDA I.

TULAGI I.

CAPE ESPERANCE   IRON BOTTOM
                              SOUND
Tenare
DOMA COVE   SEALARK CHANNEL

Gallego   TASSAFARONGA PT.
Volcano
                    LUNGA PT.   KOLI PT.   TAIVU PT.

Kokumbona   Tasimboko
Matanikau R.   Henderson
Lunga R.   Field
         Tenaru R.   Edson's
                        Ridge

BEAUFORT   GUADALCANAL ISLAND
BAY

THE SLOT

0   10   20 mi

0   10   20 km

Author's Note

"Time passes," Marcel Proust once wrote, "and little by little everything that we have spoken in false-hood becomes true."

This was certainly the case for those who flew Operation VENGEANCE on the morning of April 18, 1943. During the years following World War II, those who survived wished only to pick up the pieces of their lives, and return to some sense of normalcy. Consequently, there was little interest in revisiting the very near past with its painful memories, and events that might have been recorded with stark clarity were not. Those involved were fighting a war under the worst conditions, and had little time for journals even if they had the inclination. They were too busy staying alive to give much thought to posterity and, indeed, thinking of the future is a dangerous preoccupation in combat.

Historically, the significance of Admiral Isoroku Yamamoto's death is staggering, and has evolved into a vicious, seventy-seven-year-old debate over who killed the architect of the December 1941 sneak attack on Pearl Harbor that propelled the United States into World War II. Tens of thousands of American lives were saved from battles that were never fought, and the deadliest conflict in human history was considerably shortened. Our present world would be greatly altered if the United States had not achieved total victory from that war, and an enormous piece of this credit belongs to one extraordinary American fighter pilot. Both Captain Tom Lanphier and Lieutenant Rex Barber were awarded partial credit for this feat, sparking a bitter feud that continues today among their various supporters. Lanphier, in particular, vociferously defended his actions because his postwar political ambitions were founded on the claim that he alone destroyed "the most hated man in America."

Unfortunately, existing military reports, when written at all, tended toward the terse, brief style favored by men short of paper, who despised typewriters and were quite rightly more concerned with surviving another day than with composition. This left me a few solid, uncontestable points such as timing, routes of flight, and the names and characters of those involved. There was much to overcome here as various falsehoods had become "fact" in the decades following the war. Nonetheless, a number of men who were part of the mission, or in the Pacific Theater at the time, emerged to tell the truth. Men who had made peace with their ghosts and were now in a position to ultimately set the record straight. Regrettably, they were not aided by the government or military in this endeavor, as both organizations are loath to challenge, refute, or amend their own official records.

Official reality is not always the same as the truth, and this was certainly the case with the Yamamoto mission. Lamentably, as of this printing, rightful credit is still being withheld from the two men who deserve it, and the truth of the matter largely relegated to obscurity. In a land that prizes honor, especially on the battlefield, this will not suffice. Based on primary data, unpublished interviews with survivors, and substantial original research, I have summarized the historical context, accurately reconstructed the mission and the attack, and mathematically proven which pilot actually killed Isoroku Yamamoto.

My purpose for entering the situation is to ensure that those pilots who risked so much, and materially shortened the Pacific War by their actions, receive the long-overdue personal recognition and official accolades they merit for their valor. Perhaps Sophocles said it best: "The long unmeasured pulse of time moves everything. There is nothing hidden that it cannot bring to light."

I truly hope so.

Dan Hampton
Vail, Colorado

Foreword

by Rex Barber Jr. and Rex Barber III

How do you say the right thing about someone you knew as Dad or Grandpa but who also had a part in changing world history? A farm kid from Culver, Oregon, Rex Barber did what so many of the Greatest Generation did. He volunteered for service, went to combat, and just did his job.

Mission day was in all likelihood a suicide mission. I have often wondered what was going through Rex's mind as he turned his P-38 to attack the bomber with six Zeros above and behind him, diving to attack in a desperate attempt to save Yamamoto. Then as Rex passed over the smoking bomber, three of the Zeros were on his tail, putting fifty-two bullets into his plane. I'm sure he was mad that he had to try to escape rather than fight. I'm also sure that he had confidence in his training, his plane, his skill, and his mother's prayers. The cockpit was most likely filled with profanity, interspersed with prayer! Odd, you might say, unless you have experienced combat.

Rex's love of flying started early, listening to his uncle Edgar's stories about flying in France in World War I. Uncle Edgar was known to embellish a story. . . . Regardless, it planted the seed in Rex's mind, and as a boy, he jumped off the family barn with a makeshift parachute, and broke his arm. It was an inauspicious beginning to a remarkable flying career. Having flown in a Beech Bonanza with Rex after his retirement, it was obvious that he was a part of the plane, confident in his ability, and smooth in his touch on the stick.

History is often an odd web. Yamamoto and all of Japan were hated in the United States after Pearl Harbor. Yet growing up, Rex had a Japanese American classmate, "Doc" Akiyama, whom he helped save after Doc fell and broke his back while they were fishing in the rugged Crooked River Canyon in 1940. Three years later, Doc and his family were in an internment camp and Rex was looking over his shoulder at smoke coming out of the jungle on Bougainville. In another place and time, Yamamoto would have been a friend. There were many common interests; bridge, poker and a good wager, and love of country. I believe Yamamoto would have played bridge like Rex . . . bid no-trump if you can because of the finesse required to make it work.

Whether you were lucky enough to sit in his lap at five years old and hear this account of history firsthand, or you are hearing it now, the man known as Rex, Sir, Colonel, Coach, Friend, and Hero was truly part of the Greatest Generation. Thank you, Dad, Grandpa.

Operation Vengeance

Prologue

April 18, 1943
The South Pacific

A bead of sweat rolled down the fighter pilot's face. Gathering momentum, it furrowed a light stripe over his cheekbone, down around his mouth, and, when it could go no farther, the bead hung suspended from the end of his stubbled chin. Stretching until gravity triumphed, it dropped onto a narrow strip map on the man's left thigh and splattered across a blue area marked "SOLOMON SEA." Though it wasn't yet 7 A.M., man and machine were already draped in a thick blanket of wet heat. Condensation made the metal surfaces of the cockpit clammy, and the control wheel was slick with moisture.

Cracked and taped, the patched leather seat cushion had lost its firmness months earlier and now stank of mildew and heavy jungle funk. Everything stank; smoke from the cooking fires mixed with decaying vegetation, metal from the aircraft, and occasionally a whiff from the open-air latrines. It could be worse. There was no cloying reek from dead flesh, or the acrid stench of burned hair that hung over the island when Lieutenant Rex Barber had arrived four months earlier. Three months and twenty-eight days, to be exact.

The local people called this place Isatabu, and the few maps around said it was Guadalcanal. The American military universally referred to it as "the Shithole," or in calmer moments simply "the Canal." Today was Easter Sunday, April 18, 1943, but Rex, along with every other man stuck here, hated the island with a passion, and was having no religious thoughts whatsoever. Pushing against the rudder pedals, the pilot raised his butt off the cushion and tugged a small lever that raised the seat a bit. Looking out at the wings, then around to the tail, he cycled the flight controls, and watched everything move. Satisfied, Barber flipped the shoulder straps across his chest with practiced ease, threaded the canvas loops through the lap belt, then locked the whole thing loosely around his midsection.

Glancing around at the familiar switches, he checked that the BATTERY and MASTER SWITCH were off, set the mixture controls, and bumped both red-handled throttles a half inch forward in preparation for starting the engines. With his eyes shut the lieutenant could touch any toggle, lever, or button he wished; constant combat created that kind of intimacy. In a dogfight, there was no time for groping around the cockpit. Despite the early hour Rex already felt sweat run down between his shoulder blades and gather at his belt. The seat of his khaki pants was also damp, but he ignored all this.

This morning was too important.

Leaning forward, Rex pulled the wheel back and the control column brushed against his outer right calf. The Lockheed P-38 was the only fighter he had flown that did not have a stick, and the cumbersome column-wheel arrangement was odd in a fighter that was otherwise magnificent. Still, nothing was ever perfect. Barber normally flew number 125, which he had named *Diablo*, but it was down for maintenance, so today he had *Miss Virginia*, number 147, courtesy of Lieutenant Bob Petit. With the big wheel tucked against his chest, Rex leaned forward and checked the top of the main switch box to ensure all the lights, starters, and primers were off. The BATTERY was last in the row, and though it was obviously off he tapped it anyway.

Farthest left on the panel was a round plate with a pair of two-inch magneto levers, one for each engine, that he wriggled to make certain they were also both in the OFF position. Directly above the magnetos at the top of the plate was the rectangular MASTER switch that would, with the battery, power up all the electrical systems. It also was plainly in OFF position, but he touched it as well. Dropping his right hand down to the front of the panel, Barber ran his finger along another row of switches, tapping the two guarded covers for his generators. He did the same for the five switches mounted behind the control wheel, making certain that his cannon, machine guns, and, most important, the MASTER ARMAMENT switch, were all off. Easing the column forward Rex rolled his left forearm slightly to see the watch that he, like most pilots, wore with its face on the inside of the wrist.

0650: it was time to begin.

Leaning over the rolled-down left window he saw the crew chief looking up expectantly. No one but the pilots was supposed to know that today's mission was anything but an ordinary combat patrol, yet everyone *did* know. There were more idlers standing around, and the ground crews were snappier, their eyes bright and not from the fever that raged across the island. It was, Barber knew, a chance for them to really feel like they made a difference in this war. Not that they didn't do that every day as far as he was concerned, but today was special. Pilots got to hit back every day, killing the enemy and often being killed, but at least they got to fight. Rex had been here since December 1942 and could well appreciate the ground crew's frustration.

The crew chief put his hands on the left prop and stared at the pilot, who raised his left arm, gave a thumbs-up, then made an exaggerated circle with his left index finger. The man pulled the prop once, then again, and stepped back about ten feet. Nodding, Barber flipped the BATTERY and MASTER switches forward to the on positions, then watched the fuel-quantity gauge needles jump, so there was good power to the plane. Glancing down at the floor left of the seat, he confirmed both fuel tank selectors were in MAIN, then Rex cycled the fuel boost pump switches just behind them. Leaning forward to the bulkhead forward of the MIXTURE controls he reset the electric propellers by depressing two small circuit breakers, then flipped back the red guarded cover over the LEFT generator switch. Directly above it, the ammeter needle instantly swung right. The electrical system was good. Turning on the booster pump, Barber glanced at his watch, saw the second hand tick upward, and knew it was time to start engines.

Rex reached to the floor between his legs, pushed the black, oval-shaped ENGINE PRIMER knob, then turned it ninety degrees left. After pumping twice, he reached around the wheel to the MAIN SWITCH BOX panel with his right hand and put a finger on the LEFT starter switch. Leaning sideways and looking down, he got a nod and thumbs-up from the chief, a young sergeant wearing ragged khaki who was waiting expectantly in front of the left engine. His eyes were fixed on the pilot, sharp and alert, even though Barber knew the ground crews had worked all night attaching a newly arrived 310-gallon drop tank under one wing, and the normal 165-gallon tank beneath the other. They were absolutely essential for today's mission.

Nodding in return, Rex twirled his left hand above his head again then toggled the starter switch aft. The big three-bladed Curtiss-Electric propeller lurched once . . . twice . . . then began to spin. The fighter rocked as the powerful twelve-cylinder Allison sputtered to life, belching out a cloud of blue-black exhaust that slowly drifted toward the tails, and the smell of burnt fuel momentarily smothered the island's stink. Eyeballing the vibrating engine gauges, the lieutenant adjusted the left throttle, then repeated the process to start the right engine. With both engines idling normally at 1,000 RPM, he set the parking brake and flashed another thumbs-up to the crew chief.

Smoothly advancing the left mixture control to AUTO-RICH, Rex watched the engine revolutions stabilize. As he bumped the throttle forward a half inch to hold 1,000 RPM, the vibration stopped and he exhaled. It was a good start. *Miss Virginia* was up and running. Quickly working his way through the same procedure for the right engine, Rex then tugged his chinstrap and wriggled the flying helmet down closer to his ears. Switching on the radio, he winced as static crackled though the earphones. Quickly turning the volume down, Rex tuned to the briefed common frequency each pilot would monitor today, though no one would speak until they reached the target some four hundred miles away. Methodically working his way around the cockpit, he tested the fuel warning light and checked gauges. Peering at the attitude indicator Rex then tapped the compass to free the needle. Outside, the crew chief had vanished. Rex knew the man was checking for any leaks and closing up panels. Glancing left and right, he saw puffs of blue smoke drifting overhead from the other fighters, and the dull roaring of thirty-six engines filled the air.

Eighteen P-38 Lightnings.

And eighteen Army Air Corps pilots, mostly young lieutenants with one captain. The only two field-grade officers were Major Lou Kittel, the 12th Fighter Squadron commander, who had agreed to split the pilots and the planes with Major John Mitchell's own 339th Fighter Squadron, and Mitchell himself. A compactly built, intense combat veteran with eight aerial kills to his name, Mitchell was the Army's leading ace on Guadalcanal and today's mission commander. The sixteen primary planes, plus two spares, were divided into two groups: three flights of four fighters who would provide top cover against any Japanese fighters, and one flight of four Lightnings led by Captain Tom Lanphier, who would do the hunting. Rex was with this latter four-ship flight, and his job today was to break through whatever opposition existed, which promised to be heavy indeed, and kill the target. A target that was the solitary, vital objective of this raid, and one so critical that eighteen officers were cheerfully volunteering their own lives to destroy it: at all costs.

For a minute his eyes and hands darted around the cockpit; oil, coolant, inverters—everything was fine. With his left hand, Rex touched both four-way fuel selectors on the floor by his seat, wriggling each toggle to make certain it was locked in the RES position; he always took off and flew fifteen minutes feeding from the reserve tanks just be sure they functioned, but today would be a bit different. Today after takeoff each pilot would feed from the extra underwing tanks first to make certain they were working: five minutes from the smaller 150-gallon tank, then the rest of the inbound route from the 300-gallon tank until it was dry. The idea was to reach the target, jettison the externals, and have plenty of internal fuel for fighting and the return to Guadalcanal.

Finally, he flipped the gunsight on, adjusted the rheostat to full bright, then turned it off. Reappearing from beneath the right wingtip and angling backward to avoid the spinning prop, the crew chief stopped just past the nose. Catching Barber's eye, he nodded and flashed a thumbs-up, which he held until Rex returned the gesture. Glancing at the bottom right of the panel, the pilot checked the hydraulics then stuck both arms out sideways from the cockpit and fluttered his hands. Nodding again, the chief squatted down on the steel matting to watch as Rex cycled the flight controls. Looking left and right at the ailerons, he then turned around and checked each rudder. Satisfied, Barber sat back in the seat. Smoothing out the map on his right leg, he eased the kneeboard on his left leg into a better position. It was a good place to be, here in the cockpit of a fighter he knew so well. The powerful throbbing from both engines was comforting; everything was set as he liked it; he was ready.

Jeeps bounced past, a few with pilots riding on the hood, but most carrying ground crewmen to other fighters dispersed around the field. Now there were P-40 Warhawks of the 68th Fighter Squadron, P-39 Airacobras of the 67th Fighter Squadron, and the 339th Fighter Squadron's remaining Lightnings. The pilots were dressed haphazardly; a few wore one-piece coveralls, and others were in various bits of khaki—all were thin, and their shoes were caked with mud. Mud was everywhere, even now, but Rex knew it had been much, much worse back in August 1942, when the first planes arrived.

There had only been one airfield then, and it was the primary reason for the American invasion. Henderson Field, as it was quickly named, lay less than two miles away to the east on the relatively flat ground of the old Lever Brothers plantation.* Fighter Two, where Rex now sat, was also known as Kukum Field and was the

---

* Named in honor of Marine Major Russell Lofton, commander of Marine Scout Bombing Squadron 241, who perished on June 4, 1942, during an attack on the Japanese Fleet carrier *Hiryū* during the Battle of Midway.

northernmost of Guadalcanal's three airstrips. Just west of Lunga Point directly on the coast, it was framed on the northeast side by the Lunga River, on the southwest by the Ilu River, and to the north by the Sealark Channel. As the name implied, Fighter Two was built for fighter aircraft, with construction continuing unabated during the ground battles, naval bombardment, and sniper attacks.

When Rex had arrived on the Canal four days before Christmas 1942, the field was nearly completed. It was opened for aircraft in January. The 6th Naval Construction Battalion had built this strip, some 4,000 feet long and 150 feet wide, properly: a metal tray layered with crushed coral, topped with gravel, and finally surfaced with pierced steel planking known as Marston matting. The ten-foot-by-fifteen-inch, 66-pound steel planks were punched with holes to keep the weight down, and fastened together with hooks and slots. Pilots loved Marston mats, and Rex was no exception. Without it there was only mud, or at best, gravel on forward airstrips. Henderson had been like that during the fall of 1942, so operating an Army P-38, which weighed at least twice as much as the Navy F4F Wildcat, on a soggy, cratered surface was problematic.

Engine noises around him changed to a higher pitch, and Rex saw the first Lightning, with a faded "110" stenciled on the nose, ease forward from its revetment and jolt slightly as the pilot tested the brakes. John Mitchell had been on the Canal since early October 1942, and survived the ugly early days under some of the worst conditions. Like most pilots, Mitch, as he was known behind his back, had named his plane, and as it taxied slowly past, the word *Squinch* was plain to see above the number. Though the runway was covered with matting, some of the taxiways were not, and Mitchell's habit was to keep the engine revolutions low to avoid throwing up rock and coral. One by one, three other fighters crawled forward in the order Mitchell briefed; Lieutenant Julius "Jake" Jacobson was Mitchell's wingman with Lieutenants Doug Canning and Delton Goerke flying as Numbers Three and Four.

Rex held his arms straight up then gestured with both thumbs out for the crew chief to pull the wheel chocks. A second man yanked out the big wooden blocks from both main tires and scurried sideways from under the left wing. Holding the brakes with his feet, Barber watched the neighboring P-38 lurch ahead, the nose bobbing slightly as Captain Tom Lanphier in *Phoebe*, number 122, tapped his brakes and pulled out to follow Goerke.

With his left hand on the throttle, Rex twirled his right forefinger in the air above the cockpit. Backing up slowly, the crew chief nodded, and waved him forward with both arms. Nudging the throttle levers up slowly, *Miss Virginia* crept ahead and Rex felt the coral crunching slightly under the steel matting. After checking the brakes, he swung into line after Lanphier and trailed the others west down the taxiway. Lieutenants Jim McLanahan and Joe Moore, the other two Lightnings in the Killer flight, pulled out behind him, followed by two more flights of four. Though Barber couldn't see them, he knew from the brief that two spares flown by Lieutenants Besby Holmes and Ray Hine were at the end of the line.

Coconut trees separated the beach from Fighter Two, and they were swaying in the constant breeze as the P-38s taxied to the west end of the runway. The weather was clear now, but Rex Barber knew very well that this would likely change in the afternoon. Looking across to the south side of the runway, he could see the hillside next to the jungle where he and the others lived: Strafer Heights, they called it, in honor of the early Army P-400 fighter pilots who saved countless Marine lives by strafing the Japanese near the Lunga River. Doug Canning, who had been part of it, said they strafed so much that the rifling in the .50-caliber guns wore out and the bullets made a wild, circular pattern on their way down.

With its tricycle-type landing gear, taxiing the P-38 was considerably easier than the other "tail dragger" planes he had flown. Visibility was perfect from ten feet above the ground, and there was no need to S-turn just to see ahead. Barber set the aircraft clock with his own watch, which had been synchronized with Major Mitchell's at the morning brief. At the top of the control yoke he twisted the aileron trim to neutral, then reached down to the left bulkhead and rolled the elevator trim to zero. Up ahead, John Mitchell's fighter swung sideways next to the runway, tail facing the beach, and the others all followed suit.

Pulling up next to his flight lead, Rex set the parking brake and looked to the right. Lanphier's *Phoebe* was beautiful, like all the Lightnings; four Japanese flags stenciled on her nose just beneath the guns. Nearly thirty-eight feet from nose to tail, the long, tapering twin booms and graceful nose gave it the unmistakable look of a dragonfly. A dragonfly with a deadly sting, compliments of the four nose-mounted Browning M2 .50-caliber guns and single Hispano 20 mm cannon. As the three stenciled Japanese flags on Barber's own *Diablo* proudly proclaimed, they were the last things many of the enemy ever saw. *Miss Virginia* sported two such flags for Rob Petit's air-to-air kills, and the outline of a Japanese ship that he sank.

Rhythmic throbbing suddenly changed to a powerful roar as Lanphier ran up his engines for a final check. All down the line the fighters did the same, each nose compressing from the combined force of nearly 3,000 horses trying to pull the wings off. Leaning forward, he held the yoke in the crook of his right arm, then nudged the left throttle forward until the white RPM needle reached 2,300 at the top of the gauge. Manifold pressure and oil temperature were both solidly in the green and the electrical system checked good, so, leaving the throttle where it was, he reached around to the magnetos. In the BOTH position they stuck out like wings, and he clicked the left switch up, which turned off the right magneto. Just as they should, the revolutions on the left engine dropped a hair and Rex did the same for the second mag before carefully switching back to the BOTH position. He then checked the propeller governor, pulled the left throttle back, and repeated everything for the right engine.

Eyes flickering around the cockpit, Rex was satisfied that everything was ready. Cranking up both side windows, he checked that the ratchet locked them in place and looked left at Jim McLanahan's Lightning. The other pilot was also looking left down the line, waiting for the thumbs-up to be passed back up the line from the last aircraft. McLanahan suddenly twisted right and raised his fist; Rex nodded, turned to his right, and passed the signal to Tom Lanphier. When it reached Mitchell he pulled his four P-38s onto Runway 06, heading northeast, and waited for the tower signal. All eighteen fighters were ready, and each man sat in his compact, confined little world with a few moments for thought. Each time was different, and each time could be the last. Fighter pilots fly, fight, and die alone without the close luxury of an infantry platoon, or hundreds of buddies on a ship. Whether air-to-air or some sort of ground attack, the fighting is very personal, directed at each pilot and plane.

At precisely 0710 a green light began flashing from the midfield control tower. Flares, though common enough in peacetime, were not used here since the Japanese shot off flares before they attacked. Normally there would be some radio calls, but not today. The major had briefed absolute radio silence, and for good reason. There were too many listening ears. As Mitchell released his brakes, rolled forward, and accelerated down the runway, Rex checked that his flaps were up, the coolant and oil shutters were open, and, from long habit, switched on his weapons. Around here, anyone could be jumped by a Japanese pilot at any time, though that was becoming rare this close to home. Following Lanphier to the end, the last thing Rex did before taxiing onto the runway was pull the canopy down and lock it. Wriggling down in the seat, Barber swung the fighter left, rolling slowly ahead as his leader's plane surged down the runway. Twin dust clouds billowed back, and as Lanphier picked up speed Barber slid his own throttles forward. Both Allisons roared and he felt the familiar mix of excitement, pride, and slight touch of fear that came with every takeoff. Rex moved his feet reflexively to keep *Miss Virginia* pointed straight down the runway, just as he would on any other routine flight, but he knew that this mission was very, very different. This time they were going to kill a man. The most hated man in America.

PART ONE

". . . it is not enough that we take Guam and the Philippines, nor even Hawaii and San Francisco. To make victory certain, we would have to march into Washington and dictate the terms of peace in the White House."

ADMIRAL ISOROKU YAMAMOTO

PART ONE

"...It is not enough that we take Guam and the Philippines, nor even Hawaii and San Francisco. To make victory certain, we would have to march into Washington and dictate the terms of peace in the White House."

—ADMIRAL ISOROKU YAMAMOTO

One
Cauldron

One hot day in the summer of 1928, a stocky, dark-haired eleven-year-old boy balanced carefully on the roof of his family's barn and peered cautiously over the edge. Rex Theodore Barber had purposely chosen the back of the barn, facing away from the house and its surrounding poplars, to avoid being seen by his mother or sisters. Here, east of the looming Cascade Mountains, a flat river valley stuck up like a green thumb into the Columbia Plateau. Small hamlets followed the Deschutes River to the north, where it collided into the fast-flowing Columbia just east of the Dalles.

The barn, the boy, and the roof were on a hundred-acre farm just outside the tiny town of Culver in central Oregon. About midway up the Deschutes Valley, the town was framed between Round Butte to the north,

Juniper Butte to the south, and to the east by the vast, open Columbia Plateau. It is beautiful, open country laced with racing, icy streams filled with trout, steelhead, and salmon. Adventurous youngsters could find duck or geese along the rivers, with ample pheasant and quail out on the Marginals to the east.* As they had for generations of Paiutes, Modoc, or Umatilla Indians, the wide skies fostered superb eyesight for Rex and other boys who roamed the canyons, sagebrush, sweeping plains, or lonely mountains. East of the river the broken hills and thick forests were ideal for exploring, camping, and, if one knew where to hunt, for elk, deer, and even an elusive bighorn sheep.

Rex and his friends often rode horses across the flats and down into the narrow, dangerous gorge west of his house. The Crooked River flowed fast, deep, and cold through its gorge, but the boy never hesitated. He knew all the ways across, every splashing path through the clear water then up the rocky bank on the other side. There was steep ground here, but he could cut through a saddle in the cliffs and be on the banks of the Deschutes in no time. In the summer, Rex often

---

* So named due to their limited utility. Hit hard by the 1930s droughts, the Marginals were bought up by the U.S. government and even today are of scant agricultural value.

vanished alone into the rough wild country west of the river for days on end, camping, hunting, and exploring. This type of life bred stamina, self-reliance, and a resolute fearlessness that remained with him all his life.

It was the perfect place to be a boy.

This day was warm for Oregon, and dry: perfect for tending his family's wheat fields, which is what he was supposed to be doing, and was quite deliberately avoiding with characteristically stubborn mischievousness. But at this moment, Rex Barber was completely focused on the job at hand: he was going to fly. Well, float, actually, from the roof of his family barn to the grass thirty feet below, but he would be in the air and that was what counted. His uncle Edgar's solemn tales of piloting biplanes and the Great War always thrilled the boy, and now it was his chance to be free of the ground, even if just for a few seconds, and to fly! Carefully constructing a parachute from a pair of his mother's sheets, Rex carefully reinforced them by stitching the corners together.

Fortunately, his father, William Chauncey, disdained the use of modern farm equipment and harbored a special hatred for tractors, so there were coils of leather plow lines in the barn. Rex, like all boys, was an expert with knots; he used his best at each corner, tightly securing the leather traces, and had completed what he considered a fully functional parachute. Tying all four ends to his belt, two per side, Rex carried the parachute over his shoulders up and through the hayloft. This, he decided, was not nearly high enough, so he continued on up through the rafters and out a vent onto the roof. Though quite fearless, he was also methodical, and thoroughly checked his knots one final time. The boy glanced at the weathervane atop the nearby cupola, then he took a deep breath and jumped into the wind.

It didn't work out quite the way he had imagined.

The sheets caught the breeze all right, and thanks to the unbreakable knots successfully yanked the boy completely off the gabled roof. Unfortunately he didn't glide; he didn't even float. But he did fall, and learned a brief, valuable lesson about gravity in the process. A broken arm did not dampen his enthusiasm for flying, but twelve years would pass before he had the chance to fly again, this time under vastly different circumstances. Twelve years that saw events unfold that led to the Second World War; a global cataclysm altering millions of lives, including Rex Barber's, that shaped the course of human history as we know it today.

Though the war physically commenced in Poland on September 1, 1939, a more accurate beginning, at least for Europe, could be fixed during the final days of June 1919, with the signing of the Treaty of Versailles. The official end to the Great War, the treaty forced territorial concessions in conjunction with vast, punitive reparations: 133 *billion* marks to be paid to the victors.

Perhaps worse for the proud Germans was Article 231, the so-called War Guilt Clause, which read: "The Allied and Associated Governments affirm and Germany accepts the responsibility of Germany and her allies for causing all the loss and damage to which the Allied and Associated Governments and their nationals have been subjected as a consequence of the war imposed upon them by the aggression of Germany and her allies."

It was a humiliating and shortsighted clause written to appease France in return for a reduction of reparations. This national insult, as it was perceived in Germany, coupled with crippling payments, military emasculation, and a faltering economy, contributed greatly to the rise of National Socialism and Adolf Hitler.

A similar grievance festered in Japan. The Empire was in its Taishō period, a brief span from 1912 through 1926 when an attempt at democracy occurred. If such a system produced the British Empire, the French Third Republic, and the United States, then perhaps it could also work for Japan. Though there was no doubt in the Japanese mind that their culture was superior, the struggle to reach technical parity with the West was at least a half-century old by that time, and led primarily by the military, which for centuries has been closely intertwined with Japanese life, government, and society, so to understand the Japanese one must grasp this aspect of Imperial culture.

For more than twelve hundred years various factions of the samurai class and their daimyo overlords fought interminably, resisted contact with the West, and ruled Japan as they wished. The daimyo, like Western dukes and earls, controlled huge tracts of land named "Domains" backed by personal armies of loyal samurai, or knights, who owed military service and allegiance in return for their own lands. At the top of this feudal food chain was the shogun, which translates as "Commander in Chief of the Expeditionary Force Against the Barbarians." This supreme military ruler, created during the Heian period in 784, became a hereditary position that relegated the emperor to figurehead status.

By 1846, when American commodore James Biddle anchored the USS *Vincennes* at the mouth of Edo Bay, power resided with the 15th Tokugawa Shogun. Biddle was contemptuously rebuffed and sailed away empty-handed, which reinforced Japanese's supreme confidence in their ability to deal with the West. The fallacy of this attitude was starkly revealed during the summer of 1853 when Commodore Matthew Perry, a very different type of naval officer, and his four "Black Ships" steamed into Edo Bay.* With his eight-inch Paixhans guns trained on the nearby town of Uraga, Perry gave the Tokugawa Shogunate its first taste of American-style gunboat diplomacy backed by shockingly superior technology. Brooking no nonsense behind the guns of the USS *Susquehanna,* Perry refused to leave, and blatantly conducted surveys of the port and coastline. The Japanese, who long regarded their warrior caste as invincible, were profoundly shaken by their complete inability to prevent this, so, with Perry's threat to return hanging over their heads, they reluctantly agreed to his unequivocal terms.

Within Japan, rival factions seized this opportunity to challenge the Shogunate and restore direct control of the nation to the emperor. This led to the seventeen-month Boshin Civil War between the Imperial samurai, mainly in the south and west, and

---

* Another USS *Vincennes* would meet the Japanese off Guadalcanal ninety-seven years later. With fine historical irony, another of Perry's ships was the sloop-of-war *Saratoga*. The next ship so named would become equally well known to the Japanese: the World War II aircraft carrier USS *Saratoga* (CV-3).

Shogunate samurai in the north. The Shogunate lost, and the emperor was restored as head of state in June 1869. Prince Mutsuhito, born the year before Perry's Black Ships arrived, ascended to the Chrysanthemum Throne as Emperor Meiji and immediately embarked on widespread reforms. This included the official dissolution of the samurai class, and an unprecedented period of military modernization, especially for the newly created Imperial Navy.*

Beginning with a four-gun yacht, courtesy of Queen Victoria, and an armed Dutch-built paddle wheel steamboat, the Imperial Navy received its first modern warship from the United States. In 1869 the USS *Stonewall*, a former Confederate ironclad armed with a 300-pounder Armstrong cannon, was delivered along with French naval experts who constructed the Yokosuka dockyard. The French also taught the Japanese how to design and build modern steel vessels, and over the next twenty years the Imperial Navy ordered more warships than any other force except the British Royal Navy.† There was suddenly a desperate need for men,

---

* This is a metonymic; the actual, physical throne is called the *Takamikura*.
† CSS *Stonewall* was built in Bordeaux, and renamed *Kōtetsu* after arriving in Japan.

who were available in large numbers as ordinary sailors, and especially for officers.

Following Meiji's reforms, many samurai, by virtue of their better education, became military officers and administrators. But those in the rural north, the former Shogunate, had fewer opportunities. Many of them became teachers. Sadayoshi Takano, a schoolmaster descended from the Echigo samurai clan, was such a man, and on a spring day in 1884 his wife, Mineko, gave birth to their sixth son in the tiny hamlet of Kushige along Honshu's northeastern coast. Sadayoshi named the child Isoroku, or "Fifty-Six," which was his age when the boy was born. The family soon thereafter moved to the larger city of Nagaoka in search of better opportunities.

Isoroku grew up so poor he wore straw sandals and cotton kimonos all year round, even when winter brought snow and freezing Russian wind across the Sea of Japan. The boy could not afford textbooks for school, so he laboriously hand-copied them under the feeble heat of a little charcoal brazier. A somewhat aloof and distant father, Sadayoshi Takano nonetheless taught Isoroku calligraphy and encouraged his visits to a local Christian missionary who taught the child basic English. During summers, the boy learned the sea: how to sail, handle a boat, and fish for mackerel or octopus.

Male children also took part in large-scale military maneuvers, which often involved upward of ten thousand boys divided into opposing forces and led by regular army officers in mock attacks. Several decades of the Meiji Restoration had seen unprecedented military growth in Japan as the empire strove to make up lost centuries of progress in a matter of years—and it did. Following victory in the 1895 First Sino-Japanese War, Tokyo capitalized on a national wave of pro-naval enthusiasm by further expanding its fleet of available warships. Aware that as a potential world power the empire might have to contend with lethal Western navies, the Japanese created and funded a "Six-Six Fleet" with six modern battleships and six new armored cruisers.

By 1900, at the age of sixteen, Isoroku Takano had discovered a lifelong passion for athletics, particularly gymnastics, and American-style baseball. Given his family's samurai heritage and having grown up fishing, swimming, and sailing, he naturally gravitated toward the navy. Scoring second out of three hundred applicants in December 1901, young Takano gained admittance to the prestigious Imperial Japanese Naval Academy on Etajima Island in Hiroshima Bay. Modeled after the harsh standards of Britain's Royal Navy, the Japanese academy emphasized gunnery, technical studies, and learning the sea rather than just ships. Women, tobacco, and alcohol were banned for cadets, and each summer culminated in a thirteen-hour swim. At least 10 percent of each class dropped out every year.

At five feet three inches, Isoroku was small, even for a Japanese male, but excessively tough and resourceful. Graduating seventh in his class in November 1904, he was just in time to join the armored cruiser *Nisshin* and fight under Admiral Togo during the Battle of Tsushima Strait, the decisive climax of the Russo-Japanese War. In May 1905, three hours before a formal declaration of war was delivered, Japanese naval forces attacked Russia's Far East Fleet at Port Arthur in southern China. The Russians promptly dispatched a major part of their Baltic Fleet, including eleven battleships, to destroy the upstart Asiatics. Admiral Zinovy Rozhestvensky chose to bring his forty-two-ship armada through the East China Sea en route to the Sea of Japan via Tsushima Strait, and it was here that Togo pounced.*

At the end of the battle, the Russian fleet had lost nine of eleven battleships, with 4,480 sailors killed in

---

* Tsushima Strait was also the origin of the kamikaze, the "divine wind" of a typhoon, which destroyed an invading Mongol fleet in 1281 off Hakata Bay.

action and another 5,917 captured. Against this the Imperial Navy lost three torpedo boats, 117 dead, and 583 wounded, including Ensign Takano. When *Nisshin*'s forward eight-inch gun barrel overheated during the battle, the weakened metal burst, and the flying fragments severed the index and middle fingers from Isoroku's left hand.* He spent two months in the hospital, then was granted medical leave for the summer with his proud family. The following decade was spent on training cruises throughout Asia, Australia, and the west coast of the United States. As the Great War in Europe approached, Isoroku's father died and according to tradition he was adopted by a fellow samurai who had no sons of his own. When the thirty-year-old newly promoted lieutenant commander took up a posting at Naval Headquarters, he formally assumed his new stepfather's surname and became Isoroku Yamamoto.

Tokyo declared war against Germany on August 23, 1914, just as the German First Army crashed into the British Expeditionary Force along the French-Belgian

---

* There are conflicting accounts of this and Isoroku himself believed, for years, that enemy shell fragments caused his wound but Agawa, a former Imperial naval officer himself, states that "one of *Nisshin*'s own guns burst."

border near Mons. Though it was allied with Great Britain and on relatively good terms with the United States and France, Japan's motives for joining the fight were largely opportunistic. Already seeking to expand and perennially short of resources, the Empire snatched up Germany's Pacific possessions in the Caroline, Marshall, and Marianas islands. Rightly figuring Berlin, London, and Washington were too far away and too disinterested for intervention, Japan then landed troops on the Shantung Peninsula in mainland China. It was a gamble, to be sure, but with devotion to the emperor and the absolute conviction of cultural superiority, gambling was also a Japanese national trait.

Despite its motives, the Empire did make material contributions to the Great War. At London's request, the Japanese took on any German or Austro-Hungarian naval raiders in Chinese waters, and even aided the British in suppressing a mutiny by an Indian Army unit based in Singapore.* In February 1917 the Imperial Japanese Navy also dispatched the Second Special Squadron, which included three cruisers and fourteen destroyers, to the Mediterranean for transport duties and antisubmarine patrols. These actions earned the Empire a permanent seat in the League of Nations, and

---

* The 1915 Sepoy Mutiny of the 5th Light Infantry.

there was little doubt in Japan that they were, at last, a Great Power on par with the West.

This opinion was definitely not shared by Britain, France, or the United States. Though there was no denying Japan's impressive rise from feudalism to modern industrialism, this meteoric ascension was also quite troubling given the weakness of other Asian nations and, more important, the vulnerable concentration of European colonial resources in Asia. The Malay Peninsula, dominated by Britain and protected by the great colonial bastion of Singapore, contained over half the world's supply of tin, and nearly 50 percent of its rubber. The Dutch East Indies was a rich treasure trove of quinine, essential for combating malaria, and some 20 percent of the world's oil. It was, in fact, these very resources that Japan desperately needed, but it dared not openly challenge the combined might of the Europeans and Americans.

Not yet, at least.

As with Germany, Japan's reasons for eventually risking war can be traced to the turbulence and confusion of the 1920s. Jazz, styles of dress, movies, and other aspects of American culture were eagerly adapted by the more cosmopolitan and educated Japanese, yet this assimilation was viewed as an erosion of traditional values by many of their traditional countrymen.

Though impressed by Western technology and some of its cultural attractions, there were many who distrusted Europe and especially the United States. Asia, Japanese imperialists fervently believed, should be controlled by Asians—specifically by Japan.

Despite Japan's participation in the Great War and impressive leap forward from medieval feudalism, the prevailing belief in military circles was that the West did not view Japan as a partner, an equal. Added to this were long-standing racial tensions, on both sides certainly, but better publicized in the United States. The discovery of gold in California triggered a heavy, late-nineteenth-century influx of Asians, predominantly Chinese, to California and the Pacific Northwest. The perceived racial threat posed by this prompted America's first immigration laws in 1882, and the formation of a Japanese and Korean Exclusion League just after the turn of the century. By 1906, the situation was so polarizing that the city of San Francisco segregated all Asian children attending public schools, and this caused great offense in Japan. To alleviate the tension, President Teddy Roosevelt worked out a so-called Gentleman's Agreement, through which Tokyo refused passports for unskilled Japanese laborers in return for California rescinding its school segregation policy.

As with most diplomatic solutions, this did not solve

the fundamental issues, but merely delayed the inevitable reckoning. By 1917, the United States had entered the war in Europe, and Congress, overriding President Woodrow Wilson's veto and citing national security concerns, passed the most restrictive immigration legislation to date. Some of the conditions were quite sensible: entry was banned for anyone who could not read at least thirty words in their native language; criminals, prostitutes, anarchists, and persons with contagious diseases were also denied entry.* But the act also created an Asiatic Barred Zone, which excluded anyone from a country on or adjacent to Asia and not owned by the United States. This manifestation of anti-Asian sentiment added fuel to the smoldering Japanese fire as it was viewed as prejudicial and discriminatory. Unfortunately, this would also provide the Empire with superficial justification to act as Asia's protector.†

By this time Yamamoto had graduated from the Naval War College and received a promotion to lieutenant commander. In 1917, the Germans began un-

---

* However, if one's native tongue was not on a prescribed list then the applicant was deemed unsuitable and entry denied.
† The barred zone would continue in effect until the 1952 Immigration and Naturalization Act, and quotas would not be eliminated until passage of the Hart-Celler Immigration Act in 1965.

restricted submarine warfare and by April the United States was in the war. Yamamoto, now thirty-three, began thinking of marriage and, as these events unfolded, 4,900 hundred miles east across the Pacific, Rex Theodore Barber entered the world in Culver, Oregon, on May 6, 1917. No one, not the boy's parents and certainly not the Japanese officer, could conceive of a time when their lives would eventually overlap.

But it was coming.

Arguably, Japan's split with the West and the Empire's march toward war began with the Washington Naval Treaty of 1922. As a good part of the world enjoyed a post–World War I euphoria and the naïve hope of peace offered by the League of Nations, efforts to limit the arms races that contributed to the war seemed attainable. Naval power had yet to be eclipsed by airpower, so limiting the number of capital ships seemed quite logical.* A ten-year "holiday" was declared on new construction, and a ratio of capital ships was agreed upon for the navies of Great Britain, the United States, Japan, France, and Italy; for every five built by America or Britain, the Japanese were allowed three.

Tokyo agreed to the terms for several reasons. Ini-

---

* Armored battleships and battle cruisers, initially, displacing about 20,000 tons, and mounting heavy-caliber guns.

tially, the treaty sustained inclusion into postwar, Great Power affairs, which appealed to Japanese national dignity and created a politically advantageous position. Second, Tokyo quite correctly reasoned that the Home Islands were a long, long way from Europe and America, so there was very little that could be done if Japan acted independently of the treaty. Finally, Tokyo had insisted in Article XIX that the Allies would neither build new Pacific bases, nor fortify their existing possessions. Weary from the last war and regarding future conflicts as unlikely, especially in the Pacific, the Allies agreed. This was a huge strategic win for Japan, and would have dire consequences for Britain and the United States in less than two decades.

Diplomatic victories aside, being permitted three warships for every five available to the United States or Britain was viewed as a deliberate slight by Tokyo, and Japan's growing militarist faction was quick to demonize the treaty terms. They were aided by the 1924 passage of America's Johnson-Reed Act, which sought to plug the immigration loopholes of the 1917 law. Essentially, it restricted immigration by imposing a 2 percent quota derived from existing foreign nationalities already in the United States. This quota was based on the entire U.S. population, not just those who were foreign born and, most significant, it barred *all* Asians. The Japanese, in particular, were incensed, as they considered themselves racially superior to all other Asians, and had concluded the previously mentioned Gentleman's Agreement with the administration of Teddy Roosevelt.* This, combined with widespread perceived discrimination and the onset of the 1929 global financial depression, provided the Japanese military with leverage to gain control of the Empire and widen the chasm with the West.

For Yamamoto the 1920s had been good. He married a local farmer's daughter who, at five feet four inches, was deemed too tall for a Japanese man, but Yamamoto, never insecure, was not bothered a bit by her height. Soon after this, he left for the United States and a two-year course at Harvard University to perfect his English. As befitting an officer in this position, he made many friends, and learned all he could about America and Americans by traveling extensively. He also added poker to his natural gambling skills, and studied economics, particularly the industrial capacity of the United States.

During his summers at Harvard, Yamamoto hitchhiked southwest across America, and toured oil fields in Texas and Mexico to gain firsthand knowledge of

---

* The act was revised by Congress in 1952.

modern production methods. Following the West's prosecution of World War I, he became entranced with the potential of airpower and, though a surface warrior by training and experience, Yamamoto grasped the changing nature of naval warfare. Eugene Barton Ely flew an ungainly Curtiss Pusher off the bow of the USS *Birmingham* in 1910, then became the first pilot to land an aircraft aboard ship a year later on the USS *Pennsylvania*.* However, it was the British Royal Navy that converted a merchant ship into an aircraft carrier, HMS *Ark Royal,* in 1914, then launched HMS *Furious,* a true aircraft carrier, during September 1918. Yamamoto, a full commander now, noted each aviation development with extreme interest. Aircraft carriers, he was certain, could control the enormous areas of the Pacific upon which Japan wished to build her Empire.

Returning home from the United States, he secured command of the air training center at Kasimigaura, where, at age thirty-nine, Yamamoto learned to fly. Sent back to America in 1926, he served two years as naval attaché in Washington and continued mentoring the next generation of progressive officers. "Mix with American students as much as possible," he advised.

---

* In March 1923, Lieutenant Sunishi Kira landed aboard the light carrier *Hosho,* the first Japanese pilot to do so.

"Do not speak Japanese . . . travel by subway or bus; no one ever found out much about any city by riding in taxis . . ." Whether out of admiration, personal interest, or simply military professionalism regarding a potential enemy—probably all of these reasons—Yamamoto noticed everything, and came away from Washington convinced that the days of battleship dominance were over. Based on his now extensive knowledge, Yamamoto was also considering how he would defeat the United States if ever ordered to do so. While Rex Barber was jumping off his barn with his homemade parachute, Yamamoto did a brief stint on the Naval General Staff then went back to sea commanding the cruiser *Isuzu* followed by the aircraft carrier *Akagi*. Another naval conference was convened in 1930, this time in London, and Japan again ranked third after the United States and Great Britain in terms of allowable warship construction.*

By 1931 ultranationalists within the military had had enough, and were determined to put Japan back on the right path, as they defined it. Westernization, except for military technology, was scorned for traditional

---

* Light cruisers mounted six-inch guns, with eight-inch guns for heavy cruisers. Japan was allowed twelve heavy cruisers to fifteen for Britain, and eighteen for the United States.

values. In violation of the Treaty of Versailles, Chinese Manchuria was invaded, conquered, and occupied by the Imperial Japanese Army.

The proffered justification was railroad rights to the South Manchuria Railway granted to Tokyo by the Treaty of Portsmouth, which ended the 1904–1905 Russo-Japanese War. For three decades the extent of these rights had been in dispute, but China was in no position to contest them until 1931, and following a national conference Chinese leaders reasserted their rights over Manchuria. This was something Tokyo would not allow; Manchuria, and the Japanese puppet state of Manchukuo, were a war prize. Japan had constructed schools, hospitals, power plants, and rail lines all through northeastern China. Glass, sugar, flour, steel and, above all oil, were transported from the interior to Port Arthur for shipment to Japan. The resources were absolutely essential; the Home Islands could not produce enough food for their population of 60 million, nor did they possess enough natural resources to power a modern, industrial society. Manchuria was to Japan what the Indian subcontinent was to Britain: a breadbasket, a source of labor, and a bottomless mine of materials. It had to be retained at all costs, so when China began posturing for control, Japan acted.

Late in the evening of September 18, 1931, Lieutenant Suemori Kawamoto detonated a small bomb near the South Manchuria Railway tracks at Mukden. Entirely prearranged by a small clique of hot-blooded, nationalistic army officers acting independently of Tokyo, the explosion did no damage despite Japanese claims that "a detachment of Chinese troops destroyed the tracks." The fact that the regularly scheduled southbound train arrived on time in no way dissuaded the Imperial Japanese Army from invading and occupying Manchuria. Prime Minister Inukai Tsuyoshi, rightly viewing the incident as a usurpation of his legitimate authority, attempted to rein in Japanese army and naval adventurism, and on May 15, 1932, was assassinated for his efforts.

Following Mukden, Japan's descent into what has been aptly termed the "dark valley" by historian Ian Toll accelerated now that the military controlled the government, economy, and all foreign policy through the Imperial General Staff. Army and navy factions within this body were bitterly opposed to each other, suspicious, and territorial, which created a dysfunctional construct that would continue through the next world war. The Imperial Army favored *Hokushin-ron,* expansion of Japan's Empire into Siberia and Manchuria, and viewed the Soviet Union as their greatest threat. Conversely, the Navy fervently believed the path to imperial success lay in acquiring the rich colonies of Malaya and the Pacific Islands. This policy of *Nanshin-ron,* or "southern expansion," was viewed as risky since it would certainly provoke the Western powers. China was less dangerous, and the generals in Tokyo judged that neither Britain nor the United States would intervene effectively on its behalf.

The Mukden Incident led to condemnation by the United States, which openly supported Generalissimo Chiang Kai-Shek's Nationalists, and an investigation by the Earl of Lytton on behalf of the League of Nations. "If [the Japanese] will only consent to adopt the world's way I believe they could get all they really want and have peace at the same time." Lord Lytton wrote in 1932, but the hypocrisy of any other Great Power condemning Japan for its expansionism infuriated Tokyo, and provided additional fuel for smoldering nationalistic fires. In Geneva the following year, the League of Nations condemned Japan's Manchurian occupation, and after reviewing the Lytton Report recommended a troop withdrawal.

"Japan will oppose any attempt at international control of Manchuria," stated Yosuke Matsuoka, Japan's representative with the League. "It does not mean that we defy you, because Manchuria belongs to us by right."* He then riposted, quite accurately, with "Would the American people agree to such control of the Panama Canal Zone; would the British permit it over Egypt?" This hypocrisy from the West rankled then, just as it does now, as the Great Powers considered imperialism and colonization their province alone. A Japan ascendant would bear close watching, yet most Americans and Europeans were dismissive of any potential threat. It was one thing, professional military officers believed, to defeat the Chinese, Koreans, or even the Russians, who were all regarded as substandard militaries; a Western opponent was quite different, and there was little to fear from Japan.

This miscalculation would cost the Allies dearly in the years to come.

So, with his retinue in tow, Matsuoka stalked from the hall and Japan permanently withdrew from the League. U.S. ambassador Joseph Grew later wrote, "Nobody could miss the political significance of Japan's decision to quit the League of Nations. It marked a clear break with the Western powers and prepared the way for Japan's later adherence to the Axis." Now free of international constraints and firmly controlled

---

* Matsuoka lived in Oregon and California, and graduated from the University of Oregon Law School before returning to Japan.

by its own military, Tokyo embarked on a path of Imperial expansion throughout Asia and the Pacific. Alarmed by this and with only a year remaining on the 1922 Washington Conference, a second London meeting was called in 1935.

Yamamoto, now a vice admiral, was chosen as chief delegate representing Japan. He had personally opposed the 1931 invasion of Manchuria, so the admiral's position was politically and physically dangerous. Ultranationalist factions believed that military conquest was the only way to solve the empire's economic issues, and the Black Dragons, Heaven Spade Party, and Blood Fraternity had no hesitation utilizing assassination to achieve political goals. Yamamoto understood that any sign of weakness would be seen as capitulation to the West, and could very well be his death warrant.

"Japan can no longer submit to the ratio system," Yamamoto announced to the British press in perfect English on Southampton's dock. "There is no possibility of compromise by my Government on that point. I am smaller than you but you don't insist I eat three-fifths of the food on my plate." The conference was a nonstarter for the Japanese, though the admiral strengthened his personal prestige by gaining parity on submarine construction, and his strong stance against

Western limitations of Japanese military expansion made him quite popular with ordinary Japanese.

Returning home to a parade, Yamamoto was appointed vice minister of the navy under Mitsumasa Yonai, and became a member of the Council of Admirals. Interestingly, he never evidenced regret for shattering the 1922 Washington Conference agreement, and this is highly instructive. Despite his deep familiarity with the United States, his cosmopolitanism, and his obvious polish, Isoroku Yamamoto was, above all else, a member of the samurai caste and a product of the Japanese Imperial system. Personal misgivings aside, he was first, last, and always a loyal, dedicated serving line officer who would do anything in his power to protect his country.

As he himself would write: "To die for Emperor and Nation is the highest hope of a military man. After a brave hard fight the blossoms are scattered on the fighting field. But if a person wants to take a life instead, still the fighting man will go to eternity for Emperor and country. One man's life or death is a matter of no importance. All that matters is the Empire."

Abrogating the treaty in 1936, Japan became unabashedly militaristic. The Imperial Army invaded China again, and all through the Pacific Mandate islands airfields, ports, and roads were constructed with an eye toward future military use. The Imperial Army, modeled in many respects after the German Wehrmacht, strove relentlessly for nationalistic control just as Hitler had done, while the Imperial Navy clung to Meiji's belief in civil control of the military. The parallels between Germany and Japan are interesting and, with the benefit of hindsight, a road map to war. Both nations claimed grievances with the West, perpetuated deep-seated racial prejudices, and held an unshakable belief in the righteousness of their respective causes. They also shared a common enemy in the Soviet Union. Japan had long feared its colossal northern neighbor, and the Imperial Army regarded Russia as its principal antagonist in the fight for Asian dominance. To this end, Japan and Nazi Germany signed the Anti-Comintern Pact in 1936, pledging to defend each other's common interests, and to make no separate political agreements with the Soviet Union.*

Firmly under military control now, Japan quite naturally drifted closer to National Socialist Germany, a

---

* Other signatories included Italy, Spain, and Denmark; Hitler would abrogate the pact in 1939, when he signed a separate non-aggression treaty with Stalin in preparation for Germany's invasion of Poland.

trend the army fervently desired. Revolutionary political change orchestrated by the generals would permit a modern version of the Shogunate, and Yamamoto vehemently opposed this. The navy remained committed to Meiji's dictate that the military was subordinate to civil leadership, and this created powerful enemies for the admiral, including Vice Minister of War and future Prime Minister Hideki Tojo. With the Soviet Union now between two threats by mid-1937, Tokyo felt secure about further expansion into China, though technically the 1933 truce was still in effect. Japan had no interest in peace and, like Germany, viewed conquest as essential for the future. Land, food, and mineral resources were all necessary for national survival, so acquisition was viewed as a "right," and thus for Japan, holding China under its heel was the solution.

During the night of July 7, 1937, a Japanese soldier of the China Garrison's 1st Infantry Regiment went missing during maneuvers outside Peking. His unit commander, Major Kiyonao Ichiki, insisted on searching the little of town of Wanping, but the Chinese military refused. Tensions escalated and shots were fired. Though another truce was declared, the Japanese had the pretext they needed for "pacification" efforts deeper inside China, ostensibly to protect their commercial interests. By the end of the month, the IJA 20th Division had attacked

Peking, and the city fell in early August, leaving all of north-central China defenseless. On the southern coast Japanese units then crossed the Bazi Bridge into Shanghai on August 8, and nine days later three additional divisions were landed thirty miles north of the city. The port was vital, and with it in Japanese hands China was effectively cut in half below the Yangtze.

A bloody, three-month siege ensued that eventually involved nearly one million men, and though Shanghai inevitably fell on November 26, the casualties involved should have given Japanese military leaders pause regarding the widely touted superiority of their soldiers. This miscalculation would cost the Japanese as dearly as racial prejudice cost the Allies, and while Shanghai was taken, the latest Brussels Conference failed to resolve the Chinese conflict, so the Japanese pushed farther west toward Nanjing. Fighting a war of attrition, the Chinese believed that the enormous depth of their country would buy time until the Western powers intervened. This Fabian strategy generally avoided pitched battles while interdicting supply routes and lines of communication. Yet by December 1937, the Shanghai Expeditionary Force's 10th Army was closing on Nanjing, the capital of the Republic of China, and the stage was set for the first armed confrontation between Japan and the United States.

Most of the foreigners had vacated by this time, but a few businessmen and missionaries stayed by choice, and a handful of diplomats remained out of duty. Americans here were under the protection of the Yangtze Patrol, a division of the tiny U.S. Asiatic Fleet based in the Philippines. Formed in 1921 to safeguard American property, interests, and lives along the 1,325-mile river, by 1937 the Patrol consisted of eight flat-bottomed, shallow-draft gunboats, including the USS *Panay*, which was anchored at Nanjing by early December. Nearly 200 feet long and displacing 474 tons, when ordered to Nanjing on September 21, she covered hundreds of miles in a day, slicing through the tea-colored Yangtze at 15 knots.

By December 7, the Japanese were twenty miles east of the city and coming on fast. The U.S. second secretary, George Atcheson, had remained behind with a skeleton staff while the ambassador, Nelson T. Johnson, evacuated west to Hankow. The *Panay* was to serve as a rally point, refuge, and communications center for the last Americans in Nanjing. By Saturday, December 11, the situation was critical, and the Japanese were approaching the ship's anchorage near the Asiatic Petroleum Company's facility. *Panay*'s skipper, thirty-nine-year-old Lieutenant Commander James Joseph Hughes, moved the gunboat twelve miles upriver and anchored with several Royal Navy ships. Artillery fire from the bank forced another move during the morning of December 12, this time to the Hoshien cutoff, some twenty-seven miles above Nanjing. Each time the ship moved, the Japanese consul-general in Shanghai was informed, and en route to Hoshien, the gunboat had been boarded and identified by a Japanese army lieutenant. Lieutenant Commander Hughes also had two 18-foot by 14-foot U.S. flags painted on *Panay's* fore and aft upper awnings so they would be clearly visible from the air. He also kept both three-inch deck guns uncovered, and unlimbered all eight of his .30-caliber Lewis machine guns.

Nevertheless, at 1335 the gunboat's lookout reported aircraft circling overhead, and as the captain made his way to the bridge, bombs began to fall. Three twin-engined Mitsubishi Type 96 medium bombers had released their bombs from 11,000 feet while a dozen Aichi biplane dive bombers rolled in and dove at the cluster of ships on the river. Assigned to the Twelfth and Thirteenth Naval Air Groups, the navy planes had been ordered to attack by Third Fleet Headquarters based on flawed, incorrect army intelligence. The pilots saw what they had been told to expect, and certainly what they wanted to see—ships on the river, reportedly full of fleeing Chinese troops—and they didn't bother with visual confirmation but simply attacked, which might have been the true purpose behind the army intelligence.

The first bomb exploded on the water just off the gunboat's port side; it knocked out the forward three-inch gun, and literally blew the pants off the ship's navigation officer, Ensign Denis Harry Biwese of Sheboygan, Wisconsin. During the next twenty-five minutes more than twenty bombs impacted nearby, or hit the *Panay*. Lieutenant Commander Hughes was badly wounded, as was his executive officer, Lieutenant Arthur "Tex" Anders, and most of the crew. Three were killed, including Sandro Sandi, a famous Italian war correspondent. The Lewis guns opened fire, but with little effect, so at 1405 Hughes gave the order to abandon the sinking ship. By 1500 the survivors were swimming ashore, or being shuttled by motor sampans that the aircraft were now strafing. Two Japanese gunboats appeared and began machine-gunning the stricken vessel before boarding and searching while the Stars and Stripes was plainly flying from the mast.

Repercussions from the "*Panay* Incident," as it became known, did not include the war Tokyo feared, but reactions were quite revealing. A protégé of Yamamoto's named Kurio Toibana attempted to obfuscate and delay the initial reports, but word leaked out anyway.

The deep chasm separating the Japanese army and navy was glaringly revealed, and should have given both sides pause for consideration. The navy, more sophisticated and attuned to world affairs, eventually responded by reprimanding the involved commanders, albeit slightly. The army, fanatical, traditional, and insular, shrugged off the entire affair as irrelevant. It is quite possible, given the Japanese army's penchant for manufacturing China incidents, that they were hoping to provoke the United States into war, and were quite willing to use their naval brethren as unwitting tools.

In late April 1938, Tokyo settled the attack by paying out an indemnity of $2,214,007.36 to the United States and it was Isoroku Yamamoto, as vice minister of the navy, who officially thanked America for accepting Japan's apologies. While there was indignation in the United States, the prevailing sentiment seemed to be righteous vindication for those Americans who favored isolationism. What, postulated newspapers all over the country, could be expected when U.S. forces were forced to remain neutral in a war zone? Surely this was a sign that the United States should pull out of China, and anywhere else where national interests were not directly threatened. The *Cincinnati Inquirer* went so far as to say a few dead Americans were better than hundreds of thousands of dead or wounded Americans.

This type of attitude, combined with Washington's Neutrality Acts, convinced Japan that the United States was too indifferent or too impotent to challenge the Empire, at least over China.

Despite a well-disguised defeat by the Russians, the Imperial Army's string of easy Asian conquests created an artificial aura of invincibility that, in no small part, would eventually lead to full-scale war with the West. There was tremendous domestic political pressure to join the Axis, and Yamamoto's continued resistance put his life in grave danger from ultranationalist groups, and from army officers like Hideki Tojo. The admiral, and other ranking naval officers, believed any agreement with the Axis would inevitably lead to war with Great Britain, the United States, and Russia. Refusing to be cowed, the admiral took long solitary strolls, utilized public transportation, and even answered his own door. He could easily have been killed at any time, but as a consummate gambler with a fearless nature he took his chances.

Yet something had to be done, and soon.

"It was the only way to save his life," navy minister Yonai would recall. "To send him off to sea." So with that, in August 1939, Isoroku Yamamoto was transferred from the Navy Ministry in Tokyo and on September 1, 1939, the day Germany invaded Poland, he stepped aboard the battleship *Nagato* in Wakanoura Bay as commander in chief of the Japanese Combined Fleet.*

Rex Barber viewed the Japanese arrogance in Asia and the Pacific with a wary eye. Amid frat parties and intermittent studying, he was remembering the barn, thinking about flying, and following with great interest the latest political and technical developments in aviation. As a boy he had thrilled to U.S. Navy lieutenant Apollo Soucek's amazing climb to 43,166 feet in an open-cockpit Wright Apache, and was awestruck by Wiley Post's 1933 solo circumnavigation of the world in just one week.† The summer he left for college, Amelia Earhart and Fred Noonan vanished over the Pacific, and the U.S. Army was openly soliciting bids for new fighter aircraft.

This was noteworthy due to the Air Corps' long-standing position that bomber aircraft would win the next war. "The bomber will always get through" dictum was surprisingly well received among military and

---

* *Nagato* would end her days in July 1946 as a victim of American underwater atomic bomb detonation tests near Bikini Atoll.
† Seven days, 18 hours, and 45 minutes.

civilian airpower advocates, and was stridently promoted by Giulio Douhet, one of the more influential theorists of his day.* Pursuit aircraft, as early fighters were known, could not fly as high or as fast or as far as a bomber, so why waste money and resources on them? For the United States, separated from hostile nations by two great oceans, the superiority of the bomber seemed quite logical. With a third of Americans living in poverty in the wake of the Great Depression, there was little appetite to spend money on superfluous defenses.

In the midst of all this, a tiny California aviation company managed to survive—just barely—through a beautiful series of aircraft called Sirius, Altair, and Orion. Allan Haines Loughead and his brother Malcolm managed to eke out a business constructing about one aircraft per month until October 1931, when creditors forced the company into receivership. It was purchased the following year by three optimistic businessmen who kept the original name, and had a penchant for innovation. They decided that the Lockheed Aircraft Corporation would build all-metal, twin-engined com-

---

* The phrase became famous after being used by Stanley Baldwin, a British member of Parliament, during a November 1932 speech titled "A Fear for the Future."

mercial aircraft with an eye toward airmail contracts and the fledgling airline industry.*

In 1933, a young University of Michigan engineer named Clarence "Kelly" Johnson joined Lockheed's team. Hired as a tool designer, Johnson had aeronautical engineering expertise that was rapidly apparent and he quickly advanced to become the company's chief research engineer.† Johnson's fertile creativity and brilliant instincts found a complementary intellect in Lieutenant Ben Kelsey, a young pilot who had just been appointed head of the Fighter Projects Office at Wright Field. Despite his youth, Kelsey had been flying since age fifteen, had two engineering degrees from the Massachusetts Institute of Technology, and had flown as Jimmy Doolittle's safety/chase pilot during the latter's 1929 instrument flight tests.

To counter the bomber threat, prevailing 1930s Air Corps thinking centered around multi-seat, multi-engine holdovers from the Great War. Vigorously promoted by the French Armée de l'Air, which should have been reason enough for suspicion, unwieldy "bomber-

---

* "Lockheed" is the phonetic pronunciation of "Loughead."
† Kelly Johnson would design more than thirty airframes, from the P-38 Lightning to the Blackbird series of operational Mach 3+ aircraft.

destroyer" aircraft like the Bleriot 127 were considered state of the art. Kelsey, a visionary like Johnson, was openly appalled at such conventional designs. Disdaining multi-seat fighters in general (and gunners in particular) he was convinced that single-seat fighters, with one or two engines, were the future of tactical aviation. One limitation to this was that the Air Corps peacetime specifications for "pursuit aircraft" meant one engine, a single seat, and no more than five hundred pounds of weapons and ammunition. If a design did not fall within these parameters, then there was no access to scarce funding and the idea was dead from the beginning. In collusion with Lieutenant Gordon Saville, who sat on the Army Procurement Board, the young officers simply invented a term to fit what they wanted; the "interceptor" was born.

Ben Kelsey, who would later retire as a brigadier general, freely admitted, "This had nothing to do with the European term pertaining to fast-climbing, short-range bomber interceptors. Our nomenclature was aimed at getting 1,000 pounds of ammunition on board versus the standard 500 pounds."

But the gambit worked. Both officers were astute enough to get the requirement past the Armed Services Committee, and Kelsey was then able to publicly release preliminary requirements for two experimental aircraft. These were one single-engined and one twin-engined interceptor, both built around the most powerful engine available for production, the supercharged Allison V-1710C.

A supercharger, also referred to as a turbosupercharger, had existed in practice since 1917, when French engineer Auguste Rateau field-tested an operable unit in a Renault aircraft engine.* In America the National Advisory Committee on Aeronautics (NACA) contracted General Electric to develop a turbocharged aircraft engine for the U.S. Army Air Service, which was successfully demonstrated by Dr. Sanford Moss with a Liberty V-12 at 14,109 feet, above Pike's Peak in Colorado, during late 1918. General Electric devoted its considerable engineering expertise to perfecting the technology, and it was such a game changer that superchargers were not even exported to close allies like Great Britain.

It worked like this. A normal air-breathing, reciprocating engine fills a cylinder with air when the piston moves up and down. This air is compressed as the pis-

---

* Technically, a supercharger was driven by the engine and used primarily to boost manifold pressure for takeoff and climbs, while a turbocharger utilized exhaust gases to generate greater power at high altitudes. The terms are often used interchangeably, and components of both were often combined.

ton pushes, then injected with fuel and the mixture is ignited. The power generated from the subsequent explosion is largely dependent on the air pressure inside the cylinder. Unfortunately, outside air pressure decreases as the engine operates at higher altitudes, where the air is a fraction of its sea level weight.* This reduces the pressure a piston can generate, and therefore decreases the power available to the engine. Making bigger cylinders was the initial answer, but size and weight considerations limited this approach. Supercharging was the solution. Essentially, engine exhaust gases are used to cram extra oxygen through the carburetor into the cylinder, so a sea level pressure is maintained even when flying miles above the earth. Engine performance remains high, and the aircraft can operate in a "zone of exclusion" where nonsupercharged aircraft cannot. From a tactical standpoint, supercharging was a superb advantage for piston-engined aircraft, and though some Axis aircraft were so equipped their engines were not as effective as those utilized in P-38 or P-47 fighters.

Kelsey wrote specifications for the new plane, calling for a climb to 20,000 feet in six minutes. It needed to carry enough fuel to maintain 360 mph at that altitude,

---

* Sea level air is 14.7 pounds-per-square-inch (psi), while at 25,000 feet the same air measures 5.45 psi; a 55 percent decrease.

at full throttle, for one hour. It must have 1,000 pounds of ordnance, including a 25 mm cannon, though this was not available at the time, and hold enough internal fuel to preclude external tanks. The inclusion of a fully retractable, tricycle landing gear would also ensure very favorable consideration by the Army.

Kelly Johnson listened.

By March 1936, he had completed a design study on what Lockheed called its Model 22 twin-engined, single-seat fighter. A few months before the *Panay* was attacked, the U.S. Army formally released Circular Proposal X-608, which invited a design response from Boeing, Consolidated, Curtiss-Wright, Douglas, Lockheed, and Vultee to produce a "heavy fighter." Kelly Johnson and Lockheed's chief engineer, Hal Hibbard, created what was the only single-seat, tricycle-gear, twin-engined fighter in existence.

It was big and it was heavy.

The extra armament and 400 gallons of internal fuel generated an empty weight exceeding 11,000 pounds at a time when fighters normally weighed half as much. Yet Johnson calculated that with its polished, flush-surface skin, all-metal covered control surfaces, and powerful engines the Model 22 could reach 417 mph at 20,000 feet, nearly 60 mph faster than the army's requirement. The Luftwaffe and Royal Air Force, among others, were also actively pursuing such heavy fighter options, but most were two-seaters, and none incorporated all of Kelly Johnson's elegant aerodynamic solutions. Westland's beautiful Whirlwind arguably came closest because the British, like their American counterparts, appreciated the obvious advantages of a single-seat configuration, and they too desired heavy armament.

Ben Kelsey was thrilled by the new fighter's capabilities and by the design's obvious potential. On June 23, 1937, just weeks before Japan invaded China and Amelia Earhart vanished over the Pacific, contract AC-9974 was awarded to Lockheed.* Valued at an astounding $163,000, the contract immediately breathed new financial life into Lockheed, and the company officially gave the Model 22 its military designation: the XP-38.†

Pilots would come to call it the Lightning.

---

* Earhart was flying a Lockheed Model 10 Electra.
† Equivalent to about $2,870,000 in 2020.

Two
The Twilight

April 18, 1943
Guadalcanal

S eventy miles per hour. Ten feet beneath his seat the big tires slipped over pierced steel matting, and roaring filled the cockpit from the twin Allison engines just a few feet from his head. To the left of the runway coconut trees and parked planes began to fade, while off to the right, jeeps, trucks, and people vanished as the big P-38 rolled faster down the strip. Rex Barber's eyes shifted to the clear area ahead between his canopy supports, but dust from the preceding five fighters hung over the field and blurred the tree line ahead. With both feet on the rudder pedals and the corner of one eye on the matting, the pilot kept the big Lightning on the right half of the runway, darting glances back in at the scarred, black instrument panel as he did so.

Manifold pressure . . . then below to the RPM needles. Both Allisons were at full throttle, and all the needles were steady. Unlike in conventional tail-dragger fighters, there was no softening of the controls as the plane approached flying speed and the tail lifted. The P-38's tail was already up thanks to the tricycle landing gear, and the heavy aircraft had to be quite literally pulled off the ground.

Eighty miles per hour.

Barber's left hand was wrapped around both bulbous, red throttle knobs, jamming them forward so they wouldn't slip backward with the vibrations. And the fighter vibrated. Between the Allisons and the Marston matting covering the runway, most of the gauges were a blur, which was probably why the really important ones were so large. Squinting back at the big airspeed indicator in the center of the panel, Rex could just make out the wobbling white needle. Two marks were scored into the metal next to the indicator, and as the needle bounced to the first mark he looked up, then eased the control column back with his right hand.

Back . . . back . . .

The column grazed his right leg below the knee, and Rex held the control wheel rock steady in his fist. Up . . . the guns on the nose lifted toward the tree line, and he leaned slightly forward in the seat.

Up . . . the nose came up off the ground and Rex lightly pushed the rudder pedals to keep the Lightning straight, ignoring the rattling from the steel mat, and all the other movement around the field. Rex blocked everything else out during these crucial seconds as the fighter got airborne, because if anything was going to go wrong mechanically it usually happened now.

One hundred miles per hour.

The wings rocked a bit, but he compensated automatically and eased the control wheel back a bit more. With a final small bounce, the rattling stopped and the dust cleared as the P-38 slid upward into clear air and away from the stinking, muddy island. Rex watched Lanphier up ahead, and from the corner of his left eye turquoise water gleamed over the coconut trees. Reaching down with his left hand, he grasped a black knob next to his thigh, tapped the rudder pedals twice, then raised the landing gear. Hitting the brakes like that was a good habit, as it spun off any collected mud and kept the wheel wells clean. There was a popping sound from beneath the seat, and a few puffs of smoke drifted up from under the instrument panel, but Rex never looked away from the other P-38, which had begun a wide left-hand turn over Lunga Point.

Noise and smoke were two things that all pilots hated, but this was the normal cycling of a hydraulic pressure regulator under his seat, and the smoke came from the spinning nose wheel rubbing against the landing gear door. With the wheels up, *Miss Virginia*'s airspeed jumped past 130 miles per hour, the minimum flying speed he'd need if an engine was lost. Hydraulic pressure was back at 1300 psi, and all was well.

Keeping both throttles firewalled, Rex rolled left and dropped his plane's nose to cut *Phoebe* off on the inside of its turn to close in faster. Glancing left, he saw the first four Lightnings were already joined up in a loose formation. Number Two, Lieutenant Julius Jacobson, was on Mitchell's left wing, with Doug Canning and Delton Goerke together on his right. This was how all the four ships would fly, though once they headed out to sea everyone would loosen up. Rex pulled a bit farther left, framing *Phoebe* in his front quarter panel above the engine nacelle. This was "pulling lead," just like throwing a pass or aiming ahead of a duck on the wing. Twisting around, he looked back off the left boom but couldn't see McLanahan or Moore against the shoreline.

Well, that was their problem.

At 1,000 feet, Rex nudged the throttles back, and kicked in a bit of left rudder. The idea was to fly up the leader's wing line then stabilize in a "route" position about one hundred feet back. If a pilot came in too slow, he would have to increase power or the cutoff angle, and this would delay the whole flight's rejoin. If he came in too fast, he would overshoot, cross under the leader, then float back again to his correct side. This got in the way of Number Three and Four, delayed things, and looked bad. Fighter pilots took pride in the little things, like sounding calm and collected on the radio no matter what was happening, or flawlessly executing simple, basic flight procedures like rejoins. After all, the point of being a fighter pilot was to fight; all the basic flying stuff that transport and bomber crews worried about was taken for granted. That was, Rex fervently believed, just as it should be.

Phoebe's 52-foot wingspan was filling the right quarter panel and getting bigger by the second, so he nudged the throttles back, then stood them straight up. *Miss Virginia* slowed rapidly, but as Lanphier's fighter began moving ahead on the canopy, Barber added power, froze the forward movement, and slid into a loose position about one hundred feet off the left wing. He was close enough here to be seen, and yet far enough away that he could look around occasionally or check his instruments. Wriggling into a comfortable position, Rex loosened his shoulder straps a few inches and straightened out the map on his leg. Darting a look inside, he switched off the electric fuel booster pumps, then checked the manifold pressure, oil pressure, and temperature. The horizon seemed to slowly spin as Barber hung in the air off Lanphier's wing, and as they came through northeast he could see the dark smudge of Tulagi and the Florida Islands under *Phoebe*'s belly.

Sudden movement caught his right eye as another P-38 flashed under the tail booms. It banked up sharply to slow down, and Rex could see the other pilot staring up through the top of his canopy as he corrected, then expertly slid into formation off Lanphier's right wing. Barber frowned and glanced at the tail numbers on his lineup card. That was Joe Moore . . . he was Number Four in the Killer flight, so what happened to Number Three? Moore would never have passed up his element leader and beaten him into formation.

Where was Jim McLanahan?

A half mile ahead, John Mitchell was wondering the same thing. His plane was trimmed up for hands-off, level flight, and the throttles set to hold 155 mph, so he could turn around in his seat to watch the takeoffs. Occasionally nudging the control wheel to keep the big, easy left-hand turn coming, the major checked off each

P-38 on the back of his map as it got airborne. Each four-ship was to join up together, then maintain a half-mile spacing between each flight. Something had happened to the Killer flight, though; there had been too much space between the first pair and the third fighter that eventually joined up.

With sunlight lancing into the cockpit and hitting his right eyeball, Mitchell shallowed out the turn even more and aimed well left of the Florida Islands. Peering back and squinting a bit, he saw the problem. One Lightning was wing low in the dirt about two-thirds down the runway, and it had to be either Jim McLanahan or Joe Moore. If an engine had been lost the pilot would have stopped straight ahead, so this was something else.

This was why Mitchell had insisted on two air spares, who would stay with them for the first leg. If they were not needed, they'd return to base; now it was becoming clear that at least one would stick with them. The last spare, Lieutenant Ray Hine, was just getting airborne now.

Mitchell nudged the throttles to hold 155 mph in a gentle climbing turn as the Florida Islands passed off his right wing. Turning around in the seat again, he watched the shadows of the tail-end P-38s falling away as they banked up sharply to the north to cut across under his formation. The major knew the pair would stay low, then join up behind Major Lou Kittel's eight Lightnings unless they were needed to fill in. He thought about that. If that was McLanahan down there in the dirt, then Mitchell would move Holmes into the empty position in the Killer flight since a qualified flight lead was necessary to fly the Number Three slot. Playing the turn a bit, he leveled off at 2,000 feet, walked the throttles back to hold his airspeed, and held a very slight left bank.

Craning his neck, the major could just see Tulagi off the right wing. Down his left-wing line was the dark, spiny outline of Savo Island some fifteen miles to the west. Dipping a wing slightly, he watched the last two Lightnings rejoin low to the outside at the end of the formation. He was sure Besby Holmes was counting planes to make certain he hadn't cut anyone off, and had rejoined in the correct position. Mitchell appreciated that sort of professionalism; caution was a good trait, except, sometimes, in combat. Satisfied, he faced forward, brought the wheel a bit more to the left, then rolled out over Ironbottom Sound, pointed at the northern edge of Savo Island.

Sixteen months earlier, during December 1941, the United States was caught up in a Christmas cornucopia.

The Great Depression was a bad memory, and seemed relegated to remaining there. Largely due to passage of the contentious Lend-Lease Act in March, more than 3 million more Americans were finally back at work, and 40 million were now fully employed. Congress passed the bill, which provided $7 billion in credits and granted the president the right to transfer any defense materials he wished to "the government of any country whose defense the President deems vital to the defense of the United States." In plain English, it obviated the Neutrality Act of 1939 and pushed America closer to the war in Europe. It also jump-started the economy.

If the bill caused consternation among many, the results certainly did not.

Parents happily thumbed through catalogues for Daisy Air Rifles, roller skates, and Gilbert American Flyer train sets. High-end patent leather shoes for the ladies were $2.98, and $15.95 bought the ultimate Craftsman chrome wrench and socket set. Sears, Roebuck & Company was selling entire prefabricated houses like the ten-room Magnolia, shipped direct to your lot for construction at the eye-popping price of $6,488.00, nearly five times the annual income for the average American. RCA was even selling the wonder of television through five-by-twelve-inch sets costing $150 to $500 dollars, Or if that was too much, a "picture receiver" was available that plugged into existing radios. From either source the progressive American of 1941 could watch two fifteen-minute newscasts daily courtesy of CBS in New York.

From Ivey's in the Carolinas to Portland, Oregon's W. T. Grant, department stores lit up their front windows with amazing displays to entice and attract children. Ivey's train sets plowed through carefully crafted "snow," proving that "Ivey's Toys Make Happy Boys"; wind-up dancing mice by Marx, or Hubley's vast array of cast-iron ice wagons, airplanes, or motorcycle cops captured children's imaginations and their parent's pocketbooks. Youngsters then, as now, were enthralled, and military-themed gifts were huge sellers; dolls with Red Cross uniforms, model planes, tanks, or ships were selling fast. For ninety-eight cents a boy could have his own miniature truck-mounted antiaircraft gun, happily oblivious to the very real shadows lingering behind the toys.

Rex Barber, like many adults, was not oblivious.

He listened to Walter Winchell's *News Here and Abroad,* with Edmund R. Murrow's regular reports from Europe as the war there escalated and spread. When Poland was invaded on September 1, 1939, Rex was an agricultural engineering student at Oregon State College in Corvallis. He fit in everywhere, and was one of those fortunate young men liked by everyone. Neither brash nor loud, he was not overly reserved, loved practical jokes, and had an insatiable appetite for adventure. Naturally athletic with superb reflexes, Rex was also quite intelligent and studious when it was required, and especially when he was interested in the subject. As with most who had come of age during the Great Depression, he had never been spoiled, and was physically and mentally extremely tough. Thoroughly enjoying life off the farm, Rex found the academics at Oregon State were not excessively demanding, so he had plenty of time for girls and a relatively carefree frat-boy lifestyle.

Relatively.

Following the "Phony War" or "Sitzkreig" of late 1939 and 1940, Rex wondered if the war was all over before it really began. Tensions built again during the 105-day Soviet war with Finland, but it ended in March 1940 and barely registered with most Americans. Nevertheless, it seemed obvious that war in Europe was accelerating, despite efforts of appeasement and isolationist sentiments. Rex paid attention when the Germans moved into Norway, and then defeated Denmark in six hours. Like a huge sickle, the Wehrmacht and Luftwaffe continued moving west and suddenly in May 1940 the war was very much on again.

During the evening of May 9, German paratroopers dropped into the Hague, the port of Rotterdam, and captured the Belgian fort of Eben-Emael on the Meuse River. The German 18th Army charged straight into Belgium, bypassing the heavily defended border and hastening the defeat of the French Army, which reacted exactly as it had in 1914. Rommel's 7th Panzers poured from the Ardennes two days later, crossed the same undefended dam near Houx that was used in 1914, then surrounded Sedan. With its penchant for surrender, the French Army quickly collapsed, followed shortly by the Belgians. With its flanks exposed, Lord Gort's British Expeditionary Force had no choice but to fall back to the sea. On June 22, 1940, France and Germany signed an armistice establishing a "neutral" but pro-Axis France superficially controlled by a puppet government based in Vichy.

This was no small-scale assault on countries far away and little known; this was a knife into the heart of Western Europe. During the battle for France, the U.S. Congress passed the June 14th Naval Expansion Act, which added 170,000 tons to the navy's existing list of ships and made provision for 4,500 "useful naval airplanes." After Dunkirk, and with the impending likelihood of a German invasion of England, Congress opened its purse strings still wider with the July 19th

Naval Expansion Act; an impressive 1,325,000 tons were now authorized, including 200,000 tons for aircraft carriers alone, with more than $200 million appropriated for facilities, docks, ways, and ordnance manufacturing. That summer of 1940 also saw the U.S. Army finally expanding its size to 375,000 men, and increasing National Guard inductions with the goal of having, on paper at least, a one-million-man force by January 1941.

This was to include fifty-four new combat air groups and Rex Barber saw his opportunity. Aware that the United States would eventually be forced into the conflict, either in Europe or Asia or both, like most of his generation he felt an ingrained sense of duty to do his part. Rex's Uncle Edgar had been a U.S. Army Air Service pilot during the Great War, and his stories about France had always inspired the boy, as did the current furious air battles in the skies over England. Rex listened to nightly radio broadcasts, spellbound, as a handful of fighter pilots defended England during the Battle of Britain through the fall of 1940, and as Italy, after also declaring war on Britain, invaded Egypt.

On Monday, September 16, there was a rumor that Reichsmarschall Hermann Göring, a fighter pilot from the Great War, had bombed London personally from a Ju 88. On that same day the U.S. Congress made history by passing the Burke-Wadsworth Act, enacting America's first peacetime draft. All men from twenty-one to thirty-six years of age were required to register, which theoretically provided the military with an eligible pool of 20 million. Of these, some 10 million were initially disqualified because they lacked the minimum number of teeth, suffered from venereal diseases, had poor eyesight, or, for 340,000 men who signed their forms with an X, were illiterate.*

On September 17, 1940, Hitler postponed Operation SEALION, his invasion of England, and for nine days there was a brief respite. Hitler, it seemed, had gone as far west as he could go; the Royal Air Force had never been defeated, and without control of the air over the English Channel, the German invasion could not proceed. After France fell in sixteen days many believed the war was over.† This was not the case, of course. Britain was increasingly desperate for weapons, ships, tanks, and aircraft to hold Hitler at bay. But Americans were still overwhelmingly opposed to joining another

---

* The 1940 census listed 5.2 million Americans as illiterate, while other sources put the figure closer to 15 million.

† This measurement of France's demise begins with the Dunkirk evacuation on May 26, 1940, rather than the occupation of Paris on June 13, or by the official surrender on June 25, 1940.

war "over there," especially one that seemed to center on saving the British and French, again. Europeans also had billions of dollars in unpaid debts from the Great War, and U.S. public opinion was adamantly opposed to salvaging colonial empires with American blood.

Then, in Berlin on September 27, Saburo Kurusu signed the Tripartite Act on behalf of the Empire of Japan. With the act stating plainly in the second article that "Germany and Italy recognize and respect the leadership of Japan in the establishment of a new order in Greater East Asia," Americans from Washington, D.C., to Corvallis, Oregon, were now taking war with Japan seriously. Convinced more than ever that war was coming, and having duly registered for the draft, Rex Barber left school on September 30, 1940, quite naturally heading for the Army Air Corps.

Any new form of warfare challenges older paradigms, and military aviation had endured a bumpy ride. For the United States it technically started in 1907, but because no one could really figure out where to put balloons, the strange unit was named the "Aeronautical Division" and attached to the Army Signal Corps. The military contracted for its first fixed-wing aircraft in August 1909. Initially it was called the "Wilbur Wright machine," then the "Military Flyer," and it could manage about 40 mph on a good day with a tailwind.* As the new division grew it was renamed the "Army Air Service," and it had expanded considerably by the time of America's entry into the Great War. Having proven that aircraft were quite capable weapons, the Air Service advanced fast enough to separate from the Signal Corps in May 1918.

With the conclusion of a war to end all wars, the American public saw scant need for a large military. The Air Service promptly shrank to a minuscule twenty-two squadrons. Because the United States was bounded by the Atlantic and Pacific oceans, its first line of defense was still the Navy, with the Army providing continental or territorial defense. Indeed, world events seemed to bear out this concept as the interwar army was utilized piecemeal in Mexico, Russia, China, and the Philippines. Aircraft were still severely range limited, so the Navy maintained America's global reach, albeit on a reduced scale. But aviation technology was improving fast, and the aircraft's startling contribution during the Great War was impossible to ignore. Despite consistent pushback from the military old guard,

---

* A modified derivative of the Wright Model A, Signal Corps No. 1.

aviation as a tool of war was officially sanctioned in the National Defense Act of 1920 when the Air Service rated its own major general as commander and was recognized as a "combatant arm of the line" of the U.S. Army.

During the next decade aviation gained stature through a series of headline-making events. Naval officers Marc Mitscher and Albert Cushing Read hopped across the Atlantic in enormous three-engined Navy-Curtiss Flying Boats, while Army officers like Henry "Hap" Arnold, Jimmy Doolittle, and Billy Mitchell were willing to risk their reputations and careers to shatter traditional military glass ceilings. Then there were civilians such as Charles Lindbergh, Wiley Post, and other flyers who were always chasing aviation's next demon, solving engineering and aeronautical problems along the way as they did so. This progression was evidenced, at least for the Army, by official attempts intent on utilizing the innate potential of airpower. The Lassiter Board recommended to the secretary of war that a separate force of pursuit and bombardment aircraft be created for the Army's use while the Lampert Committee, with surprising prescience, proposed an independent "air force" with a "department of defense" to oversee American military operations.

In September 1924, President Coolidge asked

Dwight W. Morrow to study the aviation issue and arrive at the "best means of developing and applying aircraft in national defense." Rejecting the notion of an "air force," Morrow recommended the formation of an Air Corps within the Army, "thereby strengthening the conception of military aviation as an offensive, striking arm rather than a mere auxiliary service." The resulting Air Corps Act of 1926 gave aviators their own promotion list and, most significant, provided a budget independent from the rest of the Army. A five-year expansion program was also included to grant the new branch 1,800 aircraft, 1,650 officers, and 15,000 enlisted men, though a lack of funding curtailed most of this very visible sign that aviation was a viable addition to the military.

Barely retaining three wings and thirty squadrons, the Air Corps managed to survive political isolationism and appropriations cuts during the Great Depression years.* Nevertheless, with war imminent in Europe and Japan menacing Asia, the service possessed only thirteen B-17s in 1938 and its pursuit aircraft, with the exception of the developmental P-38, were already obsolete. Caught in the vacuum between quasi-peace and

---

* Twelve Bombardment, ten pursuit, six attack and two reconnaissance squadrons.

foreign turmoil, the Air Corps knew it needed to expand, but had not yet been funded at a wartime level. In his quest for rearmament President Roosevelt openly stated that airpower was desperately needed and that "a new barracks at some post in Wyoming" would "not scare Hitler one goddamned bit." With the Depression ending and war a distinct possibility, funding became somewhat easier, though Congress was still not frightened enough to make huge appropriations—yet.

Efforts to increase development and production were only one side of the coin, and without pilots to fly new aircraft the Air Corps was merely a paper tiger. This had been realized during the 1920s and addressed, somewhat, in the National Defense Act. Enlisted ranks could be filled through conscription easily and quickly enough, but commissioned officers were a different matter. Requiring a much higher education and better training, they could not simply be drafted, nor could large numbers be actively supported in peacetime. West Point graduated enough officers for a small, peacetime Army, but the tremendous Great War expansion had dramatically revealed the system's limitations in providing enough officers for a force capable of fighting a world war.

The Officers Reserve Corps (ORC) held about 100,000 World War I veterans on its lists for nearly two decades, but many were gradually replaced due to death, health, or simply age. The shortfall was filled primarily though the Reserve Officers Training Corps (ROTC) or, in the cases of Rex Barber and John Mitchell, the Aviation Cadet Program. Rex discovered that if he applied directly to the Aviation Cadets there would be at least a ten- to twelve-month delay before he could begin flying, but if he took the chance and enlisted now then he would already be in the military when and if war came. With the ensuing mass of volunteers, Rex would have the advantage of an early lead into flight school—hopefully. So, along with twenty thousand other young men, he reported to Jefferson Barracks, St. Louis, Missouri, and during November 1940 worked his way through the normal initiation to military life.

November also saw an event that, with hindsight, was ominously foretelling. Italy's September invasion of Egypt had threatened to cut the Suez Canal, Britain's lifeline to India, and if successful would give the Axis virtually unlimited supplies of Middle Eastern oil. Britain was faced with a hard, solitary fight against Germany, and was in no position to divert many resources to holding Egypt. Even those she could send had to circumnavigate Africa eastward around the Cape of Good Hope, then enter the Mediterranean via the Suez Canal. If the Regia Marina's First Squadron remained dominant east of Gibraltar, then Britain was seriously at risk.

Believing their fleet was safe from torpedoes in the shallow thirty-nine-foot-deep harbor of Taranto, the Italians were caught totally unawares on the night of November 11, when two waves of obsolete, open-cockpit British Fairey biplanes off HMS *Illustrious* attacked the 2,600-year-old port. The British lost two aircraft but severely damaged three Italian battleships, and the *Conte di Cavour* later sank. Equally important to the damage done was the demonstration that a torpedo could be airdropped successfully into a shallow anchorage by modifying its fins, which is what the Royal Navy had done with their standard Mark XII weapon. One of those aviators who instantly grasped the significance of an attack against battleships in a shallow harbor was the new commander of Japan's Combined Fleet: Isoroku Yamamoto.*

As this occurred Rex Barber endured four weeks of basic training in Missouri filled with physical training and 192 classroom hours covering military courtesy, the articles of war, hygiene, and other subjects the

---

* The average draft of Pearl Harbor in 1941 was forty-five feet. Many American naval officers considered this too shallow for an airborne torpedo attack until the British assault on Taranto.

Army deemed necessary. His college time made him immediately eligible for the Aviation Cadets, so as boot camp came to an end Rex applied for flight school and was accepted. He would begin the Civilian-AAF Pilot Training Program in the spring of 1941.

With war coming, military aviation training was frantically, desperately expanding. When Germany invaded Poland the U.S. Army Air Corps could barely train 550 pilots per year, and this was plainly not going to suffice. Hap Arnold tersely stated "to build another Randolph Field to handle 500 pilots a year would take another five years," so he turned to an alternative: civilian flight schools. Many were already established, and most of the men running them were military veterans, including T. Claude Ryan, who built the *Spirit of St. Louis*. Though most of the Army establishment didn't think much of civilians training military pilots, Arnold summoned eight of the best known to Room 1025 of the Munitions Building in Washington, D.C., looked them in the eye, and said, "There's going to be war, and it's going to bust right open, and we've got to build an air force."

Skeptics abounded, but with time short, there were no other options. The Air Corps would supply properly screened flight cadets, with current medical physicals, uniforms, and the approved curriculum. The Army would also provide aircraft, support personnel, and a commanding officer at each school to supervise training, while the civilian operators would, through their government contract, furnish mess facilities, housing, and transportation. They were also responsible for hangars, a main flying field, and athletic facilities. All the ground school and in-flight instruction would be accomplished by civilian instructors who would be periodically evaluated by their military counterparts.

The idea was a good one. These schools, eventually sixty-two of them, would do the time-consuming, basic screening of pilot candidates. Those with no aptitude would be rapidly dropped, while those who successfully completed sixty hours of flight training would progress to the Basic and Advanced flying courses, run by the military. The civilian schools were, in effect, a quality control system to ensure that precious dollars and, more important, precious time, were not wasted. Rex was thrilled to be accepted, and reported to John Gilbert Rankin's school outside Tulare, California, on March 17, 1941.

"Tex" Rankin had flown with the Aviation Section of the Army Signal Corps during World War I and opened his first flight school in Walla Walla, Washington, after returning to the west coast. A barnstormer, he toured with his Rankin Air Circus and set a 1931 world record for flying 131 consecutive outside loops over Charlotte, North Carolina.* Rankin was also a Hollywood stunt pilot and technical director who taught interested movie stars how to fly, including Errol Flynn and Jimmy Stewart. Enthusiastically joining the CFTP program, Tex chose Tulare in the San Joaquin Valley for its mild weather and opened his school in February 1941. When Rex Barber arrived, Rankin Field wasn't complete so he began his training at Mefford Field, a few miles south of Tulare.

The world was tense in March 1941, and time was running out faster than predicted. Buckingham Palace was bombed and on March 11 Congress passed the Lend-Lease Act, placing the United States at war against the Axis in all but name. Hitler, to save his hapless ally Mussolini, had dispatched the 5th Light Division under Erwin Rommel to Africa the previous month. As Rex was learning about Airplane Engine Theory, Meteorology, and Air Navigation, Rommel swept across North Africa to El Agheila, and pushed the British 7th Armored Division back into Egypt. On March 27, while Rex was taking his first flights in the PT-17 Stearman, a young Japanese naval officer named Takeo Yoshikawa arrived on the island of Oahu in the Hawaiian Islands.

---

* As of 2020, his record still stands.

He would spend nearly nine months wandering around the island, taking notes, and watching American warships. Along with technical modifications gleaned from the Taranto attack, Yoshikawa's reports were fundamentally central to Admiral Yamamoto's planning for an attack on the U.S. Pacific Fleet at Pearl Harbor.

President Franklin Roosevelt, long a naval advocate and self-styled expert, upended the U.S. Navy in late April by moving the fleet from its Long Beach and San Diego bases west to Oahu's magnificent Pearl Harbor. Roosevelt reasoned that if the Pacific Fleet was 2,500 miles closer to the Far East, Japan would be less tempted to grab the resource-rich colonies of Britain, the Netherlands, and France. The other side of that coin, which the military plainly saw, was that Japan would have no choice but to deal with that fleet when she decided to expand. Both sides were correct and, as with most political decisions, practicality was sacrificed for expediency. Everything necessary for a fleet had to be brought in from California: weapons, munitions, replacements—everything. There were no facilities for thousands of newly arrived servicemen, and most of their families remained on the mainland, to the detriment of morale.

Rex Barber wasn't much interested in the Navy, or its problems, but he did notice that with the absence of so many sailors, the bars in Los Angeles were happy to see anyone in uniform. There were Sumatra Kulus or Rhum Rhapsodies to drink at Don the Beachcomber's place, and a full Japanese Revue of Ginza Dancing Girls at the Zamboanga South Seas Club.* Flight cadets had neither the time nor money for much of the local nightlife, and as the war picked up speed in Europe flight school was now shortened to three ten-week sections; the Primary or Elementary phase was usually completed at a CFTP school, with Basic and Advanced Flight Training on an Army field.

In addition to sixty hours of flight time, Rex and others like him finished 144 hours of academics requiring a 70 percent minimum grade to pass. The tandem-seat, open-cockpit Stearman—called a "Kaydet"—was a simple and forgiving plane to learn the basics of visual, "contact" flying. Rex soloed after 13 hours and 22 minutes of dual instruction, and went on to log more than 33 solo hours during his ten weeks in Tulare. Even as he mastered basic aerobatics and simple emergency procedures, Rex heard about the German battleship *Bismarck* sinking the British battle cruiser *Hood* on May 23, 1941. England's revenge came three

---

* "Donn Beach" was actually a Texan named Ernest Raymond Beaumont Gantt, who became an Army combat pilot during World War II.

days later at the hands of aviators flying from the carrier *Ark Royal*, and out of a crew of 2,200 men only 114 Germans survived. The fact that the "unsinkable" battleship was sunk by the same obsolete Fairey Swordfishes victorious at Taranto was especially gratifying to a young man who believed that aircraft were the future of warfare.

Graduating from Tulare on June 1, 1941, Rex had one day to get up the coast to the Air Corps Basic Flying School at Moffett Field on San Francisco Bay. Here he progressed through more demanding aerobatics and instrument training, and began night flying. As always, there were academics covering aircraft systems, radio communications, and meteorology. Having completed Basic Flight with a "Very Satisfactory" overall grade, Rex entered the Advanced Flying School at Mather Field outside Sacramento in August 1941. With another eighty hours of Advanced Training, Rex earned his wings and, as the top graduates were awarded officer's commissions, he entered the operational world as a second lieutenant in October 1941.*

---

* Washouts from pilot training were sent to navigator or bombardier schools, and if they also failed there the men were sent to gunnery school. Pilots who did not win commissions were graduated as flight officers.

Even as London burned, and turncoat Vichy French pilots bombed Gibraltar, the British fought on across North Africa, implored Washington for aid, and warily watched the Pacific. So did the Americans. Days after Rex Barber gained his silver wings, Prince Fuminaro Konoye resigned as Japan's prime minister and was succeeded by General Hideki Tojo. A career army officer, Tojo was a die-hard nationalist who absolutely believed in Japan's right to conquer and rule China, Southeast Asia, and the Pacific. The perceived ABCD (American, British, Chinese, Dutch) encirclement and containment of the Empire was, in his opinion, reason enough to strike, as were the continued U.S. embargos aimed at forcing Japan from China. America supplied 95 percent of Japan's copper, 74 percent of its scrap iron, and virtually all its oil. Negotiating with the Dutch proved useless, as the United States had frozen Japan's cash assets and there was no way to pay for available oil. So critical was the situation that in 1941 the Imperial Navy estimated it possessed a stockpile of bunker oil sufficient for only one year of war. The grim choices were therefore reduced to diplomatic concessions or attack.

On November 26, the "Outline of Proposed Basis for Agreement Between the United States and Japan," commonly known as the "Hull Note," was delivered to the Japanese. It was a final attempt to alleviate tension and avoid war, but Section 2, Point 3 was quite pointed and stipulated that Japan "withdraw all military, naval, air and police forces from China and from Indo-China." Japan would never give up its puppet state of Manchukuo, and due to the crippling U.S. embargo, the Empire was economically unable to do so. Even if Tokyo could consider this, Tojo certainly would not. Interpreted as an ultimatum, the Hull Note is widely regarded by the Japanese as a diplomatic Rubicon, though this is attaching too much significance to statecraft, since Yamamoto began outlining Operation Z, the destruction of the U.S. Pacific Fleet, back in January 1941.

At 0600 on November 26, 1941, thirty-two warships of the Imperial Navy weighed anchor from Hitokappu Wan, a bleak, horn-shaped bay in the Kurile Islands.* Six fleet carriers accompanied by a pair of battleships, their escorts, and eight supply ships slid out to sea under cold, gray skies.† Slowly clearing the snow-covered volcanic shoreline cloaked in ice fog and blow-

---

* This is November 26 dated from Washington, D.C., in the Eastern Time Zone. The fleet sailed on November 25, Tokyo time.
† Two destroyers, *Sazanami* and *Ushio*, separated from Nagumo's Air Attack Force and steamed for Midway.

ing sleet, the warships swung southeast toward their target, more than three thousand sea miles away: the Hawaiian island of Oahu, home port of the U.S. Pacific Fleet.

That same day seven transports of Convoy 4002, escorted by the heavy cruiser USS *Pensacola*, departed San Francisco outbound for Pearl Harbor. Crammed with artillery, aviation fuel, and ammunition, the convoy also carried eighty-seven pilots and seventy crates of aircraft, including eighteen P-40 fighters for the 35th Pursuit Group. Sailing on from Hawaii on November 29, bound for Manila, the convoy was followed days later by the *President Johnson*, *Tasker H. Bliss*, and *Etolin*. Lieutenant Rex Barber, after a short visit home to Culver, embarked with the *Johnson* from San Francisco on December 5, 1941, to join the 35th in the Philippines. Everyone in uniform believed that when the Japanese attacked, the U.S. bases in the Philippines would be the target.

The blow, when it came, was 5,300 miles farther east from Manila. Very few saw it coming, and those who did were largely ignored. As dawn touched the North Pacific on Sunday, December 7, 1941, thirty Japanese warships materialized on a patch of open ocean that the world, and certainly the U.S. Navy, expected to be empty. With dawn glowing faintly on the horizon, the big fleet carrier *Akagi*, followed by five others, swung into the trade winds and began launching her fighters, bombers, and torpedo planes. First off was the leader of all 43 Zeros, *Akagi*'s Lieutenant Commander Shigeru Itaya. The other fighters followed, then 49 high-altitude bombers, 51 dive bombers, and 40 torpedo planes—183 aircraft in all that launched and rejoined in fifteen minutes before turning south for Pearl Harbor.

Less than two hours later the first Zeros appeared off Oahu's Kahuku Point and the strike commander, Mitsuo Fuchida, tapped out in Morse code, "TO . . . TO . . . TO," the abbreviation for *Totsugeki:* "charge!" This was followed four minutes later by a message back to the fleet: "Tora . . . Tora . . . Tora," signaling that complete surprise had been achieved. By 0800 the harbor was burning. Six inches of fuel oil covered the water in places, and it all seemed afire. Admiral Husband E. Kimmel, commander of the Pacific Fleet, sent the now famous wire to Washington:

AIR RAID, PEARL HARBOR—THIS IS NO DRILL.

In 110 minutes, 18 ships were destroyed and 2,403 Americans were killed. Aboard the battleship *Nagato* in Japan's Inland Sea, Isoroku Yamamoto was excited and relieved. His ultimate gamble had paid off, sinking five American battleships. He and his staff celebrated with sake toasts and dried squid, and the glorious victory was announced all over Japan to the accompaniment of "Umi Yukaba," a favorite martial song:

Across the sea, corpses in the water
Across the sea, corpses in the field.

Reports from Hawaii electrified the world. Fans listening to the Giants-Dodgers game were the first American civilians to hear of the attack when WOR in New York interrupted its broadcast for the breaking news. Latent fury swept across America, and even vehement isolationists supported immediate war with Japan. Charles Lindbergh, who adamantly opposed fighting for Britain and France, said, "Our country has been attacked by force of arms, and by force of arms we must retaliate."

President Roosevelt did just that.

On December 8, 1941, he addressed a joint session of Congress to ask for a declaration of war and deliver his "Infamy Speech," which in part states:

Yesterday, December 7th, 1941—a date which will live in infamy—the United States of America was suddenly and deliberately attacked by naval and air forces of the Empire of Japan.

The United States was at peace with that nation and, at the solicitation of Japan, was still in conversation with its government and its emperor looking toward the maintenance of peace in the Pacific.

No matter how long it may take us to overcome this premeditated invasion, the American people in their righteous might will win through to absolute victory. I believe that I interpret the will of the Congress and of the people when I assert that we will not only defend ourselves to the uttermost, but will make it very certain that this form of treachery shall never again endanger us.

Hostilities exist. There is no blinking at the fact that our people, our territory, and our interests are in grave danger. With confidence in our armed forces, with the unbounding determination of our people, we will gain the inevitable triumph—so help us God.

Congress took less than an hour to deliver the declaration, and with it America was at war again. Some, like Prime Minister Winston Churchill, were relieved. "I thought of a remark," he later said; "the United States is like a gigantic boiler. Once the fire is lighted under it there is no limit to the power it can generate." Others, like Rex Barber, who even at the time were sailing into harm's way, felt what most men feel when going to war. Trepidation, pride, and a bit of fear. But they go anyway, of their own free will, if their nation has been attacked and those they cherish are threatened. With America's declaration, the conflict had now become a world war, soon to be the most costly and violent war in history. Raymond Clapper, eminent journalist for *Life* magazine, perhaps phrased this best when he wrote, "So ends our reverie in the twilight over the dear, dead days." Yet wherever they were, and whatever they were doing, men and women all over America knew that the world had just changed forever, and it could never again return to what it was before.

Three
Down but Never Out

April 18, 1943
The South Pacific

Rex Barber stuck to *Phoebe*'s left wing during the turn past Tulagi, his left wrist flexing slightly as he made small throttle adjustments, and his feet moving reflexively on the rudder pedals to hold his position. Tom Lanphier flew silky smooth, and at two thousand feet they were comfortably above the bumpy air lower down over the Sound. Directly ahead, the four P-38s of Major Mitchell's flight were rolling out, and Lanphier played his turn a bit to the outside. As *Phoebe*'s left wing lifted toward the horizon, Rex pushed forward slightly to stay lower than his leader, and as they leveled off Joe Moore appeared on Lanphier's right wing. He was holding his normal Number Four spacing, leaving room for one of the spares to slide into the Number Three slot. Stealing a glance back, he could see Lou Kittel's eight P-38s, each distinctive H-shaped fighter perfectly silhouetted against the brightening eastern horizon as they rolled out heading west.

Mitch had briefed an automatic change from the external tanks once everyone was rejoined and headed toward Savo. Without looking down, Rex reached the four-way tank selectors near the floor with his left hand. Touching the long, slender switch on the forward selector, he clicked it left one notch from three o'clock to the twelve o'clock position so fuel would now feed from one of his two reserve tanks. He did the same with the rear selector, glancing down quickly to confirm both switches were in the RES ON quadrant. A pilot could never be too careful where fuel was concerned, since gas was literally life. Forward of the selectors were both fuel boost pump switches and he toggled them off, then checked the fuel quantity gauges on the bottom left instrument panel. Staying in formation with his peripheral vision, Rex ran his eyes over the hydraulic and oil gauges, confirming his RPM needles were rock steady and the temperature gauges were all in the green as they should be.

Suddenly Mitchell rocked his wings, and Lanphier did the same. Up ahead Barber saw the wingmen ease into close formation, so he inched the throttles forward and nudged the wheel right. Lining up Tom's head with the supercharger atop *Phoebe*'s left engine nacelle, Rex slid up the wing line, playing the throttles fore and aft until he was six feet away. Freezing in that position, he noticed Joe Moore hadn't moved in. Tom rocked again, and this time Number Four angled in slowly. As he closed the distance, across the top of Lanphier's plane Barber could see Joe Moore's helmeted head shaking back and forth.

Not good.

His gear looked fully retracted so it could only be a problem with an engine, or maybe fuel. As Rex watched, Moore put his thumb to his mouth, tilted his head back, then made a cutting motion across his throat.

Fuel. Had to be one of the new external tanks. Lanphier nodded then gently kicked his rudders and the tail booms waggled. Joe Moore raised a hand, looked right, and banked away slightly till he was well clear. At a hundred yards away, his P-38 suddenly zoomed up and Rex watched him gracefully roll over the formation before disappearing astern back toward Fighter Two. Lanphier's face turned toward Barber, who passed him a thumbs-up and got a nod in return. *Phoebe*'s booms yawed again and Rex eased back to his loose position off the left wing. Dawn had spread quickly, as it does in the islands, and the sea around Savo was dark blue now instead of black. At 0730 as he looked left, Barber could see all of Guadalcanal; from two thousand feet it was difficult to imagine the lives lost and blood spilled so he and the others could fly from this mottled speck of earth.

But it all happened.

Japan's drive across Asia and the Pacific in the six months following Pearl Harbor had been impressive, but as Yamamoto himself grimly stated to the prime minister, Prince Konoe, "If I am told to fight regardless of consequence, I shall run wild for the first six months or a year, but I have utterly no confidence for the second or third years." In fact, recent battles at the Coral Sea and Midway with the "decadent and weak" Americans had already shown that sand was leaking from the Japanese hourglass.

Certain that the racing Imperial train could be derailed, with ruthlessness the Americans were already striking back. This surprised the Japanese, who were about to suffer a profound shock. On April 18, 1942, seventeen days after leaving Naval Air Station Alameda in San Francisco, the USS *Hornet* was 650 miles east of the Japanese Home Islands. Joined by the *Enterprise*, both carriers and their escorts crossed the Pacific in absolute secrecy: until 0738 on the morning of April 18, 1942. The *Nittō Maru* spotted Task Force 16, and though immediately blown apart by the light cruiser *Nashville*, the small 70-ton picket had time to radio the information. Less than forty minutes later, *Hornet*, under the command of Captain Marc Mitscher, turned into the wind and began launching the sixteen B-25B U.S. Army Mitchell medium bombers on her flight deck.

Well aware that they were ten hours and 170 miles early according to his plan, Lieutenant Colonel Jimmy Doolittle and seventy-nine other "Raiders" never hesitated. Six hours later, just after noon in Tokyo, the unimaginable and, for the Japanese, the impossible occurred; bombs began falling on their capital, the port of Yokohama, and four other cities. Each bomber carried only four 500-pound bombs, three packed with high explosive and one with incendiary. Such a light load could not cause much physical damage, though at least 112 buildings were destroyed and others, including Showa Electric and warehouses belonging to the Japanese Steel Corporation, were heavily damaged. But damage was not the point. The point was to demonstrate to the world, and especially to the Japanese, that America was in no way defeated. If such a strike was possible within months of Pearl Harbor, then what would be forthcoming the following year, and the years after that?

However, the aftermath from the raid had far-reaching implications that began immediately. The Imperial Staff finally realized that China was a massive Achilles' heel where defense of the Japanese Home Islands was concerned. If the Americans could sneak in from an aircraft carrier, what could they do with bombers based on the Asian mainland? Accordingly, a Japanese force of more than 100,000 men swept across China to secure the eastern provinces and to exact bloody revenge for local assistance given to Doolittle's flight crews. Any who helped the raiders were captured and tortured. One group was forced to eat feces, then lined up and shot. A Chinese man who aided Lieutenant Harold Watson was tied to a chair and wrapped in a kerosene-soaked blanket while Japanese soldiers made his wife throw the match that burned him alive.

Rev. Frederick McGuire, a missionary serving in China, wrote, "Soldiers rounded up 800 women and herded them into a storehouse outside the east gate. For one month the Japanese remained in Nancheng, roaming the rubble-filled streets in loin clothes much of the time, drunk a good part of the time and always on the lookout for women. The women and children who did not escape from Nancheng will long remember the Japanese—the women and girls because they were raped time after time by Japan's imperial troops and are now ravaged by venereal disease. . . ."

Another clergyman, Father Wendelin Dunker of Ihwang, recalled:

They [the Japanese] shot any man, woman, child, cow, hog, or just about anything that moved. They raped any woman from the ages of 10–65, and before burning the town they thoroughly looted it . . . none of the humans shot were buried either, but were left to lay on the ground to rot, along with the hogs and cows.

Deciding that the conquest and pacification of China was an ideal testing ground for bacteriological warfare, a top-secret Japanese unit based at the Zhong Ma prison camp in northeastern China was given carte blanche for experimentation with captured civilians. Unit 731 infected prisoners with bubonic plague, typhoid, anthrax, and cholera, among others, then let them loose to mingle with the general population.* Contaminated water, rolls, and biscuits were also left, and starving Chinese became carriers. Between the military butchery and bacteriological experimentation, more than 250,000 Chinese were murdered by the Japanese army.

For Isoroku Yamamoto, commander of the Combined Fleet, Doolittle's raid was a mixed blessing; it was a tangible warning for the Imperial General Staff, and for those officers prescient enough to be justifiably wary of their enemy. Yamamoto was one of these, and he knew time was a luxury the Empire did not possess. The raid proved that Japan was not invulnerable, as many supposed, and that the Americans must be dealt with decisively before they had a chance to gain a foothold in the Pacific.

No doubt he felt a pang of fear thinking of the United States, a country where he had lived and studied, a country he knew quite well. Its immense industrial capacity was frightening, as was the character of its people. The admiral understood Americans regarded treachery with intense hatred, and through poor dip-

---

* Under Shiro Ishii, a Japanese Josef Mengele, Unit 731 continued research all through the war. In 1945, bacteriological attacks against San Diego were planned, but never carried out. Ishii and nearly all the other members of Unit 731 were never tried for war crimes.

lomatic timing delivering Japan's declaration of war this was precisely how his masterstroke against Hawaii was viewed. The attack stirred a wrath in the United States that he knew would overwhelm and destroy the Empire if enough time elapsed, and the shipyards and factories began turning out war material for millions of angry young American men waiting to fight.

Yamamoto understood the message of the Doolittle Raid, and that it was no rash, emotional action. It was a very real harbinger of America's rage, and for this reason the consummate gambler was advocating another shrewd gamble. By invading Midway Island, the admiral sought to lure the remaining U.S. aircraft carriers into a strategically tactical counterstrike. Once committed and isolated in midocean, Yamamoto would spring his trap with at least four frontline carriers and nearly 250 aircraft. It would finish the job he had begun at Pearl Harbor, and be a deathblow to the Pacific Fleet. With no defense for Hawaii or the U.S. west coast, Washington would be forced to negotiate a peace. Japan would have won the war and, with the vast resources of her newly acquired territories, the Empire would be secure. It was bold, audacious, and entirely in keeping with Yamamoto's personality. Nevertheless, until Doolittle's B-25s appeared over Tokyo, he had not been able to obtain approval for it.

That all changed on April 18, 1942.

Yamamoto's plan, though overly intricate and based on several large assumptions regarding American actions, suddenly seemed the best chance of decisively dealing with the United States Navy. But before luring the Americans into the trap, Operation MO, the previously planned "Southward Thrust" into the Solomons and New Guinea, had to go forward. Envisioned as a three-pronged plan, the eastern assault would come through the Solomon Sea and take the Florida Islands opposite Guadalcanal. Simultaneously, a western prong would slip through the Louisade Archipelago off New Guinea, traverse the Jomard Passage, and round the southern tip of the peninsula to invade Port Moresby. This would put the Imperial Army within striking distance of Australia, and essentially seal off the southwest Pacific. The main prong was intended to catch the U.S. fleet in open water and destroy it. Japanese control of the Solomons and New Guinea meant control of the Coral Sea, where carrier air strikes could be launched against northeastern Australia and New Caledonia and thereby sever the U.S.-to-Australia sea routes.

Two 5th Division fleet carriers, *Zuikaku* and *Shokaku*, sortied from Truk on May 3, headed into the Coral Sea. They were to support the light carrier *Shoho* and the Port Moresby invasion force, then return north if able to add their weight to the Midway operation. Flawed Japanese intelligence, generally based on saving face, and racial contempt for their enemies hindered the operation from the onset. A tendency to favorably interpret information fueled an overly optimistic, simplistic, and quite dangerous assessment of American naval assets in the southwest Pacific. Despite being constantly proven wrong, these surprisingly poor intelligence practices continued throughout the war, and would cost the Japanese dearly.

In fact, the reality was starkly different. Admiral Nimitz and Admiral King both agreed that halting the Southward Thrust and maintaining the eastern sea routes to the U.S. west coast was *the* strategic priority in the Pacific Theater. For King it was the line in the sand; Japan's stab must be blunted, and the myth of their invincibility shattered. Both admirals knew that island hopping worked both ways, and if the Solomons were held by American forces, then other islands up the chain could be eventually captured. This meant naval bases and, above all, airfields, from which subsequent counteroffensives could be launched against Rabaul. With the sea routes secure and Australia safe, it would then be possible to knock Japan onto the defensive and force the Empire back into a steadily diminishing perimeter around the Home Islands.

But first and foremost the Solomons had to be held.

To this end, Nimitz, who was also capable of bold gestures, decided to commit his fleet, meet the Japanese Navy in the Coral Sea, and thwart the Port Moresby invasion. There wasn't sufficient fuel or enough tankers for a conventional fleet, so Nimitz sent his seven battleships back to California and decided to face the Japanese navy with fast carrier task forces. This was a truly historic decision with lasting implications for modern naval warfare, and it ended three centuries of battleship dominance over naval tactics.

Task Force 11, commanded by Rear Admiral Aubrey Fitch, centered on the USS *Lexington* and in late May was already in the South Pacific. The *Yorktown* and Rear Admiral Frank Jack Fletcher's Task Force 17 were ordered to the Coral Sea to join up with the other carrier, and by May 4 was some hundred miles southwest of Guadalcanal.* Opening the fight the day earlier, Japanese forces invaded the Florida Islands and captured Tulagi. *Zuikaku* and *Shokaku* swung around San Cristobal at the southern end of the Solomons and entered the Coral Sea from the north, hoping to ambush the

---

* Task Force 16, with the *Enterprise* and *Hornet,* was returning to Pearl Harbor following the Doolittle Raid, and could not make it so far south in time to make a difference.

U.S. carriers. Blanketed by heavy rain, the two fleets missed by less than one hundred miles as *Yorktown* rendezvoused with *Lexington,* then set off on May 6 westward toward New Guinea.

Knowing most of the Japanese route to Port Moresby, Fletcher planned to lie in wait on the southern end of the Jomard Passage, and when the enemy fleet emerged he would cut it to pieces in an ambush of his own. Deciding to hedge his bets, Fletcher split his force by sending his cruisers to cover the west exit while he stayed to the north. At 1100 on May 7, *Lexington*'s SBD-2 Dauntless dive bombers and *Yorktown*'s TBD-1 Devastator torpedo planes caught the *Shoho* at the north end of the passage just as she was launching her aircraft, and the ninety-three American planes made short work of the little 12,000-ton carrier. After thirteen 1,000-pound bomb hits and at least seven torpedo strikes, nothing remained but an oil slick. Commander Bill Ault, who led the strike and was *Lexington*'s Air Group commander, famously radioed back, "Scratch one flattop!" as the first major Japanese warship to be lost in the war went down.

Unfortunately, the next day's battle was quite different.

At 0530, *Lexington* turned into the west wind and launched her morning scout planes. About the same time, some two hundred miles to the north, Admiral Chuichi Hara launched as well. Several hours later, both sides blundered into each other at approximately the same time and scrambled to get strike forces airborne. *Lexington* and *Yorktown* put up thirty-nine dive bombers and twenty-one torpedo planes escorted by fifteen Wildcat fighters; Hara launched thirty-three dive bombers, eighteen torpedo planes, and eighteen Zero fighters. Both Japanese carriers were spotted at 1032, but the U.S. planes fussed around for twenty-five minutes trying to coordinate an attack, which allowed *Zuikaku* to hide under a convenient rain squall. The American strike commenced at 1057 against *Shokaku,* and though all the torpedoes missed, a pair of 1,000-pound bombs hit squarely and set the flight deck on fire for one hundred feet down the port side. Minutes later another bomb struck the carrier and put her out of action, and while the pilots believed they sank her, *Shokaku* managed to withdraw north to fight another day.

Not so for the crews of forty-three planes lost in the quick battle, or for the U.S. carriers that were under attack at virtually the same time. *Yorktown,* smaller and more agile, evaded all the lethal Type-91 Long Lance torpedoes used by the Japanese, but did take one 800-pound bomb forward of her superstructure that penetrated fifty feet through three decks before exploding. Concussions from near misses sprang some plates below her waterline but the tough carrier, as always, fought on.

Lexington was not so fortunate. Coming in from both sides, the Japanese scored two torpedo hits on her port flank, and two bomb hits that started deadly fires below decks. Damage control was a focus of the prewar U.S. Navy, and this was well proven as the "Lady Lex" continued to hold 25 knots and recover returning aircraft. Her damage control officer, Lieutenant Commander Healy, informed Captain Frederick Sherman that the torpedo damage was contained, then added with characteristically tough, humorous professionalism, "but I suggest sir, that if you have to take any more torpedoes, you take them on the starboard side."

Within minutes the big carrier was rocked by a powerful, teeth-rattling explosion from deep below decks. Fuel vapor had leaked out from her ruptured tanks and, rising upward undetected, was ignited by sparks from her generators. Some of her aircraft got back aboard, and others went to the nearby *Yorktown.* Some, including Bill Ault, who destroyed the *Shoho,* were lost forever. He was out of fuel and wounded; his last transmission was simply, "Okay . . . so long people. We've got a 1,000 lb. hit on the flattop!" At 1707, Admiral Fitch ordered the ship abandoned. Captain

Sherman, with his cocker spaniel, Wags, was the last off, and shortly thereafter five torpedoes from the destroyer *Phelps* sent Lady Lex to rest 14,400 feet beneath the Coral Sea.

The first carrier battle in history was over.

This was the first time ships from opposing fleets fought without sighting each other, and the battle was won or lost by pilots. Both sides figuratively blinked after the Coral Sea; those who had not grasped it before now realized the decisiveness this form of warfare could provide. The Americans in particular saw the potential, especially when carrier airpower was utilized in conjunction with amphibious assaults. Both sides also claimed victory. The Imperial Navy sank the *Lexington* but lost the *Shoho*. More damaging were the losses of seventy-seven aircraft and most of their trained crews, which were never adequately replaced. American attacks also prompted the recall of the Port Moresby invasion fleet, and this was a tremendously decisive victory, as there would never be another chance to invade by sea again, and the entire Japanese strategic plan for the southwest Pacific had been derailed. This loss of momentum, and the psychological ramifications on both sides, would be highly significant in the months to come. Following on the heels of the Doolittle Raid, the Battle of the Coral Sea further cracked the mythical wall of Japanese invincibility.

Shokaku returned to the Home Islands for a ninety-day refit and *Zuikaku,* which had lost fully half of her air group, was also forced to return to Japan. This left Yamamoto with four fleet carriers, instead of six, for his Midway operation, and the lack of these two air groups would prove crucial. For the Americans, losing the *Lexington* was a blow and though *Yorktown* was badly damaged she was steaming back to Pearl Harbor under her own power. Nevertheless, only the *Enterprise* and *Hornet* now remained fully operational in the Pacific to counter the greatest gamble of Yamamoto's life.*

While Commanders Joe Rochefort and Ed Layton burned themselves out breaking the new Japanese five-digit naval code, a battered American warship limped back into Pearl Harbor. Sirens blared, horns honked, and sailors lined decks as the big carrier, trailing a

---

* The USS *Saratoga* had been torpedoed in early January 1942 and sent back to the Bremerton Navy Yard for repairs. She would sail from San Diego on June 1 and did not fight in the Battle of Midway.

ten-mile oil slick, steamed slowly up the channel past Fort Kamehameha and Hickam Field. As she rounded Hospital Point on May 27, 1942, waiting tugs eased her into the Navy Yard's Dry Dock Number One, south of Ford Island.* The USS *Yorktown* was home.

But not for long.

Admiral Nimitz himself, wearing boots and gloves, inspected her damaged hull and concluded that welded steel plates would serve well enough as temporary patches, and he ordered her to sea again in seventy-two hours. Like ants, some 1,400 dockyard workers and specialists of all types swarmed over Fletcher's flagship. The wounded were taken ashore and replacements brought aboard. A hurried conference took place at CINCPAC headquarters, a three-story, concrete motel-type building surrounded by chain link fence on Makalapa Drive. Rochefort had broken the code, and based on this Commander Layton staked thousands of lives and the short-term fortunes of the war on his analysis of Yamamoto's plan. "They'll come in from the northwest on a bearing 325 degrees and they will be sighted at about 175 miles from Midway, and the time will be about 06:00 Midway time." Nimitz,

---

* This same dry dock held the battleship USS *Pennsylvania* during the Pearl Harbor attack.

like Yamamoto, also gambled and had formulated a riposte: a risky, bold plan that appalled Washington, and frightened many senior officers who believed remaining American strength should be used defensively to protect Hawaii and the U.S. west coast.

Nimitz thought otherwise. The Japanese were certain *Yorktown* had been sunk in the Coral Sea, and the other American carriers were far away down in the South Pacific. Yamamoto's plan was to attack and invade the Aleutian Islands, which was U.S. soil and he believed had to be protected. He would also target Midway, a vital speck of coral that, in Japanese hands, would threaten Hawaii and possibly open the west coast to invasion, or at least make Washington consider that threat.* The Americans would *have* to counter, and Nimitz would *have* to commit the Pacific Fleet to meet such a threat. When this happened, it would be caught between three powerful fleets and annihilated in a classic Japanese hammer-and-anvil sudden strike centering on the Combined Fleet's battleships. This tactic had worked for the Japanese against the Russians

---

* Japan did not have the logistical or material capacity to invade the United States, but most Americans did not know this in 1942 and Yamamoto believed that such a threat would compel Washington to open peace negotiations.

in 1904, and to a lesser degree more recently against the British.

But these were Americans, not Russians. They were unpredictable and often illogical in the conventional military sense, so predicting how they would act was fraught with danger. Given his experience in the United States and close acquaintances with many officers, Yamamoto should have known better, and perhaps he did; but the admiral was a chess player, and was well aware that his time to "run wild" was slipping away. He believed his American counterpart would act according to training and experience, thereby deploying his remaining assets defensively. This assumption was the fundamental weakness in an already overcomplicated battle plan, a plan that also divided the Combined Fleet, was hampered by radio silence, and was lacking two carriers due to the Coral Sea action.

These considerations aside, the overwhelmingly weak link in Yamamoto's gambit was that the Americans already knew the details. Combined with the deep-seated anger toward the Japanese, thirst for revenge, and the rapidly blossoming tactical skill of its pilots, the U.S. Navy was a much more formidable adversary than the admiral allowed. Nimitz intended to use all these conditions to his advantage and turn the

Japanese attack back on itself, thus doing to them what they intended for the Pacific Fleet.

Unlike Yamamoto's surprising battleship-centric plan, the Americans based everything around their three available aircraft carriers, which is precisely why *Yorktown* put to sea on May 30, forty-eight hours after *Enterprise* and *Hornet* steamed west to the rendezvous some two hundred miles northeast of Midway. Though the Imperial Navy switched codes on May 28, U.S. intelligence had deciphered enough of the plan so that Nimitz was in no way deceived when, on the morning of June 3, 1942, air strikes from the carriers *Junyo* and *Ryujo* swept in over Unalaska Bay to hit Dutch Harbor in the Aleutians.

A few hours later, some 1,400 miles to the south, a solitary Catalina from Navy Patrol (VP) Squadron 44 out of Midway picked up a large body of ships west of the atoll. Ensign Jack Reid mistakenly identified the fleet as the Japanese "main body," and a B-17 strike was immediately ordered. Admiral Nimitz, quite correctly, deduced that this was the invasion fleet, not the enemy carriers, but Yamamoto's plan was exposed. American code breakers, and Nimitz, had been right.

At 0130 on June 4, pilots from both fleets were at breakfast. Tea, soybean soup, and sake for the Japanese, while the Americans had steak and eggs washed down with black coffee. Admiral Raymond Spruance was certain the enemy carriers would appear northwest of Midway, and before sunrise his Catalinas were outbound flying spokes on an enormous wheel. As for Admiral Chuichi Nagumo, optimistic assumptions regarding the American carriers, coupled with copious amounts of false aviation radio traffic in the South Pacific, lured the Japanese into complacency.* He knew where Midway was, so there was scant need of reconnaissance. At 0620 the first wave of 108 aircraft had blown through the Marine fighters of VMF-221 and appeared over the atoll. Fortunately, everything flyable was already airborne headed northwest; six Navy TBF Avengers and four USAAF B-26s were followed by a second wave of sixteen Marine Dauntless dive bombers, fifteen B-17s, and eleven obsolete Marine Vindicators. Thirty minutes later the Japanese disappeared, leaving rising columns of smoke from burning oil tanks, hangars, and the powerhouse. However, repeating their errors at Pearl Harbor, they failed to ac-

---

* The heavy cruiser *Salt Lake City* and seaplane tender *Tangier* created very realistic communications simulating a carrier task force.

complish the primary objective and the atoll's airstrips were still functional.

This initial failure set up the rest of a very long, critical day. Midway's air attacks failed, but the strike did pinpoint the Japanese carriers and create mass confusion—especially in the mind of Admiral Nagumo. He was now faced with a still viable threat from the atoll, which would put his force in a vise if American carriers appeared. After vacillating and delaying, his ninety-three aircraft that were standing by to attack ships were ordered rearmed with bombs for a second strike on Midway's runways. He planned to launch this attack before the first strike returned. Those aircraft would then be refueled and armed to attack the U.S. Navy, which, unbeknownst to Nagumo, was less than two hundred miles east and turning into the wind.

Hornet and *Enterprise* launched everything available; sixty-seven Dauntless dive-bombers, twenty-nine Devastators, and twenty Wildcat fighters joined up until a Aichi E13A1 "Jake" floatplane from the cruiser *Tone* was discovered overhead. Fearing an attack, Spruance ordered his dive bombers out alone to find and destroy the Japanese carriers. Nearly thirty miles behind *Enterprise* and *Hornet,* the *Yorktown* sent up its own strike of seventeen dive bombers and sixteen torpedo planes escorted by six Wildcats. Three separate waves totaling 155 American aircraft were now headed for the Japanese carriers. Learning of at least one U.S. carrier within two hundred miles of him panicked Nagumo, who was still rearming and preparing to recover his first strike aircraft. At this critical moment, the second wave of attackers appeared from Midway, led by Major Lofton R. Henderson, the commander of VMSB-241. It also failed, and half the dive bombers were lost, including Major Henderson, who died attacking the *Hiryu*.

Twenty minutes into rearming, Nagumo finally made the decision to halt yet again and those planes already serviced were to be taken below to give a clear deck for the recovery of all airborne aircraft. Tired, harassed, and short of time, the Japanese crewmen left the torpedoes on trolley, and stacked fully fused bombs wherever they could rather than return munitions to the magazines. Fuel hoses were everywhere, tempers were short, and the four carriers were in various states of confusion when the *Hornet*'s torpedo bombers appeared off the *Akagi*'s starboard quarter at 0920. Fifteen clunky Devastators of VT-8 bored straight in without fighter escort, and all were shot down in flames by the Zeros or from curtains of intense antiaircraft fire.

As Lieutenant Commander John Waldron and his

men died, another fifteen torpedo planes from the *Enterprise* appeared, splitting to attack the *Kaga* and *Akagi*.* More of the Zeros came down, using up fuel and ammunition to fight off the Americans, and ten Devastators were destroyed. As the carriers sliced through the water at 30 knots, *Yorktown's* squadron of twelve torpedo planes attacked at 1000; only two made it out. Including lost Wildcats, in less than one hour forty-one aircraft went down and eighty men died. But by this time, there were no Zeros overhead and those still in the air were short of fuel, while rearming planes on the carriers had been disrupted. Nagumo was trying to regain some sense of order when Lieutenant Commander Wade McClusky, commander of Air Group Six off the *Enterprise*, came screaming out of the sky with thirty-seven Dauntless dive bombers, aiming directly for the red "meatball" insignia on the *Akagi's* flight deck.

"Call it fate, luck or what you may," McClusky later recounted, "I spied a lone Jap cruiser scurrying under full power to the north-east. Concluding that she possibly was a liaison ship between the occupation forces

---

* U.S. Naval Academy class of 1924, Waldron was a North Dakota native and part Sioux Indian. Ensign George Henry Gay, the sole survivor of VT-8, was rescued by a Catalina after thirty hours in the water. Fifty-two years later, his ashes were spread on the spot where his squadron perished.

and the striking force, I altered my Group's course to that of the cruiser . . . that decision paid dividends."*

The other half of his bombers went for the *Kaga*, hitting it with four bombs that killed her captain and turned the big carrier into a blazing wreck. Within minutes of McClusky's attack, Lieutenant Commander Max Leslie and eighteen Dauntless bombers from the *Yorktown* dove into the fight, and within minutes the *Sōryū* was uncontrollably afire. The American hammer stroke lasted about six minutes; by 1047, turbines dead and flaming puddles of aviation fuel washing over her deck, the *Akagi* was abandoned by Admiral Nagumo, who slid out of the bridge on a rope ladder. *Sōryū* would sink just past 1600 later that afternoon, and the *Kaga* would follow some ninety minutes later.

Aboard *Hiryū*, Japan's finest carrier tactician was alternately shocked and angered. Rear Admiral Tamon Yamaguchi was aggressive, talented, and flexible in his tactical thinking. Like Yamamoto, he also had spent time in America: two years at Princeton and a further three years as naval attaché in Washington. There was no doubt in his mind what would happen if the initia-

---

* The Japanese warship was actually the destroyer *Arashi*, which had been attacking the USS *Nautilus*, an American submarine that later sank the *Kaga*.

tive were not seized, so he immediately ordered every remaining plane into the air to follow the Americans back to their carrier. Just before noon the *Yorktown*'s radar picked up an unidentified formation inbound from the northwest, and at 1205 eighteen dive bombers began their attack. Only six would survive, but the carrier took three direct hits and two near misses that left her a drifting, listing inferno.

Fittingly, it was a scout from the *Yorktown* that pinpointed *Hiryū*, the last of Nagumo's carriers, about an hour later, and the *Enterprise* immediately launched a strike while the last ten torpedo bombers and six Zeros took off from the *Hiryū*. By the time they arrived, the American carrier was making 19 knots and thanks to superlative damage control she appeared undamaged. The Japanese pilots thought they had discovered yet another carrier and promptly attacked, putting two torpedoes into *Yorktown*'s port side, bringing the ship to a stop with a 23-degree list. That was the final piece of good news for the Japanese that day, as the Americans caught up with the *Hiryū* and by 1700 that afternoon four direct hits turned her into a floating pyre. She would survive the night but followed the *Akagi* to the bottom of the sea the following morning.

Yorktown would be abandoned, but she refused to die. Captain Elliot Buckmaster boarded with a damage control party, extinguished all the fires, and reduced her list. The minesweeper *Vireo* was able to tow the carrier at three knots, while the destroyer *Hammann* provided power. Unfortunately, the Japanese submarine I-168 managed to slip inside the screening vessels and on at 1331 on June 6, fired four Type 89 torpedoes at the carrier. One blew the *Hammann* in half, and two others hit *Yorktown* squarely on the starboard side. At 0501 on the morning of June 7, the great carrier rolled to port, settled, and finally sank with her battle flags still flying.

Far to the north, damage to the Aleutians was minimal, as there wasn't much to be damaged. Despite this victory, the battle was an overwhelming tactical defeat for the Japanese, one that would have far-reaching consequences they knew nothing of until after the war. On the morning of June 3, while the carriers were swapping strikes north of Midway, a Catalina flying boat flown by Lieutenant Bud Mitchell tried to escape from Dutch Harbor. A flight of three Zeros off the *Ryūjō* shot down the ponderous amphibian, and then strafed the crew as they struggled into life rafts. After participating in killing the helpless men, Flight Petty Officer Tadayoshi Koga in Zero No. 4593 with the other two fighters began strafing flying boats in Dutch Harbor.

The next day the same three Zeros, led by Chief

Petty Officer Makoto Endo, attacked gun emplacements around the harbor until ground fire hit Koga's
plane, severing the return oil line and damaging the
engine coolant system. Venting oil, the smoking fighter
veered off toward the nearest designated emergency
landing area, about twenty-five miles away to the
northeast: Akutan Island. On the southern side Koga
found what he took as a flat pasture about a half-mile
inland from Broad Bight, circled, then dropped his
landing gear. The pasture was actually a swamp covered with knee-high grass, and as the fighter touched
down its gear instantly sank into the bog, and the Zero
flipped onto its back in a spray of mud.

Endo and the other pilot, Flight Petty Officer Tsu-
guo Shikada, were supposed to strafe and destroy the
wreck, but they thought their fellow pilot might be
alive inside and did not. Returning to their carrier,
Endo reported the combat loss, but said nothing about
the wreck. For a month, Koga's body rotted in the
cockpit, his head partially submerged in water, until
July 10, when a patrolling VP-41 Catalina flown by
Lieutenant Bill Thies and Ensign Robert Larson spotted the plane. The U.S. Navy sent a team in and with
a tractor dragged the plane to the beach, where it was
crated and loaded aboard a transport ship. Taken to
North Island Naval Air Station in San Diego, Koga's

Zero was rebuilt to flyable condition and Lieutenant Commander Eddie R. Sanders made two dozen evaluation flights during September and October 1942.

Less than four months old when it went down, tail #4593 was the latest-model Zero, but Sanders discovered significant limitations. At speeds above 200 knots the aileron responsiveness was poor, so high-speed maneuvering was slow, and it utilized a float-type carburetor so any negative-g maneuvers would cut out its 940-hp radial engine; very bad in a dogfight. The plane also rolled left much easier than to the right and lacked self-sealing fuel tanks, so one good burst would light it up like a torch. Koga's Zero was used to formulate counter tactics, and as a result many American lives were saved while Japanese lives were taken. It was also used to evaluate the performance of Wildcats, Corsairs, P-39s, and the Army's best fighter aircraft in the Pacific: the P-38 Lightning.

Four
Shoestring

Following news of the attack on Pearl Harbor, the *Pensacola*'s convoy was rerouted to Australia and made it to Brisbane two days before Christmas 1941. Rex Barber, aboard the *President Johnson,* was turned around midocean and she returned to San Francisco, where the pilots disembarked on December 9, 1941, to the Polo Grounds in Golden Gate Park. Twenty-seven days later Rex left again, this time on board another Dollar Steamship liner called the *President Monroe* and bound for Suva on Viti Levu in the Fiji Islands.

It was here, three thousand miles south of the battles around Midway, that Rex Barber and John Mitchell also waited. Both pilots, along with 41 other officers and 217 enlisted men of the 70th Pursuit Squadron, had finally made it to the Fijis late in January 1942. Just as the 67th was doing, Mitch and Rex were to become acclimated to the tropics, protect convoys, and be prepared to move fast when called. Their P-39 Airacobras were only marginally better than the P-400s flown by the 67th, but they were all there was, so Mitchell and Barber made do. John Mitchell was generally appalled by the gunnery skills of most of his pilots, and that became a priority as they flew from Nadi airfield on the west coast of Viti Levu, largest of the 330 Fiji islands. Peacetime training had been just that—peacetime. The emphasis was usually on pretty flying, aerobatics, and formations as there had been little prewar funding for ammunition, bombs, and tactical exercises. That had all changed on December 7, and a pilot who could not hit a target was not a fighter pilot in Mitchell's mind.

Known for his no-nonsense, professional leadership, John Mitchell did not tolerate bravado or foolishness. He cared as much about bringing his men home alive as he did about killing Japanese. Born in northwest Mississippi during the summer of 1914, he entered the Army in 1934 as an enlisted man and served with Battery F, 55th Coastal Artillery, at Fort Ruger on Oahu. With a bit of college under his belt, Mitchell applied for the Aviation Cadet Program and was admitted on November 10, 1939. The stocky, dark-haired young man was sent to Randolph Field outside of San Antonio, Texas.

Earning his silver pilot's wings and a second lieutenant's commission by the end of July 1940, Mitchell flew P-40 Warhawks for the 20th Fighter Group for the next seventeen months, until the attack on Pearl Harbor. Stuck in North Carolina with a broken P-40, he chafed at the delay and wanted to get into the action. By the time his plane was ready to fly back to Hamilton Field, outside San Francisco, the United States had declared war on Japan. Stopping off in Texas long enough to marry a beautiful San Antonio belle named Anne he'd met during flight school, Mitchell volunteered to go anywhere there was fighting. Henry Vicellio, then a captain, was the commander of the newly formed 70th Pursuit Squadron, and his unit already had orders for the distant Pacific. He needed all the experienced pilots he could find so Mitchell, who overnight found himself as second in command, was charged with getting his pilots as ready as possible in the limited time remaining. Worse still, the 70th was going to war in the Bell P-39 Airacobra instead of the tough Curtiss-built Warhawk, which was needed for rumored operations in North Africa.

Mitchell did what he could.

Every day his pilots flew whatever was available just to get some air beneath their butts. Above all, he wanted gunnery practice for his green lieutenants, among them a young, quiet Oregonian named Rex Barber and a dark, extroverted Idahoan named Tom Lanphier. The prewar lassitude had vanished, and with it the gentlemanly "flying club" mentality so common in the peacetime Army Air Corps, so the pilots shot up targets dropped off the coast and practiced dive bombing over Rogers Dry Lake. John Mitchell also faced the logistical nightmare of packing up a fighter squadron, then deploying to the other side of the world, which is exactly what occurred during late January 1942.

Nearly nine months before Mitchell took off with his Lightnings, the island was just an unknown smudge on a map to most Americans. Most, but not all. During the night and early morning of August 6–7, 1942, a convoy of dark ships approached it from the south, passed through a squall line, and emerged into the moonlit sky of the Solomon Sea. Eighty-two warships slid out of the storm front, then split into two separate groups. The American fleet carriers *Enterprise*, *Saratoga*, and *Wasp* swung away with the battleship *North Carolina* to provide air support from a position one hundred miles south from the task force's objective: a slug-shaped island called Guadalcanal.

A second formation of ships, the amphibious group of Task Force 62 carrying 959 officers and 18,146 men of the 1st Marine Division, continued north under the command of Rear Admiral Richmond Kelly Turner. A 1908 Naval Academy graduate, "Terrible Turner" was just that: short-tempered, brash, and highly intellectual when he so chose. He had earned his aviator's golden wings in 1927 at age forty-two. A tenacious fighter with a superb brain, Turner was "brilliant, caustic, arrogant, and tactless—just the man for the job," according to Chester Nimitz, commander in chief of the U.S. Pacific Fleet.

Aboard the *Bellatrix, Betelgeuse, George F. Elliot,* and other transports, thousands of young men watching from the decks smelled Guadalcanal before they could see it: the stench of wet, rotting vegetation that smothered the clean, salty sea air. At 0240, with silver light brushing the rolling waves, the ships swung northeast at the bottom of New Georgia Sound, then glided past Cape Esperance into the Sealark Channel near Savo Island. Menacing silhouettes of warships, led by the heavy cruiser USS *Vincennes,* headed farther into the channel, their gun turrets rotating toward a sliver of sand along Guadalcanal's northern shoreline. Sharklike destroyers moved inshore to the beach, while their older, four-stack brothers crept closer to sweep the shallow waters for the small, airdropped naval mines favored by the Japanese. Separating at Savo, the eight transports of Group "Yoke," and some five thousand Marines, went north around the dark coast before turning east toward Florida Island and Tulagi. Group "X-Ray," the remaining fifteen AK/AP transports, chugged slowly though the channel before drifting to a stop 4.5 miles off Lunga Point on Guadalcanal's north shore.

Windy, rocky, and steep along the southern "weather coast," the ground climbed sharply to the 1,514-foot summit of Mount Austen. Dropping off north of the mountain, the central plain had a few relatively flat spots that tailed off into a fetid, coastal plain that dropped into the water where the Marines now waited. It was hot, wet, and steamy during the rainy season, which was most of the time, and more than 160 inches of rain each year kept the air thick and always humid. The few native hand-cut pathways were narrow, clogged with thorn-encrusted vines, and crisscrossed by enormous, twisted roots. Beaches stank of rotting vegetation, decayed coconuts, and dead fish. Swarms of biting insects were always present, along with rabbit-sized rats, snakes, and screeching monkeys. Huge, strange butterflies flitted silently through dark shadows at the massive bases of hardwoods more than 150 feet tall. Tenaru, Matanikau, Ilu, and other stagnant, tepid streams shortly to be infamous were home to ugly crocodiles and thick clouds of mosquitoes.

No one, with the possible exception of the native Melanesians or a few hardy foreigners making money from the plantations on the central plain, had much use for the place. However, it was this very central plain, the only flat area on the island, that made it valuable to the Marines who were now awaiting the command to storm ashore. They were not the first recent strangers to stare at Guadalcanal from the water. Three months earlier the Japanese landed in the Florida Islands across the Sealark Channel, and deployed the Yokohama Air Group's seaplanes to Tulagi. They reported that a central plain existed on Guadalcanal large enough for an airfield to stiffen Japan's outer defenses. The Solomons, which they called Soromon Shoto, were at the extreme limit of this, but protected the sea approaches to New Guinea and Japan's great South Pacific bastion: Rabaul.

Anticipating the impending defeat of the U.S. Navy, the Japanese knew these islands would be an ideal springboard to invade the Fijis and New Caledonia. To this end, in early July 1942, twelve transports carrying about 2,500 men of the 13th and 11th Construction Units commanded by Imperial Navy captain Tei Monzen landed on Guadalcanal and wasted little time. A primitive dock was knocked together, and a narrow-gauge railway quickly laid between the dock and central plain. Grass was burned off, and work commenced immediately on the one feature that could make the island valuable: a thirty-six-hundred-foot packed-earth runway. When completed, the airfield would permit Japanese control of the air around the southern Solomons.

But for the waiting Americans there was no indication yet of how vital this piece of earth would become in the next few months. It was, at the moment, just ground to be taken. Reveille sounded at 0300, and the 959 officers and 18,146 men of the 1st Marine Division breakfasted on hard-boiled eggs, fruit, and black coffee. Equipment and weapons were checked, again, and the men with extra time came topside to stare at the islands. Operation WATCHTOWER, the first American counteroffensive of the war, was about to commence. Sunrise, a watery pink glow along the far eastern horizon, changed the sky from deep black to light gray tinged with purple. Shades of green on the island were discernible now, and the white flecks of breakers could be seen just off the beach.

There wasn't much else to see until 0600, when the Dauntless dive bombers and Wildcats fighters arrived overhead to shoot up the airfield, docks, and anyone foolish enough to fire back. Just after the air strikes, nine 8-inch guns from the heavy cruiser USS *Quincy* opened fire from the Sealark Channel, commencing the first Allied counteroffensive of World War II. F4F Wildcat fighters from VF-72 off the USS *Wasp* dropped through the haze and destroyed eight Nakajima A6M2 Zero float fighters along with seven big Kawanishi H6K4 "Mavis" flying boats moored in Halavo Bay. Other heavy cruisers and all the destroyers joined in while the rest of the air strikes hit suspected coastal batteries, wharfs, and the unfinished airfield on Guadalcanal.

The Marines, wearing new sage green cotton battle dress and modern M-1 helmets, began lining up on deck. They went over the side and clambered down cargo nets dyed brown in drums filled with Navy coffee. Armed with the same Springfield '03 bolt-action rifles their fathers used during the Great War, the average enlisted Marine was twenty years old, and their officers just a few years older. At full strength, the 1st Marine Division of 1942 was allocated 19,500 men and officers with a "triangle" organization of three subordinate units.

Major General Alexander Archer Vandegrift's division comprised the 1st, 5th, and 7th regiments, each commanded by a colonel. However, in August 1942 the 7th Marines were on Samoa, so for WATCHTOWER the 2nd Marine Regiment was borrowed from the 2nd Marine Division. Every regiment was further broken down into three battalions: the 1st, 2nd, and 3rd, respectively, each commanded by a lieutenant colonel. Battalions consisted of companies, lettered alphabetically, which were led by a captain. Companies, also lettered alphabetically and commanded by a lieutenant, consisted of three rifle platoons, nominally of forty-two men each, and a weapons platoon. Unlike their Army counterparts, Marines were Marines first: they were riflemen trained to use every light or heavy weapon their unit possessed. Aviators, technicians, cooks, and support personnel were also all combat troops. This long-held doctrine would prove decisive, and a salvation, in the campaign to come.

By 0910 the aerial and naval bombardment had ceased, so the forty-five-foot-long, open-topped Higgins boats pushed away from the transports, hit the rally line, and headed toward a 1,600-foot stretch of shore east of Lunga Point.* Nine minutes later Lieutenant Colonel Bill Maxwell and his 1st Battalion of the 5th Marines waded ashore on Beach Red near the mouth of the Te-

---

* Officially an LCVP (Landing Craft Vehicle, Personnel), its rear and sides were made of plywood.

naru River, exactly eight months to the day after the Japanese attack on Pearl Harbor. It had been forty-four years since the last American amphibious assault, led by Lieutenant Colonel Bob Huntington, stormed into Guantanamo Bay during the Spanish-American War.*

Maxwell was pleasantly surprised with an unopposed landing, but justifiably suspicious. Too many reports had filtered back from China, Malaysia, and other areas of Japanese conquest to take the enemy for granted, and there was ample evidence of recent occupation. Shore emplacements for two antiaircraft guns, and a triple 25 mm cannon were found, as well as for two 75 mm mountain guns and all the ammunition required. Bivouacs had been abandoned, many with rice and fish on the tables. At Kukum, the future site of Fighter Two, there were split-toed *tabi* boots, soap, and tents with bedding.

The Japanese construction units, along with eighty-one men of the assigned Guard Force, had fled west from Lunga Point to the far bank of the Matanikau River. A subordinate unit of the Base Forces, the Guards were essentially garrison sailors who manned antiaircraft positions and provided rudimentary pro-

---

* The debut assault was made by Continental Marines in 1776 during the Battle of Nassau.

tection for a base or outpost. Like the construction workers, the Guards were not true combat units. The landings on Beach Red would have been opposed if the 3rd Kure Special Naval Landing Force of 247 men had been on Guadalcanal rather than Tulagi.*

This may have given the Marines a false view of the Japanese, but that would change rapidly. As elements of the 1st Marines pushed west toward the high ground past the central plain, some 556 miles to the northwest Rear Admiral Sadayoshi Yamada, commander of the 25th Air Flotilla in New Britain, canceled his group's morning mission to Milne Bay on Papua New Guinea. He intended to throw everything he had at the Americans on Guadalcanal and the Florida Islands.

Eighteen Zeros were airborne by 0830 from Rabaul, escorting nine Vals and twenty-seven Betty bombers southeast toward Guadalcanal. At 1037 over southern Bougainville near Buin they were spotted by Paul Mason, a forty-one-year-old, bespectacled Australian coastwatcher who immediately radioed, "Twenty-four

---

* Often and erroneously referred to as Japanese "marines," the SNLF was composed of sailors trained as light infantry. Like the U.S. Marines, their specialty was fast, surprise amphibious assault but they were not a separate service. SNLF units were typically battalion-sized, and generally lacked heavy weapons.

bombers headed yours," to Melbourne. The message was retransmitted to Pearl Harbor, then to Admiral Turner's invasion fleet in less than thirty minutes. With a two-hour warning the Americans were waiting over Savo Island with eight Wildcats from VF-5 off the *Saratoga*. Splitting into two flights of four, the Navy fighters came in high out of the sun to simultaneously attack the Betty bombers and fighter escorts. The Japanese pilots, though Imperial Navy aviators, were shore-based, so they had not fought during the battles of Coral Sea or Midway, and had never encountered the stubby little American fighter.

Though outclassed by the Zero in slow-speed turn performance, rate of climb, and acceleration, the Wildcat possessed a faster roll rate, cockpit armor, self-sealing fuel tanks, and six rapid-fire .50-caliber Browning M2 machine guns capable of chewing the Japanese fighter to pieces. In such a situation of offsetting capabilities, individual pilot skill combined with some measure of luck would make the difference. Zero pilots would nearly always forgo their escort or protection duties to dogfight, and were amazed to see the first four Wildcats ignore them and attack the Betty bombers. It worked. The Wildcat payloads splashed into the sea, and five bombers were lost. Saburo Sakai, one of the leading aces at the time, was equally startled to see one of the Wildcats attacking three Zeros by himself. "I gaped," Sakai, who survived the war, later wrote. "The Zeros should have been able to take the lone Grumman with no trouble. . . . I had never seen such flying before."

Lieutenant James Southerland of VF-5 shot down two of the Bettys, and then went after one of the Zeros, only to find that his guns were jammed. By this time Sakai had dived into the fight and the two pilots were suddenly in a twisting, gut-wrenching "furball" of a dogfight. "Never had I seen an enemy plane move so quickly or so gracefully before . . . he would not be shaken," the Japanese pilot recalled. "There was a terrific man behind that stick." Nicknamed "Pug" by his academy classmates, Southerland was a typically aggressive, tenacious, and skilled fighter pilot, but by working together the three Zeros eventually got a shot. Sakai was able to put a 20 mm burst into Southerland's left wing root that ignited gasoline vapor from the fighter's holed fuel tanks. As Southerland recounted:

> The after part of my fuselage was like a sieve. She was still smoking from incendiary but not on fire. All of the ammunition box cover on my left wing were gone and 20mm explosives had torn some gaping holes in its upper surface. . . . My instrument

panel was badly shot up, goggles on my forehead had been shattered, my rear view mirror was broken, my Plexiglas windshield was riddled. The leak proof tanks had apparently been punctured many times as some fuel had leaked down into the bottom of the cockpit even though there was no steady leakage. My oil tank had been punctured and oil was pouring down my right leg.

As his fighter burned, Southerland tried rolling out the cockpit to the right. Briefly hung up by his .45-caliber pistol, the Navy pilot got clear and parachuted into the jungle. Suffering from eleven wounds and now unarmed, Pug Southerland evaded the Japanese on Guadalcanal and eventually, with help from local people, made it back to American lines.

But the Navy lost nine Wildcats, and one Dauntless dive bomber flown by Lieutenant Dudley Hale Adams off the *Wasp*. Spotting several Zeros, Adams actually attacked and caught Saburo Sakai completely by surprise.

"For the first time in all my years of combat an enemy plane caught me unawares." Sakai was shocked by a bullet that passed within two inches of his face. "The audacity of the enemy pilot was amazing; he had deliberately jumped four Zero fighters in a slow and lightly armed dive bomber." The Japanese ace rapidly repositioned, killed the gunner, and sent the Dauntless spinning toward the ocean.* Minutes later while trolling for targets, Sakai jumped what he believed to be a formation of Wildcats. Only at sixty feet did he discover that they were eight TBF-1 Avenger torpedo bombers, and he was caught like a bug on a pin between sixteen turret-mounted machine guns that all opened fire.† With his plane shredded and himself badly wounded, Sakai dove away from the fight. Hours later, blinded in one eye and paralyzed on the left side from a bullet that traveled through his skull, the Japanese pilot managed to land back at Rabaul.

The planes that failed to return, and the sorry state of a top ace, shocked the Japanese. There were surprises on both sides that began stirring doubts, at least among the combatants, that what they had been told of their enemy might not be accurate. One Betty bomber pilot who pancaked into the sea next to the USS *Zane* climbed up onto the wing of his plane and didn't move until the destroyer drew close to try to save him. Draw-

---

* Badly wounded, Adams ditched alongside a destroyer and was saved. Unsurprisingly, after his recovery he transferred to fighters and later commanded Fighting Squadron 104. Like Southerland, he was killed in a postwar crash.

† Probably from VT-3 off the USS *Enterprise.*

ing his pistol, the pilot began shooting at the bridge, so the destroyer promptly responded with a 20 mm cannon, and the pilot and his plane disappeared in a welter of bloody spray.

It had been a costly mission: five Bettys, all nine Val dive bombers, and two Zeros, and due to his wounds, one of Japan's top aces had been put out of combat for two years. The attack utterly failed; none of the transports were hit, and the only damage was from a single bomb strike on the destroyer *Mugford*. If the Battle of the Coral Sea and their defeat at Midway had not given Japanese leadership pause, then the unexpected invasion of Guadalcanal should have done so. The Americans, it seemed, were not going to be easily defeated. They intended to remain on Guadalcanal.

Monkeys screamed, bird calls filled the air, and the underbrush crunched in the darkness. The Marines fanned out from the beachhead and entrenched themselves against a Japanese counterattack. Night in a jungle on enemy territory understandably made the young Americans jittery, and no one got much rest. Gunfire popped sporadically and a Navy corpsman was killed by accident, though with the dawn on August 8 came the promise of a better day.

It was an illusion.

By 0800 in Rabaul, the newly arrived Misawa Air Group was airborne with twenty-seven Bettys armed with torpedoes, and escorted by fifteen Zeros headed southeast for the Guadalcanal invasion fleet. Since the planes were spotted by coastwatcher Jack Read, the Americans were again ready, though this time the Japanese mission commander swung away north of Savo, then swept in from the east over the Florida Islands at treetop level. Only three Wildcats from the *Enterprise*'s Fighting Six were able to intercept, but they downed five Bettys and one Zero. The clustered transports, each with a dozen 20 mm antiaircraft mounts, got thirteen of the rest.

Of the twenty-three Bettys that made it to the Sealark Channel, only five returned to Rabaul, bringing the two-day total Japanese losses to thirty-six aircraft with their highly trained, irreplaceable crews. In addition to the single Dauntless, the Americans lost nine Wildcats, but recovered three of the pilots. Two destroyers were damaged, the *Jarvis* and *Mugford,* and the transport *George F. Elliot* had to be scuttled with a battalion's worth of supplies aboard.

While the Navy battled the Japanese in the Sealark Channel, the 1st Marines pushed inland to the airfield, and by late afternoon were in control of Guadalcanal's sole attribute. Again unopposed, they found wooden barracks, repair shops, a radio station, a refrigeration plant, and a medical clinic. The fleeing Japanese had left an astonishing array of supplies and tools behind: picks and seventy-five shovels; three cement mixers and six hundred tons of cement; four tractors; six earth rollers; wood and nails; forty-one trucks; and at least three dozen bicycles.

Yet the best news was the airfield. Planned for thirty-six hundred feet end to end, it was intended for sixty fighters of the 26th Air Flotilla. Construction was rudimentary by U.S. standards; Japanese planes were lighter than their American counterparts, so a graded earthen or coral surfaced airstrip was sufficient. It had also begun to be built from both ends and an uncompleted 180-foot gap remained in the middle that would require five thousand cubic feet of earth to fill. With their heavy equipment aboard ship or back in New Zealand, this left hand shovels and backbreaking labor for the 1st Marine Engineer Battalion. However, in their haste to flee, the Japanese left behind a treasure trove of equipment and supplies: six heavy trucks, four generators, ample explosives, an air compressor, six road rollers, and three cement mixers for a cache containing the six hundred tons of concrete. There were also fifty handcarts, two cartoonish gas-powered locomotives, and 150,000 gallons of gasoline.

The Marines made two other significant discoveries that afternoon. The first was a strange piece of equipment atop a concrete slab housed within a wooden shed. An alert officer recognized it as a radar, and it was hauled to the beach for shipment back to the United States.* Second, among the papers in the pagoda-shaped administration building, another officer recognized a bound sheaf that that contained a copy of the latest JN-25C naval code. This was immediately passed to U.S. Navy code breakers in Hawaii and Washington, D.C., where it was instrumental in deciphering encoded Japanese naval dispatches.

The situation was less celebratory back on Lunga Point. Boats were constantly running from the five anchored transports to the shore, but the beach was a now a logjam. Vital supplies of ammunition, and especially food, were not getting through. Part of the problem stemmed from the necessity of repacking each transport for combat with ammunition, food, medical supplies, and weapons at the top so they could be accessed

---

* This was actually a search radar prototype, and the first Japanese radar captured by the Allies. Later identified as a Type 11, Mark 1 set, it had a maximum detection range of about thirty-five miles. The American specialists at the Naval Research Laboratory discovered that most of the components were copies of existing U.S. equipment.

immediately. In a shameful display of arrogance, the longshoremen at Wellington's Aotea Quay refused to work in the rain, even to help men going into harm's way to protect New Zealand. The Marines ignored the arrogant Kiwis and did it themselves, but hurriedly, so now there was no clear idea of what supplies were where.

Added to this, Rear Admiral Fletcher had grown increasingly nervous following the three Japanese raids, and radioed Kelly Turner that he was withdrawing Task Force 61. Just after 1900 on the evening of August 8, the *Enterprise*, *Saratoga*, and *Wasp* steamed away to the southeast, leaving the 1st Marines with no air cover. Turner was now in a bind because less than half of the division's supplies had been offloaded but, commanding the only American transport fleet in the Pacific, he could not risk staying without air cover. Nevertheless, he told the Marine commander, Major General Alexander Archer Vandegrift, that he would offload as much as possible before departing the next morning.

Vandegrift understood that the three carriers were the only ones available until 1943 and that Fletcher had fought at both Coral Sea and Midway, yet he was nonetheless appalled by such a craven act. Kelly Turner was incensed and embarrassed: "He's [Fletcher] left us bare ass!" Fletcher's flaccid excuse was that he was down from ninety-nine to seventy-eight fighter aircraft, and that fuel was running low. This cut no ice with either Turner or Vandegrift as they knew full well that the entire task force had refueled in the Fiji Islands, and that five fleet oilers were with the warships now. Four of these were new *Cimarron*-class fast tankers, each capable of holding 147,150 barrels of fuel oil, diesel, and aviation gasoline. In fact, logbooks later revealed seventeen days of fuel remaining when Fletcher deserted the 1st Marine Division.

Vandegrift epitomized the "Old Breed" Marine: an exceptionally tough, no-nonsense careerist who knew he and his division were on Guadalcanal because they, and no one else, could do the job. At fifty-five, he was a veteran of the Banana Wars and Mexican Revolution who had written a prescient article in 1909 titled "Aviation, the Cavalry of the Future." With this in mind, he hunkered down, patched together a defensive perimeter, and ordered the airfield completed as soon as possible. Besides survival, this was the top priority; once aircraft could operate from Guadalcanal he would not be forced to depend on the Navy.

This dependence proved more tenuous than even Vandegrift imagined, and the weakness of his position was violently illustrated less than eight hours after

Fletcher retreated. The initial Japanese reaction to the invasion had been understated at best, as both the Imperial General Staff and Combined Fleet Headquarters were still suffering from what was later termed "Victory Disease." A long string of relatively easy victories, which in Japanese eyes included Pearl Harbor and Manila, undermined the ability to make sound tactical decisions.

By virtue of its experiences at the Coral Sea and Midway, the Imperial Navy had glimmers of the truth, but the Imperial Army was another matter altogether. The outright animosity between the branches precluded cooperation an anything approaching a joint level. In fact, the army had no idea that the navy lost at Midway, nor did the services share information of any kind if it could be avoided. The majority of officers were kept in the dark, and most seemed to prefer it that way, yet there were exceptions. The commander of the Combined Fleet, Admiral Yamamoto, was one such man, and Vice Admiral Gunichi Mikawa, commander of the 8th Fleet at Rabaul, was another.

Mikawa had foreseen the American interest in, and invasion of, Guadalcanal because he shared the same strategic interest in the island. But when the admiral broached the topic in July, he was chided for his concerns by the Imperial General Staff, and told that such an event was impossible; the Americans were too weak, too disorganized, and lacked the ability to face Imperial forces. Nevertheless, when rumors began circulating about Tulagi and Guadalcanal, he assumed they were true and acted instantly. Even as the U.S. Marines moved inland during the afternoon of August 7, Mikawa cobbled together an ad hoc strike force and sortied from Rabaul's Simpson Harbor. It was a simple plan: steam down through the New Georgia Sound, pass Savo Island, and attack everything in sight. American warships were the first target, and then the anchored transports in the Sealark Channel. Mikawa calculated that if he struck by 0130 on August 9, then he could wreak his havoc and be beyond range of American carrier aircraft by dawn.

From the beginning, the small Japanese fleet was favored with luck, and a combination of American errors or flawed assumptions. Mikawa was detected twice on August 8, once by USAAF B-17s and again by the S-38, a U.S. submarine prowling to the northwest of Guadalcanal, but his fleet was misidentified as a force of seaplane tenders, and the reports were dismissed. In any event, U.S. commanders did not believe any enemy force could reach the Sealark Channel by August 9, and by then Kelly Turner's transports would be gone. Land-based American planes carried out an air search pattern, but not quite far enough up New Georgia Sound to discover the "seaplane tenders" were actually five heavy cruisers, two light cruisers, and a destroyer, and that they were headed southeast into the Solomon Islands. Buoyed by its recent victory at Midway, the U.S. Navy was temporarily suffering from the same Victory Disease that afflicted the Japanese. The Imperial Navy was generally scorned, and because night fighting was not yet among the American skill sets, it was not attributed to the enemy.

In fact, night naval combat was a Japanese specialty, and torpedoes were the weapon of choice, at least for the initial strike. Building on lessons learned during the Sino-Japanese War (1894–95) and the Russo-Japanese War (1904–1906), during the 1930s the Imperial Navy fielded the Type 93 *Sanso gyorai,* the "oxygen torpedo." Exceptionally lethal, the 6,000-pound, 29.5-foot monster could send its 1,090-pound warhead 11 miles at 49 knots, or an incredible 20 miles at a slower 36 knots. Nicknamed the "Long Lance," it employed pure oxygen mixed with kerosene rather than the compressed air utilized by the U.S. Navy Mark XV. The oxygen-kerosene mix emitted carbon dioxide, which was rapidly soluble in water and thus did not leave the telltale trail of bubbles in its wake. Japanese warships used flashless powder to delay revealing their positions and had superb optical equipment but, oddly enough, very limited radar capability. Unlike the U.S. Navy, the Japanese had practiced extensively for night combat, so what happened that evening should have been anticipated.

It was not.

Passing down the New Georgia Sound under an overcast sky with no moon, at 2312 Mikawa launched four floatplanes. Exactly at midnight, the Japanese Striking Force went to battle stations, and fifty minutes later sighted the dark cone of Savo Island. Sliding undetected through a rain squall, the five heavy cruisers slipped past the picket destroyer USS *Blue* into the south channel between Cape Esperance and Savo. This approach to the transports anchored off Tulagi was guarded by two heavy cruisers, HMAS *Canberra* and the USS *Chicago*, in company with two destroyers. One of the Japanese floatplanes was spotted near Savo and as it began dropping illumination flares the USS *Patterson*, screening for the southern Allied cruisers, spotted the Japanese surface ships and blinkered, "WARNING-WARNING-STRANGE SHIPS ENTERING HARBOR."

Canberra reacted instantly to the flares, but the Long Lance torpedoes were already in the water, and before she could fire the Australian warship was hit. Four Japanese cruisers then zeroed in and pummeled the *Canberra* with at least thirty large-caliber shells. Her captain and most of the senior officers dead, both boiler rooms out and aflame, the Australian warship drifted to a burning, listing stop. *Chicago* rang up 25 knots and charged west toward what Captain Howard Bode believed to be the enemy position—he was wrong. After striking hard, the Japanese cruisers turned northeast and attacked the second Allied squadron patrolling the northern edge of Savo.

Watch officers aboard the USS *Vincennes*, *Quincy*, and *Astoria* had seen the gunfire flashes against the low clouds, but with all the fighting on Guadalcanal they were not certain of the cause. *Patterson*'s warning had also been missed, so it was a shock when searchlights cut across the dark water and transfixed the *Vincennes*. Thus began the massacre of the American warships, and within forty-five minutes the USS *Quincy*, which had fired the first shots of the previous day's invasion, rolled to port and sank by the bow. By 0300 the *Vincennes*, which proudly led the amphibious fleet into the Sealark Channel just two days earlier, also sank.

At this point Admiral Mikawa did the math and determined it would take ninety minutes to rejoin his scattered cruisers, re-form, and accelerate across to the transport fleet anchored off Tulagi. Unaware that Fletcher had panicked and withdrawn the American carriers, Mikawa decided to withdraw before he could be caught by daylight and counterattacked. Though the Battle of Savo Island cost the Allies four heavy cruisers and 1,077 sailors, the Japanese victory was diminished by Mikawa's failure to destroy the only cargo ships available to the Americans and then hold the Sealark Channel for Japanese reinforcements.* Had he done so, the 10,819 Marines on Guadalcanal would have been completely defenseless, and their temporary seizure of the airfield a moot point. In any event, the Japanese did not capitalize on their tactical victory and the Marines remained in possession of the most essential asset on Guadalcanal. Still, their hold was precarious, at best, and the Americans abandoned on the island were keenly aware of this. Facing limited supplies with no air cover, and having been deserted by the Navy, for those on the island WATCHTOWER had rapidly become Operation "Shoestring."

---

* Heavy cruisers HMAS *Canberra*, USS *Vincennes*, *Quincy*, and *Astoria* against light damage to three IJN cruisers and the loss of 129 Japanese sailors.

Five

The American Toe

April 18, 1943
The Solomon Islands

F lying over the graves of the *Quincy* and *Vincennes* northeast of Savo, Rex Barber knew those lives had not been wasted. He and every other pilot remembered this every time they took off from Henderson Field, or the Cow Pasture, or Fighter Two. Control of Guadalcanal meant more than just controlling the air for hundreds of miles; it was a rebuke to Japanese confidence as well. In the spring of 1943, the Imperial Army and Navy now knew that they were not invincible, and that Americans were neither decadent nor weak. Today, April 18, 1943, the island also meant one

more thing: because the Marines held on, Guadalcanal was America's opportunity to avenge the lives lost
at Pearl Harbor, the Coral Sea, Midway, and all those
buried back on Edson's Ridge or along the Matanikau.
If John Mitchell could get his Lightnings to exactly the
right place at precisely the correct time, and if Rex or
one of the others could kill Yamamoto, then vengeance,
at least for some of America's dead, would be satisfied.

Up ahead, the leading four Lightnings banked up
to the left and descended, their twin booms starkly
outlined against the horizon. Rex pulled the throttles
back, cranked his wheel over, and stared at Tom Lanphier's left wing as the Killer flight followed their
leader. Savo Island, and the ghosts of the men who
perished there, drifted aft along his port tail boom as
the P-38 dropped toward the water in a left turn. Gliding toward the sea, Barber reached under the wheel,
and put his left hand on the teardrop-shaped CANNON
CHARGE knob. Turning it counterclockwise ninety degrees, he pushed it in, which electrically charged, or
cocked, the 20 mm cannon.

Sunlight glinted on the wavetops and surf was breaking along the gray ribbon of Savo's northern shoreline.
His eyes flickered to *Phoebe*, then he reached for the
large black handle mounted on a cylinder that pro-

truded six inches from the instrument panel between the throttles and control wheel. A flat, coaster-sized knob engraved with a white arrow was mounted on the front of the cylinder, and Rex put his fingers over the knurled edge then twisted it left to the position marked UPPER RIGHT. He had to manually cock each of the four .50-caliber machine guns, and grasping the handle, Rex pulled back sharply, felt it snap in place, then he shoved it back forward. Reaching to the knob, Rex twisted it left again to the LOWER RIGHT position, and cocked the second gun. He repeated the procedure for the LOWER LEFT and UPPER LEFT guns, then leaned back. Though the Japanese mainly operated farther north, these days one never knew, and Guadalcanal had been raided just a few days ago, so the pilots expected combat at any time. Ignoring the heat of the morning sun beating through the canopy, and the sweat oozing from beneath his leather helmet, he loosened the lap belt a few inches. Heat brought out the ever-present odors of mildew and urine, but he ignored those as well. Up ahead, Mitchell's P-38 bobbed up and down as he "porpoised" the plane; it was the briefed signal for everyone to spread out for the long flight. Lanphier did the same thing, and Rex eased away to five hundred feet as *Phoebe* rolled out heading west. Rex walked the throttles a bit to hold position off Lanphier's wing, and the sixteen fighters leveled off fifty feet above the water, then vanished in the haze above the Solomon Sea.

We have gained, I believe, a toehold in the Southwest Pacific," President Franklin Roosevelt wrote, "from which the Japanese will find it very difficult to dislodge us." Optimistic words certainly, but Admiral Fletcher's hasty withdrawal of Task Force 61 left no air cover for Kelly Turner's vulnerable transports, so he also was forced to weigh anchor and the whole operation was now in serious doubt. Fully half of the 1st Marine's essential material went with him, including the medical and surgical supplies, all the heavy earth-moving equipment, and most of the food. Marines on the island had seventeen days of field rations, plus whatever could be scrounged from captured Japanese stores, and fortunately this was considerable: about ten days' worth of canned fruits, salmon, crab meat, and fish. There were ample supplies of socks, always valuable in the wet tropics, but most were too short for the Americans. Underwear as well, though the traditional Japanese loincloths were much too small to be of much use. On the bright side, a stockpile of 12 million rounds of .30-caliber and .45-caliber ammunition made it ashore, and a few field guns that were offloaded before the navy's retreat.

It would have to do.

If the island could be held and the airstrip made operational, Vandegrift knew help was on the way. Five days before the Guadalcanal landings, a stubby, flat-topped little ship put to sea from Pearl Harbor, headed southwest across the Pacific to the Solomon Islands and a muddy airstrip on Guadalcanal. Originally a cargo liner, the SS *Mormacmail* had been acquired by the government in March 1941, rechristened the USS *Long Island*, and designated CVE-1; the U.S. Navy's first escort aircraft carrier. With a length of 492 feet and a narrow 69-foot beam she was a little more than half the size of her larger fleet carrier sisters. Also called a "jeep carrier," she was lightly armed and could barely manage an unimpressive 19 mph top speed. Yet for all her limitations, the *Long Island* was carrying a load that would change the fate of thousands, and allow the men on Guadalcanal a fighting chance. Her tiny flight deck was crammed with thirty-one aircraft belonging to Marine Air Group (MAG) 23, and stuffed below were forty-five pilots.

Nineteen F4F-4 Wildcat fighters made up Marine Fighting Squadron 223, a unit patched together from at least two other squadrons and commanded by Captain John Lucian Smith. The dozen Dauntless dive bombers belonged to Major Richard Mangrum's Scout Bombing Squadron, which had been thrown into the newly formed air group on Oahu just ninety-one days prior to the Guadalcanal invasion. Twenty-six of Smith's thirty-one fighter pilots and nine of Mangrum's aviators were green second lieutenants right out of flight school, but without air cover the island would be lost, so the situation was desperate. However, after Savo and the navy's withdrawal, the little carrier put into Suva on Fiji, before continuing forward as far as Efate. Here the greenest pilots of VMF-223 were swapped for eight veterans from Major Joe Bauer's VMF-212, and the carrier continued northwest toward the Solomons.

In the meantime, the Marines dug in and held on. They were prepared to be outnumbered, and in tight spots—that's what Marines were for, so rumors about massive attacks did not have the effect the Japanese wished. Nor did the grunts believe in the invincibility of their enemy; they believed in plenty of ammunition and sharp blades. Passwords were created and changed every night, usually L words like "Lollygag," "Lollipop," or "Lilliputian" that Asians had trouble pronouncing. Of course, so did some of the Americans. Bob "Lucky" Leckie remembered one night as a sentry when a comrade was coming back after relieving himself:

"Halt!" Leckie hissed.

"Fer Gawd's sake, Lucky, don't shoot. It's me, Briggs."

"Gimme the password."

"Lily-poo . . . luly . . ."

"C'mon, c'mon! The password, or I'll let you have it."

"Luly-pah . . . lily-poosh . . . aw shit-shoot!"

Vandegrift quickly built up a perimeter from the Ilu River east of the beachhead west to the Matanikau, with the airfield in the center. This protected his supply line to the Sealark Channel, and kept the airstrip secure—if the Marines only had air cover any Japanese counterattack would be a difficult proposition. Though most of the Navy had pulled out, there were glimmers of hope over the next week. On August 12, five days after the landings, the engineers managed to have a 2,600-foot runway patched together and several acres of banyan trees dynamited away from both ends of the runway.

Anxious for air support, Vandegrift nevertheless sent a message stating "Airfield Guadalcanal ready for fighters and dive bombers." At the moment, the only Marine aviator on the island was Major Ken Weir, who christened the ugly little strip Henderson Field after Major Lofton Henderson of VMSB-241, who died attacking the *Hiryu* during the Battle of Midway. He wanted it named after a fighting man, "not some potbellied SOB behind a desk in the Pentagon." To prove the point and garner support for the Marines, Rear Admiral John Sidney McCain sent his personal PBY-5A to Guadalcanal and that afternoon Lieutenant William S. Sampson landed the first aircraft on the island.

On August 15, the destroyers *McKean, Gregory, Little,* and *Colhoun* slipped into Ironbottom Sound, as the Sealark Channel had been aptly nicknamed after the Savo debacle, and put ashore Major Charles H. "Fog" Hayes, USMC, to get the airfield up and running. The destroyers also brought belted ammunition, 282 general-purpose bombs, tools, pumps, and 400 gallons of aviation gasoline along with Ensign George W. Polk, two other officers, and 188 men of Construction Unit Base (CUB) One. CUB-1 was an advanced element of the 6th Naval Construction Battalion, which itself had only arrived at Espiritu Santo in the New Hebrides on August 11, 1942.

Fortunately, for several years prior to the war, much thought had been given to the logistics of fighting in the immense Pacific. Barely three weeks after Pearl Harbor, the Navy Bureau of Yards and Docks, in conjunction with the Civil Engineer Corps, put the planning into action by forming Naval Construction Battalions. Quickly and famously abbreviated to "Seabees," these men were specially recruited for their engineering and construction expertise and by August 1942, there were six battalions of about 1,100 men each in the Pacific.

The same day Polk arrived, a barefoot British coast-watcher named Martin Clemens appeared on the beach east of the Marine positions on the Tenaru River with twenty native scouts. Born in Scotland and educated at Cambridge, Clemens had joined the British Colonial Service at twenty-three and been in the Solomons since 1938. Commissioned a captain in the Protectorate Defense Force, he was recruited into Operation FERDINAND, the net of coastwatchers scattered through the islands, by the redoubtable Lieutenant Commander Eric Feldt.* Of Feldt and the contribution of his men, Admiral William Halsey stated, "I could get down on my knees every night and thank God for Commander Eric Feldt. . . . the coast watchers saved the Guadalcanal and Guadalcanal saved the South Pacific."

"We closed column. . . ," Clemens later wrote, "and marched in two ranks with rifles at the slope; I figured

---

* Feldt chose the name after Munroe Leaf's story of Ferdinand the Bull to emphasize that the coastwatchers were to observe, rather than actively fight, the Japanese. By war's end the organization had saved 321 Allied airmen and 280 sailors, and had rescued 75 prisoners of war from the Japanese in addition to supplying vital intelligence regarding the enemy.

no Japanese would march in this stupid manner, and we would therefore be regarded as peculiar, rather than hostile!" It was a wise precaution given the proximity of thousands of young, heavily armed U.S. Marines, though Clemens was already well known, at least by name, to General Vandegrift. Taken to see the Marine commander the following day, Clemens was given the responsibility of "all matters of native administration and intelligence beyond the perimeter." It was a prescient move by Vandegrift that would to prove invaluable for the survival of the Marines during the coming months.

Surprised, but dismissive of the U.S. invasion, the chief of the Imperial Navy General Staff, Admiral Osami Nagano, told Emperor Hirohito, "It is nothing worthy of your Majesty's attention." Others, especially Yamamoto, were more concerned. He moved the Combined Fleet Headquarters forward to Truk, and ordered his 1st and 2nd Fleets to prepare for a reconquest of Guadalcanal. Astonishingly, at least from an Allied standpoint, the Imperial Army had no notion that the Navy had been building an airfield on Guadalcanal, but now that they were informed, Lieutenant General Hyakutake's 17th Army at Rabaul was instructed to deal with the Americans. August 15 also saw Kiyonao Ichiki of the 1937 Wanping incident, now a colonel and the commander of the 28th Infantry Regiment, embark immediately with six fast destroyers for Guadalcanal. Intelligence reported no more than one thousand Americans on the island, so to Ichiki's mind his 2nd Battalion of 917 men was more than enough to deal with an enemy he considered "effeminate" and "cowardly."

After easy victories over the Russians, Chinese, and colonial troops, the Imperial Japanese Army believed absolutely in its superiority. It was held that each soldier gained his spiritual strength from *Yamato-damashii,* an indomitable indigenous spirit produced from a super ordinate culture; in essence, a Japanese master race. Added to this was the individual's *seishin,* the physical and mental strength quite naturally derived from being Japanese. Combined with *bushido,* the Japanese warrior code, this canon of beliefs would sustain each soldier, sailor, or airman, and render the Imperial forces invincible. Surprise attacks against tiny American garrisons on Wake Island and Guam, and the victory at Pearl Harbor did nothing to dissuade the Japanese from the cherished notion of their military prowess. There was no mention by the 17th Army to Ichiki that the U.S. invaders in the Solomons were not soldiers but

Marines, and in any event the distinction would have been meaningless at the time. The type of foe did not matter; Japan would always prevail.

Guadalcanal would change this attitude forever.

On August 17, two days after the Ichiki Detachment sailed, the destroyer *Oike* dashed down the New Georgia Sound to land 113 sailors of the 5 Yokosuka SNLF near Tassafaronga west of the Matanikau. They were to secure a beachhead for resupply efforts and gather what intelligence they could. Ichiki came ashore twenty-four hours later at Taivu Point, twenty-five miles east of the Marine positions along Alligator Creek.* He was also supposed to secure a beachhead and await the arrival of his second echelon of 1,411 men, plus the battalion's heavy weapons and supplies. Ichiki had been a revered instructor at the army's infantry school at Chiba so this expertise, combined with success in China and his opinion of Americans as "very effeminate and very cowardly," combined to brook no delay. Leaving a 125-man rear guard, the colonel set off immediately toward

---

* The "creek" was actually the Ilu River because initial maps mismarked the fetid stretch of water as the Tenaru River. Incidentally, alligators prefer fresh water and are not found the South Pacific, so the inhabitants of the Ilu were actually crocodiles— but in August 1943, this was a distinction of supreme indifference to the U.S. Marines.

Lunga Point and the airfield, intending a classic night-time frontal assault to sweep the Americans into the sea.

Supremely confident, he saw no reason to reconnoiter in force and only bothered to send ahead a thirty-eight-man advance party to establish a base camp. Ichiki's postdated diary entries read: "18 Aug. The landing. 20 Aug. The march by night and the battle. 21 August. Enjoyment of the fruits of victory." Assuming they had nothing to fear, the Japanese marched openly along the beach. There they ran straight into a sixty-five-man combat patrol under Captain Charles Brush, A Company, 1st Marines, some five miles east of the airfield at Koli Point. In short order thirty-three of Ichiki's men were killed, and the remaining five fled back into the jungle. Brush, described by Bob Leckie as a "bear in overalls," lost three Marines, but personally searched the dead Japanese officers and discovered very accurate sketches of the American positions. He also noted the corpses had no beards, wore polished boots, and that their insignia was the five-pointed gold star of the Imperial Japanese Army rather than the chrysanthemum worn by naval troops. Reinforcements had obviously arrived, and Brush correctly deduced that this was a patrol in advance of a much larger force.

The next day would prove historic. On the afternoon of August 20, accompanied by the USS *Helena* and the destroyer *Dale,* the *Long Island* rounded San Cristobal southeast of Guadalcanal and swung into the wind. Led by Lieutenant Colonel Charles Fike, the first thirty-one aircraft of MAG-23 got airborne and turned northwest toward the island. None of them had any idea what to expect, and no news had reached them beyond Vandegrift's declaration that the field was ready, so each plane was crammed with extra parts, plugs, starter cartridges, and even spare tires. The aviators belonged to the same Marine Corps as the grunts on the Canal, and they were prepared to do anything to save them. That same day Lieutenant Commander Joe Blundon, commanding officer of the 6th Naval Construction Battalion, arrived from Espiritu Santo. He took a quick look around and promptly requested that two complete companies of Seabees be sent as soon as possible.

A bizarre encounter occurred south of Guadalcanal that gave the Marines a proud smile and dismayed the Japanese. A Kawanishi H8K flying boat, called a "Mavis" by the Allies, was returning to its base at Shortlands after reconnoitering American positions when a string of rapid hammer blows struck its belly. Sunlight appeared through jagged holes and, thinking he was under attack by a fighter, the pilot began weaving frantically. Suddenly, and quite shockingly, an American B-17 Flying Fortress appeared from beneath the flying boat's tail. Captain Walter Lucas of the 19th Bombardment Group was also returning to his base after scouting for Japanese ships when he spotted the lumbering enemy patrol plane. Lacking the bristling armament that later Forts would carry, Lucas still had one .30-caliber and six .50-caliber guns available, so as he slipped the bomber back, Sergeants Vernon Nelson and Chester Malizeski poured multiple bursts into the Mavis. With three of its engines gone, the huge aircraft managed to belly-flop into the sea, and as the frantic Japanese pilot attempted to taxi away Sergeant Ed Spetch put a final burst into the flying boat, which blew up and burned.

Late in the afternoon the Marines heard the familiar sound of aircraft engines and dove into their foxholes. For twelve days the Japanese had raided at will, so through the jungle canopy the grunts were surprised to see light gray bellies and white stars on the approaching aircraft. Americans. A wave of cheering erupted all around the airfield. "That's the most beautiful sight I've ever seen," one Marine admitted. Others cried. A big Dauntless dive bomber circled the field, dropped the gear and flaps, then bounced down on the dusty runway. Taxiing clear and shutting down his big Wright Cyclone engine, an astonished Major Richard Mangrum was greeted by General Vandegrift himself.

Finally, late that evening, Jacob Vouza, a native member of Solomon Islands Protectorate Armed Constabulary, staggered into the Marine lines east of Henderson Field on the Ilu River. He had been captured by the Japanese, and personally interrogated by Colonel Ichiki about the U.S. positions. Refusing to speak, Vouza was staked out over a red ant bed, beaten with rifle butts, and finally bayoneted six times as he hung from a tree. Left for dead, the fifty-one-year-old Vouza chewed through his ropes, got to the Americans, and confirmed earlier reports that the enemy were coming.

Skirmishes began around midnight as the advance party of Japanese engineers made contact with the 2nd Battalion grunts dug in on the west bank of Alligator Creek. By 0215 the Marine outposts had been called in and at 0310 on August 21, Ichiki's 2nd Company led the first assault across the narrow, forty-five-yard-wide sandbar. Caught in the single strand of barbed wire the Marines were able to lay across the sand, they "waved their arms wildly, they shrieked and jabbered." Lieutenant Colonel Edwin Pollock's 2nd Battalion opened up with everything they had, and the sound of battle carried all the way to Henderson Field: the heavy hammering of .50-caliber machine guns, the unmistakable sawlike rasp of Browning Automatic Rifles, and the hollow *whung* from mortars. Deadliest of all at close range was a 37 mm antitank gun that was blasting canister shot into the packed Japanese.

"Fuck Babe Ruth!" and "You die, Marine!" rang out under red and white flares as streams of tracers cut down the charging Japanese: they never stopped. They had been inculcated with the belief that no enemy could withstand their bamboo-spear charge and this had been largely true against the Chinese and Allied soldiers earlier in the war. Nothing prepared them for a foe who was quite capable of fighting back just as viciously as themselves, and all through that long, bloody night the Marines proved it. The sky glowed pink with continuous fire; the coconut palms were clearly silhouetted against the black sky. A few Japanese inevitably broke through and were met by the shockingly ferocious Americans. Private Dean Wilson, infuriated over his buddy's death, jumped out of his foxhole and hacked three Japanese to death with a machete. Another private, George Turzai, was attacked by seven Japanese soldiers; he killed five with a pistol and a sixth with his bayonet. Leading a platoon on the front line, Lieutenant George Codrea took fragments from two grenades, yet bloodied and in terrible pain he refused to leave his command until noon the following the day.

Unlike their Japanese counterparts, who never deviated from a plan, Pollock and his officers continuously shifted and adapted to each new situation. When Ichiki committed two more full companies to the attack, the Marines responded by shifting their machine gun positions and calling in heavy artillery fire support, which decimated the charging infantrymen. As the sky lightened on Saturday, August 21, Pollock turned the table on Ichiki. A platoon of Stuart light tanks were sent across the forty-foot sandspit at the mouth of Alligator Creek, and three companies of Lieutenant Colonel Leonard B. Cresswell's 1st Battalion circled south through the jungle to envelope Ichiki from behind. A fourth company penetrated farther east to cut off any Japanese retreat toward Taivu Point. Dawn also brought the very welcome sound of American Pratt & Whitney aircraft engines as the VMF-223 Wildcats warmed up.

Boxed in on three sides, the remnants of Ichiki's vaunted shock battalion was truly caught between the anvil and the hammer. Cut to pieces as they scattered through the palms, the Japanese's sole escape route seemed to be the waters of Ironbottom Sound.

But many who tried swimming to safety were chewed apart by strafing Wildcats. The devastation was complete. "Never had I seen such terrible destruction occur in such a short time," Martin Clemens wrote, and others had similar recollections. "Everywhere one turned there were piles of bodies," said correspondent Richard Tregaskis, who had witnessed most of the battle. "Here one with a backbone visible from the front, there a charred head, hairless but still equipped with blackened eyeballs, pink, blue, yellow entrails drooping . . ."

Private Robert Leckie of H Company, 2nd Battalion, wrote of "swarms of flies; black, circling funnels that seemed to emerge from every orifice: from the mouth, the eyes, the ears. The beating of their myriad tiny wings made a dreadful low hum." Exhausted, wary, and expecting further attacks, the Marines along Alligator Creek let the crocodiles take care of the dead Japanese. Leckie recalled, "We never shot the crocs because we considered them a sort of 'river patrol.' They kept us awake, crunching."

But not every dead enemy was truly dead, and many wounded Japanese preferred to take an American with them than surrender. Paul Buelow, a Navy pharmacist's mate, attempted to treat a wounded enemy soldier, who jumped up and stabbed him to death with a bayonet. Others threw grenades or tried to fire weapons at close range, so prisoners were rarely taken, and if the Japanese wished to fight to the death for their emperor, then the Marines would let them do it.

As for Ichiki, there are several versions of his death. One states that when his command's annihilation became clear, he burned his regimental flag, prayed, then shot himself. One of the ten survivors who straggled back to Taivu Point reported the colonel was last seen walking toward the battle, and he never returned.

In the end it didn't matter how he died; his arrogance and hubris cost the lives of 813 men, and with the U.S. Navy gone and no real air support, Ichiki's recklessness cost the Empire its best chance of retaking Guadalcanal. All told, the 1st Marines lost thirty-four dead and seventy-five wounded during the sixteen-hour attack, but the precarious American foothold was still secure and Henderson Field had been saved. These young Americans, and thousands more like them, proved on land what the U.S. Navy had proven in June at Midway: the Japanese myth of invincibility was just that—a myth.

Beyond surviving the night, Sunday, August 22, brought the Marines tentative good news—the U.S. Army had sent reinforcements. Richard Tregaskis, having lived through the battle at Alligator Creek, recalled, "Back at the airport I found some long-nosed fighter planes, painted Army brown, coming in for a landing. They were pursuit ships, the first Army planes to arrive in Guadalcanal. The planes bore bright insignia and spectacular individual crests." Led by Captain Dale D. Brannon of the 67th Fighter Squadron, a grand total of five USAAF P-400 fighters had departed from New Caledonia, far to the south, and flew the first 325 miles to Efate. Refueling, they pressed another 180 miles to Espiritu Santo and spent the night. The following morning, full of gas, they crossed the final 640 miles to Henderson in company with a B-17 bomber. Brannon remembered the bomber navigator's final radio call before they headed away: "Hold this course for twenty miles. When you get there, check the flag on the pole at the edge of the field. Make sure it's American." The ground echelon and maintenance contingent of thirty enlisted men commanded by Lieutenant Robert E. Chilson arrived off Lunga Point the following day aboard the transport *Fomalhaute*.

Entering operational life as the export version of Bell's P-39 Airacobra, the shark-nosed P-400 had a curved belly and somewhat pleasing lines, but the beauty ended there, save for the big Hispano-Suiza 37 mm cannon in the nose. The P-400 was initially intended for the Armée de l'Air Française, but following the collapse of France in May 1940, the remaining initial order was diverted to the Royal Air Force.* Unfortunately Bell Aircraft, not known for quality designs, had indeed fudged the fighter's performance figures by basing them on an unarmed and unarmored prototype, so by late 1941 even the embattled British found the plane unsuitable for combat on Western Front. Some two hundred of these were sent to the Soviet Union, and then finally, desperate for aircraft after Pearl Harbor, the U.S. Army Air Force grabbed all the remaining P-39s and P-400s available.

More capable fighter designs were entering production, but until they were fielded in sufficient numbers the Army had to make do with what was available. Large numbers of P-400s and P-39s began arriving in Australia during winter of 1943, including ninety P-39s to the 8th Pursuit Group for the defense of Port Moresby and Australia. One hundred P-400s, split into five squadrons, went to the 35th Pursuit Group and were dispersed to Fiji, Palmyra, Christmas Island, Canton, and New Caledonia as a stopgap until better aircraft became available.

---

* French prime minster Paul Reynaud telephoned Winston Churchill on May 15, 1940, to say, "We have been defeated. We are beaten; we have lost the battle."

Brannon and his squadron entered Nouméa harbor on the southwest tip of New Caledonia aboard the *Thomas S. Barry* on March 15, 1942. After a thirty-eight-day journey from New York via Australia, New Caledonia was the last link in the island chain protecting the fledgling, but absolutely vital, South Pacific convoy system running between the U.S. west coast to New Zealand and Australia. Forty crates, each weighing ten thousand pounds, were unloaded on the Nickel Docks, and when the first was opened the pilots and their maintenance crews received a nasty shock. Expecting to find a dissembled P-40 Warhawk, they found instead a P-400, a plane none of them had ever flown, and the maintenance manuals were for the P-39 Airacobra; D, F, and K models, but nothing for the P-400. Apparently forty of these planes had been outbound for the Soviet Union when Pearl Harbor was hit, and the shipment was promptly diverted to the Pacific Theater for the U.S. Army.

With no other option, Brannon and his men trucked the crates one at a time thirty-two miles northeast over the single-lane, treacherous "road" through the mountains to Tontouta, a French-built base near Vincer Bay. There was one farmhouse for the forty-four officers, and the enlisted men slept outside beneath partial shelters. In between rainstorms and swatting off mosquitoes, the men learned how to assemble the Bell aircraft with only basic tools; it was a challenge. One plane had been wired completely wrong, so when the flaps were lowered the landing gear retracted, and when the gear was raised the cannon fired. Fuel lines were stoppered with plain Scotch tape instead of electrical tape, and this had dissolved into a gooey mess that had to be cleaned out by hand. Nevertheless, within three weeks there were forty-one aircraft assembled. The pilots taught themselves to fly the recalcitrant little fighter, listened to the war news, and waited.

Brannon's few pilots were as ready as he could make them when they were thrown into the Canal meat grinder on August 22, 1942. However, nothing but combat is anything like combat. The day the Army P-400s landed Ichiki's dismayed survivors began tottering back to his base camp at Taivu Point. A radio message was sent on August 22 to the 17th Army that read, "The detachment [Ichiki] was annihilated before dawn before they reached the airstrip." Shocked, but more puzzled than alarmed, Japanese staff officers refused to believe it until a surviving communications lieutenant sent a formal dispatch describing the action. Fifteen hundred men of Ichiki's 2nd Echelon, plus the

5 Yokosuka SNLF, had been at sea since August 16 and were due to land shortly on Guadalcanal. Rear Admiral Tanaka with three transports, the light cruiser *Jintsu*, and eight destroyers had made the inaugural run of the "Tokyo Express," as Japanese seaborne reinforcement operations became known.

High-speed passage or destroyer transports, submarines, and fast troop carriers down "the Slot" of New Georgia Sound would become a cornerstone of efforts to retake Guadalcanal. As Yamamoto saw it, the Japanese faced two main obstacles in retaking the island: the American carriers lurking southeast of the Solomons, and the troublesome "Cactus" Air Force— the land-based aircraft flying from Henderson Field. Both had to be eliminated before Guadalcanal could be retaken, and Yamamoto planned the operation personally. Befitting his reputation, the admiral viewed the invasion as another opportunity to lure the American carriers into a trap and destroy them. Subtlety, deception, and surprise were hallmarks of Japanese naval tactics going back to their first significant victories at Port Arthur and Tsushima against the Russians. Bait the trap, then spring it.

Even though this had been attempted against the U.S. Navy at Coral Sea and Midway with dismal results, the admiral believed he could pull it off this time.

As with the island of Midway, Yamamoto believed the U.S. carriers would be forced to protect Guadalcanal and the Marines, and in so doing they would be vulnerable to a combined Japanese assault. If this occurred, his previous defeats would be erased, and control of the strategic situation in the South Pacific would be undeniably in his hands.

Fifty-eight ships and 177 aircraft steamed past Truk on August 23, refueled at sea, then headed for southeast for Guadalcanal. The late Colonel Ichiki's contingent, already approaching the island from the north, was to cover the initial ground assault and had been alternately steaming south, then retreating north each time it was discovered. Several hundreds of miles behind the convoy were six cruisers and six destroyers of Vice Admiral Kondo's Advanced Force. They were screening for Vice Admiral Nagumo's Main Force: two fleet carriers, one light carrier, a pair of battleships, and eleven destroyers. *Zuikaku* and *Shokaku* had recovered from their mauling during the Battle of the Coral Sea, reconstituted their air groups, and were out for blood.

The little carrier *Ryujo*, with her twenty-four Zeros and nine dive bombers, was split off from the Main Force as a diversion to attack Henderson Field. As at Midway, Yamamoto planned to lure the carriers out by threatening a garrisoned island protected by its own aircraft. He had reacted quickly after the initial invasion, but hastily committed the Combined Fleet's best assets without a coherent plan, unified objectives, or clear command. This became quickly obvious on the morning of August 24, with the opening moves of the Pacific War's third carrier battle, though Admiral Fletcher's reactions were scarcely better. A PBY discovered the *Ryujo* at 0935, but the American admiral disbelieved the information and did nothing until another report came through two hours later. Steaming north now, patrolling Wildcats began shooting down Japanese scouts, which clearly indicated a larger fleet in the area. East of this, *Ryujo* launched fifteen Zeros and six Kates at 1220 to hit Henderson Field and draw the American carriers into a trap.

One hour after launch, the *Saratoga* picked up the strike on her radar and passed the information to Guadalcanal. Fletcher then finally launched thirty Dauntlesses and eight Avengers off the *Sara* to attack the *Ryujo*. At 1400 a floatplane from the cruiser *Chikuma* found both U.S. carriers about two hundred miles due east of Guadalcanal, and at 1455 twenty-seven Vals and ten Zeros flew off *Shokaku* and *Zuikaku* headed for the American fleet. However, while this was happening, *Ryujo*'s small strike force ran smack into the Cactus Air Force in the violent skies over Guadalcanal. Three

Wildcats went down in the melee, but took six of the attackers with them. At roughly the same time, SBD scouts found Kondo's cruisers, then shortly thereafter sighted Nagumo's big carriers.

Confusion reigned supreme for the next several hours with both sides missing opportunities, yet blood was drawn as *Ryujo* was hit multiple times by the *Saratoga*'s air group. As this occurred, a second strike from the big carriers put another twenty-seven dive bombers and nine fighters inbound toward Fletcher's task force, which were initially detected by the *Enterprise* some eighty-eight miles to the northwest. Poor fighter direction and flawed communications prevented most of the fifty-three Wildcats from engaging, and some of the Vals got through. During a bloody two minutes, three bombs struck the "Big E" and by 1646 she was afire. The fifteen-minute battle cost the Japanese Navy eighteen dive bombers and six Zeros, with U.S. losses at eight Wildcats, though five of the pilots were recovered.

American damage control procedures once again paid off, and within an hour the *Enterprise* was making 24 knots and recovering her aircraft, though luckily the second Japanese strike force missed the battle entirely, and returned north without engaging. *Ryujo* was not so fortunate, and would sink later that evening.

Under brilliantly moonlit skies early the next morning, a PBY found Tanaka's convoy about 180 miles north of Guadalcanal with the rest of Ichiki's detachment aboard. By 0808, Cactus dive bombers rolled in on the *Jintsu* and the biggest of the three transports. The cruiser was heavily damaged, and the transport dead in the water when a flight of three B-17s appeared far overhead and dropped 12,000 pounds of bombs on the smoldering Japanese ships. For once the Fortresses hit their seaborne targets, and the destroyer *Mutsuki* went down in forty-seven minutes, and the transport was scuttled. The landing was canceled and the remaining ships limped off northwest toward Truk.

Savo, though a decisive Japanese tactical victory, was a strategic loss since the Marines remained on Guadalcanal. This Battle of the Eastern Solomons was something else; the U.S. carriers were not destroyed, an invasion convoy blunted, and air superiority of the southern Solomons continued to elude the Japanese. Most of all, it was yet another warning of what to expect against an angry, alert, and vengeful enemy. Yamamoto, at least, recognized this and the immediate need to switch tactics. It was his ability to do so, and his willingness to fly in the face of Japanese tradition, that made the diminutive admiral the most lethal adversary faced by the Americans in the South Pacific.

While the Japanese licked their wounds the Marines patrolled, fought, and protected the perimeter, especially the airfield. Without Henderson and air cover there was no survival. Pilots went up every time a warning of inbound raid arrived, or close air support was needed around the perimeter. Everyone became weaker; everyone got sick to one degree or another. After the first five days of air combat only eleven Wildcats, nine Dauntlesses, and three P-400s remained flyable. Four days later Captain John Thompson brought in nine additional P-400s from New Caledonia and the 67th Fighter Squadron was more or less at full strength.

Landing during an air raid and taking pot shots from Japanese snipers around the field, Thompson's pilots were immediately pressed into the Cactus Air Force, and on August 29 they struggled into the air in three flights of four against eighteen Betty bombers and their escorting Zeros. Unable to climb past 14,000 feet, Brannon had to watch with extreme frustration as the Wildcats slashed into the Japanese formation, shooting down four bombers and four Zeros. Coming back to land, the Army pilots were surprised to see bushes seemingly sprouting from the runway. Avoiding the plants and bouncing past working groups, they discovered that the shrubs were used to mark craters for returning pilots. Jumped by Zeros on August 30, five of eleven P-400s limped back stitched with holes, and four did not return at all; Lieutenants Robert E. Chilson and K. W. Wyethes were killed in action, though two others made it back on foot.

Conditions were deplorable, yet until the Navy reappeared there wasn't much to be done. Clustered together near the airfield in a coconut grove they named "Mosquito Gulch," the mix of Navy, Marine, and Army pilots lived in muddy dugouts or ragged tents. Those who had cots were fortunate—many only had old Japanese straw mattresses. After a few days of gut-wrenching, high-performance combat it didn't matter. Pilots did not have the luxury of armed buddies close by, and when they died they died alone; a bloody or burned corpse in a cockpit, or a lonely, thirsty death at sea. Sometimes a man just disappeared with no trace; all that remained were a few letters, tattered clothes, and a picture of a sweetheart, a wife, or a child stuck to his cot. Cactus Air Force pilots ran odds of about one in five of death or serious wounds; those for an infantryman, either Army or Marine, were closer to one in fifty.

Spam, canned hash, and an occasional sausage added some variety to the awful dehydrated potatoes left over from the Great War. There was also no liquor yet, which was very nearly a post-combat essential to calm shredded nerves and put an exhausted man to sleep, and the only cigarettes remaining were Japanese. There was lots of hot, black coffee, and occasionally a stray cow would wander close enough to be shot for dinner, but the stringy meat didn't last long. The mud Marines were a bit luckier with local meat, and could shoot a cow through the eye at two hundred yards.

Everyone on the Canal lost weight: at least twenty pounds per man, and often twice that. Morale wasn't bad—the Marines were too professional for that—but they rightly felt abandoned by everyone but the Cactus Air Force. Still, they counted the planes taking off every time, and saw fewer and fewer return. There was a defiant pride in being at the Canal, presumed forgotten, always outnumbered, and seemingly alone. The U.S. Army, with the exception of Dale Brannon and his P-400 pilots, earned their special enmity:

> They sent for the army to come to Tulagi
> But Douglas MacArthur said "No!"
> He said, "There's a reason, it isn't the season,
> Besides, there is no U.S.O."

Aerial attacks came daily, weather permitting, and the dwindling number of fighter pilots usually had a thirty-minute warning courtesy of the coastwatcher chain. The surviving Americans had been quick studies, and gifted, aggressive pilots like Captain John Smith and Marion Carl had proven several viable countertactics against the Japanese. They dove on the Betty dive bombers from at least 5,000 feet above, and at oblique angles to avoid the 20 mm tail gun and 7.7 mm guns in the three turrets. These high to low slashing attacks, usually out of the sun, minimized the danger to the Wildcats while exposing the bomber's unarmored fuel tanks to heavy .50-caliber machine gun fire. As for the Zeros, no one turned with them if it could be avoided.

However, the commanding officer of VF-3, Jimmy Thach, had devised a solution until better fighter aircraft were fielded. It was based on a "fighting pair" working together to defeat a superior turning adversary. Essentially, the pair, or section, would fly a multidimensional weave across the sky. This spoiled initial shots by a foe and, more important, made him choose one fighter out of the pair, leaving the other free to attack. As the preferred Japanese method mirrored the Samurai philosophy of individual combat, American fighting pairs were effective countertactics. In fact, Saburo Sakai described his first encounter with this new American tactic and its effects on Tadashi Nakajima, Japan's leading ace in 1942: "Two Wildcats jumped on the commander's plane. He had no trouble in getting on the tail of an enemy fighter, but never had a chance to fire before the Grumman's teammate roared at him from the side. Nakajima was raging when he got back to Rabaul; he had been forced to dive and run for safety."

Koga's captured Zero had made it from Akutan to Seattle and was presently being reconstructed at North Island, so no hard data was yet available and the new two-ship tactic was the best chance pilots had. It spread rapidly among the U.S. Navy and Marine Corps aviators, who, in turn, shared it with their Army brothers on Guadalcanal. Thach called it the "Beam Defense Position," but it became known universally as "the Thach Weave." Nevertheless, there were soon fewer than a dozen operational fighters remaining to the Cactus Air Force, and at the end of the month things came to a head.

August 30 saw a concentrated effort by Imperial Navy fighter pilots to destroy the Cactus Air Force—and they nearly succeeded. At 1145, eighteen Zeros of the crack Tainan Kobutai (Air Group) appeared overhead in a carefully planned fighter sweep. They intended to engage and destroy as many Cactus aircraft as possible to soften up Guadalcanal for the next raid later that day. Coastwatchers down the island chain alerted the Americans, who were up in force with three formations of fighters; four P-400s were low over Tulagi protecting a stranded cargo ship, while another seven "Klunkers," as their pilots now called them, orbited at their top altitude of 14,000 above Henderson Field. High over it all at 28,000 were John Lucian Smith's eight remaining Wildcats—waiting and watching.

Tainan pilots were the very best Japan had. Veterans of the Sino-Japanese War, they had been first into the fight over the Philippines against the U.S. Army Air Force. Transferred to Lae, New Guinea, the Tainans battled the P-40 Kittyhawks of the Royal Australian Air Force and U.S. Army P-39s until the Americans landed on Guadalcanal. Saburo Sakai had been a top ace, and his loss due to wounds infuriated his squadron mates. However, overconfidence was not limited to the Imperial Navy; despite Sakai's loss, the Tainan pilots could not conceive of an enemy as skilled as themselves. Moreover, they were not adaptable, as were their U.S. counterparts, and even with their superb aircraft persisted in flying close, three-plane formations while employing largely ineffective individual tactics. The Wildcats fought as pairs, utilizing their much heavier armament and armor plating to largely negate the Zero's turning ability. American fighters also used radios for communication and coordinated attacks, while the Japanese had removed their own radios to save weight.

It was over quickly.

In a matter of minutes eight of the Tainan's best had been shot to pieces, and one would ditch in the ocean later. Japanese pilots, who valued death in combat, did not wear parachutes, so if they went down not only was the plane lost, but a skilled, trained aviator as well. Americans thought differently, and considered it their duty to fight another day. The only U.S. planes lost were four P-400s, and two of the pilots were recovered. So when the second raid of thirteen Zeros and eighteen Betty dive bombers appeared overhead, the Cactus Air Force was still alive and fighting. Nevertheless, the destroyer *Colhoun* was sunk, and when the Japanese disappeared there were only five flyable aircraft remaining at Henderson Field. Temporary salvation arrived shortly thereafter as Colonel William Wallace, commander of MAG-23, brought in Major Robert Galer's VMF-224 with nineteen remaining Wildcats, and a dozen additional Dauntlesses led by Major Leo Smith.

However, elation was always short-lived on the Canal and the following morning began badly for the Americans. At 0748, cruising 260 miles south of Guadalcanal, the USS *Saratoga* had just launched her morning flights when a Long Lance torpedo slammed into her starboard side. Commanding the fleet submarine I-26, Lieutenant Commander Minoru Yokota spotted the carrier and fired a spread of six torpedoes before crash diving.* In a narrow escape, the submarine's super-structure actually scraped destroyer *Macdonough*'s keel on her way down. The carrier took on a four-degree list from a flooded fire room, but damage control parties controlled the fire and she was taken under tow by the cruiser *Minneapolis*. Admiral Fletcher got a cut on his forehead, which added to his overall nervousness, and headed southwest past the Fijis for Tonga, then on to Pearl Harbor. With the *Enterprise* also out for repairs, this left the *Wasp* and *Hornet* as the sole American carriers in the South Pacific.

In Tokyo, the Imperial General Staff belatedly con-cluded that the U.S. toehold in the Solomons was genu-ine, neither a raid or a reconnaissance in force, but a real effort to blunt Japan's southern thrust and restrict Yamamoto's movements. The admiral agreed. He was also adamant that the island could only be retaken by

---

* On December 7, 1941, *I-26* was the first Japanese sub to sink a U.S. merchantman. Patrolling off the American West Coast, she dispatched the *Cynthia Olson* with her 5.5-inch deck gun. The Doolittle Raiders narrowly missed her at Yokosuka in April 1942, and by June *I-26* was back off the U.S. west coast, where she shelled the Estevan Point lighthouse on Vancouver Island. She was sunk with all hands off the Philippine coast during the fall of 1944.

ground forces, but without air superiority this could never occur. His solution was Operation KA. Named for the first syllable in the Japanese name for Guadalcanal, this was a massive counterstroke that aimed to destroy the U.S. carriers, sweep the skies of the fledgling Cactus Air Force, and give the Imperial Army unfettered access to the island. Enemy forces began to gather and ominous rumors reached the Canal.

By this time, it was becoming obvious that the battle for Guadalcanal was a line in the sand, a Yorktown or a Gettysburg, and the Americans rotting there fervently hoped it would not become an Alamo. To this end, Major General Kiyotake Kawaguchi embarked his 35th Infantry Brigade from Shortland Harbor, three hundred miles northwest off the coast of Bougainville, and headed southwest down the Slot toward Guadalcanal. Supremely confident that he would retake the island with his 5,000 veterans, Kawaguchi's advance force consisted of nearly 1,000 men from Ichiki's Second Echelon, and the 124th Infantry had already landed at Taivu Point.

There was some good news for the Americans as well. Twenty-one Dauntlesses and torpedo bombers accompanied by nine Wildcats under Lieutenant Commander Leroy Simpler flew off the damaged *Saratoga* and landed at Henderson Field to augment the Cactus

Air Force. Rear Admiral John McCain also arrived on August 31 to see his friend Archer Vandegrift and appraise the situation for himself. Tall and spare, the Marine general produced his coveted bottle of bourbon for the wiry little admiral—just in time for an air raid. Crouching in a dugout, they heard the bombs whistle down and watched the dirt jump from the concussions. After night fell a Japanese cruiser slid in close enough to shell the airfield. Those stuck on the Canal, McCain was told, had grown used to such events. The admiral responded: "By God, Vandegrift, this is your war and you sure are welcome to it. But when I go back tomorrow I am going to try to get you what you need for your air force here."

He immediately wrote to MacArthur and Nimitz that "40 flyable high altitude fighters" were absolutely necessary on Guadalcanal if the island was to remain in American hands. Specifically; "2 full squadrons of P-38s or F4Fs in addition to present strength should be put into Cactus at once . . . the situation admits no delay whatever. Cactus can be a sinkhole for enemy air power. . . . [I]f the reinforcement requested is not made available, Cactus cannot be supplied and hence cannot be held."

To the men fighting and dying on the Canal, the situation was clear and unambiguous, but the United

States was struggling to catch up after years of low budgets and technical deficiencies. Her latent economic and industrial might was beginning to flex its muscles, but the Axis powers were still very much on the offensive. The 4th Panzer Army was closing on Stalingrad and Rommel's Afrika Korps was within fifty miles of Alexandria. If he was not stopped, then Egypt would fall and the Germans would seize the Suez Canal, thus slitting England's throat by denying her resources in India. The scarce P-38s, argued the Army, were needed for the upcoming invasion of North Africa and to stop Rommel in Egypt. MacArthur, ever arrogant and myopic, also refused any assistance to Guadalcanal. His reason was there were only eighteen Lightnings in theater, and they were needed to defend Port Moresby *if* it was attacked. That, MacArthur believed, was more important than the Solomons, and in any event Guadalcanal was within the Navy's area of responsibility, though he saw no hypocrisy in demanding aircraft carriers to support his own intended operations in New Guinea. Eighteen P-38s would not have made much difference during a Port Moresby invasion, which did not happen, but they could have saved lives on Guadalcanal.

The only piece of good news was the recall of Frank Jack Fletcher by Admiral Nimitz. Using Fletcher's scratched forehead as a pretext, the Pacific Fleet commander sent him back to California with the *Saratoga*. Fletcher's perennial caution and craven abandonment of the 1st Marine Division on Guadalcanal finally caught up with him, and he spent the remainder of the war holding shore commands where he could do no damage. Though men under his command accounted for six Japanese carriers, Fletcher himself reacted to situations rather than seeking out and destroying the enemy. This does not suffice in war, and condemnation of his actions, or lack thereof, was thinly veiled in a message from Nimitz to the Pacific Fleet: "We cannot expect to inflict heavy losses on the enemy without ourselves accepting the risk of punishment. To win this war we must come to grips with the enemy. Courage, determination and action will see us through."

Action, at least, was a constant, the surface Navy notwithstanding. The first day of September saw the arrival of *Betelgeuse*, a cargo ship carrying 387 men and five officers of the 6th Seabees; Joe Blundon had kept his promise of ten days earlier. They brought along a pair of bulldozers to put the finishing touches on Henderson Field, and immediately began clearing an auxiliary strip about a mile to the east. Officially known as Fighter One, the pilots simply referred to it as the "Cow Pasture," since it was little more than a cleared field of cut kunai grass. Two days later the first transport aircraft bounced onto Henderson and rolled to a stop amid a cloud of dust, and out jumped Roy Stanley Geiger, Brigadier General, USMC, commander of the 1st Marine Air Wing. Short and stocky, with close-clipped gray hair, Geiger was a hard-eyed, "Old Breed" Marine. A veteran squadron commander during the Great War, he held a law degree, had fought in Nicaragua, Santo Domingo, and Haiti, and was an old friend of Archer Vandegrift. Officially designated as Marine Corps Aviator #5, Geiger was an aviator version of Admiral Bull Halsey. He could fly anything with wings.

He was just the man to get things jumping and put some order in the Cactus Air Force, and that is exactly what happened. Geiger established a wing staff and moved it to Espiritu Santo to facilitate the flow of replacements, spare parts, fuel, and ammunition, while he remained on Guadalcanal; the jungle didn't bother him much after the Banana Wars. He set up shop in the "Pagoda," the wooden, Japanese-built operations center in the very center of the bull's-eye of Henderson Field. Geiger and his indomitable chief of staff, Colonel Louis Woods, also got radar up and running at Henderson to augment information provided by the coastwatchers. With radar there would be little guesswork, and fighters would be sent directly at inbound enemy formations just as they were at sea.

Elements of the 3rd Marine Defense Battalion had come ashore on August 7 with fire control and early warning radars, but these were already out of commission due to battle damage and lack of spare parts. Detachment A of the 5th Defense Battalion landed early in September with a mobile SCR-270B Early Warning radar and its nine-man crew. Ideally, the system could detect aircraft formations at 20,000 feet at a range of about one hundred miles, though actual performance was somewhat worse than this—still, anything helped.* Two days later Lieutenant Colonel Wyman Marshall landed an R4D under fire at the airfield bearing a special cargo: three thousand pounds of candy and cigarettes courtesy of MAG-25.† He flew back the same day for New Caledonia with a fuselage full of wounded Marines, and the South Pacific Combat Air Transport (SCAT) began regular resupply operations.

---

* The SCR-270 had a resolution of about 50 feet, so it could not pick out individual targets, but was good enough against large formations. Incidentally, the Marine Corps opened its first radar school at Quantico, Virginia, in July 1941.

† This was the venerable "Gooney Bird," the USN/USMC version of the C-47 Skytrain.

The next day, September 6, a skinny, dirty man wearing a shredded flight suit approached the American lines west of Henderson Field. Lieutenant Richard Amerine of VMF-224 had gone missing on August 31 near Cape Esperance, where he'd lost his oxygen system then his engine. Bailing out, the young pilot swam ashore and found himself some thirty miles into enemy territory. Coming across a sleeping soldier, Amerine killed him with a rock, then took his pistol and shoes. Over the next few days the lieutenant carefully made his way east, killing two more Japanese soldiers with the butt of his pistol and shooting a fourth before making it to the Marine positions near the Matanikau River. Correspondent Richard Tregaskis interviewed the young officer and asked what he'd eaten. Amerine shrugged and answered, "Red ants and snails." His degree in entomology from the University of Kansas had finally paid off.

By September 9 the Cow Pasture was ready for operations, but only for lightweight fighters as it was not paved. All the concrete and Marston matting went to Henderson so it could accommodate heavily laden bombers and cargo planes. Two days later the 67th Fighter Squadron lost Dale Brannon during a noon air raid. Diving toward a dugout with four of his pilots, Brannon was still in midair when a thousand-pound bomb detonated just a few feet away. Mud, branches, and pilots spun across the encampment before landing hard. Somehow they all survived, but Brannon and two others were badly wounded and had to be evacuated.

Finally, later on September 11, the "Nameless Wonders of the Bastard Air Force," as the Cactus pilots called themselves, got a much-needed break—and just in time. They all had chronic diarrhea by this time, and the continuous stress of combat had worn down even the strongest of them by now. There were also only twelve flyable Wildcats remaining, and all indications pointed to a renewed Japanese assault on the island. There was nothing to do but keep fighting, yet hope was running out. "Better to fight it out," Geiger snarled at his exhausted men, "than to get a Jap bayonet up the ass." But at 1620 that afternoon, weary smiles crossed the dirty, bearded faces at Henderson Field when Lieutenant Commander Leroy Simpler brought in two dozen F4Fs from *Saratoga*'s VF-5, and not an hour too soon.

The epic battle for Guadalcanal was about to begin.

As Richard Amerine recovered, and Fighter One prepared for flight operations, Major General Kawaguchi and most of his brigade had moved west from Taivu toward the village of Tasimboko and then on to the tooth-shaped Marine perimeter around Lunga Point. With 5,200 men, plus another thousand under Colonel Akinosuka Oka moving in from the west, the general was confident of crushing the Americans once and for all. But Kawaguchi did not know the terrain, and failed to reconnoiter. It wasn't necessary, Kawaguchi believed, since he had a numerical superiority and surprise.

In fact, he had neither.

Kawaguchi was outnumbered three to one by the Marines, but like Ichiki before him he was unaware of this. Not that it would have mattered. The general's first taste of combat had been in Malaysia during December 1941, and later in the Philippines. No enemy he had encountered challenged the notion of Japanese superiority, and he expected very little from the Americans. Surprise had been compromised from the beginning. Martin Clemens and his coastwatchers had been keeping Vandegrift apprised of the situation and on September 8, Colonel Merritt "Red Mike" Edson and his 1st Raider Battalion, accompanied by the remnants of the 1st Marine Parachute Battalion, nicknamed "Chutes," landed at Taivu behind Kawaguchi. They found field guns, antitank guns, and mounds of supplies. There was also a detailed set of instructions for the elaborate ceremony planned for the Marines' imminent surrender, including taking General Vandegrift's sword.

The Raiders demolished a radio station, stuffed their pockets with tinned crab and beef, and then destroyed everything else, everything but twenty-one cases of beer and seventeen half-gallon containers of sake, which they couldn't bear to burn and took with them. They also took a chest of clothes belonging to Kawaguchi that included the dress white uniform he intended to wear before Vandegrift was flown to Tokyo and paraded through the streets. Moving west toward Tasimboko, Edson's men found the 35th Brigade's base camp, but Kawaguchi had already moved off farther west. Killing the few Japanese who remained, the Marines tossed the gun breeches into the water, gathered up the papers, maps, and code books, then boarded the destroyers *Manley* and *McKean*, which were standing just offshore from the Tenaru with two smaller boats. Once the area was clear, Cactus P-400s and SBDs bombed and strafed whatever was left. Off to the west, Kawaguchi heard the gunfire and bombing, but discounted it as a raid and, displaying the Japanese penchant for fixed plans, would not turn back.

For their part, the Raiders and Chutes returned to Lunga, passed on their captured documents, and bivouacked near Kukum village on the coast. Edson and other officers were convinced that a large enemy force had landed, and was making its way around the Marine lines to attack from the south, the weakest part of the perimeter. Vandegrift disagreed and refused to reinforce his southern position. The Japanese would attack his flanks, either from Alligator Creek or west from the Matanikau, as they always had done, or possibly come ashore on Lunga at night. Vandegrift's reaction was understandable—to a point. There was no way to land on the southern shore of the Canal, and even if it had been done the jungle would slowly kill any force coming up from that direction. Enemy troops had to be landed to the west, east, or from the north, and that's where his Marines had to remain.

He had also received a message, hand delivered on September 11 by Admirals Turner and McCain. Ghormley, from the safety of his anchored headquarters, had written that there were too few ships, too few assets, long supply lines, that in light of massing enemy forces he could no longer support the Marines on Guadalcanal. General Henry Harley "Hap" Arnold, bombastic chief of the newly established Army Air Force, also refused another request to deploy P-38s to Guadalcanal, as he considered it a lost cause. Turner was having none of it. He was planning on landing the 7th Marine Regiment wherever Vandegrift wanted them as soon as possible. With the Cactus Air Force steadily diminishing and an official message leaving the Marines to their own resources, the situation was grim. Nonetheless, Colonel Edson persuaded the general to let him move his 840 men up away from the airfield so they could rest, and he chose the ground south of Henderson and east of the Lunga River: three small hilltops linked by a north-south ridgeline, and exactly where Yamaguchi planned to attack.

Just past 2100 on the night of September 12, the cruiser *Sendai* opened up with her eight-inch guns and, along with three destroyers, shelled the ridge for an hour. Kawaguchi, who crossed the Tenaru well south of the perimeter, was now trying to assemble his force without effective radios, and in the darkness of the jungle. Impatient and impetuous, he launched a disorganized attack from his center with three battalions of 2,506 men. Confused and disoriented, most of these missed the ridge and ended up in the low, swampy ground around the lagoon. Kawaguchi's left wing tried to cross the fast-flowing Lunga River and intermingled with lost units from the center attack. The right wing, Ichiki's surviving 2nd Echelon, staggered out of the jungle into the Raiders and Paramarines on Hill 80, the farthest south position, where they were cut apart by accurate, preregistered artillery fire from Colonel "Don Pedro" del Valle's 11th Marine Artillery.

Kawaguchi himself ended up in the Lunga River,

and by dawn was muddy and exhausted. As the Marines on the ridge shortened their lines, ate cold hash and potatoes, and tried to rest, the Japanese general spent the day trying to gather his forces and coordinate the next attack. "The time has come," he scolded his commanders, "for you to give your lives for your Emperor." Three separate air raids occurred during the day. The Japanese lost 11 aircraft against 5 from the Cactus Air Force, but then that night Kawaguchi threw everything he had available at the ridge. A red flare arced out of the jungle at 2230, and Major Masao Tamura's 2nd Battalion charged up the south slope of Hill 80 firing weapons and throwing grenades. Smoke was confused with a gas attack, and the Marines fell back briefly before Major Ken Bailey, one of the finest officers in the Corps, rallied the men. The combination of this and del Valle's 105 mm howitzers shredded the Japanese. "A curtain of metal descended behind the retreating paratroopers," historian Joseph Wheelan writes. "Carving gaps in the Japanese ranks and spraying the ridge's approaches with blood and severed limbs."

Nevertheless, the situation was desperate as wave after wave of Kawaguchi's men poured from the jungle. Two Marines were captured, and by torturing them with knives the Japanese hoped to lure others into the open. It didn't work, but their screams thoroughly enraged the Raiders. Captain Harry Torgerson led a bayonet counterattack from Hill 123 shouting, "Do you want to live forever?" Despite a 40 percent casualty rate, he drove the Japanese 3rd Battalion off the ridge. "The Japanese attack was almost constant," recounted Captain William J. McKennan. "Like a rain that subsides for a moment and then pours the harder. . . . When one wave was mowed down—and I mean mowed down—another followed it into death."

With courage, rage, and guts the Marines held on through the long, long night of September 13–14, 1942. As Edson, with bullet holes through his clothes, fell back toward Hill 60, there was nothing between the Japanese and the airfield but his three hundred or so remaining Marines. At 0530, the remnants of Major Tamura's 6th Company made it north onto Fighter One, and were within one thousand yards of Henderson Field when finally stopped by C Company engineers. Some did break through, and Ensign Harold Buell recalls nearly tripping over a dead Japanese soldier on the way to his plane that morning. There was blood splashed all down one side and as the pilot approached a Marine Raider climbed out of the cockpit. Colonel Edson had detailed a man to guard each aircraft, and it was well he did so. A Japanese soldier had clambered up on a wing to toss a grenade inside the cockpit when the Raider stuck his Browning Automatic Rifle against the man's chest and pulled the trigger. "Then I pulled him off the wing so you guys can fly this thing."

Fly they did.

Just after 0400, Captain John Thompson of the 67th Fighter Squadron was called to the Pagoda on Henderson Field.

"The Marines had been fighting on the ridge all day and all night," he recalled.

> Several Marines from the ridge were there, including one of their company commanders. He was very tired, caked with mud—a bullet hole through his helmet and blood streaming down his face. He told me their situation was bad and they desperately needed our help. He grabbed a pencil and a scrap of paper and drew a rough diagram of the ridge showing the positions of both sides. He said the Japanese were expected to make a big push at daybreak.

The officer with the bullet hole through his helmet was the indomitable Major Ken Bailey, and the massing Japanese totaled well some 1,700 men from two battalions; the Marines simply could not hold out against those numbers. The enemy was gathering below the southern ridge and could not be hit by del Valle's artillery fire—only an attack from the air could stop them. Would Thompson do it? He had five flyable P-400s remaining, but only enough fuel to get three airborne.

I shoved that map in my pocket, went back to the flight line and picked a couple of other pilots, Lieutenants B. E. Davis and B. W. Brown. We took off at dawn and made a wide circle around the field to stay out of sight.

The ridgeline was covered with Japanese bodies, sometimes three deep. Arms and legs were everywhere; coconuts too, which puzzled the pilots since there were no trees nearby. Then they realized the coconuts were severed heads. Craters pockmarked any open surface, large holes from the artillery and naval guns, with hundreds of smaller, scorched marks from grenades. Turning to run in from the east, Thompson put the sun behind him and into the eyes of the Japanese below the ridge.

We came in low over the trees, pulled up and saw the Marine positions. It was just daylight. In the clearing were hundreds and hundreds of Japanese, ready to charge. I lowered the nose, pressed the trigger and just mowed right through them. The next two pilots did the same thing.

Infantrymen in any army feared and loathed enemy close air support aircraft, and the Japanese were no exception. Opening up with chattering Nambu machine guns and their Arisaka rifles, they put a curtain of lead into the sky as the twelve-cylinder Allisons roared overhead. Pulling up from the attack over the Lunga River, Lieutenant Davis's P-400 took a hit in the vulnerable cooling system. Wounded, and with no engine, the young pilot glided back over the ridgeline and dead-sticked the shark-nosed fighter into the Cow Pasture. Thompson and Brown came around again, dropped their noses toward the antlike enemies swarming on the slope, and opened fire.

For all its shortcomings in aerial combat, the Klunker packed a deadly punch against ground targets. John Thompson emptied his guns into the exposed infantrymen: 60 rounds from his Hispano 20mm cannon, 540 rounds from a pair of Browning .50-caliber guns, and fully 3,000 rounds out of his four .30-caliber guns. This time he took the hit in the pullout, and zoomed up over the cheering Marines to glide into Fighter One after Davis. Lieutenant Brown made one more pass over the blood-soaked ridge and watched the annihilated Japanese battalions scatter back into the jungle.

Clambering out of his smoking, hissing Klunker, Thompson waited for his one remaining P-400 to land, then took a jeep over to the Pagoda to report. Apparently the Marines on the ridge had already done it for him, and reported more than five hundred chewed up Japanese corpses on the hillside. The astonished pilot was greeted by Vandegrift himself. "Captain Thompson," the general said, shaking his hand and giving him a bottle of precious scotch. "You won't read about this in the newspapers, but you and your flight of P-400s just saved Guadalcanal."

PART TWO

"The only good Jap is one that's
been dead six months."

ADMIRAL WILLIAM F. "BULL" HALSEY

Six

Borrowed Lives

Rumors surrounding the Japanese defeat were all bad.

Despite initial setbacks, Yamamoto, determined to recover the initiative, was preparing a joint, coherent counteroffensive in the wake of Ichiki's and Kawaguchi's shocking defeats. This plan centered on the high-speed convoy capability of the "Tokyo Express" and its twenty-seven destroyers. These were intended to dash into Ironbottom Sound, land the 2nd Division and elements of the 38th Division of General Hyakutake's 17th Army, and retake Guadalcanal.* As Henderson Field's

---

* The Japanese called this *Nezumi*, or "Rat" transportation. Destroyers could not carry many men or extra supplies, but they were extremely fast and capable of self-protection.

defiant pilots had not been negated or defeated by the vaunted flyers of the Imperial Navy, then Yamamoto would pound the Americans into submission by the powerful guns of his battleships and heavy cruisers. Recapturing the island had become the number one priority for the Combined Fleet, and was directed by the admiral himself, who recognized the danger of an American toehold in the Solomons.

His counteroffensive had three main prongs. First, at 0800 on October 11, a Reinforcement Group commanded by Rear Admiral Takatsugu Jojima sailed from the Shortlands. Consisting of two seaplane tenders and five destroyers, it would steam 220 miles down the Slot, pass south of the Russell Islands, and enter Ironbottom Sound as close to Cape Esperance as possible. A Bombardment Group consisting of three heavy cruisers with two destroyers, commanded by Vice Admiral Aritomo Goto, also sortied from the Shortlands at 1400 on the same day. Much faster, Goto's force would pass Jojima to arrive in Ironbottom Sound by midnight, then blast Henderson Field while the destroyer convoy landed its reinforcements.

In the meantime, Yamamoto assembled the most powerful elements of the Combined Fleet at Truk, including all five of his remaining aircraft carriers, to deliver the hammer blow he planned for Guadalcanal.

Zuiho, Shokaku, and *Zuikaku* made up the fast carrier strike group commanded by Vice Admiral Chuichi Nagumo, of Pearl Harbor infamy, who later forced the Royal Navy from the Indian Ocean and was subsequently outfought at Midway. The other pair of carriers, *Junyo* and *Hiyo,* were grouped with the battleships *Kongo* and *Haruna* and screened by four cruisers with ten destroyers under the command of Vice Admiral Nobutake Kondo. The battleships *Hiei* and *Kirishima* were escorted by three heavy cruisers and fifteen destroyers under Rear Admiral Hiroki Abe. Despite setbacks and ongoing combat losses, Yamamoto knew he had to strike now so "X-Day," the full-scale assault in conjunction with the 17th Army, was set for October 15, 1942.

Both sides used the comparative lull in large-scale fighting during the latter half of September to reorganize and regroup somewhat. Admiral Chester Nimitz toured the South Pacific to see the situation on Guadalcanal for himself, something Admiral Ghormley had never bothered to do. Afterward, he insisted that the island receive all the aid they could provide. Roads, docks, communications, and reinforcements: everything they could give. Most important, as Nimitz saw it, was Henderson Field. It needed to be completed, surfaced, and expanded with first-class repair facilities. "Planes," Nimitz said, "were too expensive and too hard to get to let only minor damage render them permanently unserviceable."

Aircraft were useless without pilots to fly them and the admiral also wanted medical and mess facilities, permanent fuel storage, and Quonset huts instead of tents. It took years to fully train a pilot, so to lose one unnecessarily was a shameful and dangerous waste of resources. In the early days of the campaign this could not be helped, but Nimitz made it clear that America was in the Solomons to stay, and success or failure rested squarely on air superiority. Additionally, the Seventh Marine Regiment landed on September 18, with Mitchell's newly arrived pilots the first visible sign of Army aid for the beleaguered defenders.

The second sign was the 164th Regiment of the 23rd "American" Division, which was ordered out of New Caledonia to Guadalcanal. On October 9 the transports *McCawley* and *Zeilin* sailed from Nouméa with 2,837 "Doggies" under Colonel Bryant Moore, a competent and charismatic West Pointer who had taken over from the National Guard commander during the previous month.* In preparation for the Army landing, four

---

* The 164th was an activated unit of the North Dakota National Guard.

cruisers and five destroyers under Rear Admiral Norman Scott formed Task Force 64, and were ordered to
secure the approaches into Ironbottom Sound.

A fighting admiral, Scott was a 1911 graduate of the
Naval Academy who had battled U-boats in the Atlantic during the Great War.* A surface Navy gunnery
specialist, he was nonetheless a firm believer in modern technology who incorporated radar and aviation
into his battle plans. Scott was also a fierce advocate
for realistic combat training, especially night fighting. Patrolling south between Guadalcanal and Rennell Island, Scott drilled his task force as a unit, honed
their gunnery skills, integrated every piece of technology available to put his guns on target, and waited for
the Imperial Japanese Navy. But not for long. Jojima's
group was sighted by a pair of Cactus Air Force Dauntlesses at 1445 some two hundred miles up the Slot off
Choiseul. The dive bombers immediately transmitted
the information as they were attacked by Zeros. Both
pilots were wounded yet they continued sending radio
reports on the Japanese ships. Fortunately, the seaplane
tenders and transports were misidentified as cruisers

---

* Scott was the executive officer of the destroyer *Jacob Jones*
(DD-61) when it was torpedoed and sunk by *U-53* on December 6, 1917, near the mouth of the English Channel.

and destroyers, though Goto's surface force was still behind the convoy and undetected. This was enough for Scott, who came north for the intercept with the heavy cruisers *San Francisco* and *Salt Lake City,* with the light cruisers *Boise* and *Helena,* and his destroyer screen.

During his fifth night on Guadalcanal, Mitchell and his pilots were awakened by the rumble of gunfire out to sea northwest of Cape Esperance. At 2200 Scott's task force had passed Cape Hunter, launched three floatplanes, then headed north to take up station off Savo Island. Twenty-three minutes later Jojima's ships were sighted attempting to slip into the Sound, but the American admiral rightly guessed there was another force west of Savo Island. Two minutes later his instincts were proven correct when radars aboard *Helena* and *Salt Lake City* caught Goto's Bombardment Force less than five miles distant. At 2333, Scott, who had been steaming northeast, brought his ships about to the west in a badly timed left turn, and for the next few minutes his ships were in temporary disarray as they attempted to regain formation. By 2345 the two groups were less than three miles from each other and within visual contact. The U.S. ships had been sighted minutes before by the Japanese flagship's lookouts, but Admiral Goto aboard the *Aoba* believed them to be Jojima's convoy.

One minute later, at 2346, *Helena* opened up with her fifteen six-inch guns and Goto realized his fatal error—briefly. *Salt Lake City's* and *San Francisco's* eight-inch guns immediately zeroed in and within minutes dozens of shells struck the *Aoba,* killing nearly eighty men and mortally wounding the Japanese admiral. U.S. destroyers darted in, quickly illuminating targets with searchlights, firing torpedoes, then disappearing back into the darkness. Captain Edward "Mike" Moran of the USS *Boise* ordered "Pick out the biggest one and fire!" and his crew did so, pouring more than three hundred six-inch shells into the enemy warships. Communications mishaps notwithstanding, the American cruisers shifted their ferocious, concentrated fire to the *Furutaka,* which was attacked by a bold U.S. destroyer and took a pair of torpedoes along with scores of heavier eight-inch shell hits. Just before midnight she, and the destroyer *Fubuki,* were hit hard and afire. Pursuing his retreating enemy northwest down the Slot, Scott ordered a cease-fire at 0120 and turned back toward Guadalcanal.

The Japanese, acknowledged masters of night naval combat, had been just been dealt a bloody blow that cost the lives of at least four hundred sailors. Joining *Fubuki* at the bottom of the Solomon Sea, the heavy cruiser *Furutaka* sank at 0228, while *Aoba* limped up the Slot with *Kinugasa*, finally crawling into the Shortlands at 1000 that morning. The destroyer *Duncan*, which had so bravely attacked the *Furutaka*, took a pounding in return and was the only American ship sank that night, along with forty-eight of her crew. Her skipper was Commander Edmund Battelle Taylor, a former all-American lacrosse player from the Naval Academy who jumped from his burning bridge then clambered back aboard to fight fires and save his crew. The destroyer *Farenholt* was also damaged by friendly fire that cost the lives of three sailors, graphically illustrating the dangers inherent in night fighting. Most of the 163 American casualties were aboard the *Boise*, which took several heavy hits from *Kinugasa*, including one that detonated in her forward magazine. Captain Moran's quick decisions and his superb damage control parties saved the ship, but the light cruiser spent the next five months in the Philadelphia Navy Yard under repair.

Captain John Mitchell awakened to another eventful day in a week of excitement. He shot down a reconnaissance floatplane within forty-eight hours of his arrival on the Canal, and had just witnessed America's first successful night naval battle of the Second World War. It was surely a much-needed U.S. tactical victory, and as much a boost to the morale of the surface

Navy as the victories over Japan's ground forces on the Canal had been to the Marines. Overestimation of an enemy is as equally dangerous as underestimation, and now the specter of Imperial infantry invincibility was dispelled as well. However, as Scott was mauling Goto west of Cape Esperance, the Reinforcement Group did slip into Ironbottom Sound and land 728 soldiers, a pair of field guns, and four howitzers in Doma Cove, northwest of the Matanikau.

For Mitchell and the other aviators, the naval victory seemed to give the Cactus Air Force some breathing room: a chance to repair aircraft, reorganize, and perhaps rest a bit. There were now twelve P-39 Airacobras with forty-five Navy and Marine Wildcats in the kunai grass of Fighter One, along with six Avenger torpedo bombers and sixteen Dauntlesses. C-47/R4D Skytrains from SCAT flew in as much aviation fuel as possible, though each transport carried only enough fifty-five-gallon drums to keep a Wildcat squadron in the air for an hour.

Two Marine heroes were also finally evacuated; Major John Smith and Captain Marion Carl of VMF-223, with nineteen and sixteen kills respectively, left Guadalcanal on October 11 for home. Major Richard Mangrum, commander of VMSB-232, was the only pilot from his squadron left standing and he would leave the next day. Out of his nineteen total pilots, seven had been killed, four wounded, and the rest evacuated from sickness. For the Marines the Battle of Cape Esperance was a sign that the U.S. Navy had their backs at last, and could hold Yamamoto at bay while they killed Japanese soldiers on Guadalcanal.

This pleasant illusion was about to be literally shattered.

The *McCawley* and *Zeilin*, which sailed from Nouméa two days earlier, anchored off Lunga Roads at 0547 on the morning of October 13 and offloaded the 164th Infantry Regiment with 3,200 tons of supplies. The transports also brought 210 men of the 1st Marine Air Wing, plus 85 replacement riflemen and an assortment of badly needed equipment: forty-four jeeps, thirty-seven trucks, a dozen 37 mm guns, and even sixteen British Bren gun carriers. Loading up with the battered remnants of the 1st Marine Raider Battalion, the ships sailed for New Caledonia before dark, quite fortunately as it turned out. A Japanese cruiser-launched floatplane known as "Louie the Louse" periodically flew over the Canal at night, spotting for naval bombardments and generally harassing the American defenders. The Marines told the jumpy Doggies of the 164th to relax; it was their first night here and they'd get accustomed to it. But at 2330 on the night of October 13 the Louse's normal annoyances turned ominous. He dropped a bright green flare directly over Henderson Field, and the Marines hunkered down for the expected naval bombardment.

What happened was unlike anything they'd experienced before.

Dashing unopposed down the Slot at 25 knots, the battleships *Haruna* and *Kongo* glided into Ironbottom Sound, slowed to 18 knots, and rotated all sixteen of their fourteen-inch guns toward the green flares over Henderson Field. They had sortied from Truk on October 10, with personal orders from Yamamoto to "apprehend and annihilate any powerful forces in the Solomons area, as well as any reinforcements," and they meant to do just that. Built as battle cruisers, the pair were heavily armored, fast, and carried eight fourteen-inch guns apiece. Their immense steam turbines could muscle the 702-foot long warship through the water at 27 knots, and at slower speeds they could travel 8,000 nautical miles without refueling. Designed by British naval architect George Thurston, *Kongo*'s keel was laid down at Vickers Limited at Barrow in Great Britain and the ship was commissioned in 1913. Her age was irrelevant that morning, when the first of 973 fourteen-inch shells thundered from her gun turrets and arced toward shore. The ships were so close and the trajectory so flat that Americans near the beach felt the heat of passing shells. Bob Leckie with the 1st Marines later recalled: "Gouts of flame gushed from their muzzles, and huge red blobs went arching through the blackness with the effect of strings of lighted boxcars rushing over a darkened hill."

Many of the rounds were 2,998-pound Sankaidan "Beehive" shells packed with nine hundred incendiary tubes. These would fan out into a 20-degree cone and impacting at 2,000 feet per second they were murderous on soft targets like personnel or parked aircraft. The shell casing fragmented also for good measure, which threw out deadly metallic splinters that shredded tents, pierced metal, and killed men. Using the Pagoda, Henderson Field's operations center, as a reference point, the watching Japanese had carefully surveyed headings and ranges to vulnerable American positions. Both airfields, their revetments, parking aprons, and the fuel dump were methodically shelled.

In a valiant attempt to distract the attackers, at 0200 four U.S. motor torpedo boats commanded by Lieutenant Commander Allen Montgomery slipped out of Tulagi, rounded the north tip of the island, and roared out to confront the battleships.* The American boats

---

* PT-38, PT-46, PT-46, and PT-60.

fired torpedoes, made smoke, and caused some confusion, but the nine destroyers screening for *Kongo* and *Haruna* chased them off with no damage. At 0256 the big guns fell silent and both battleships steamed out of the Sound heading northwest away from Guadalcanal. Circling Japanese aircraft then dropped bombs on burning spots, and at 0530 field artillery lobbed shells into the American perimeter. Alternately referred to as "The Night of the Battleships," or "All Hell's Eve," the naval assault of October 13–14 exacted a terrible toll from the defenders of Guadalcanal.

John Mitchell, like everyone else, crawled from his dugout when the sun rose. Red-eyed, head ringing, and dizzy, the American defenders were dazed and forty-one men were dead, including Major Gordon Bell, commanding officer of VMSB-141. The damage was appalling. Henderson Field was a mass of twisted Marston matting, and the 5,000-gallon fuel dump was completely gone. *Hornet's* Avenger torpedo bombers from VT-8 were all destroyed, but Lieutenant Commander Harold Henry "Swede" Larsen and his pilots scavenged their plane's .30-caliber machine guns and took to the hills with the 7th Marines. Of the thirty-nine Dauntlesses on the field, only a handful were still flyable. Mechanics immediately began cannibalizing wrecks for spare parts to get as many operational as possible.* Fighter One had been spared most of the pounding and there were still thirty flyable fighters: twenty-four Wildcats, four P-400s, and a pair of P-39 Airacobras that John Mitchell took up on a morning patrol.

Horrific as this was, the overall situation was better than the lonely days in August when the Marines were isolated and alone, or even during Kawaguchi's assault on Edson's Ridge. The Marines could handle any Japanese ground force, and the Cactus Air Force had held their own in the air, but what was possible against such huge naval guns? There was nothing to keep Henderson operational, or the Marines alive in the face of such uncontested bombardments. To emphasize the point, on the night of October 14 the heavy cruisers *Kinugasa* and *Chokai* idled unopposed offshore and blasted 752 eight-inch shells into the American positions.

"I don't think we have a goddamn Navy," General Roy Geiger snapped, and it was hard to argue with him.

That same night, six Japanese transports ran up onto the beach near Tassafaronga and began offloading another 4,500 soldiers from the 16th and 230th Infantry Regiments, plus 824 men of the 4th Maizuru Spe-

---

* Sources differ; Sherrod says four remained, while Miller lists seven operational. In either event, it was far too few.

cial Naval Landing Force. Two artillery batteries and a company of light tanks also came ashore, and Tokyo Express destroyers landed 1,100 additional men, plus food, supplies, and ammunition. General Hyakutake had landed on October 10 to personally lead the attack, with approximately 23,000 troops available at a time when the Cactus Air Force was all but wiped out— exactly as Yamamoto had intended. Conditions seemed so dire that a Marine staff officer, Lieutenant Colonel J. C. Munn, briefed the surviving pilots: "I want you to pass the word along that the situation is desperate. We don't know whether we'll be able to hold the field or not. After the gas is gone we'll have to let the ground troops take over. Then your officer and men will attach themselves to some infantry outfit. Good luck and good-bye."

Nevertheless, the American fighting spirit was undiminished on Guadalcanal and morale was certainly higher than in the rear area. Major "Mad Jack" Cram perfectly demonstrated this on October 15, as the Cactus Air Force scrounged up everything flyable to hit the enemy transports off Tassafaronga Point. "Jap troop transports were already landing reinforcements at Tassafaronga and they were all but unopposed. Only an occasional F4F or P-39 broke through the fierce anti-aircraft screen put up by the Jap destroyers."

Cram piloted General Geiger's personal plane, a gigantic Consolidated PBY-5A Amphibian named *Blue Goose*, which had flown in a load of torpedoes for VT-8 that were no longer needed. A dozen Dauntlesses were going to hit the transports, and Cram suggested jury-rigging two torpedoes under *Blue Goose* so he could join the attack. Knowing nothing about torpedo bombing and with Swede Larsen out on the line with the grunts, the major's only source of information was Major Joe Renner, a fighter pilot whose brother-in-law flew Avengers.

Determined to fight nonetheless, Cram got airborne amid Japanese shelling and rendezvoused with the Dauntlesses east of Henderson Field. Eight Wildcats under Major Duke Davis with three P-39s and the sole remaining P-400 led by Captain John Mitchell distracted the Zeros while the dive bombers nosed over from the landward side and attacked the transports. Cram arced out over Ironbottom Sound and, while the antiaircraft gunners were busy with the Dauntlesses, dove in from over the water. Designed to cruise at 125 mph, the Catalina was never meant to fly faster than 195 mph, yet Cram came lumbering in at 240 mph like a huge blue whale.

Bob Leckie, who saw the whole attack, wrote: "Cram pulled the stick back. He leveled off at one thousand feet, then went over again. Blue Goose came thundering over two transports at seventy-five feet. She shuddered and bucked in their flak blasts. Cram sighted off his bow at a third transport. His first torpedo hit the water and began running straight and true. He yanked again, and the second fell. It porpoised, righted, and followed the first into the transport's side."

Cram later recalled, "I pulled the Cat up into a left turn and headed for Henderson Field. Back behind, one of our torpedoes scored a direct hit on a transport while the other one missed." In any case, the *Sasago Maru* was so damaged her skipper beached it, and five furious Zeros attacked Cram. Jinking, bunting, and diving, the Marine pilot ran all out for Henderson Field. The fighters raked it so many times that when the PBY came racing over the field, those on the ground heard whistling through its holed skin. Gunners got two Zeros, and a Wildcat got a third while Cram pancaked the damaged Catalina into the kunai grass of Fighter One; he and his crew were unhurt though the plane had 175 holes in it. Summoned to see his boss, Cram stood at attention while Geiger vented.

"Goddamit Cram! I ought to court-martial you for deliberate destruction of Government property!" Glancing over at Geiger's aide, Cram saw the man trying not to burst out laughing. The aide winked, and

Geiger walked up, shook the major's hand, smiled, and said, "Jack, that was a damn fine job!" Later that same day the general wrote out a recommendation for the Navy Cross.*

Fighting continued all through the day, and less than an hour after Mad Jack's torpedo escapade two dozen Bettys bombed Henderson Field. B-17 Flying Fortresses from Espiritu Santo also hit the anchored transports as well, eventually adding two more ships to Cram's kill. By the end of the day *Azuasan, Sasago,* and *Kyushu Maru* were sunk or beached, and the Japanese were having serious doubts as to supposedly "defeated and demoralized" Americans. Unfortunately, for those few days in late October, such desperate acts were all the Cactus Air Force had left. *Hornet* was the only U.S. carrier in the immediate area, but she was refueling and Admiral Scott's cruisers were also off station replenishing and refueling.

A lack of aviation fuel was perhaps the most critical issue, for without it the planes were useless and with no air cover the Canal was isolated. Fortunately, the first Cactus aviators had cached some 465 gallons around the airfields and groves, and these were rapidly exca-

---

* "Mad Jack" survived the war, fought again in Korea, and retired as a brigadier general.

vated but still it wouldn't last long. Several attempts to tow fuel barges into Ironbottom Sound were met with disaster, so the submarine *Amberjack* was hastily modified to hold nine thousand gallons of aviation fuel and dispatched to the Canal.

Rear Admiral Aubrey Fitch, who succeeded Admiral McCain as commander, Air South Pacific in late September, acted at once. Essentially emptying Espiritu Santo, he dispatched twenty Wildcats under Harold "Indian Joe" Bauer, now a lieutenant colonel, and all seventeen Dauntlesses to the Canal. Fitch was no Ghormley. Another fighting admiral, he was a Great War veteran and in 1930, at age forty-six, he earned his gold wings as a naval aviator. Fitch had commanded *Langley*, the first U.S. aircraft carrier, followed by *Lexington* and *Saratoga*. A veteran of the Coral Sea, he flew into the combat zones under his command to assess developing situations for himself.

MAG-23 was relieved by MAG-14 and October 16 saw the departure of the last Marine aviators who landed on Guadalcanal in August, leaving only the 67th Fighter Squadron from the original Cactus Air Force. That same day, following the bombardments and enemy landings, Admiral Ghormley continued with his consistent pessimism, by dispatching a message that read:

THIS APPEARS TO BE ALL OUT ENEMY EFFORT AGAINST CACTUS POSSIBLY OTHER POSITIONS ALSO. MY FORCES TOTALLY INADEQUATE [TO] MEET SITUATION. URGENTLY REQUEST ALL AVIATION REINFORCEMENT POSSIBLE.

Though Admiral Nimitz was renowned for his calm demeanor, this latest missive visibly upset him. The admiral was aware for some time that Ghormley, a superb planner and staff officer, was not the man for offensive combat action in the South Pacific. Though the men had been friends for more than forty years, this was no time for personal inclinations, and Nimitz probably knew he'd delayed too long in replacing Ghormley. But now there was no more time; the Japanese were massing to retake the island and Nimitz needed a man who could fight. If anyone stood a chance of defeating Yamamoto, it was Admiral William F. "Bull" Halsey, and he was handed the "hot potato," as he put it, on October 18, 1942.

French administrators on New Caledonia had bullied Admiral Ghormley, refused his requests, and generally been of no material assistance. With the Japanese threatening the entire Pacific, Georges Thierry d'Argenlieu, Free French high commissioner and a Gaullist to the core, publicly stated that "the United

States was nothing more than a democratic country with imperialistic ambitions." Nevertheless, Halsey had Marine lieutenant colonel Julian Brown repeatedly make formal, polite requests for shore facilities and when Governor Auguste-Henri Montchamp had the temerity to ask what he would receive in exchange, with a straight face the colonel answered, "We will continue to protect you as we have always done." The governor, a devoted Gaullist who did not grasp that France had been conquered in 1940 and was in no way on equal footing with the United States, merely shrugged. Colonel Brown's acidic reply was, "We've got a war on our hands and we can't continue to devote valuable time to these petty concerns. I venture to remind Your Excellency that if we Americans had not arrived here, the Japanese would have."

Halsey finally had enough quibbling and simply came ashore with a Marine escort and seized what he wanted. Considering the circumstances, a world war in which a defeated France had no significant role, the governor's typically Gallic complaint to his superiors would have been simply ridiculous rather than appalling. The Americans, Montchamp whined, "were trying to kill French life, by suppressing little by little through requests based on military considerations, all our organization—to substitute for it some American

form which would lead to the ruin of all that is French."
With fighting men dying every day and the Pacific War
intensifying, the United States merely brushed aside
such foolishness and did what was necessary. As the
situation in the Solomons worsened there was no time
for anything else.

John Mitchell and everyone else on Guadalcanal
felt *something* was coming—the signs were all there.
Thousands of Japanese troops had been landed in the
first three weeks of October. Air raids had intensified,
and at least two dozen submarines lurked around the
southern islands while the big battleships and cruisers
stayed just out of range to the north. Rumors abounded,
most of them untrue: the U.S. Navy had pulled out;
ships were more valuable than Marines; there was no
more aviation fuel. In fact, the Navy was rushing *Enterprise* and *Hornet* to the area, along with two new,
radar-equipped fast battleships, *Washington* and *South
Dakota*. The dithering Ghormley was gone, and Bull
Halsey was firmly in command. "On Guadalcanal,"
Bob Leckie remembered, "men who had never once
lost hope of victory, who were entering their eleventh
week of battle still confident of it, heard the news with
shouts of jubilation. A real tiger was taking over."

Unfortunately, there were true rumors, among them
that Henderson Field was out of gas. The Navy made

desperate attempts to resupply the Cactus Air Force, but most failed. Barges holding two thousand gallons each were towed north to the island by cargo ships, tugs, destroyers, and anything else capable of making the trip. The seaplane tender (destroyer) *McFarland* made it to Lunga Roads with 40,000 gallons of aviation fuel, which she was offloading onto barges when nine Vals attacked. The destroyer cast off the barges and tried to get under way, but took a bomb through the stern that damaged her rudder and engine. In the midst of this attack, "Indian Joe" Bauer and nineteen Wildcats of VMF-212 arrived over *McFarland* and the Canal. Nearly out of fuel after the long flight in, Bauer never hesitated, dove straight, and shot down four Vals before gliding in with empty tanks.

"The Chief," his excited wingman recounted, "stitched four of the bastards end to end!" *McFarland* limped across the Sealark Channel and beached at Tulagi, where some of her fuel and ammunition was salvaged. *Meredith,* another destroyer, was not so fortunate and went down fighting south of Guadalcanal; fewer than 90 men of her 273-man crew survived their wounds and the sharks. "Thus did the Navy suffer," Bob Leckie recalled, "to keep the Marines and soldiers on Guadalcanal alive and fighting."

Another true rumor was that Admiral Yamamoto

had taken personal command of the operation, committing his Combined Fleet to the destruction of the U.S. Navy in the Solomons and the annihilation of those on Guadalcanal. His naval forces had been at sea since October 11, and were holding a vulnerable, fuel-consuming station northwest of the Solomons. The USS *Hornet* was somewhere nearby and the *Enterprise* was returning to the South Pacific, though neither carrier had been spotted yet. The 17th Army's difficulties on Guadalcanal perplexed him, and the admiral was running out of time. From Buin, Buka, and Rabaul the Zeros and bombers of the 11th Air Fleet were attacking every day in a determined, but piecemeal, attempt to whittle away the Cactus Air Force.

October 23 dawned as always: humid, fetid, and certain of rain. Marine captain Joe Foss and a flight of Wildcats escorted a Catalina off Henderson and he flew perfectly, as always, though this time was different. General Archer Vandegrift was aboard, along with Lieutenant General Thomas Holcomb, commandant of the Marine Corps, on their way to Nouméa for a conference with Admiral Halsey. Turning back to the Canal, the fighters were just in time to intercept an inbound strike of sixteen bombers and eighteen Zeros. John Mitchell with his P-39s also rose to join the fight, and in a matter of minutes five bombers were damaged or destroyed. None of the Zeros returned to their bases; Joe Foss got four, but landed safely in a smoking Wildcat riddled with bullet holes. John Mitchell also surprised a low-altitude Zero and sent it down in flames over Tulagi.

The obvious failure to subdue Henderson Field was bad enough news for Yamamoto, but while John Mitchell was dogfighting Zeros, the admiral received a message that General Maryuma's forces had not reached the reattack assembly area. This was east of the Lunga and south of the north-south rise the Americans called Edson's Ridge, so the attack would have to be delayed twenty-four hours: again. Maryuma now realized that his predecessor, General Kawaguchi, had been quite accurate concerning the terrible terrain and the Sendai Division spent five days hacking through twenty-nine miles of the jungle from their base at Kokumbona. Their plan was to attack from the southwest, where they would not be detected and certainly not expected, but after five days of exhaustive marching there were still six miles remaining. Each man was carrying sixty pounds of equipment, including an artillery shell, and subsisting on half rations. None of the division's howitzers or 37 mm antitank guns had made it thus far; all the horses used to pull them had been left in Rabaul, and due to constantly patrolling American aircraft any movement had to be done at night.

But this was the Sendai Division, arguably the best unit in the Imperial Army, with a long fighting record against the Chinese, Russians, and Dutch East Indies colonial forces. Americans, the Japanese knew, would fare no better against their spiritual power and hand-to-hand combat skills. Maryuma, like Ichiki and Kawaguchi before him, had absolute faith in the strength of his soldiers and the weakness of his enemy. The assault plan called for a western diversionary attack across the Matanikau from Major General Tadashi Sumiyoshi, commander of the 17th Army's artillery. With remnants of the Fourth Infantry Regiment and a company of tanks they were to breach the Marine lines, then drive eastward along the coast.

Maryuma's Sendai Division, having crossed the Lunga River undetected from the west, would split into two parts, then assemble in the jungle south of Edson's Ridge. While the Marines were distracted at the Matanikau, Kawaguchi would charge north from the same basic position he had the previous month, take the ridge, then press down onto Henderson Field itself. The second prong, under Major General Yumio Nasu, would also come north while paralleling the east bank of the Lunga River, flank the ridge, and continue north toward the coast. All forces would converge on Lunga Point, and Henderson Field would be Japanese once more. Owing to his delay, Maryuma passed the word that an attack on October 23 was not now possible, and X-Day would occur the following day.

Terrain aside, there were several problems with this. Though initially undetected, Marine Scout-Snipers picked up the Sendais as they hacked their way through the jungle. Noise, singing, and smoke from cooking fires all indicated a force of five thousand to seven thousand men was moving south of Edson's Ridge. The other problem was that Maryuma's vaunted Sendais faced two of the toughest American officers on Guadalcanal: Lieutenant Colonel Lewis Burwell "Chesty" Puller and Lieutenant Colonel Herman Henry Hanneken, commanding the 1st and 2nd Battalions, respectively, of the 7th Marine Regiment. Both were veterans of the Banana Wars and Haiti, where Hanneken had won the Medal of Honor for personally killing Charlemagne Péralte, the Haitian rebel commander. "Old Breed" professionals to their core, they had two thousand Marines dug in along a 2,500-yard front and were simply waiting; Henderson Field had to be held at all costs. Maryuma's final problem was that due to confusion, wet batteries, or poor radio transmission from the jungle, the western force did not receive word about the postponement, and attacked on schedule: alone.

At 1800 that evening the jungle west of the Matanikau lit up in orange and yellow as Sumiyoshi's Type 4 150 mm howitzers and Type 41 mountain guns opened fire on the Marine positions east of the river. Colonel Nakaguma's 4th Infantry massed on the bank and was promptly ripped to shreds by ten battalions of Colonel Pedro del Valle's 11th Marine Artillery. Nine tanks led by Captain Maeda of the 1st Independent Tank Company charged out of the jungle and tried to cross the sandbar at the river's mouth. Responding with mortars, 37 mm antitank guns and machine guns, the Marines blew apart eight of them in three minutes.

The lead tank was the only one to clank across the sandbar, and as it rumbled over Private Joe Champagne's foxhole the young Marine stuck a grenade in the tracks and rolled away to safety. The explosion put the little tank out of control, and before it could escape a 75 mm gun mounted in a Marine half-track fired twice, hit the ammo locker, and blew pieces of Maeda twenty yards into the sea. Not one infantryman made it across the river. "Marines along the Matanikau heights could look down upon a silent sandbar clogged with broken, burned-out tanks and the bodies of the enemy," Bob

Leckie of the 1st Marines later wrote. "Nothing moved but the crocodiles swimming hungrily downstream."

The next day, October 24, brought the *Enterprise* and *Hornet* to a rendezvous south of the New Hebrides. They then steamed north together toward the Solomons. On the Canal it was raining and exposed ground turned to mush while the jungle became a steamy, boggy nightmare. Rain delayed Japanese air raids, however, though Henderson was damaged and Fighter One too muddy for flight operations. Thinking the previous evening's western assault was the main attack, Hanneken's 2nd Battalion was pulled off the ridge and sent to plug gaps along the Matanikau, which left Chesty Puller's seven hundred-man 1st Battalion to cover the entire southern sector.

Lieutenant Colonel Robert Hall's 3rd Battalion, 164th Infantry, was alerted and by 2300 rain was again pouring down. Maryuma, impatient for his victory, ordered the attack. Led by Colonel Furumiya's 29th Infantry, his exhausted, disoriented men charged into the American guns and the long, bloody night began. Firing until the gun barrels turned red, the Marines beat off the Japanese, who, typically, committed themselves in the wild charges that had defeated the Chinese and Russians. Ammunition ran short, but when Chesty

Puller was told about it he replied, "You've got bayo-nets, haven't you?"

The Sendai charged at 0130 and were again repulsed with heavy casualties, so by 0200 Hall's Doggies were ordered up to the ridge. There was no question of the Army National Guard soldiers acting on their own, and they were intentionally intermingled with Marines. Refusing to believe he could be beaten, Maryuma charged again at 0300, and the 164th became a combat unit as they fought back side by side with the Marines. As the sun lightened the horizon at 0400, Maryuma watched the remnants of his shattered division slink back into the jungle, "bands of hollow-eyed men stumbling woodenly back to their assembly areas."

The line had held. Henderson Field was safe for an-other day, and at least one thousand Japanese lay dead on the slopes surrounding Edson's Ridge.

Sunday, October 25, dawned with more rain and with the Americans ringed in on the sea, the air, and from two directions on land. The *Amberjack*, carry-ing two hundred 100-pound bombs and more than four tons of aviation fuel, made Lunga Roads as the sun rose. With the attacks on Henderson Field she had been diverted to nearby Tulagi, and for good reason. Cautiously approaching, Lieutenant Commander J. A. Bole idled at periscope depth, and what he saw was not reassuring. Two old four-stack U.S. destroyers, *Trever* and *Zane,* were coming out of Tulagi Harbor after delivering fuel, and the fleet tug *Seminole* was towing a gasoline barge across the sound to Lunga Point. What caught the submariner's eye were the unmistakable low-slung silhouettes and raked-back funnels of three Japanese destroyers charging into the bay. Based on Maryuma's ecstatic, but premature, victory message, the *Akatsuki, Shiratsuyo,* and *Ikazuchi* were running in three hundred men of the 228th Infantry Regiment to Koli Point, east of the Marine positions. They were to land, cut off any American retreat to the east, and secure another beachhead for future reinforcements.

The 0800 Japanese reconnaissance flight was shot down by antiaircraft fire over Henderson Field, and three Wildcats managed to slosh their way through Fighter One's mud, get airborne, then climb up over the east end of the island. Sighting the old U.S. ships, all three Japanese destroyers rang up flank speed and lunged after them. Both ships were more than twenty years old and had been refitted as destroyer-minesweepers, so their heavier armament was gone. Nevertheless, Lieutenant Commander Dwight Agnew in *Trever* disdained his option of hiding up the Maliala River, and at 1014 turned to fight. Well out of range from the tiny American three-inch guns, the Japanese destroyers opened fire at 1030. Fortunately, they were loaded with high-explosive rounds to bombard Henderson Field, not the normal armor-piercing shells for ship-to-ship action.

Zane was hit by a 5-inch shell that destroyed her Number 1 forward gun and three sailors were killed, so the American ships turned for the Niella Channel, a narrow passage laced with shoals, but as Commander Yusuke Yamada in *Akatsuki* closed the distance, Wildcats dove down from the clouds. The fighters had no bombs, but they let loose with four .50-caliber Brownings apiece and at 1040 the destroyers turned away, perhaps recalling their mission was to land troops at Koli Point. In the turn they ran straight into the *Seminole* and a little patrol boat, YP-284, trying to make Tulagi harbor, and sank them both.

But all three enemy ships were now within range of the Marine 5-inch guns on Guadalcanal, which immediately opened fire, damaging *Akatsuki*'s Number 3 turret at 1053. It was too much; the presence of U.S. destroyers, an air attack from a field that was supposed to be neutralized, all convinced Commander Yamada to make smoke and flee northwest back up the Slot without landing the 228th Infantry at Koli Point.

Nearly thirty Zeros escorted several waves of bombers between 1000 and 1430, but by this time the sky had cleared and the sun was "blistering hot," Leckie wrote. "Its scorching rays shone with dissolving intensity upon the corpses laying outside the lines beneath buzzing, conical swarms of black flies. Already these bodies were beginning to turn lemon yellow, to swell and burst like overripe melons. . . ."

Fighter One was dry enough for operations, and "Smokey Joe" Foss shot down five Zeros during this wild day as other Cactus fighter pilots sliced through the bombers. One group of nine Bettys attacked the "bone yard," the area where wrecked aircraft were parked so spare parts could be scavenged. "I couldn't have picked anything I'd rather have them hit," Geiger, now a major general, chuckled. Just after 1300, Lieutenant Commander John Eldridge with five SBDs from VS-71 attacked the light cruiser *Yura* and her escorts in the Indispensable Strait, east of the Florida Islands. Eldridge put a 1,000-pound bomb into her engine room, and another pilot put a 500-pounder in the same hole. The cruiser and her escorts were the Second Assault Unit for the Koli Point landings, and had not been informed that the destroyers carrying the First Assault Unit were running away back up the Slot.

John Mitchell attacked the *Yura* at 1415 with three Airacobras and scored two near misses, which are nearly as lethal as direct hits. The Imperial Navy turned around and headed northwest back up the strait but were slowed down considerably by the cruiser, which was flooding. Wildcats and P-39s continued strafing any ships they could find, sometimes tangling with the escorting Zeros a few thousand feet over the waves. Lieutenant Jack Conger of VMF-212 found himself in a low-altitude dogfight just off Lunga Point with a pair of Zeros. Due to his strafing the Marine was short of ammunition, but he managed to put his last burst into one of the fighters and sent it down in flames.

Low-altitude fighting leaves little room for vertical maneuvering. As Conger went head-to-head with the last Zero the only direction he could go was up, and that's what he did. With no ammunition remaining, he rammed the fighter and sawed off its tail, counting on the Wildcat's sturdy construction to save him—and it did. The Zero broke in two, but Conger managed to tumble out and get two swings in his chute before hitting the water about a half mile away from one of the Japanese pilots. A Higgins boat came out from the beach, picked up Conger, then turned toward the Zero pilot. The sailors, having seen what the Japanese did to captured Americans, wanted to kill him outright, but the lieutenant forbade it. The enemy aviator tried to swim away, but his sodden, heavy flight suit made that impossible.

When they pulled up close, Conger used a boathook to snag the other pilot and yank him toward the boat. The Japanese flyer fought back, snarling and spitting, and when the Marine leaned out to help him he got a pistol pushed in his face, a big Mauser to be specific, and the enemy fired. Falling backward to get clear, the lieutenant only heard a wet snap, no gunshot, and realized the gun misfired. The other pilot then put the weapon to his head and pulled the trigger, but there was only a second snap. The Americans had had enough at this point, so the sailors pummeled the enemy pilot with paddles, while Conger smacked him over the head with a water can and knocked him out. Unconscious, but still alive, Pilot Officer 2nd Class Shiro Ishikawa lived out the rest of the war as a prisoner in New Zealand.*

By 1600 Eldridge and Mitchell were airborne again, following the *Yura*'s smoke up north of the Indispens-

---

* Ishikawa survived the war and returned to Japan, where he spent the next thirty years at the Tokyo branch of Chase Manhattan Bank. He and Jack Conger, who retired as a colonel after fighting again in Korea, met for the first time since 1942 in April 1990.

able Strait toward Santa Isabel. They caught her rounding Cape Astrolabe, making for Fera Island near Buala Bay. Mitchell's fighters put a 500-pound bomb directly through her and *Yura* was doomed, a burning, flooded hulk. The cruiser was abandoned by her crew and adrift when two of her escorts torpedoed the wreck later that night. In light of the ferocious American resistance and the loss of at least a dozen aircraft, the Imperial Navy came about and steamed back to the north leaving Maryuma's infantry on their own.*

Still in the dark, or denial, regarding the ground situation on Guadalcanal, 17th Army headquarters in Rabaul urged Maryuma to expedite its attack and get on with the American surrender so reinforcements could be sent. In between the day's air attacks, Hall's 3rd Battalion and Puller's 1st Battalion sorted themselves back into separate units and regrouped; the Doggies took the eastern 1,100 yards of the ridge while the Marines dug into 1,400 yards along the western edge. One battalion of Marines was kept in reserve immediately behind the line as the Japanese massed in the dark jungle

---

* Japanese records admit to two bombers lost and ten fighters, while the Cactus Air Force claimed twenty-one plus the reconnaissance plane downed by anti-aircraft fire. As always, the truth lies somewhere in between.

to the south. At 2000 on the night of October 25, what remained of the Sendai Division's artillery shelled Edson's Ridge, and small waves of fewer than two hundred men attacked the American positions. It was typically Japanese: piecemeal, uncoordinated, frontal assaults aimed at quickly closing to hand-to-hand range.

They all failed.

By October 29 the Japanese were retreating back toward Kokumbona and their safe area in northwest Guadalcanal, though these "havens" were temporary illusions, as the remnants of the 17th Army would shortly discover. American casualties were light, though that is a relative term to men who lost buddies, and their families back home. Total U.S. deaths for the past five days were 86 killed in action and 192 wounded. Of these, 61 were Marines or Doggies killed on Edson's Ridge or along the Matanikau. A preliminary 1st Marine Division report compiled on October 26 estimated enemy dead at 2,200, but this was extremely conservative. Japanese figures put losses from the 29th and 16th regiments at 3,568 killed, with an equal number wounded. This included both regimental commanders, half the total officers, and Major General Nasu. "Fighting the Chinese," one Japanese officer recalled after the war, "was nothing like this."

The Sendai Division was finished as a fighting force.

The 16th and 29th Infantry Regiments had each landed with 2,300 men, but were both down to about 700 effectives by November. The 4th Infantry reported a mere 400 men fit for combat, one-sixth of its total, and the division would spend the remainder of the war garrisoning Singapore in British Malaya. The 11th Air Fleet was also finished. Cactus Air Force fighters claimed 228 enemy aircraft of all types, though the confusion of dogfights and fog of war no doubt added to the total. Official Japanese combat losses, though usually understated, listed forty-three Zeros, twenty-nine Betty bombers, one reconnaissance plane, six Vals, and four flying boats. Sixteen floatplanes were also shot down, and twelve carrier-based aircraft, for an aggregate total of 111 combat losses against 49 for the Cactus Air Force.

Whatever the actual cost, the Battle for Henderson Field was a crushing defeat for the Japanese, and the airfield would never again be seriously threatened. Heavy B-17 bombers, Dauntlesses, and fighters of all types were now free to operate with impunity, and it was this control of the air, paid for by the Cactus Air Force, that decided the issue. Despite their tenaciousness, the Marines could not have held the island without naval resupply, and this would have been impossible if the Japanese were free to bomb the transports. Without Henderson Field no Cactus Air Force could exist, and with no Guadalcanal there would have been no forward American base in the Solomons in early 1943 from which to stab deep into Japanese territory.

Guadalcanal became to the South Pacific, in a much smaller sense, what England was now for the war in Europe: a generally secure, unsinkable aircraft carrier. Offensive operations, modest at first, could now be launched against an empire that had suffered its first series of defeats. Momentum in war is vital, and because of the indomitable fighting spirit of those men on Guadalcanal, Japan's momentum came to a bone-jarring halt in the fall of 1942. The battle marked the zenith of Imperial offensive operations, and the limit of Japanese expansion. However, Yamamoto and his Combined Fleet, as well as an Imperial Army nearly one million strong, were in no way defeated, and the war was still far from decided.

For both sides, the Guadalcanal campaign was a revelation of capabilities and weaknesses from which tactical blueprints might be drawn. The Americans used what they had learned immediately. Training and organization, especially for the Marines, was modified to reflect hard lessons from the Canal. The basic rifle platoon would now contain three twelve-man squads, with three 60 mm mortars added to each company. The cumbersome, water-cooled, Great War vintage machine guns were replaced with lighter, air-cooled models, and the old bolt-action Springfields gave way to semiautomatic M1 rifles or carbines. Vulnerable plywood landing craft were rapidly improved with armored and tracked variants that could get men ashore fast while providing heavy fire support. Close-quarters fighting including extensive hand-to-hand combat training was expanded, as was the creation of Scout and Sniper platoons.

Logistics, the heartbeat of a modern military, was overhauled, streamlined, and refined all through the remainder of the war. In 1936, the U.S. Navy possessed nine deepwater transports, but less than a decade later numbered more than five thousand. Squabbling between the Army and Navy continued, but the American genius for logistics steadily improved. The roughly eight-thousand-mile supply line from the U.S. west coast to New Zealand, and on to the Solomons was much too long. Admiral Halsey set about rebuilding Nouméa into a forward support base.

By the time the first P-38s arrived and were towed through the streets, the harbor was servicing sixty ships per day, and facilities to stockpile 400,000 gallons of fuel or oil were under construction. This would be vital in the coming months, when Cactus Air Force planes were using 1,000 to 3,000 gallons every day to hold the

Japanese at bay. Seabees, the Naval Construction Battalions (see page 164), would continue to expand and improve their outstanding capabilities. In addition to building a 1,300,000-gallon storage facility on Guadalcanal, over the course of the Pacific War they would construct hospitals for 70,000 casualties, 111 airfields, and housing for 1.5 million men.

By comparison, the Japanese had no comparable logistical or engineering equivalent. They had planned for a short, fast war, and once Guadalcanal prevented this there was nothing in place to match American capability. Strategically, this was precisely the danger Yamamoto had foreseen after his extensive travels through the industrial heartland of the United States. Tactically, Japanese army hubris and arrogance combined with inflexibility to hasten their battlefield defeat on Guadalcanal. Repeated negligent misjudgments of terrain, logistics, and the enemy exacerbated the situation, as did a shocking lack of coordination between the army and navy. Much of this stemmed from Japan's contempt for America and her fighting men; it just was not possible to lose, Imperial officers believed, so why waste time with reconnaissance, coordinated assaults, and tactical adaptation?

There were, to be sure, exceptions among Japanese officers. Men who had been to the West, lived in America or Europe, and knew something of what they faced. They were the only ones now who could, in the wake of Midway, Coral Sea, and Guadalcanal, alter the Japanese concept of war enough to have a fighting chance against the "sleeping giant" of the United States. Men who could, with the weight of the Combined Fleet and the balance of the Imperial Army, gain enough time and draw enough American blood to stave off national disaster. If the United States could be forced into a protracted war, while also gearing up to fight in Europe, then a separate armistice might be negotiated. If not, then a slow, bloody, delaying war could be fought until the cost to America became too great to bear. These Japanese officers knew that Americans felt differently about death, and would not blindly sacrifice themselves for a national figurehead. If the death toll rose high enough, anything, they believed, was possible. Unfortunately for the Allies, first among these men who understood what must be done was the extremely capable Admiral Isoroku Yamamoto.

Seven
Magnificent Courage

Like all his buddies, Rex fretted through the fall of 1942, wanting to get into the war he'd come all this way to fight. When John Mitchell left, he'd assumed the rest of the squadron would follow quickly, but that had not occurred. No one was certain then if the Japanese might bypass the Solomons and strike New Caledonia or Fiji to cut off reinforcements from the United States. Anything was possible during those dark days, so the fighter squadrons stayed in exile and waited for attacks that never came. After the Battle of Henderson Field, the 70th squadron prepared to move forward, and Rex was certain they'd be in action soon, but during Dugout Sunday the opposing fleets closed in on each other for the fourth carrier battle of the war.

Enterprise and *Hornet* had joined to form Task

Force 61 under Rear Admiral Thomas Kincaid, and by this time were three hundred miles due east of Santa Cruz, while the carriers *Shokaku*, *Zuikaku*, and *Zuiho* hovered the same distance northwest of the island. Vice Admiral Nagumo, in charge of the carrier strike force, was waiting for the 17th Army to take Henderson Field before attacking Kincaid. To his mind it was Midway all over again, and he had no intention of being caught between the anvil of Kincaid's carriers and the hammer of land-based aircraft from Guadalcanal. While the Sendai Division was being cut to pieces during the night of October 26, Nagumo received premature notice that Henderson was recaptured, and promptly reversed course toward the southeast. By sunrise his ships had closed to within two hundred miles of the American carriers and launched search aircraft.

This time the Japanese attacked first.

A sixty-four-plane strike collided with twenty American aircraft off the *Enterprise* and the resulting melee cost four Zeros against a pair of Avengers and three Wildcats. Nevertheless, some twenty Japanese aircraft broke through and attacked the *Hornet*. Hit by three bombs, two torpedoes, and two damaged dive bombers turned kamikazes, the carrier that launched the Doolittle Raid was adrift and on fire. Hit by another torpedo from a subsequent strike, she was abandoned and eventually sunk in the early hours of October 27 by four torpedoes from the destroyers *Makigumo* and *Akigumo*. The *Enterprise*, hit by three bombs, was once again out of the fight and forced to withdraw for repairs, leaving no American carriers in the South Pacific, which is why Rex Barber and the other scattered Army fighter pilots remained where they were.

Though the Imperial Navy lost no ships, the battle took a fearsome toll on its remaining aircrews, with *Zuikaku* and *Junyo* returning to Japan to scrape together replacements. Air-to-air combat accounted for some, of course, but the new U.S. radar-guided antiaircraft systems were proving lethal. Those aboard the battleship *South Dakota* and antiaircraft cruiser *San Juan* alone knocked down more than thirty-two aircraft. In all, nearly one hundred aircraft were lost and 148 Japanese aircrew perished, including twenty-three veteran squadron or flight leaders. Fifty percent of Yamamoto's prewar, highly trained, irreplaceable dive bomber crews were gone forever, and a carrier with no aviators is just an oversize barge; planes and crews were the weapons, so Yamamoto was in serious trouble. Against this, the Americans lost eighty-one aircraft; twenty crews were killed and four taken prisoner, but fifty-seven were recovered and lived to fly again.

Most important, the Canal was still firmly in

American hands and, with dwindling hope for retaking the island, the Japanese soldiers west of the Matanikau were solely dependent on seaborne resupply. Their situation was now desperate; men were eating their leather belts, tree bark, and berries, with an occasional roasted lizard as a treat. Malaria and dysentery racked them all, and General Hyakutake would be hard-pressed to field 13,000 effective combatants from the 28,000 or so he had remaining. Believing he had sunk both American fleet carriers at Santa Cruz, Yamamoto now planned to again bombard Henderson Field with his battleships while reinforcements were landed near Tassafaronga. The Combined Fleet could muster two carriers, four battleships, eleven cruisers, and thirty destroyers to protect eleven transports carrying the 14,500 men of the 38th Infantry Division and 8th Special Naval Landing Force. This would be enough, he believed, with Hyakutake's survivors, to finally retake the island.

Kicking into high gear, the Tokyo Express made at least sixty-five destroyer runs into Ironbottom Sound during the first ten nights of November, and submarines were stripped down to bring in thirty to fifty tons of supplies each. Floating containers were used, and the *unpoto*, a sort of supply sled attached to a pair of torpedoes, then fired at the beach. Far from defeated, the tenacious Cactus pilots attacked anything that moved on land or floated on the water, which generally limited Japanese efforts to nighttime. Even though the P-39s had replaced all but one of the original Klunkers, the Airacobra was still not much of a match against the Zero unless it was caught at low altitude.

November 7 was a good day for John Mitchell because he did just that. Eleven Tokyo Express destroyers packed with fresh troops were sighted late in the afternoon coming down the Slot, and the Cactus Air Force attacked with a vengeance. Every enemy they killed at sea was one less that had to be fought on the Canal, and there were more than 1,300 soldiers on those destroyers. Catching the destroyers in the middle of New Georgia Sound near Santa Isabel, Major Joe Sailor's Dauntlesses dive-bombed the ships and Avengers swept in low with torpedoes while John Mitchell's P-39s flew top cover. Ten "Rufe" floatplane fighters swarmed up from Rekata Bay on the north end of Santa Isabel and Mitchell sent one down in flames. Marine Wildcats jumped the others, and six Japanese pilots bailed out, then "unbuckled their parachutes and plunged into the sea."

Mitchell also heard a rumor that Dale Brannon, now a major, was bringing in the new P-38F twin-engined fighters any day now. It had been decided to combine the pieces and parts of all the Army flying remnants on Guadalcanal into one unit: the 339th Fighter Squadron, activated on September 29, 1942, and initially called the "Sun Setters," with Brannon commanding.* The Army was at last committing itself to Guadalcanal, so in addition to the Lightnings, two battalions of the 182 Regiment, an activated unit of the Massachusetts National Guard, was due to arrive as part of Task Force 67 with a Marine replacement battalion. Four transports, *President Adams, President Jackson, McCawley,* and *Crescent City,* anchored in Lunga Roads on November 11 and 12 to begin offloading more than five thousand fresh troops. Responding with several air raids, the 11th Air Fleet was unable to prevent the American reinforcement and, in the midst of this, Brannon landed on Guadalcanal the morning of November 12 with eight Lightnings.

Nevertheless, Rear Admiral Nobutake Kondo's Bombardment Force of two battleships, a cruiser, and eleven destroyers came on down the Slot determined to blast Henderson Field into oblivion and cover the 38th

---

* Sources disagree, but the most likely explanation is that the 339th would "Set the Rising Sun" of the Japanese Empire. The squadron would be officially renamed the "Gremlins" on December 2, 1943.

Infantry Division's landing at Doma Cove. Admiral Turner, in overall command of Task Force 67, knew well the value of massed firepower and gave Rear Admiral Dan Callaghan's support group every heavy ship he had on hand in order to face the oncoming Japanese. Most recently Admiral Ghormley's chief of staff, Callaghan also served as President Roosevelt's naval aide. He was a blue water sailor, USNA Class of 1911, but seemed more comfortable with the life of a staff officer than that of a fighting admiral like Norman Scott.

Scott, the victor at the Battle of Cape Esperance, was junior to Callaghan by fifteen days, so despite the latter's lack of combat experience, Callaghan commanded Task Force 67.4 when its thirteen ships put to sea on Friday, November 12, to meet the Japanese threat.* Turner, Callaghan, and Scott believed, rightly so, that the vulnerable American transports in Lunga Roads were best protected by offensive action in open water rather than the confined battleground of Ironbottom Sound. The resulting battle was "one of the most furious sea fights in all of history," Bob

---

* The USS *Fletcher*, DD-445, was the thirteenth ship in Callaghan's line; her hull number also added up to thirteen. Incidentally, the ship was named for Admiral Frank Friday Fletcher—the uncle of Admiral Frank Jack Fletcher.

Leckie recalled. "Never before had the iron tongues of midnight bayed with such a maniacal clanging."

Fanciful, perhaps, but Rear Admiral Callaghan's cruisers and destroyers surprised the battleships, whose guns were loaded with high-explosive Type-3 shells for surface bombardment rather than armor-piercing projectiles for ship-to-ship combat. At 0124 the USS *Helena*'s SG surface search radar picked up two groups of Japanese ships, at 27,100 and 28,000 yards, respectively, heading into Ironbottom Sound. Callaghan's lack of experience commanding a fleet in combat showed immediately. He had issued no written battle orders, did not appear to understand, or care, how to best utilize his SG-radar equipped ships, and began second-guessing his ship captains. In his indecision, Callaghan simply drove straight into the enemy ships, denying his destroyers permission to launch torpedoes, and delaying fire until within a few thousand yards. The resulting close-quarters knife fight devolved into a confusing, slashing mess of a battle.

Rear Admiral Norman Scott, the victor at Cape Esperance, would have very likely conducted the battle differently, but he died early in the battle when his flagship, the cruiser *Atlanta*, was caught by Japanese searchlights and badly pummeled. Callaghan's heavy cruiser took on the battleship *Hiei* while U.S. destroyers darted in close with torpedoes, but *San Francisco*'s bridge was hit by forty-five shells, including four fourteen-inch shells each packing a fourteen-hundred-pound punch that killed nearly every officer on the bridge, including the admiral.*

Dawn of November 13 found the cruiser *Atlanta* afire and drifting toward the Japanese-held shore near Cape Esperance. She had been torpedoed, probably by *Inazuma*, then hit by at least nineteen eight-inch shells from the *San Francisco* as it fired at the Japanese cruiser. The *Atlanta* was so battered that Captain Samuel Jenkins would not risk power for steerage way, so the ship was towed toward Lunga Point, where she dropped anchor. After the crew was removed, Captain Jenkins and a demolition crew exploded a charge, which sank her that evening. The destroyers *Barton, Cushing, Laffey,* and *Monssen* were also gone, and *San Francisco* so badly mauled that the only recognizable piece of Dan Callaghan was a hand bearing a 1911 Naval Academy class ring. Bloodstains and body parts were everywhere; the dead were identified by dog tags and once their personal effects were removed they were placed in a bag with a dummy five-inch shell and carefully eased over

---

* Both Norman Scott and Daniel Judson Callaghan were posthumously awarded the Medal of Honor.

the side. *Portland* and *Juneau* were badly damaged, and with *Helena* the three cruisers limped toward Espiritu Santo. AT 1101 *Juneau* was hit by a pair of torpedoes from *I-26*, broke into two pieces, and went down in less than thirty seconds.

Henderson Field remained unscathed.

Callaghan's and Scott's sacrifice, with that of 1,439 other Americans, once again stopped the Imperial Navy from blasting the airfield and potentially retaking Guadalcanal.* Unknown to the Japanese the sole American carrier remaining in the South Pacific was coming north to get back in the fight. *Enterprise* had been damaged at Santa Cruz and her forward elevator was jammed, fortunately at the flight-deck level. She'd left Nouméa with welders still aboard, and was steaming north to add the weight of her aircrews to this latest fight on the Canal.

During the night the battleship *Hiei* was savagely attacked by U.S. destroyers and their five-inch guns wrecked her superstructure, wounding Admiral Abe and killing his chief of staff. At point-blank range, *San Francisco* blasted her steering compartments, which subsequently flooded. This jammed her rudder and

---

* The Navy's casualties on November 13 alone nearly equaled those of the Marines for their entire tenure on Guadalcanal.

left her circling at 5 knots some thirty miles north of Savo Island. Despite poor weather, just after 1000 eight Avengers off the *Enterprise* found the smoking battleship and put three Mark 13 torpedoes into her, then at 1110 fourteen B-17s of the 72nd Bomb Squadron from Espiritu Santo dropped fifty-six 500-pound bombs on the *Hiei;* one hit and one was a near miss.

The Cactus Air Force got into the game by 1120, with successive waves of Dauntlesses and Avengers attacking until sunset. In *The Cactus Air Force*, Thomas Miller writes that "by sunset of that day she [the *Hiei*] lay sinking off Savo, having absorbed eighty-five shell hits from Callaghan's cruisers and destroyers, and five bombs and ten torpedoes . . ." The big battleship, at one point Emperor Hirohito's personal transport, was scuttled and sank later that evening about five miles north of Savo Island.* Due to the savagery of Callaghan's attack, Yamamoto ordered the invasion force of eleven transports back up New Georgia Sound until

---

* *Hiei* was the first Japanese battleship lost in the war, and her destruction was a psychological blow to Admiral Yamamoto as the emperor had used the ship during the mid-1930s as an official transport. Hirohito's younger brother, Prince Takamatsu, had once served aboard as well. Thirteen Imperial Navy battleships would eventually be sunk during the course of the war, the highest number of any combatant nation.

they could re-form with the remaining Imperial warships, which they did during the night, and proceeded south again toward Guadalcanal.

While the Japanese regrouped, the heavy cruisers *Maya* and *Suzuya* with a pair of destroyer escorts slipped into Ironbottom Sound to pummel both airfields with more than one thousand shells. Forty-five minutes later they slid again, heading northwest for Rendova Island, but leaving behind eighteen destroyed aircraft, and at least thirty holed by shrapnel. Fortunately, none of the new P-38s was damaged, and by sunrise on November 15, Fighter One was back in operation and the morning air search missions were launched to find the incoming Japanese.

They were discovered at 0830 steaming through the heart of the Slot between Santa Isabel Island and New Georgia: eleven transports crammed with the 38th Infantry Division and escorted by eleven destroyers. Due to the actions of Scott and Callaghan, not only was Henderson still fully operable, but the Japanese were forced into this daylight attempt to land these crucial reinforcements. Well aware that this was an invasion by a full division, John Mitchell and every other plane the Cactus Air Force could muster got airborne: fourteen Wildcats, seven newly arrived Lightnings, three Airacobras, nineteen Dauntlesses, and nine Avengers.

"Mission Accomplished!" by Roy Grinnell: A superb depiction of Yamamoto's Betty bomber (G4M1 Type-1 Attack Bomber #323) seconds before impact over southern Bougainville. Note that the left engine is dead as a result of Barber's attack, causing the aircraft to heel over sharply. Three escorting Zero fighters can be seen behind *Miss Virginia*'s left boom. *(Courtesy of Irene Grinnell)*

Admiral Isoroku Yamamoto. *(U.S. National Archives)*

LEFT: Yamamoto supervising the Pearl Harbor attack. Though he personally did not favor war with the United States, the admiral would do his best to destroy the American Navy. *(U.S. National Archives)*

BELOW: The aftermath of December 7, 1941. The operation was Yamamoto's brainchild, and the only way he felt victory was possible against the United States. *(U.S. National Archives)*

ABOVE: Henderson Field, Guadalcanal, 1942. The airfield was the primary reason for the U.S. invasion, and the cause of months of bloody fighting. The "Cow Pasture" fighter strip is visible in the top right. *(Courtesy of the U.S. Museum of the Pacific War)*

LEFT: Fighter Two on the Canal's north shore. The P-38 Lightnings were based here, and from here the April 18, 1943, attack was launched. *(Courtesy of the U.S. Museum of the Pacific War)*

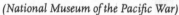

(National Museum of the Pacific War)   (Courtesy of Rex Barber Jr.)

LEFT: Major John Mitchell, who planned and led the Yamamoto Mission. In an astonishing feat of airmanship, Mitchell used only a map, a Navy compass, and his wristwatch to bring his fighters some four hundred miles over open water and intercept Yamamoto exactly as intended. / RIGHT: Lieutenant Rex T. Barber, April 1942. The man who killed Admiral Isoroku Yamamoto. / BELOW: The Fork-Tailed Devil. A flight of four P-38s in close formation, 1943.

RIGHT: Strafer Heights on
Guadalcanal, 1943.
*(National Museum of
the Pacific War)*

LEFT: Rex Barber's tent
on Strafer Heights, Gua-
dalcanal, 1943.
(Courtesy of Rex Barber Jr.)

The New Guinea Club, Rabaul. This beautiful colonial-era building was used
as Imperial Japanese Navy Southeast Area Headquarters, and by Yamamoto
days before his death. *(National Museum of the Pacific War)*

VENGEANCE mission pilots. Photo taken April 19, 1943, on Guadalcanal. *(Courtesy of Guy Aceto)*

Rear row left to right: Lt. Roger Ames, 12th FS; Lt. Lawrence Graebner, 12th FS; Captain Tom Lanphier, 70th FS; Lt. Delton Goerke, 339th FS; Lt. Julius Jacobson, 339th FS; Lt. Eldon Stratton, 12th FS; Lt. Albert Long, 12th FS; Lt. Everett Anglin, 12th FS.

Front row left to right: Lt. William E. Smith, 12th FS; Lt. Doug Canning, 339th FS; Lt. Besby Holmes, 339th FS; Lt. Rex T. Barber, 339th FS; Major John W. Mitchell, 339th FS; Major Lou Kittel, 12th FS; Lt. Gordon Whittaker, 12th FS. Not shown is Lt. Ray Hine, 339th FS; posted missing in action, April 18, 1943.

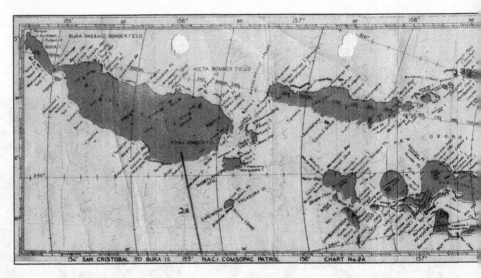

Rex Barber's VENGEANCE mission map, April 18, 1943. *(National Museum of the Pacific War)*

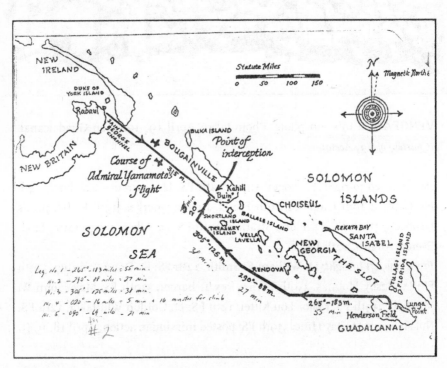

VENGEANCE route map. Sketched later by John Mitchell. *(National Museum of the Pacific War)*

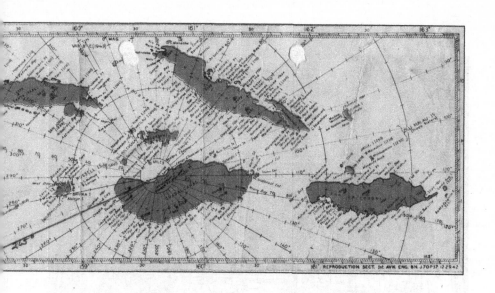

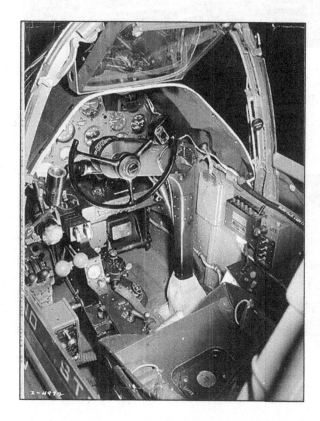

P-38G cockpit,
December 1942.

ABOVE: P-38G cockpit. Note the gun-charging handle, left of center.

BELOW: Yamamoto killer—P-38 Lightning #147, *Miss Virginia*. *(Courtesy of Rex Barber Jr.)*

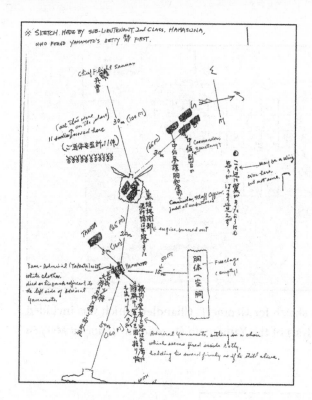

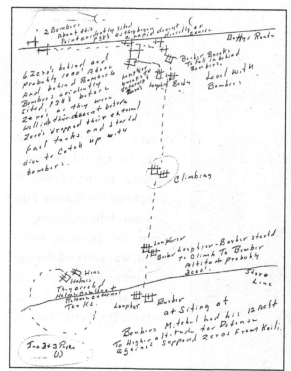

Japanese Lieutenant Hamasuna's original hand-drawn sketch of Yamamoto's crash site, April 1943.
(Courtesy of Rex Barber Jr.)

John Mitchell made this sketch for George T. Chandler, which was included in his June 5, 1989, analysis of the Yamamoto shootdown. *(National Museum of the Pacific War)*

Flight Warrant Officer Kenji Yanagiya of the 204th Kokutai was the only escort pilot to survive the war. His account of the engagement, from the Japanese viewpoint, was provided during oral testimony on April 15, 1988, at the National Museum of the Pacific War.

Rex Barber after receiving a Navy Cross for killing Japan's greatest admiral. A Medal of Honor nomination was endorsed on April 20, 1943, by Admiral Marc Mitscher, Commander Air, Solomon Islands. This was disgracefully downgraded by Admiral William F. Halsey in a fit of interservice pique.

The admiral's remains are carried aboard the battleship *Musashi* in a white-covered box, May 7, 1943.

Isoroku Yamamoto's final resting place. Tama Cemetery, Tokyo. Half his ashes were placed here and an urn containing the other half rests in the Chokoji Zen temple in his hometown of Nagaoka.

Brothers-in-arms together again. Colonels John Mitchell (left) and Rex Barber in the early 1990s.

Colonel John Mitchell's final resting place: Golden Gate National Cemetery, California.

Rex Barber's last landing. Redmond Memorial Cemetery, Oregon, looked after by his grandson, Rex Barber III (left), and his son, Rex Barber Jr. *(Dan Hampton Collection)*

Unknown to the Japanese, the *Enterprise* had steamed northwest at flank speed during the night and closed to within two hundred miles of Guadalcanal. She was now within striking distance and at dawn added Air Group 10 to the lineup.

At 1100 the Cactus Dauntlesses and Avengers found Tanaka's transports 150 miles up the Slot and attacked; *Canberra Maru* and *Niagara Maru* were sunk outright while the *Sado Maru*, carrying the 38th Division's commanders, was so badly hit by dive bombers that she turned back for the Shortlands. For the next five hours planes cycled off Henderson Field, refueling and rearming, then heading back up the Slot to hammer the transports. *Enterprise*'s carrier air group pounded at the heavier warships, sinking one cruiser, damaging three more, and joining the Cactus planes on Henderson for the remainder of the afternoon to save time. By late afternoon the *Brisbane Maru, Shinanogawa Maru, Arizona Maru,* and *Nako Maru* joined their sister ships at the bottom of New Georgia Sound.

At the end of that long day six transports were gone, and the seventh was crawling back north to safety. Hundreds of Japanese corpses bobbed in the water and five thousand wet, bedraggled soldiers were taken off burning ships onto destroyers that also turned northwest for the Shortlands. There were so many dead that the waters surrounding the gutted transports were actually red with blood. "They were red," Bob Leckie later recorded in his firsthand accounts. "[A]nd so were bunks and bulkheads glowing with heat and visible beneath decks torn open." Painfully aware of the 17th Army's dire situation on Guadalcanal, Yamamoto himself ordered Tanaka to proceed with his four surviving transports south toward Cape Esperance. Vice Admiral Kondo was similarly ordered to gather his still-formidable fleet of *Kirishima,* two heavy cruisers, two light cruisers, and nine destroyers, to cover the landing.

The Japanese plan was essentially a pincer around Savo Island; a Screening Force of the light cruiser *Nagara* with six destroyers would lead the Bombardment Force composed of *Kirishima* and two heavy cruisers counterclockwise around Savo to enter Ironbottom Sound from the west. A Sweeping Force led by the light cruiser *Sendai* with three destroyers would enter east of Savo, enter the Sound, and proceed clockwise down to Lunga Point. While the warships dealt with the PT boats from Tulagi and any U.S. surface ships and shelled American shore positions, the Reinforcement Unit under Rear Admiral Tanaka would unload the 38th Division survivors from its remaining four transports and nine destroyers.

It was a workable plan but for three main flaws. First, the Japanese had again incorrectly assumed that Henderson Field was out of service due to the cruiser assault the night before. This assumption, even more than most Japanese underestimations, is perplexing given the mauling of Tanaka's transports that very afternoon. Second, the Japanese had no warning that a pair of American battleships—Task Force 64—were coming north at flank speed to intercept their invasion fleet. Though search aircraft had sighted the *Washington* and *South Dakota* one hundred miles south of Guadalcanal they were misidentified as cruisers, and dismissed by Admiral Kondo. This was a somewhat understandable error, as the last time a Japanese aviator had seen a U.S. battleship where it was a stationary, unsuspecting target was in Pearl Harbor.

Tonight promised to be vastly different.

Both were new ships. *Washington* was commissioned in May 1941 and *South Dakota* in March 1942. Displacing some 45,000 tons, they could make 28 knots, had at least foot of hull armor, and each possessed nine radar-guided 16-inch guns. The first time *South Dakota*'s guns were all tested together the resulting back pressure ripped her captain's pants off. Properly handled, they were more than a match for their Japanese counterparts in the Solomons, and they were in superb hands, which was the third flaw in Kondo's plan. Rear Admiral Willis Augustus Lee was short, nearsighted, and as unprepossessing as he was deadly. A 1908 graduate of the Naval Academy, he was a member of the rifle team and participated in the 1914 U.S. occupation of Vera Cruz. Coming under fire while leading a shore party, the young officer sat in the open to attract fire, then calmly killed three snipers at long range. He served on destroyers during the Great War, and won seven personal medals in the 1920 Olympics as a member of the U.S. Rifle Team.*

Willis Lee was quite likely the Navy's foremost authority on radar, and had worked unceasingly to maximum the effects of his big guns coupled with precision fire control. Unlike Dan Callaghan, Lee also had a plan, and was able to effectively control his ships so the Second Naval Battle of Guadalcanal, as it was later known, was no disorganized melee from the American side. Utilizing a widely spaced, tactical formation with his four destroyers far out front, Lee came up from the south, passed Savo, and entered Ironbottom Sound from the north with a counterclockwise flow toward the west. *Washington*'s radar got a clear picture of the *Sendai* and her escorts at 2300 and sixteen minutes later

---

* Five gold medals, one silver, and one bronze; the record stood for sixty years.

Lee opened fire at 18,700 yards, catching the Sweeping Unit completely by surprise as it rounded Savo.

Rear Admiral Hashimoto, badly shaken at facing 16-inch guns, tried to withdraw under a smoke screen that was utterly ineffective against Lee's radar. Kondo was informed that the American cruisers were really battleships, but again he discounted the possibility and continued with his Bombardment Force around Savo heading south. Intending to blast Henderson Field to pieces while the 38th Division landed, the Japanese admiral was astonished to meet the *South Dakota* heading west from behind the island. The U.S. battleship had suffered a massive electrical short circuit at 2333 that disabled her guns, and she was unable to return fire to the Japanese Bombardment Force. *Washington* suffered from no such limitation. Lee had ordered his battered destroyers to safety and charged alone with his battleship straight through channel directly at the *Kirishima.*

The Imperial battleship vanished under immense towers of salt water as Lee fired everything he had exactly at midnight. Every massive 16-inch projectile weighed 2,700 pounds, and each of the twenty that hit the Japanese battleship left a thirty-foot hole in her; *Kirishima* had no chance at all, and was a listing, burning hulk in a mere seven minutes. A shocked Kondo, commanding from the cruiser *Nagara*, ordered a withdrawal and abandoned the plan to bombard Henderson Field. Having sortied from the Shortlands two days earlier with twenty-three ships, Rear Admiral Tanaka crept toward Cape Esperance. Flying his flag from the destroyer *Hayashio*, he gained Yamamoto's approval to beach his remaining four transports on Guadalcanal so at least some of the critical supplies and vital reinforcements would reach Hyakutake's 17th Army.

As the heavily laden, damaged transports crept toward Cape Esperance, the *Kirishima* was scuttled and at 0320 settled beneath the dark waters of Ironbottom Sound.* By 0400 in the gray, dawn light of November 15 the *Yamaura Maru*, *Manatsuki Maru*, *Hirokawa Maru*, and *Kinugasa Maru* ground to a halt on the Japanese-held beaches at Tassafaronga and Doma Cove. Wraithlike, skeletal soldiers appeared from the jungle and worked frantically with the sailors. They managed to offload approximately two thousand fresh

---

* This was the only battleship-versus-battleship sinking in the Pacific Theater. Interestingly, the *South Dakota*'s sister ship *Massachusetts* sank the French battleship *Jean Bart* a week earlier during the Naval Battle of Casablanca.

troops, 260 cases of ammunition, and four days' worth of rice before the Cactus Air Force appeared.

Major Joe Sailor's Dauntlesses were first off at 0555, immediately spiraling up over the Sound and gaining altitude to attack their targets just fifteen miles up the coast. All day long five-hundred- and one-thousand-pound bombs rained down on the transports. There wasn't much air combat, as most of the Zeros had been squandered providing air cover over the Slot rather than attacking the Cactus Air Force, so the American fighters strafed the ships, the ad hoc supply dump, and any Japanese they could find. By the end of the day the beached transports were burned-out hulks and Guadalcanal was free from invasion.

"We believe the enemy has suffered a crushing defeat," Archer Vandegrift wired to Admiral Halsey. "We thank Lee for his sturdy effort of last night. . . . Our own air has been grand in its relentless pounding of the foe. These efforts we appreciate, but our greatest homage goes to Scott, Callaghan and their men who with magnificent courage against seemingly hopeless odds drove back the first hostile stroke and made success possible. To them the men of Cactus lift their battered helmets in deepest admiration."

Life on the Canal began changing fast.

Three days after the battle, Bill Halsey collected his fourth star and became a full admiral. The following day, November 19, Major General Alexander McCarrell Patch, commander of the American Division, arrived on Guadalcanal. The best of all rumors had been true; the Marines were finally being relieved and the mop-up of the remaining Japanese was in the hands of the U.S. Army. Patch, known as "Sandy" to his peers, was the son of a cavalryman, a West Pointer, but also a veteran of the Great War battles at St.-Mihiel and the Meuse-Argonne. On November 25, the 339th Fighter Squadron also received a new commander: John Mitchell.

Like so many others, Major Dale Brannon was going home to pass on hard-learned combat lessons and Mitchell, who had spent the past few weeks getting checked out in the Lightning, was his obvious replacement. By the end of the month there seventeen P-38s on the Canal, in company with seventy-one Wildcats, sixteen Airacobras, and a single indestructible P-400 to watch over a growing collection of Dauntlesses and Avengers. Eight B-17s were assigned to Guadalcanal for long-range strike and surveillance, and the first of several night-flying "Black Cat" PBYs arrived.

Henderson Field was growing up. Officially designated as a Marine Air Base, construction was nearly completed on Fighter Two over at Kukum since the

Cow Pasture at Fighter One was unusable when wet, or for heavy aircraft like the Lightning. There was an increasing number of roads, depots, and combat missions that were now consuming 45,000 to 80,000 gallons of aviation fuel per day, depending on the number of operational planes. There were enough aircraft now that pilots got a breather, and even a bit of baseball. A Liberty ship with thirty thousand cases of beer arrived, and most of the brew "disappeared" into a secret supply dump that remained secret because it was behind the Japanese lines. Hooch was also popular. Made from limes and papayas mixed with grapefruit juice, it got its kick from alcohol drained out of the Mark 13 torpedoes carried by Avengers.

But despite the improving situation on Guadalcanal, Yamamoto was still very much in the game, though with significant issues. Due to its critical losses fighting the Cactus Air Force, Rabaul's 11th Air Fleet was unable to put waves of aircraft over Henderson Field anymore, and with the Imperial Navy's failure to resupply the 17th Army, the Guadalcanal campaign was fast becoming a lost cause for the Japanese. Unwilling to concede defeat, Yamamoto directed the construction of forward air bases farther up the Slot to protect Bougainville and the approaches to Rabaul. If this could be accomplished, primarily at Munda on New Georgia, then if Hyakutake's starving men could be sustained an eventual counteroffensive was possible. With hindsight, given the growing American strength in the South Pacific, this was a pipe dream, though as a consummate gambler Yamamoto was prepared to roll the dice.

Roll them he did on the moonless night of November 30, 1942, with the redoubtable Rear Admiral Tanaka and nine destroyers. Of the 30,000-odd remnants of 17th Army, only about 4,000 were combat capable and they were subsisting on one-sixth rations. They were eating anything now: roots, dead fish washed up on the beach, and even, if some reports are accurate, each other. Submarines could not carry enough, airdrop attempts failed miserably, and without control of the sky, seaborne supply was extremely risky. The final method was to use fast destroyers, dash into Ironbottom Sound at night, and drop fifty-five-gallon drums off the coast. Carefully cleaned, each drum was filled halfway with barley and rice, then lashed together in lines of one hundred drums each that would drift ashore. Each destroyer could manage 240 drums, and after each line was dropped into the sea the warships would dash back out again to get as far up the Slot as possible before dawn.

Tanaka's plan called for six of his destroyers to drop 1,360 drums off Tassafaronga Point near the mouth of

the Umasani River. A decoded messaged alerted Halsey
of a Tokyo Express run departing the Shortlands on
November 30, just after midnight. Task Force 67, six
cruisers and five destroyers commanded by Rear Admiral Carlton Wright, was dispatched to intercept the
Japanese. Rather than steam straight down the Slot,
Tanaka hugged the northern edge of it and entered
Ironbottom Sound from the Indispensable Strait, then
passed into the channel between Cape Esperance and
Savo. Wright's Task Force, confident with its radar
and heavier firepower, entered from the east via the
Lengo Channel along Guadalcanal's northern shoreline. At 2306 the *USS Fletcher*, 4,000 yards in front of
the cruisers, picked up the enemy destroyers on radar,
23,000 yards ahead and approaching Tassafaronga.
They were splitting into two groups, one to cover and
one to proceed inshore to drop the drums, but abandoned this when the American warships were visually
sighted six minutes later.

Twelve minutes after detecting Tanaka's destroyers,
Commander Bill Cole of the *Fletcher* asked permission to launch his torpedoes and, astonishingly, was
denied by Admiral Wright. When clearance to engage
was finally given at 2318, the U.S. destroyers sent at
least twenty Mark 15 torpedoes splashing into the
water, but the Japanese had already turned to attack

and were passing abeam of the American destroyers. Leading the U.S. line of cruisers *Minneapolis* opened on the *Takanami* with her nine 8-inch guns, and her five sisters immediately followed suit. Four minutes later the Japanese destroyer "glided to a halt wrapped in flames." Unfortunately, all the Mark 15s missed and while Wright's cruisers concentrated on *Takanami*, the other Japanese destroyers did what they did best: a point-blank-range night fight with torpedoes.

Standing inshore near Tassafaronga, their low silhouettes were nearly impossible to see visually, and the island's landmass obscured the U.S. radar picture. Purposely not firing his deck guns, Captain Torajiro Sato in the *Oyashio* slipped past the cruisers then turned to attack, aiming at the cruiser's white-yellow gun flashes. At least twenty-four Long Lance torpedoes sliced through the dark water and *Minneapolis* took a torpedo forward that ignited her aviation fuel and another that wrecked the Number Two fire room. All down the American line, huge columns of oily, burning water shot upward as the torpedoes impacted; *New Orleans* took one in the forward magazine that blew her bow off and *Pensacola* took a Long Lance squarely amidships. The light cruiser *Honolulu* instantly went to flank speed, began zigzagging, and evaded the torpedoes meant for her, but the heavy cruiser *Northampton*, last in line, inexplicably did neither. She took two Long Lances from the *Kawakaze* and heeled over steeply to port, drenched in flames.

Amid the confusion Tanaka was already withdrawing. The entire engagement, from first radar sighting to the final torpedo hit, lasted forty minutes, but there was no chance now to complete his mission and after fighting the U.S. Navy for three months the Japanese admiral knew when to run. In the last few weeks a few pilots who returned from strikes over Henderson Field recounted stories of a strange new American fighter. It was oddly H-shaped, with two engines and twin booms, but if its appearance was strange the new plane's capabilities were frightening. The fighter was extremely fast, could outclimb anything flying, and had a cluster of weapons in its nose that would shred a Zero or Betty. Tanaka had no wish to be caught by a swarm of them.

Takanami went down just as the Japanese artillery near Tassafaronga opened fire on the drifting *Northampton*. Fires raged out of control and the heavy cruiser's list slowly increased until 0304, when she rolled over and sank stern first, four miles northeast of Doma Cove. The other three cruisers made it across the Sound to Tulagi, where they were camouflaged, and rudimentary repairs were performed by their own crews with help from the Seabees. *New Orleans* was given a temporary bow made from coconut logs, and to ease the strain she steamed backward all the way to Sydney Harbor, Australia. The Cockatoo Island Dockyards made her seaworthy enough to sail for home, which she did, stern first, all the way to Puget Sound. *Minneapolis* left Tulagi and made it to Mare Island, while *Pensacola* steamed to Espiritu Santo, then on to Pearl Harbor.

The Battle of Tassafaronga was a major U.S. tactical disaster that revealed the awful price of overconfidence, and the loss of 19 officers with 398 men graphically illustrated the absolute necessity for competent combat commanders. However, not a single supply drum made it ashore that night, so the brief fight was a strategic defeat for Japan that symbolized the irrevocable loss of Guadalcanal, and the limit of Imperial expansion. Nevertheless, Tanaka came back again on December 3 and managed to drop 1,500 drums near the beach. Cactus Air Force pilots strafed most of them, and fewer than five hundred were recovered by Hyakutake's starving soldiers.

Another attempt was made four days later and fittingly, one year to the day since Pearl Harbor, it failed due to Cactus air strikes and PT boats in the channel. December 7 also saw the launching of America's largest battleship to date when the 887-foot-long, 45,000-ton USS *New Jersey* slid into the Delaware River from the

Philadelphia Naval Shipyard. Pedro del Valle, now a brigadier general, treated the Japanese positions west of the Matanikau to a December 7 anniversary barrage with "Tojo. Dec. 7, 1942" scratched into each shell. The following day on Guadalcanal saw the 132 Infantry Regiment come ashore at Lunga Point; the Army's Americal Division was now fully in place and the Marines could begin leaving.

At 0703 on the Wednesday morning of December 9, PT-59 put a torpedo into the stern of IJN submarine I-3 and it sank three miles northeast of Kamimbo Bay, off Cape Esperance. Later that morning Marine major general Archer Vandegrift formally turned command over to Army major general Alexander Patch and by 1400, after 125 days in hell, and the 1st Marine Division began leaving Guadalcanal. Battered and shabby, many wearing fragments of their original green dungarees held up with rope, the emaciated Marines were shuttled out to their transports.

Most had lost at least twenty pounds, and some were so weak they couldn't climb the netting onto their ships, but they'd broken the back of the Japanese advance and stalled its momentum. Their adaptability and ferocity shocked their enemy, who'd been told all their lives there was nothing fiercer than the invincible Japanese soldier. The U.S. Marines taught them differently and wore severed Japanese ears on their belts, made necklaces from the enemy's teeth, and kept the little skulls for good luck charms to prove it.*

Sailors cried openly and bodily pulled their fellow Americans back aboard. The officers and men of the 1st, 2nd, and 5th Marines had held out despite Frank Jack Fletcher's timidity and the indecisiveness of Robert Ghormley. The division left 774 of its men on the island in a cemetery aptly named Flanders Field; another 2,736 would bear physical wounds the rest of their lives. Sick and walking invalids accounted for another 3,000 to 8,000 men from the original 19,000 who landed in August.

Always covered by the Cactus Air Force and eventually by the fighting Navy, the Marines never gave up and Henderson Field, the single asset that made Guadalcanal worth fighting for, was still in American hands. December 11 saw Yamamoto personally directing a Tokyo Express run of eleven destroyers with 1,200 supply drums in one final desperate attempt to break through to Hyakutake, whose soldiers were dying at a rate of forty to fifty every day. It failed. Once again, American code breakers knew what ships were leav-

---

* Later in the war President Roosevelt was given a letter opener carved from a Japanese soldier's arm bone.

ing the Shortlands and when they intended to arrive off Guadalcanal.

Once again the Japanese, caught in a fatal pattern, never considered that their naval codes had been broken. By 0115 the destroyers cut loose their drums and were turning back up the Slot when PT 37, 40, and 48 fired a spread of torpedoes. One hit *Teruzuki*, the admiral's flagship, and knocked Tanaka out cold. Eighteen minutes later he transferred his flag and fled back up New Georgia Sound, leaving his ship to sink two hours later. This was the last run of the Tokyo Express in 1942 and, due to the American's shockingly unexpected resistance, the Imperial Staff began to plan the unthinkable: the extraction of a Japanese army from a combat zone.

As the dark days of 1942 drew to a close, a new phase of the war opened as the outward limit of the Axis was reached all over the world. After losing at El Alamein and Tobruk, Field Marshal Erwin Rommel was retreating to Tripoli. American forces had landed in northwest Africa and were moving east to fight the Afrika Korps. December found the German 4th Panzer Army in retreat after failing to break through to Stalingrad. More than 300,000 of Germany's finest soldiers were now cut off with no hope of escape. The Japanese Empire had also advanced as far as it could, blunted and bloodied by a small group of American Marines, soldiers, airmen, and sailors. From now on the battles would increase in ferocity as Japan fought to hold the outer island perimeter it had seized, and to make any reconquest as expensive as possible in terms of Allied lives.

Both sides in the Pacific had thus far made significant and costly mistakes; that is normal in any war, especially against a new foe, but America's strength lay in learning from those errors and adapting training, equipment, and tactics accordingly, while, with a few exceptions, the Japanese never did. To now win the war in the Pacific, the Allies, principally the Americans, had to drive north and east across millions of square miles to get within heavy bomber range of the Home Islands. From here the Japanese Empire could be killed at its heart, physically smashed to pieces in advance of the necessary but appalling cost of invasion—unless another option was developed.*

---

* On December 2, 1942, the first man-made, self-sustaining fission reaction occurred in a reactor built on an old squash court under the west viewing stands of the University of Chicago's Stagg Field. Ironically, eight years earlier Yamamoto, who loved American-style football, had watched a game between Northwestern and Iowa in Evanston, not twenty miles from Stagg Field.

Nonetheless, the Combined Fleet remained the greatest naval threat to the United States. Japan could muster ten battleships, including the *Yamato* and *Musashi,* the greatest warships in the world. The Imperial Navy had dozens of cruisers, more than one hundred destroyers, and some fifty fleet submarines. Additionally, there were nine aircraft carriers of various types, and several under construction. Tokyo, like Washington, was focused on other theaters for much of 1942 and both believed the "real" war would occur elsewhere. For the United States this was Europe and North Africa, while the Imperial General Staff's priority was to hold China against an invasion from the Soviet Union. By the end of 1942, the Imperial Army had fifty-four divisions in the field, but twenty-five of these were committed in China, leaving only a handful for the South Pacific. The Japanese Army Air Force was also late in being redeployed, and if those aircraft had been available in the fall of 1942 it is very possible the struggle for Guadalcanal would have ended differently.

Yet even with these assets, Japan was walking a tightrope. Evidence of America's awakening power was visible everywhere; aviation fuel, ammunition, toothbrushes, soap, the capability to replace lost equipment all spoke to a long, complex logistical system that kept men fighting. By December 1942, there were more than ninety cargo ships carrying 180,000 tons of supplies in line to offload in Nouméa Harbor. New technology was particularly envied: radars, mobile heavy weapons, and aircraft like the deadly Grumman F6F Hellcat, F4U Corsair, and Lockheed's P-38 Lightning. But the Allies had their own tightrope to walk; desperate enemies will commit desperate acts, and this was certainly true of Japan.

What it lacked in industrial capability and technology was, for the foreseeable future, compensated for with a fanatical devotion to a deified emperor and deep-seated hatred for the West, particularly the United States. As long as these could be harnessed and utilized in the most advantageous manner, it was believed that the war could be drawn out past American national will to fight. How long would the United States tolerate thousands of dead boys in return for fly specks of land in the Pacific? Admiral Isoroku Yamamoto was the one man capable of bringing this stratagem to fruition, to inflicting so many casualties on America's fighting men that peace could be negotiated. The Axis would be fractured, and the United States could devote its wrath to Nazi Germany and Fascist Italy; Japan would not have won the war, but it also would not have lost it, either.

Four days before Christmas in 1942, eleven P-39

Airacobras swept in over Guadalcanal's north coast, touched down on Fighter Two, and taxied to a stop; the 70th Fighter Squadron had joined the other Army units now spreading over the island. One young man, a stocky twenty-five-year-old fighter pilot from Oregon, climbed stiffly out onto his left wing, stretched, sniffed the heavy, foul air, and looked around at his new home. He didn't know it, of course, any more than the fifty-eight-year-old Yamamoto did, but their destinies were now linked and rapidly coming together.

Lieutenant Rex Barber was in the war at last.

Eight
At Any Cost

John Mitchell rolled the elevator trim wheel back with his left hand until he could feel no pressure against the control yoke in his right hand. The big fighter was very stable, and could be trimmed to fly "hands-off" as he did now, which would make the long mission a bit easier, physically at least. Normally this wasn't an issue; fighter combat hops in the Pacific were usually very short, and trimming a plane up for hands-off flight was an invitation to have your tail shot off. Today was different, however, and arriving over Bougainville exhausted would not suffice. His plan was simple: four inbound legs totaling 412 miles; two hours and five minutes to roar in, hopefully undetected, over Empress Augusta Bay and catch the Japanese by surprise. Mitchell knew from long experience that the real trick was the execution, in making it work, and no one could do that for him.

It was a good plan. Mitchell should know. He created it.

The previous afternoon, April 17, he had been lying on his cot in the 339th Fighter Squadron Ops Tent trying to doze. He'd already flown a morning mission and was on the board for another later in the afternoon, so he was irritated when the tent flap was yanked back and Henry Vicellio stepped in. Mitchell's former 70th Pursuit Squadron commander was now a lieutenant colonel and officially the acting director of operations for the 13th Air Force Fighter Command. This was largely administrative, but his dual position as commander of Guadalcanal's newly formed 347th Fighter Group was not. Skinny, like everyone on the Canal, Vicellio had narrow eyes, oddly protruding ears, and a receding hairline.

"Mitch, they want you over at the Opium Den," he said tersely as John Mitchell later recalled. "They've got something for you."

The Opium Den was a reinforced dugout over on Henderson Field, and the headquarters of the Commander Air, Solomon Islands: Rear Admiral Marc Mitscher. A 1910 graduate of the U.S. Naval Academy,

"Pete" Mitscher was a grizzled, hard-bitten professional. Designated Naval Aviator No. 33 in 1916, he gained early fame by piloting Navy Curtiss Flying Boat One (NC-1) during the first attempt at a fixed-wing, transatlantic crossing in May 1919.*

More than two decades later Mitscher, then a captain, commanded the USS *Hornet* for the April 1942 Doolittle Raid on Japan, and during the epic Battle of Midway. Soft-spoken, direct, and decisive, he had the overall command for fleet air before Bull Halsey handpicked him in December 1942 to lead the air assets in the Solomons during this most critical time. "I knew we'd probably catch hell from the Japs in the air," Halsey later recalled; "that's why I sent Pete Mitscher up there. Pete was a fighting fool and I knew it."

Mitscher's command had only been in place since February 1943, after the Japanese on Guadalcanal were killed or evacuated. It was part of a reorganization that was only possible due to the hard-won victories of late 1942, and reflected growing Allied optimism in the South Pacific. Mitscher's Air Solomon command was

---

* Mitscher, then a lieutenant commander, went down at sea, but the entire crew was rescued. NC-4, flown by Lieutenant Commander Albert Cushing Read, hopped across from NAS Rockaway in Queens, New York, to Plymouth, England, and landed safely on May 31, 1919.

subordinate to Air South Pacific, based in Nouméa, and contained, among other units, the 1st and 2nd Marine Air Wings, and units of the Army Air Force's 13th Air Force. Nevertheless, the Japanese, though bloodied and temporarily back on their heels, were far from beaten, physically or psychologically. In large part this had to do with the extreme compartmentalization of "bad" information, such as the Imperial Navy's loss at Midway or the army's defeat on Guadalcanal. Soldiers, sailors, and airmen who knew the truth because they'd been there were simply transferred to other stations or kept in combat. Flag officers and the Imperial General Staff were still supremely confident for two reasons. First, they continued to underestimate the Americans, and the second cause for extreme confidence was Isoroku Yamamoto; as long as he commanded in the Pacific they were unconcerned with defeat. The admiral would find a way.

Rolling out of his sweaty cot on that steamy Saturday afternoon, Mitchell left with Vicellio, then picked up Captain Tom Lanphier and Major Lou Kittel, the bearded commander of the 70th Fighter Squadron, and drove slowly over two miles of pockmarked coral road toward Henderson Field. By April 1943, Guadalcanal's original airstrip was now a full-fledged airfield with a real runway, taxiways, and hangars. It was a far cry from the muddy patch of dirt that so many had died for during the previous eight months. The former Cow Pasture auxiliary strip was now officially Fighter One and was utilized by the remaining Marine fighters while the Army flew from Fighter Two. If the irony of his situation occurred to him, Mitch would not have shown it. Two years ago he had been a lowly first lieutenant in the 70th Pursuit Squadron, and now he was a major, and since November 1942 a combat squadron commander. However, being summoned to the Opium Den was far from ordinary—not that there was any such thing as ordinary on Guadalcanal in the spring of 1943.

This was certainly the case on the afternoon of April 17, 1943.

"There were 15 to 20 people crammed in there," Mitchell remembered. "It was mass confusion . . . lots of smoke, and everyone was talking. When we showed up, they stopped and looked at us then a marine major handed me a message."

The message was, in fact, a more detailed translation of Admiral Yamamoto's proposed itinerary intercepted on April 14 by the Fleet Radio Unit, Pacific (FRUPAC) in Pearl Harbor, and also by the Fleet Radio Unit, Melbourne, Australia (FRUMEL). In part, the encoded telegram 131755 from the Japanese Southeast Area Fleet Headquarters read:

THE INSPECTION TOUR OF THE COMMANDER IN CHIEF TO BALLALE, SHORTLAND AND BUIN ON APRIL 18 IS SCHEDULED AS FOLLOWS:

1. 0600 DEPART RABAUL BY MEDIUM ATTACK PLANE (ESCORTED BY SIX FIGHTERS); 0800 ARRIVE BALLALE. IMMEDIATELY DEPART FOR SHORTLAND ON BOARD SUBCHASER (1ST BASE FORCE TO READY ONE BOAT), ARRIVING AT 0840. DEPART SHORTLAND 0945 ABOARD SAID SUBCHASER, ARRIVING BALLALE AT 1030. 1100 DEPART BALLALE ABOARD MEDIUM ATTACK PLANE, ARRIVING BUIN AT 1110. LUNCH AT 1ST BASE FORCE HEADQUARTERS (SENIOR STAFF OFFICER OF AIR FLOTILLA 26 TO BE PRESENT). 1400 DEPART BUIN ABOARD MEDIUM ATTACK PLANE; ARRIVE RABAUL AT 1540.

The officer who handed Mitchell the message was Major John P. Condon, USMC, operations officer for Guadalcanal's Fighter Command. Condon, who was very open about his dislike of the Army pilots, had already put a strip map together with routes and timing; it was how *he* would fly the mission, and how he expected Mitchell to do it. Obviously this was a Navy show, and besides Mitscher there was his chief of staff, Brigadier General Thomas Field Harris, with a bevy of other Marine colonels and Navy commanders. The Army pilots were the lowest-ranking officers in the stuffy little dugout and it was plain that they were just needed to fly the fighters, not actually have anything to say about the mission.

"There was big discussion . . . a real hassle . . . as to how to get Yamamoto," Mitchell later recounted. "The reason we were called in was because we were flying P-38s, the only fighter planes that could fly the distance from Guadalcanal to Bougainville and back. The navy and marine pilots would never have let us army pilots in on a mission like that if any of their F4F and F4U fighters could have made the trip."

The only way the Marines or Navy might have flown the mission is from a carrier, but that would have meant penetrating deep into Japanese-held territory to within a few hundred miles of Bougainville. This would put the carrier at extreme risk from land-based aircraft at Rabaul, or from Kahili on the southern tip of Bougainville. Unwilling to risk this, the navy was forced to turn to the army for assistance. Also, if the mission was flown from Guadalcanal, the Navy could control it to some degree, as the southern half of the Solomons belonged to the South Pacific Area and Admiral Nimitz. Roughly halfway up the Slot, control officially passed to the Southwest Pacific Area and General Doug MacArthur, and no one wanted to deal with him.

Mitscher turned the planning over to the ComAirSols Fighter Command executive officer, Lieutenant Colonel L. S. "Sam" Moore, who, with Condon, did all the initial legwork. They figured on a low-altitude inbound route outside of the Slot to avoid radar detection or visual sightings from any ships. But neither marine knew much about the P-38, so their timing was incorrect because their planned airspeeds were wrong. "If I had followed Condon's route," Mitchell related to noted historian Carroll V. Glines, "we would have been forty to fifty miles offshore from where I wanted to be."

The other dugout debate revolved around how exactly to kill Yamamoto. The Navy pilots, perhaps understandably, thought it best to attack the minesweeper transporting the admiral from Ballale to the Faisi Naval Anchorage at nearby Shortland Island. But Mitchell saw several problems with this plan. First, there was the issue of identifying the boat. "I didn't know one boat from another . . . a subchaser from a sub," he recalled. And even if they got the correct one, "[h]e [Yamamoto] could swim for it, and would certainly have a life preserver. If we got him the air, well, the chances of survival were practically nil. He's dead. Period."

Even if they managed to find the vessel and sink it there was no guarantee that the admiral would die; he could swim quite well, and once in the water how could Yamamoto be distinguished from other survivors? Admiral Mitscher, who had sat back and listened while his subordinates argued, finally waved a hand to shut everyone up, and squinted at Mitchell:

"How do you want to do it?"

"I want to get him in the air, sir. We're fighter pilots, that what we do."

The admiral nodded gently, and glanced around at his gathered officers. "Since Mitchell's got to do the job, let's let him do it his way."

On his way back to the operations tent the major thought about the seventy to eighty enemy fighters just fifteen miles northwest of Ballaleat Kahili Airfield, on the southern tip of Bougainville. The Japanese called it Buin, but 11th Air Fleet carrier planes were always rotating in and it had been a major base for operations against Guadalcanal. According to U.S. Navy Intelligence, Kahili was now home to at least three air groups: the 201st and 204th fighter units, plus the 582nd composite group and a few more Zeros of the Hiyo Detachment. As of late May, there were also thirty-six fighters at Buka on the northern tip of Papua New Guinea, about one hundred miles from Kahili. The message from Halsey mentioned six fighters as an escort, but those were with him from Rabaul; it was highly likely that others would join up along route to escort their famous and indispensable commander in chief into Ballale.

Mitchell, and every fighter pilot on Guadalcanal, had done that on January 21, 1943, when Secretary of the Navy Frank Knox, Bull Halsey, and Admiral Nimitz had flown into Henderson Field, so it was reasonable to assume the Japanese might do the same. Far from beaten, the Japanese were planning another offensive. However he personally viewed the war, Yamamoto was a professional naval officer and proven warrior, so doing his duty was a foregone conclusion, though the admiral had also been stung by the defeats of late 1942. Personally promising the emperor that he would again attack the Allies, Yamamoto planned to retake the captured territory and reclaim Japan's honor.

In April 1943, the Combined Fleet could still muster the fleet carriers *Shokaku* and *Zuikaku*, and five more were under construction. Two fast battle cruisers, the *Hiei* and *Kirishima*, had been lost off Guadalcanal during November 1942, but the Imperial Navy still had ten heavy battleships, including the *Yamato* and *Musashi*—the largest battleships in the world—as well as hundreds of cruisers, destroyers, and submarines.* The Allies were fighting back, but the large-scale offensives were still to come. Also, and perhaps most critical, the Japanese did not suspect that the Allies had broken their codes. They certainly had reason to consider this after their crushing defeat at Midway, and subsequent disasters at Cape Esperance, and the Bismarck Sea, but this very plausible option never seemed to occur to the General Staff. How could Westerners, especially Americans, grasp the intricacies of the Japanese language? They could not, the Imperial Army had long ago decided, and therefore breaking codes was impossible.

Nevertheless, Americans in Washington and Pearl Harbor worried about what the Japanese would think after Operation VENGEANCE. How could the sudden appearance of sixteen American fighters in precisely the right place and time be explained? Many believed the mission would finally convince the Japanese that

---

* *Yamato* and *Musashi* were more than eight football fields long and displaced 69,988 tons. By comparison, the infamous *Bismarck* displaced 49,500 tons, roughly the same size as the mighty American *Iowa*-class battleships.

their message traffic was being intercepted and read. The question was whether the life of one man, however hated by America and essential to the Imperial war effort, was worth compromising and losing such a tremendous capability. Chester Nimitz decided that it was, and Bull Halsey certainly concurred, which is how John Mitchell found himself back at the 339th Fighter Squadron Ops tent late Saturday afternoon staring at a map of the Solomon Sea.

Not knowing the P-38's exact capabilities, Condon plotted a route far too close to the Japanese-held islands up the Slot, and his timing was incorrect. Mitch also figured he'd have to fly lower than the Marine officer planned, fifty to a hundred feet above the waves at the most, to completely avoid detection. There were obvious problems with this. Navigation, for one. There were no landmarks at sea; one wave looked just like another. The fighters would be too far out to sea for visual checkpoints, and far too low to see anything anyway. Pilot fatigue would be another concern, and the margin of error at fifty feet was nil, but Mitch knew his pilots, and knew that adrenaline would work its magic inbound to the target. Finally, despite the long range of the Lightning, more than four hundred miles at such a low altitude would increase fuel consumption, so even with two 165-gallon external drop tanks the fuel figures were on a razor's edge. However, before leaving the Opium Den and returning return to Fighter Two, Mitchell was told that every available 310-gallon external tank was being flown in from New Guinea, courtesy of the 90th Bomb Group at Port Moresby.

Knowing this, Mitchell tossed Condon's plan aside and started from scratch. Any attack plan began with the objective and what were known as "absolutes." The objective was obvious: shoot down the medium bomber and kill Admiral Isoroku Yamamoto. Good. Objectives always sounded simple, but he knew they hid a multitude of potential disasters, and this mission was rife with them. The Japanese might alter their plan or the admiral's itinerary; every Zero fighter on Bougainville might show up to make an impression on their commander; the whole thing might be a trap. Nevertheless, Mitchell had made a point of intercepting the bomber transport, and that was his hot potato.

So, how to do it?

Two intelligence officers had followed him back from Henderson, Army captain William Morrison and his naval intelligence counterpart, Lieutenant Joe Mc-Guigan. They brought everything available from the Opium Den, which wasn't much, and spread it out on the battered wood table in the 339th Fighter Operations Center, a glorified name for a moldy, Armbruster

M1934 OD canvas tent. While they began to examine several maps of the Solomon Islands, Mitchell sent his runner out after the maintenance officer. Leaning over the larger map he could plainly see the crescent shape of New Britain with Rabaul at the top. Drawing a circle around it, the pilot ran a finger down to Ballale, off Bougainville's southern tip, where Yamamoto would land, and drew another circle there. Assuming they flew direct, and there was no reason to believe otherwise, the Japanese bomber would cross the St. George Channel, skirt the southern edge of New Ireland, then cross about 170 miles of the northern Solomon Sea over to Bougainville.

Would Yamamoto's pilot fudge east to stay over land, or fly the route direct? Mitchell chose the latter. The Japanese did not deviate from a plan once it was made, and in any event the admiral would certainly want to get into Ballale as soon as possible. Measuring the straight black line between Rabaul and Ballale, Mitchell jotted down 315 miles. A Betty bomber—the most common type—would average about 180 mph, roughly three miles per minute. There was no way to figure his exact takeoff time, nor did it really matter. What did matter was that Yamamoto expected to land on the island at 0945, Guadalcanal Time, so figuring on the admiral's fanatical obsession with punctuality, that meant that at 0935, ten minutes prior to landing, the bomber would be . . . here. He touched an empty spot of jungle between the slopes of Mount Takuan to the north, and the southeast coast. It lay almost half-way between Empress Augusta Bay and Kahili, so if the Zeros weren't already airborne, Mitchell's pilots would have a few precious minutes to do their work. This was the time, then, and the point of interception, just as the bomber was slowing down, descending to land, and the fighter escorts would be relaxed with the destination in sight.

The dogleg route around the Slot was necessary, as was the low altitude. Intelligence figured any land-based search radars would be Imperial Navy models, most likely Type 11 sets identical to the one captured on Henderson Field. Copied from the American-built SCR-268, the 19,200-pound Japanese monster could detect a formation of aircraft at 20,000 feet out to about 150 miles, and surface ships to ten miles on a good day. However, even though sixteen to eighteen fighters generate a much, much smaller radar return than a warship, Mitchell calculated that at fifty to one hundred feet, the best detection range would be no farther than ten miles, and he planned the route accordingly. At no point over the three legs he plotted would the fighters be any closer than thirty miles to enemy-held territory until turning in toward Empress Augusta Bay on the fourth leg. So unless the Lightnings happened across a stray Japanese ship, they had an acceptable chance of getting to Bougainville undetected.

But how long could they remain over the island, deal with any fighters, and find Yamamoto's bomber? Fuel was indeed life, and in this case the chances of success of failure were measured in gallons of 100-grade aviation gasoline. Gas and flawless aerial gunnery of course, but Mitchell wasn't worried about his pilots in a dogfight. Fuel, however, was another matter. The P-38G carried 306 gallons internally, which was quite sufficient for defending an island, or for short missions in the area of Guadalcanal. This, though, was something else, which was why each Lightning could carry a 165-gallon drop tank under one wing, and the larger 310-gallon tank under the other.

This gave each fighter a total of 781 gallons. At maximum cruise airspeed, at high altitude, this meant nearly six hours of flying for well over a thousand miles. But they weren't at high altitude, so Mitchell figured flying at fifty feet would increase fuel consumption by 25 percent. Then there was the wind. "The only weather we could get from the Navy said it would be a little hazy," he remembered. "With a quartering wind of the port [left] bow at 5 knots." That was nearly

6 mph, and when he calculated the angle it dropped his ground speed from 203 mph to 197 mph.

Just to arrive over the Bougainville coast was 412 miles, plus another 30 miles to rejoin after takeoff: 442 miles, if nothing went wrong, and if his navigation was perfect. Ground operations, taxiing, and the takeoff would consume 75 gallons per aircraft, and the next 412 miles, with the added increase in low-altitude consumption, and a full power climb to intercept the bomber would burn another 363 gallons. Total fuel then, just to get up, get together, and fly the route to the intercept point was 438 gallons. That was one of his "absolutes." Another was the return-to-base distance and fuel. Once clear of Bougainville by twenty miles, each P-38 could safely climb to altitude, pull the throttles back, and head southeast down the New Georgia Sound some 220 miles direct to Guadalcanal.

There were Japanese bases scattered about on the way home, but due to fuel limitations the Lightnings would have no choice but to run the gauntlet, starting with Vila Airfield on Kolombangara Island. Nestled in the Kula Gulf between Vella Lavella and New Georgia, Kolombangara looked like an immense horseshoe crab capped by an ominous volcanic crater. Built in the fall of 1942, the airfield was on the southern shore, away from New Georgia Sound, and as far as intelligence knew it was used as an emergency landing strip for damaged aircraft returning from Guadalcanal. However, the same had been said for Munda Field, about halfway down the Slot, and that was proving inaccurate. Since December 1942, the 3,500-foot-long airstrip had initially belonged to Zeros of the 252 Kokutai, but was attacked so viciously that the surviving pilots were evacuated by bomber. Mitchell knew that less than a month ago, coastwatcher Donald Kennedy reported Zeros of the 204 and 582 Kokutai were operating on the field.

Interestingly, due to the Imperial Navy's heavy losses, as of mid-December 1942, Japanese Army Air Force (JAAF) units were rather belatedly being deployed into the South Pacific. The first Ki 43 "Oscar" fighter units arrived at Rabaul's Vunakanau airfield, and in early January 1943, the 1st Sentai (Group) deployed forward to Ballale. From here the JAAF initially entered combat against Guadalcanal on January 27, losing six Oscars in the fight.

Since then, JAAF fighters, including the new Ki 61 "Tony," could be found on any of the forward bases like Munda. If any were there now, and Mitchell acknowledged the possibility, then it was another calculated risk they would take. In any event, Munda lay on the extreme south side of New Georgia island, at least forty miles laterally from where his pilots should be flying, and by the time any fighters were scrambled and got to altitude the Lightnings should be well past the danger—at least those in front. There was also a seaplane base in Rekata Bay, across the Slot from New Georgia, on the north shore of Santa Isabel Island. Seaplanes didn't bother Mitch a bit, but there could also be fighters there as well.

It didn't matter. He had no choice.

At maximum range airspeed the return flight to the Canal would take about ninety minutes, and at least 188 gallons of fuel—another absolute. Adding the 438 gallons required to fly to the intercept point gave a total of 626 gallons. So much for the hard math. The southern end of Bougainville was a nest of Japanese bases: Kahili, Ballale, and the Shortland Islands. Especially Kahili. It was the main fighter base south of Rabaul, and assuming Mitchell's ambush was successful the Zeros there would instantly turn into an angry swarm, so flying over it was a bad idea. Another egress choice, depending on how far inland the intercept actually took place, was to skirt the south slope of Mount Takuan, then fly east over the Bougainville Strait, and turn south into the Slot near Choiseul. However, if they got the bomber on the west side of Bougainville then his pilots could turn south near Moila Point, avoid the Shortlands, and head home down the south side of the Slot. Either way, it was about twenty minutes at full MIL power with both engines together burning 5.5 gallons per minute, which meant another 110 gallons.

A full 736 gallons out of 781 total.

That left 45 gallons for combat; actually, 40 if he tried to keep a five-gallon reserve. That was seven minutes of dogfighting at full MIL power, not much at all. Under normal circumstances, whatever those were in a war, it would be an unacceptable margin, but this was not normal. Of course, Mitchell's pilots would save a few gallons by executing a long, en route gliding descent when they were close enough to Guadalcanal, and they would be much lighter since most of the gas was consumed. But there was no way to calculate that, and no way to plan it. Everything past the intercept was situation dependent, and that phrase could cover a multitude of disasters. His men would know that they had, best case, seven minutes of fighting time over Bougainville. It wasn't much, and if Yamamoto was late, or the weather was bad, or the Lightnings had to fight their way through a horde of Zeros it would not be enough time. The odds weren't good. "At that time," Mitchell recalled forty-five years later, "I figured the odds at about a thousand to one that we could make a successful intercept at that distance."

Nevertheless, once the framework was built around his absolutes, the major could devise a tactical plan that fit the circumstances. He had no idea when a Betty bomber normally lowered its gear and slowed down for landing, but he'd flown enough with B-17s and B-26 Marauders to know they preferred long, gradual descents, unlike fighters that flew tight, overhead patterns. This bomber was also carrying an admiral, and would let down as gently as possible, so it was likely to begin twenty to thirty miles away—right where he planned the intercept. The Betty would be slow, vulnerable, and its pilots preoccupied with the approach. Over friendly territory and close to the final destination the fighter escorts would also be relaxed. Finally, the P-38s would not be expected, and would pop up from the least likely direction: low latitude from over the sea. It was, ironically and satisfyingly, like Pearl Harbor in reverse.

As Captain Morrison and Lieutenant McGuigan inked over Mitchell's lines, pilots began stepping into the tent. Secrets were hard to keep on the Canal, and impossible within the close-knit brotherhood of fighter pilots. More than forty men from three P-38 squadrons—the 12th, 70th, and 339th—all shared the twenty-odd aircraft and everyone wanted to be a part of this. The major shooed the pilots out and told them to stand by; they'd get word soon enough. The maintenance chief stopped by and informed Mitch that he could put up eighteen operational P-38s for the mission. Several were down for mechanical issues and one pilot, Lieutenant Rex Barber, had lost three feet of his right wingtip on an earlier mission. Mitchell told them to do the best they could, and to stand by for the inbound drop tanks. They *had* to be installed during the night or the mission was a nonstarter. They discussed fueling, and the ammo load out. Despite the weight Mitch insisted on a full load: 500 rounds for each of the four .50-caliber Brownings, and 150 rounds for the 20mm Hispano cannon.

The target area tactics were fairly straightforward. Based on the number of Zeros available, Mitch decided to put four Lightnings into an "Attack" flight that would ignore the dogfighting and destroy the bomber at all costs.* They would all stay together in a string of four-ship flights until the Betty was sighted. At that

---

* Other accounts call it a "Killer" flight but John Mitchell, who created the plan, designated the four P-38s who were to get the bomber as the "Attack" section.

point the attackers were on their own, and the other P-38s, hopefully fourteen altogether, would climb up to 18,000 to 20,000 feet to keep the Zeros busy. That might include the close escort of six, but certainly those coming up from Buka or up from Kahili. However many there were, Mitchell and his top-cover flight were obliged to take them on. If they couldn't get to the escorts, then two of the Attackers would deal with them while the other two bounced the bomber. It was simple, and easily adaptable if the situation changed. *When* it changed; combat situations always did. The pilots he chose would accept that, and had to make the most of what time they had.

That was next: the pilots.

There were forty-one available, all members of the 339th Fighter Squadron, though about half officially came from the 12th and 70 Fighter Squadrons. Mitchell had arrived on the Canal in early October 1942, with ten pilots of the 70th Fighter Squadron, and together with a few survivors from the 67th they had begun combat missions immediately.* By now, he

---

* Official Cactus Air Force records list Captains Mitchell and Sharpstein, Lieutenants Dinn, Farron, Shaw, Jacobson, Gillon, Purnell, Stern, Banfield, and Dews arriving on October 7, 1942.

knew many of these forty-one men very well. Using a lantern and flashlight, he chalked the flight lineup on a blackboard from those he knew on Fiji, or who had fought with him here on the Canal. "There wasn't any great deliberation on my part," Mitchell related, "except I guess I was going a little heavy on the pilots I knew. I knew what they could do. They were good pilots and I could depend on them." These included Captain Tom Lanphier, with Lieutenants Doug Canning, Besby Holmes, and Rex Barber.

Major Lou Kittel, now acting as the deployed 12th Fighter Squadron commander, returned to the Ops tent after running down the maintenance and armament details, and asked Mitch to add a few more of "his boys" from the old 12th Fighter Squadron. Kittel had deployed to Christmas Island, a tiny speck of coral a thousand miles south of Hawaii, during March 1942, with a handful of 12th Fighter Squadron pilots, and remained there a year. The North Dakota native lived in a hut he'd pieced together from abandoned crates and driftwood, kept a dog and motorcycle, and, much to his disgust, missed the "hot times" during the fall of 1942 in New Guinea and Guadalcanal. His newly arrived pilots had done well, so Mitchell agreed to give Kittel eight slots, including himself. The final lineup for April 18, 1943, read:

- Major John Mitchell, 339 FS CO, Mission Commander (Top Cover Flight)

- Lt. Julius Jacobson, 339 FS

- Lt. Doug Canning, 339 FS

- Lt. Delton Goerke, 339 FS

- Captain Tom Lanphier 70th FS Killer Flight Lead (Attack Flight)

- Lt. Rex Barber, 339 FS

- Lt. Joe Moore, 70 FS

- Lt. Tom McClanahan, 339 FS

- Major Lou Kittel, 12 FS, Acting CO (Top Cover Flight)

- Lt. Gordon Whittaker, 12 FS

- Lt. Roger Ames, 12 FS

- Lt. Lawrence Graebner, 12 FS

- Lt. Everett Anglin, 12 FS (Top Cover Flight)

- Lt. William Smith, 12 FS

- Lt. Eldon Stratton, 12 FS

- Lt. Al Long, 12 FS

- Lt. Besby Holmes, 339 FS (airspare)

- Lt. Ray Hine, 339 FS (airspare)

Mitchell finished up the details and left the intelligence officers to make copies of the strip map for each pilot. Word was passed to every P-38 pilot that the major wanted them all awake by 0500, to have breakfast and then report to the Ops tent at 0600 for a mass briefing. There had been indications all day that something big was up. Every P-38 on the line was being checked and rechecked, even those that were scheduled for routine maintenance, and a rumor was floating around about a request for bigger drop tanks. The intelligence officers knew but they weren't talking, nor, surprisingly, was Tom Lanphier. Rex, like most combat pilots, was too tired to care much. Whatever the mission was would be revealed in the morning, and until then he could forget about it. Mitch went back to his tent and got a few hours' sleep, but it was a busy night for the non-flying folks of the 339th Fighter Squadron. Once the 310-gallon tanks, which no one had ever seen before, arrived, the maintenance crews worked all through the night to get them on board and checked. Armorers loaded the heavy .50-caliber belts, and 20 mm cannon rounds, then each aircraft was fueled.*

Arising at 0430, the major, who slept in his clothes like everyone else, rolled out of his canvas cot and walked to the mess tent. With the arrival of the 164th Regiment in October the food had improved drastically from the early days on the Canal. Any U.S. Army prepackaged K rations were an improvement over Japanese rice, but chow now also included hotcakes, sausages, and even canned fruit. As always, the coffee was hot, black, and strong. At Operations, Mitchell rechecked the weather, and got the status on his Lightnings; eighteen were operational, and the last 310-gallon tank was being secured now. When the pilots crammed into the tent, he synchronized watches and told them the scoop; it was Admiral Yamamoto, commander in chief of the Japanese Combined Fleet, that they were ordered to kill. "We were to get that bomber no matter what." Mitchell had no illusions regarding the mission. "That was it."

---

* P-38 pilot Colonel (then Captain) Charles W. King held that this was widespread practice. The trajectory was different from a normal round, and tracers instantly alerted enemy aircraft they were being attacked.

"They were an eager bunch," he chuckled at the memory. "Everyone wanted to go." He told them the mission was highly classified, passed out the strip maps, then briefed the specifics: the time to step to their planes, when to start engines, and when to taxi out. There would be a "hard" takeoff time of 0710, and the entire mission was to be "comm out," or silent operations, from the beginning. Anything information that needed passed would be done with hand signals. The major went over the lineup, and carefully explained the route. He would set the course and speed, and the others would fly off him. Fuel consumption was critical, so he briefed easy, wide formations once they descended down to low latitude so throttle movements could be minimized. They would be out of sight of land the entire way in to Bougainville, and only on the short final leg would they climb up to make the intercept. Just before crossing the coast they would jettison the now-empty drop tanks, and the attack section would split off to get the bomber.

"The rest of us," he recalled, "would climb rapidly to altitude to be top cover . . . and also be ready to bounce any of the seventy-five to one hundred Zeros based at Kahili near Buin." This, Mitchell believed, would be the real fight. He could have led the attack section, but figured the action would be much higher up with the enemy fighters, and saw this as a great chance to add a few more Japanese flags to the eight on *Squinch*'s nose: "I wanted to get after those Zeros." No other targets were to be attacked. There was to be no strafing of the Japanese bases at Kahili or Shortland, and after the bomber was down everyone was on their own to get back home. Mitch reviewed the routes down the Slot, and talked about landing in the Russell Islands. There were some typical questions, but no one flying today was new to the Pacific War. "I had the utmost confidence in all of them. If anybody could do the job, I knew they could."

With that, those on the mission broke up into their individual flights and discussed specific details while the others, gloomy to a man, wandered off to the mess tent or out to watch the takeoff. Mitchell reviewed the timing, standard hand signals, and reinforced radio silence—under all circumstances until the enemy was sighted over Bougainville. The recap didn't take long. Each man was a veteran and knew what was expected. The major had the route diagrammed on a piece of tablet paper that he folded up and put into his chest pocket as they left the tent. His flight members—Doug Canning, Julius Jacobson, and Delton Goerke—then walked over to collect their flight gear.

Tom Lanphier's flight was also getting dressed for

combat and, as with all combat pilots, Rex Barber had a routine that he never varied. That would be unlucky. Like everyone else, Rex wore khaki pants and a long-sleeved shirt with the sleeves rolled up. Some pilots buttoned the cuffs down around their wrists, believing it was added protection in case of fire, but most did not. Same thing with flying gloves. Rex liked to touch switches and feel everything in the cockpit, and even the thin rayon glove liners some used were too thick.

Stooping, he tightened his boot laces so they'd stay on if he bailed out, then buckled a canvas belt around his waist. This ran through a battered leather holster holding his personal Model 1917 Colt .45-caliber pistol, which he checked and loaded. Two faded canvas pouches holding extra bullets were in front of the pistol on his left hip because Rex flew with his right hand, and found anything on that side could snag when he moved the control column. The only thing on his right hip was twelve-inch Marine Ka-Bar fighting knife that he'd found in the mud one day at Fighter One. Everyone carried weapons on the Canal, even though the Japanese were long gone, and shoulder harnesses for pistols were becoming more popular. Major Mitchell had always worn one.

Next, the lieutenant carefully inspected his yellow life vest, checking the straps and especially the pair of cords attached to the bottom front edge. These connected to cartridges filled with fluid carbon dioxide and, if he yanked on them, gas would instantly fill two rubberized cloth chest pockets and keep him afloat. Faded black stenciling on the bottom right corner read VEST, LIFE PRESERVER, TYPE B-3, but Barber and every other aviator called it a Mae West since the inflated pockets gave the wearer an instant bosom rivaling that of the famous movie star.*

Pulling his flight helmet off its nail, Rex flipped it over and checked the radio comm cord, especially the red jack on the end he would plug into the aircraft. Today was not a day for exposed wires, rot, or rust on the metal surfaces. The cord was clean. The helmet itself was made of canvas for tropical or summer use since leather rotted quickly out here. Some pilots had the newer ANH-15 types with huge earphones, but he

---

* The vest was invented by Peter Markus of Minnesota, originally for fishermen. Granted U.S. Patent No. 1,694,714, for an "inflatable life preserver," on December 11, 1928, he improved it and the U.S. government enthusiastically produced it for military aviators. It saved thousands of lives and during the war Markus canceled his patent rights, happy that his invention was so useful. Counterclaims by inventor Andrew Toti are without merit; he never received a patent and was eleven years old when Markus invented the vest.

liked his old A-9 helmet. It was lighter and the hard rubber earphones, which he checked now, were smaller. Inside the helmet was a padded liner covered with soft chamois, though it was badly stained by sweat. Satisfied, he tugged on the helmet, wriggled it into place, then removed his goggles from the same nail. Pilots could choose any type they wanted, and again he preferred the older 6530 type as they were smaller and more streamlined.

Rex wiped the goggles with his handkerchief and looked closely for scratches. This was important; errant marks could block his vision at a critical moment, and there were no second chances in a dogfight. They were clean. Pressing the goggles to his forehead, the pilot ran the strap along the back of his head then snapped the three retaining bands into place. The final piece of equipment was his S-2 seat-type parachute. Enlisted riggers checked them before and after each flight, but pilots always did as well unless they were scrambled during an emergency. The heavy coffee-colored straps had once been white, but were now permanently discolored. What mattered to him was sturdiness, and there were no cuts, tears, or loose threads on the straps or the parachute pack itself. Fighter pilots usually wore the seat-type parachute, as opposed to bomber crews who used back or chest chutes so they could clamber through their big planes. Rex had no such luxury, and had to be able to get clear in a hurry. The seat chute was uncomfortable, though, so a cushion was snapped onto the top and it helped a bit. Fighter missions were usually so short it didn't matter much, though today would definitely be an exception.

Holding his strip map and notes, Rex ducked outside and joined the other waiting pilots. It was already hot, but that meant the ground was dry and there was no sticky mud to contend with. The chalkboard from the Ops tent was leaning against a post with every pilot's name and aircraft side number written in neat columns. Any last-minute changes would be reflected here, and Rex noted that *Diablo,* his own personal Lightning, was still not flyable. He was borrowing Lieutenant Rob Petit's *Miss Virginia.*

Clustering in their respective flights, some pilots chatted quietly while others smoked or reviewed maps. There were no obvious displays of nervousness—that would be bad form—but it was there just under the surface. It always was. A tapping foot or a short laugh a bit higher than it should be. These were usual pre-combat signs accompanying symptoms that couldn't be seen. Rex, and every other fighter pilot, controlled these other symptoms in his own way. A tightening gut, shallow breathing, and the drumbeat of his heart.

The trick was to focus only on today; forget home, family, and the secret deals made with God during the night. This mission. Only this mission. Despite this, Rex knew today was different from any he'd yet flown. It was a strike deeper into enemy territory than he'd ever flown. There would be no rescue if he went down over the Japanese-held jungle. Rex could deal with that all right, he did it every day, but Major Mitchell, over the Navy's objections, had revealed their true target. Nailing the bomber over Bougainville would be more than just a slap in the enemy's face; it would mean the death of the Combined Fleet's commander. That, Rex decided as he climbed into a waiting jeep, was worth any cost.

PART THREE

"With unshakeable resolve I will drive deep into the enemy's positions and let him see the blood of a Japanese man. Wait but a while, young men! One last battle, fought gallantly to the death."

ADMIRAL ISOROKU YAMAMOTO

1943

Nine
Sharks and Dolphins

April 18, 1943
The Solomon Sea, west of Guadalcanal

A bead of sweat rolled down the fighter pilot's face. At 1,000 feet, Mitch shallowed out of the dive, then deliberately eased down to a mere fifty-foot wingspan over the water. Glancing at the big Mk II ship's compass as he did so, the twenty-nine-year-old major steadied up on 265 degrees and looked at his wristwatch. It was a prewar Waltham B-1 with black enamel numbers, except for the red 12 against a white face. Manufactured as a "trench watch" for the Army, it had a second smaller, second-hand dial within the face and a brown, sweat-stained leather wristband.

Fifty-five minutes at a cruising speed of 200 mph should carry the sixteen fighters 183 miles out into the Solomon Sea, depending on the wind, and this was well beyond the range any of the primitive Type 11 search radars the Japanese had on Rendova or Vella Lavella. No one knew exactly what was there, so he had to account for the possibility, and the chance of running across stray enemy ships. Nudging the throttles up to hold his airspeed, Mitchell twisted the silver-dollar-sized friction lock to hold the throttles in place, then let go of the control wheel. The fighter's nose immediately sagged and he pulled it up, then rolled the elevator trim wheel back until he let go again and remained level.

Like all the other pilots, he took a few moments to check his gauges: manifold pressure, RPM, oil temperature . . . all were in the green as they should be. Already hot, Mitchell then opened the ventilator by his left knee to let in some outside air, not that it was any cooler, but it did circulate the hot air in the cockpit a bit. Loosening his lap belt, the major twisted left, then right to check his wingmen. Satisfied, he squirmed back in the seat a bit, then pulled the map out from under his clipboard. Leg Two would run the P-38s northwest and parallel to the islands before turning back toward their target. It was a good plan, simple and adaptable.

The sun was shining over his shoulders into the cockpit, but the Navy compass was so large Mitch only squinted a little to read the heading. It was still steady on 265 degrees, and he didn't need to look at the strip map for the other numbers; he had planned the route, done the math, and the numbers were burning the inside of his eyelids. Once past the Russells, they would head away from New Georgia and Rendova before turning to parallel the Slot northwest toward Papua New Guinea. Another methodical clockwise scan around the cockpit showed everything was fine: fuel, oil, temperature . . . there was nothing else to do at the moment but fly flawlessly and pray for luck.

Guadalcanal had fallen away behind them, but the long struggle for that place made the chance of success today possible. Mitchell, and all the others on the island, had heard that just before Christmas 1942, the Japanese had finally realized Guadalcanal could not be held, much less retaken. Christmas Day itself was exactly as it always was in a combat zone: a parody of the real thing. This appeared strange to those safe back in the United States, who figured fighting men had much to be thankful for if they were alive and celebrating, and they would cherish Red Cross packages filled with gifts. Not that knit sweaters or winter scarves weren't appreciated, but they only punctuated the immense distance between home and the reality of war in the Pacific.

By Christmas there were some 40,000 Americans on Guadalcanal, and nearly 45,000 gallons of aviation fuel were used every day for the two hundred aircraft of the 2nd Marine Air Wing and five squadrons of Army Air Force fighters. It was a far cry from the 14,000 Marines and thirty-odd aircraft holding on by their fingernails just four months earlier. Now the tents had wooden floors, there were shower stations, and a movie theater nicknamed the "Coralcobana." Food, unlike at the beginning, was not a problem now and Mitchell had eaten turkey, mashed potatoes, and cranberries for Christmas dinner. The 15,000 remaining Japanese, holed up in the northwest, were eating tree bark, grass, and lizards, losing fifty to one hundred men every day, and that suited the Americans just fine. The Japanese had started this war, and Mitchell, Barber, and the others blamed them for the fact that they were still stuck on Guadalcanal dreaming of home.

"Let them all die" was a common sentiment, and the Americans meant it.

Yamamoto was not willing to do that. Every man saved was one who could continue the fight, and in December he forwarded a message from General Hyakutake to Tokyo that read, in part, "Seventeenth Army now requests permission to break into the enemy's positions and die an honorable death rather than die of hunger in our own dugouts." On Christmas Day, while the Americans sang real Christmas carols like Bing Crosby's newly released "White Christmas" or "Silent Night," an emergency conference took place at the Imperial Palace in Tokyo and the stage was set to evacuate the army from Guadalcanal under the guise of a renewed offensive.

Part of this illusion included troop and ship movements, a flood of false radio traffic, and the completion of a new enemy air base at Munda, some 180 miles up the Slot on New Georgia's south coast. The Japanese had been clever, moving largely at night, and tying the tops of coconut trees together while they graded and finished a 3,282-foot runway. Satellite fields on Vila and Kolombangara Island were also operational, so though the counteroffensive was an illusion, Yamamoto's plan to hold the central Solomons was not.

The bases were attacked nearly every day, and though the Royal New Zealand Air Force (RNZAF) sent Hudson bombers when it could, the strikes were overwhelmingly American. Within that category, the true hard hitting was done by the Army Air Force, which had finally gotten into the air war in force. B-17 heavy bombers of the 5th Bombardment Group, with B-26s from the 69th and 38th Bomb Groups, were escorted in by P-39s and, whenever possible, P-38s out of Guadalcanal. The Lightnings were a godsend for high-attitude, long-range escort, though the pilots hated it, and by New Year's Eve there were still only forty-one operational P-38s in the entire theater. Hindering the Japanese buildup in the central Solomons became the main American objective for early 1943. Yamamoto would never stop, and he knew that any hope of ending the war meant spilling so much American blood in an island campaign that Washington would be forced to negotiate.

There was still time, but not much.

Rex Barber, comfortably flying a hundred feet off Tom Lanphier's left wing, had been part of beating up Munda and the central Solomons. All through December, John Mitchell's and Lou Kittel's pilots had bombed, strafed, and fought. After Rex arrived days before Christmas, he and the other new P-39 pilots got a very brief refamiliarization in the Lightning. This consisted of reading the battered manual in the cockpit, then going through the engine sequence, radio operations, and emergency procedures with a current P-38 pilot. Back in October at Tontouta Air Base on

Nouméa, Rex and the others were given rudimentary checkouts in the new fighter, but they were just that: rudimentary.

Rex had passed the blindfolded cockpit check and could locate all the switches. As there were no two-seat Lightnings, the only way to learn about the plane in the air was to cram into the small space aft of the seat, and fly "piggyback" looking over the pilot's shoulder. He then did several solo flights around New Caledonia with another P-38 to practice formation flying, aircraft handling, and aerobatics, but it was nothing like a true checkout program. Nothing had been set up yet to train new pilots on different aircraft in theater and there wasn't time; this was combat, not the peacetime Army Air Force, and men were expected to just make it happen: and they did. As a qualified fighter pilot he was supposed to already know weapons and gunnery, so Barber just needed as much flying time as possible. When the scarce Lightnings weren't available he flew the Airacobra, which was how he was leading a two-ship element over Munda three days after Christmas. With Lieutenant Bill Daggitt as his wingman, Rex was trolling around New Georgia looking for targets.

He had found one.

A big two-engined, twin-tailed bomber with meatballs on top of the wings was descending through

1,000 feet on final approach to Munda. Rex, like all fighter pilots, had a little yellow box of government-issued recognition cards for all Japanese ships and aircraft. He'd never seen this one before, but knew it was a Mitsubishi G3M Type 96 bomber. The Japanese called it a "Rikko"; Americans nicknamed it the "Nell."

Yanking back on the big red handles jutting from either side of the instrument panel, Rex charged the four .30-caliber Brownings in the wings, and both .50-caliber Brownings mounted in the nose cowling. Dropping his left hand down to the panel in front of the stick, he pulled a smaller handle to charge the cannon. Leaning back again, Barber slid the throttle aft, flipped the little fighter on its back, and dove down steeply to avoid the 20 mm cannon turret on the bomber's rear dorsal. The plane felt sluggish and, remembering that he'd forgotten to skin off his hundred-gallon belly tank, Rex roundly cursed himself, then jettisoned it. The tank came off, and the fighter bounced up suddenly. Swearing again, and with the Nell filling his N-3 optical gun sight, Rex simultaneously squeezed the trigger and mashed down on the cannon button atop the stick.

Shuddering from the recoil of six Brownings and the big cannon, the Airacobra seemed to slow down until he quit firing three seconds later. The bomber's

82-foot wingspan looked enormous at a few hundred feet and Barber yanked back on the stick with his right hand while slamming the throttle forward with his left. Slashing past, Rex saw pieces of the plane come off as the heavy lead chewed through it. He'd heard Japanese planes weren't very sturdy, and this was proof. Orange and yellow plumes burst from the right engine, and thick black smoke boiled up over the fuselage as it dove into the Solomon Sea. No self-sealing tanks either, he noted, pulling away hard to avoid the air base and its antiaircraft guns. That was just as he'd been told. American or British aircraft, and a few German designs, lined fuel tanks with layers of rubber. U.S. manufacturers tended to use an outer vulcanized layer over an inner layer of natural rubber, which, when pierced, swelled up and absorbed the fuel. This prevented many explosions, obviated the extra weight of armored gas tanks, and made American aircraft much more survivable.

Fuel was always on a pilot's mind somewhere, even in combat. Fuel was life, and today's mission to Bougainville was absolutely no exception. Rex, according to procedure, had started up and taken off with his RESERVE tanks selected to ensure they were feeding correctly. After all sixteen fighters joined up and began descending, he'd rotated both fuel system selectors to the DROP TANK ON position. Dropping his left hand down to the side panel by his thigh he touched both selectors anyway out of habit. They would remain in the three o'clock position until the drop tanks fed out. It would be different this time because they were of different capacities, and the smaller 165-gallon tank under his right wing would empty sooner.

In any event, he'd jettison both drop tanks over Bougainville because they weren't self-sealing, and had a nasty habit of exploding if hit by bullets. The extra weight and drag would also slow him down and make the Lightning less maneuverable. There should be sufficient internal fuel to get him home as long as he didn't get into a prolonged dogfight, which was an excellent way to die anyway. The Lightning had four internal tanks: two on the left side and two on the right in the wings between the engines and his gondola. The large main tanks were farther back, and the smaller reserves were directly off his shoulders. Between them they held more than three hundred gallons of fuel. It would be enough. It *had* to be enough.

Just short of an hour into the mission, John Mitchell's wings suddenly waggled up ahead, and Rex tensed slightly. After a few seconds the major's right wing dropped, and the P-38 smoothly banked up to the right. His wingmen followed and for a moment all four beautiful H-shaped fighters were poised on the fuzzy gray horizon as they came around heading northwest. Lanphier flew on till he reached the spot; Mitchell turned then did the same. Rex eased the power back, dropping slightly aft and low as the turn was into him. Playing the throttles and wheel, he kept his head lined up with the superchargers atop *Phoebe*'s right wing throughout the shallow bank.

Formation flying was basic for a fighter pilot and he did it unconsciously, yet Rex loved the technique and precision. His hands instantly converted what his eyes were seeing, and the Lightning moved accordingly, adjusting and readjusting constantly. He could see it all: the graceful curves of Lanphier's gondola, sunlight on the canopy so bright that the support railings vanished and the whole thing looked like a teardrop. The corner of his right eye caught Mitchell's flight rolling out, and Rex felt an unwelcome twinge of vertigo as those four planes were now straight and level and he was still turning. The lack of a horizon made it worse, but that's what *Phoebe* was for, a reference, so Barber simply flew off the other plane and ignored his own inner ear.

As Lanphier slowly and gently rolled out, Rex nudged the wheel left and added a bit of power. Sliding smoothly forward again, he moved out to thirty yards off *Phoebe*'s left wing, took a deep breath, and automatically scanned his gauges. Top right first; manifold pressure, RPM, and oil were all in the green. His eyes flickered up and left to Lanphier, then back down to the oil temperature and pressure. All good. His peripheral vision told him *Phoebe* was rock steady, so Rex squinted at the bifurcated engine coolant gauge on the panel over his left knee, then all the way over to the fuel. Everything was purring along as it should.

Hot. It was hot.

Leg Two had the fighters heading 290 degrees and the rising sun was directly behind them now. Rex glanced down at his strip map and squinted at the numbers: 83 miles to the next turn . . . 27 minutes. Though he was a flight lead himself, he was flying a wingman position on this mission and wasn't worried about navigating. That was Mitchell's and Lanphier's job today, so he'd simply jotted down the course, time, and distance in three columns on the back of his map. There was nothing to see anyway at fifty feet, so the best thing Rex could do was fly perfectly and in position. Vangunu was maybe thirty miles off his right wing, and farther north was Rendova. Just past it, on the southern tip of New Georgia, was Munda, and Barber's thoughts drifted back to Guadalcanal.

Nine more missions were flown against Munda in the month after Christmas, and also against other targets as far north as southern Bougainville. The

Japanese also intensified their raids on Guadalcanal in order to disguise their real intention to evacuate the 17th Army. By the end of the month, Rex wasn't certain the island was secure. General Patch, who believed a counteroffensive was imminent, did not move quickly to attack the beleaguered Japanese holed up on the northwest side of Guadalcanal, and the 339th ranged as far north as Papua New Guinea to harass the Japanese. Aircraft revetments, previously lacking on enemy airfields, suddenly appeared and this substantiated the belief that Yamamoto was determined to hold the line in the Solomons. Photo reconnaissance discovered at least seventy-two, and forty-four of them were on Munda.

On January 5, John Mitchell and Besby Holmes each shot down a floatplane over Tonolei Harbor east of Buin, and Rex built up P-38 time escorting bombers or shooting up targets in the central Solomons. Mid-January saw the activation of the 13th Air Force at Nouméa under Major General Nathan Twining, who promptly moved his headquarters five hundred miles farther forward to Espiritu Santo. P-38 production and delivery was picking up, and at least five more fighters were guaranteed in theater every month by spring, and more if the worldwide demand allowed.

Mitch got his seventh kill at the end of the month,

and it was a particularly sweet victory. Since August 1942 several types of Japanese planes had been making annoying night bombing runs over Henderson Field, interrupting repair work, occasionally killing Americans, and always costing precious sleep. Single-engined floatplanes launched from cruisers or Rekata Bay were collectively named Louie the Louse, while the twin-engined Betty bombers from Rabaul became "Washing Machine Charlie" because it "sounded like an old Maytag washer with a gasoline motor." Everyone on the Canal hated them, but without night fighters there wasn't much to be done about it. Mitchell was given permission to try and on January 29, 1943, just before sunrise, he caught up with the last Charlie of the night. After a concentrated burst of .50-caliber bullets and 20 mm cannon shells it spun down into the Slot in flames.

Three nights later Yamamoto sent twenty-one Japanese destroyers under Rear Admiral Shintaro Hashimoto down New Georgia Sound toward Guadalcanal to conduct a daring, superbly executed operation. Hashimoto was sighted north of Vella Lavella at 1320 and attacked by a fifty-one-aircraft wave, including four 339th Lightnings, yet he did not turn back and arrived off Guadalcanal by 2210. Making 30 knots toward

Cape Esperance the Japanese destroyers were suddenly confronted by at least eight PT boats from Squadrons 2, 3(2), and 6, and a furious night battle ensued as escorting floatplanes spotted the torpedo boats by their wakes. Nevertheless, twenty of Hashimoto's destroyers fought their way through, and two hours after midnight 4,935 soldiers of the 38th Infantry Division were evacuated near Cape Esperance and Kamimbo.

"What a sad and pitiable sight they presented," a young soldier aboard ship later wrote. "Hardly human beings, they were just skin and bones dressed in military uniform." Six months of combat, starvation, and unrelenting American attacks had reduced the Imperial Army's finest to walking bones. "[T]heir beards, nails, and hair had all stopped growing . . . their buttocks were so emaciated that their anuses were completely exposed . . . they suffered from constant and uncontrollable diarrhea."

The following day, February 2, 1943, John Mitchell led four P-38s on a B-17 escort mission to Shortland harbor, and shot down another Nakajima A6M2-N "Rufe," his third floatplane fighter and eighth kill of the war. This was the same day Americans on the Canal heard that the entire German Sixth Army had surrendered to the Russians at Stalingrad, so it seemed the Japanese were not the only parts of the Axis learning the price of hubris and arrogance.*

All day long the retreating Japanese lit campfires, then moved north toward their embarkation points to deceive the American Army—and they succeeded. General Patch was of the opinion that the nightly destroyer runs had recommenced to bring in reinforcements, not evacuate the 17th Army.

Forty-eight hours later, under a clear, moonless night, the Tokyo Express was back, and in two hours pulled out 3,921 soldiers, including General Hyakutake. They reached Bougainville at 1250 on February 5, 1943. While Patch's Doggies slogged their way across the Bonegi and Segilau Rivers, John Mitchell, Rex Barber, and the other 339th pilots patrolled the northwest coast of Guadalcanal, but the Japanese rear guard under Colonel Matsuda remained concealed. Other flights of Wildcats, P-40s, and Dauntlesses headed up the Slot to attack eighteen destroyers of the incoming Tokyo Express, but were intercepted by forty-nine Zeros, who blunted their assault.

Three minutes past midnight on February 7, 1943,

---

* Out of 91,000 taken prisoner, fewer than 5,000 would eventually return to Germany in 1955.

the last of 1,796 men who could be taken off the island were aboard ship and the evacuation from Guadalcanal was complete. Stopping long enough to snatch the Russell Islands garrison, the destroyers headed up the Slot for the last time. From nearly 36,000 men who landed on the Canal, the 17th Army evacuated 10,652, but left behind 14,800 killed or missing, 1,000 captured, and another 9,000 dead from disease or starvation. The Imperial Navy lost 138,000 tons of warships, including two battleships and a light aircraft carrier. Most damaging, some 620 aircraft with 900 to 1,600 highly trained aircrews were dead, and could not be replaced. The 11th Air Fleet effectively ceased to exist as a fighting force after Guadalcanal.

At 1650 on the afternoon of February 9, 1943, the 1st Battalion, 161st Infantry joined up with the 2nd Battalion Task Force at Tenaro, just short of Cape Esperance. General Patch wired, "Total and complete defeat of Japanese forces on Guadalcanal. . . . Tokyo Express no longer has a terminus on Guadalcanal." To arrive at that historic day cost the United States 1,207 Marines killed, and another 2,894 wounded, while Army losses stood at 1,298 killed with another 562 wounded. Two fleet carriers, *Hornet* and *Wasp*, were sunk along with six heavy cruisers, two light cruisers, and fifteen destroyers. Though 264 aircraft and 420 crews were lost, the United States could recover while the Japanese could not.

Rex Barber was well aware that without the American victory on Guadalcanal there would be no reason for Isoroku Yamamoto to leave the safety of his flagship and travel to the forward area at Ballale. There would be no airfield at Fighter Two from which *Miss Virginia, Phoebe,* and the others could launch to reach the Bougainville coast. He also knew that this mission was much more than a fighter sweep to shoot down Japanese planes; it was even more than the chance to kill Yamamoto and avenge Pearl Harbor.

Today was a symbol of how far the United States had come in the sixteen months since Pearl Harbor. That America had the ability to hit hard, deep, and suddenly into enemy territory; to strike at the heart of Japan's morale, and threaten their spirit as nothing yet had done. If Rex and the other fighter pilots were successful today they would send a message not even the Japanese could misunderstand: Your days of offensive operations are over, and your god-emperor cannot save you. Everything you believe is going to get you killed because we are coming to get you. The battle for Guadalcanal was over: it was time to go get the man responsible.

Rex followed the war news and rumors like everyone else. War clouds were still heavy in early 1943, and though the Allies were fighting back hard, the issue was still very much in doubt. Hitler's Sixth Army was surrounded at Stalingrad, and with the Japanese clearly foundering on Guadalcanal, President Roosevelt buoyantly announced, "The Axis knew they must win the war in 1942 or lose everything." His January 6 State of the Union address was proud and optimistic, just what the nation needed, and the pilots on Guadalcanal chuckled at the text. "I suspect Hitler and Tojo will find it difficult to explain to the German and Japanese people just why it is that 'decadent and inefficient democracy' can produce such phenomenal quantities of weapons, munitions and equipment—and fighting men!"

By the time Roosevelt made his speech some 70 percent of U.S. manufacturing was dedicated to the war effort, with stupendous results that confirmed Yamamoto's dire predictions. It had taken a year to renovate old factories, construct new ones, and retool them all for war production. Machine tools were the key; virtually any product could be mass produced with the right lathes, saws, grinders, and drill presses, but in 1940 only a few hundred firms in America manufactured every machine tool. This changed quickly.

Electrified by the grim threat of the Axis, capitalistic initiative coupled with the flexibility and capability of a free-market economy was turning out matériel on an unprecedented scale.

Ironically, the Soviet Union took delivery of 20,380 two-and-a-half-ton General Motors trucks that the "worker's paradise" was unable to manufacture for itself, along with some 14,000 aircraft and more than 12,000 tanks. When the Red Army eventually marched into Berlin it did so in 15,417,000 pairs of American-made boots. Future marshal of the Soviet Union Georgy Zhukov later stated, "[T]he Americans gave us so many goods without which we wouldn't have been able to form our reserves and continue the war. We didn't have explosives, gunpowder. We didn't have anything to charge our rifle cartridges with. The Americans really saved us with their gunpowder and explosives. And how much sheet steel they gave us! How could we have produced our tanks without American steel? Without American trucks we wouldn't have had anything to pull our artillery with."

Baldwin Locomotive, Chrysler, and the American Car Foundry were all producing tanks. Not one had been manufactured in the United States in 1940, yet 29,495 would roll off various assembly lines in 1943 alone. Companies all over the nation had become defense contractors; Underwood Typewriters of New York, along with jukebox maker Rock-Ola of Chicago, were now turning out M1 carbines; Ames constructed 11 million trenching tools; and Frigidaire was manufacturing .30-caliber machine guns.

Due to wartime censorship, Rex, in Oregon, had not heard about the shipbuilding boom, which would perhaps do as much to win the war as those actually fighting. Winston Churchill eloquently wrote that "the foundation of all our hopes and schemes was the immense shipbuilding program of the United States." Though not glamorous, the "Liberty" shipbuilding program made the transport of men and vast amounts of matériel possible. They were small: only 441 feet long, and displacing a mere 14,245 tons. They were ugly: boxy, straight lines whenever possible so the plates could be welded, instead of riveted, to save time. They were slow; diesel engines went to submarines, and precision-made, powerful steam turbines were for fast surface warships, so the new merchantmen got what was left: reciprocating engines that nudged them forward at a stupefying top speed of 12 mph.

There were no creature comforts. No running water, and no electricity; oil lamps were used. The entire vessel was steel, except for concrete in the toilet areas and wooden hatch covers that doubled as floatation devices in case the ship went down, as nearly three hundred did. *Star of Oregon*, the first Liberty ship commissioned, took 253 days to construct and outfit. This would decrease to an average time of 42 days, and 160 new cargo ships were launched per month by mid-1943. It seemed that most of Oregon, with exceptions like Rex Barber, were employed by one of Henry J. Kaiser's three shipyards turning out Liberty ships, tankers, and new escort carriers that only carried a few dozen aircraft, but were invaluable for the accelerating Pacific campaigns, or protecting merchant convoys bringing ammunition and fuel to far-flung islands like Guadalcanal.

Yet despite the desperate global situation in 1943, a perennial thorn in industry's side were labor unions. Worker strikes during the darkest days of the war were common, and while American fighting men were dying in the Pacific and North Africa, thousands of Pennsylvania coal workers stalked from their mines demanding a two-dollar-a-day raise. This was at a time when the base pay of enlisted marines in the Pacific was $50 per month, and fighter pilots officers like Rex Barber made $167.67 each month.*

---

* U.S. Army Pay Table (effective June 1, 1942). All the services utilized the same table, and those with extra-dangerous duty like paratroopers or pilots received additional allowances.

U.S. Marines died on Cape Gloucester, and heavy bombers went down over Kiel, while 60,000 draft-deferred miners sulkily dropped their tools and walked off the job, as did workers at two dozen vital plants in Detroit. Reviled by the press and universally despised by the millions of families with loved ones in combat, the workers returned to their jobs after President Roosevelt threatened to rescind their deferments and put them into the very fighting they had avoided. In 1943 alone, such contemptible actions cost 13.5 million man-days, enough to build some 15,000 B-24 bombers, or six *South Dakota*–class battleships. Nevertheless, U.S. war production was twice that of the combined output from Germany and Japan.

But the German military was over three million strong, and the Japanese had twenty-five divisions in China alone that could be committed to the Pacific. U-boats were sinking 500,000 to 600,000 tons of shipping *per month* for most of 1942, and in March 1943, ninety-seven Allied merchantmen went to the bottom of the ocean. Without the flow of matériel to Britain or the Soviet Union the war could not be won—yet. American industrial might combined with millions of men under arms had not triumphed yet, and if the Japanese could exact a high cost in blood, Washington might consider a separate peace in order to deal with Hitler.

This was Yamamoto's strategic hope, at any rate, so he needed every soldier possible to make it happen. By January 14 the Imperial General Staff approved Operation "KE," the evacuation of the 17th Army from Guadalcanal. It was formally called *tenshin,* or an "advance in another direction," but those Japanese in combat against the Americans did not doubt its true meaning. Warrant Officer Saburo Sakai, Japan's top ace who was mauled in a dogfight over Guadalcanal and sent home to recover, later wrote: "I had lost all my optimism, and that our Navy fliers at Rabaul, despite their many successes, were now waging an uphill battle . . . the American Navy pilots we encountered over Guadalcanal were the best I have ever fought, and their tactics were superb. And their planes are certain to improve."

Rex Barber was certain of that.

He was completely at home in the Lightning and knew it to be the best fighter currently in theater. Rex had heard about the Navy's new F6F Hellcat, a larger, tougher replacement for the venerable Wildcat, and rumored to now be operational aboard the new carrier *Essex.*★ There was also a big, new fighter with a huge engine and an eighteen-foot propeller that the Navy had

---

★ The Hellcat became operational with Lieutenant Commander Philip Torrey's VF-9 in February 1943.

trouble landing on carriers, so it was given to the Marines. Major Bill Gise, commander of the "Wild Aces" of VMF-124, led a dozen of the impressive, gull-winged F4U Corsairs onto the Canal in February 1943, but Barber loved the Lightning.

Especially this version of it, the P-38G.

For him, the biggest difference was the power plant: a pair of Allison V-1710 engines that could sustain 1,150 hp, or 400 mph, each at 25,000 feet. This made the P-38 a true high-speed, high-altitude fighter, which meant Rex could reach a target much faster, and use less fuel getting there. He could climb over bad weather, stay above antiaircraft fire, and fly high enough to make interception by a Japanese aircraft impossible. Of course, he had to eventually descend to attack, but the Lightning's magnificent engines always gave him an out; no Japanese plane could accelerate fast enough to catch him once he firewalled the throttles, nor could a Zero follow him six miles above the earth. Supercharged engines made this possible, just as it had with the earlier-model Lightning Rex had flown, and the P-38G used the new General Electric B-13 turbo superchargers. Engine technology such as this had changed tactics and was giving U.S. aircraft a measurable advantage in the air, all else being equal.

The other big improvement was visible on the right

bulkhead: the SCR-274N radio. Silent for now, and it would be until they were over Bougainville, the Very High Frequency (VHF) radio was another technical advantage that revolutionized air-to-air tactics. Rex, like all other American fighter pilots, was trained to use it on each mission. With plane-to-plane communications, a basic four-ship flight of aircraft could split into two fighting pairs; they could locate each other if separated and, most critically, they could combat an enemy in coordination with each other. Mutual support and the ability to protect each other, conduct search and rescue for a downed brother pilot, and combine firepower as a fighting team added up to a tactical advantage the Japanese could not match.

The Japanese didn't have workable radios; in fact, most of their fighter pilots removed the set to decrease weight. They exclusively used World War I–era hand signals, and did not fight as pairs. The ingrained Japanese doctrine of attack, even in a modern high-performance fighter, was their only tactic, and they would instantly swarm as individuals once a formation was broken. Mutual support was only available if one happened to see the other, which was extremely difficult in the big, three-dimensional sky of a dogfight. Japanese failure to recognize this deficiency and solve it was inexplicable, but Rex was happy for every mistake they made. They'd die quicker and he could go home.

By 1943 the captured Akutan Zero 21 flown by Petty Officer Koga had been fully exploited by the Navy and the results disseminated in several reports.* However, there were limits to the secrets it betrayed; the reconstructed Zero had lain in a bog for five weeks after crashing, and the subsequent evaluations were based solely on this one aircraft, but in late 1942 and early 1943 any hard information regarding enemy capabilities was useful. There were also wrecks of other Zeros that had been recovered, including one from China and nine from Pearl Harbor. This data, combined with the flight analysis of Koga's Zero and combat lessons derived by American pilots returning from the Pacific, painted a fairly complete picture.

All fighter pilots received intelligence briefings when there was time, and something to discuss. Mitchell's 339th was no exception, so Rex Barber and the others knew to stay fast against the Zero, and whenever

---

* "Flight Characteristics of the Japanese Zero Fighter Zeke," Informational Intelligence Summary No. 85, Intelligence Service, U.S.A.A.F., December 1942. "Performance and Characteristics Trials, Japanese Fighter," Technical Aviation Brief #3, Aviation Intelligence Branch, Navy Department, November 4, 1942.

possible avoid a low-altitude, slow-speed dogfight as the Japanese fighter could easily turn quicker, thereby bringing its guns to bear first. If a Zero got behind you they'd also been taught to dive away, preferably with negative g's, until above 200 knots, then turn hard right since the Zero's aileron's became stiff and hard to use above that speed. The P-38's top speed of 400 mph was at least 50 mph faster than the Zero's, and the Japanese fighter could not follow a Lightning in a full-power climb. It was another area of exclusion that Barber and the others were keen to utilize in combat whenever possible.

Rex also knew to attack from above, whenever possible, which is one reason he thought today's mission stood a decent chance of success; Lightnings were rarely seen *below* Japanese fighters since the preferred tactic was to dive through an enemy formation, scatter them, then pick the Zeros off one by one. The Japanese would not be expecting a low-altitude attack from the Solomon Sea side of Bougainville and would not be looking in that direction. His enemy's ongoing arrogance puzzled Rex, and many others, as by April 1943 the Japanese had ample proof of American fighting ability.

Hot. It was hot. The Allisons were throbbing rhythmically, level flight was monotonous, and there was nothing to look at except Lanphier's Lightning. Despite the strain of flying low over water and deep into enemy territory, Rex felt the first dragging claws of drowsiness. Lifting the dangling mask to his face, Rex reached between his legs and selected 100 percent oxygen, then inhaled deeply. It tasted like dry plastic, but as the pure oxygen flowed into his lungs and entered his bloodstream Rex's vision felt sharper, and his mind cleared. This model of P-38 also carried an improved oxygen system that incorporated a low-pressure bottle for lower altitudes, and a high-pressure demand regulator that he could select that would force oxygen through his mask. There was also an independent emergency bottle that he could use if the main system failed, which enabled a pilot to stay conscious long enough to descend to low altitude, where no oxygen was needed.

Combat loaded to 15,800 pounds, the P-38G could also carry a 2,000 general-purpose bomb under each wing. This made the plane 4,000 pounds altogether, only 800 pounds lighter than a B-17 Flying Fortress. Rex's eyes continued their automatic cross-check of the cockpit gauges, then to *Phoebe* and back again. Keeping awake was tough; he tried counting dolphins and whales, but there were too many. One thing the Lightning did not have was a decent cockpit cooling system, or a heater for that matter, not that he'd need that today. Still, the heat would continue to be a problem if he wasn't flying at fifty feet over shark infested waters, though he wondered how the major, leading the flight with no one to watch, was faring. Even as he glanced ahead, Rex saw the lead four-ship come slightly right and he knew Leg Three had begun.

In fact, John Mitchell *was* having trouble with the heat.

"Oh, man it was hot," he later recalled. "Just like every day was out there, and at that altitude . . . the heat in the cockpit . . . and one wave looks just like another, so I probably dozed off once or twice."

He'd just made a small, 15-degree check turn to the right. A touch of the rudders, actually, barely a turn at all. Squinting at the glare shield, he was thankful again for the big, six-inch-diameter ship's compass. The white line over his heading was easy to see: 305 degrees. Peering down, he flattened the torn piece of notepaper with his hand. Like the back of Barber's map, it was very basic: three columns labeled "Course," "Time," and "Distance." This leg would take thirty-eight minutes and bring the fighters 125 miles closer to Bougainville.

After this leg they'd make a 90-degree right turn toward Empress Augusta Bay, and the island's southeast coastline. Mitchell had two worries and one hope.

The first worry was that Yamamoto would not be on time; early or late, it would have the same effect on the mission. If Mitch led his fighters over land they would most certainly be mobbed by enemy planes, and he couldn't very well orbit over Bougainville waiting for the admiral to show up, nor could he reverse course and disappear back out to sea they way they'd come in. There wasn't enough fuel for that. The major had, of course, already thought it out because thinking ahead to handle contingencies was something a flight lead did. If Yamamoto did not show up on time, the only thing Mitch could do was sweep southeast over the island, shoot down anything in his way, then climb up above 35,000 feet out of Japanese reach and fly straight home down the Slot.

The other nagging concern was being discovered before he made landfall and attacked. By necessity, the route carried his fighters over the exact piece of the Solomon Sea used by Japanese warships steaming from Rabaul down to Buin or the Shortlands. One thing about the P-38 was that it could not be mistaken for anything else, so if the major was sighted he knew their location would be immediately transmitted to the eighty Zero fighters waiting at Kahili. Honestly, that was also a hope as long as it didn't interfere with his mission, and was the main reason Mitch was leading the cover flight rather than the Killer flight; he wanted to mix it up with the Zeros and chew them to pieces. The five-to-one odds didn't bother him a bit. "I had wanted for a long time to make a fighter sweep up there with the whole squadron," he recounted. "We were told there were at least 75 Zeros at Kahili, and I wanted a piece of that. I thought we'd have a real turkey shoot. If I'd have known they weren't going to send the fighters up, I would have made the attack."

Of course, the true hope was that Yamamoto would show up where the code-breakers said he would be, at exactly the right time, and completely unaware of the fighter ambush. If that happened, Mitchell's Lightnings would kill the admiral for Pearl Harbor, for all American blood lost since December 7, 1941, and to deprive the Japanese of the one leader capable of prolonging the war. If Yamamoto did appear where U.S. intelligence predicted, then John Mitchell, Rex Barber, and the other fighter pilots on today's mission would send Yamamoto straight to hell in a broken, burning airplane—or die trying.

Ten
The Eight-Fingered Samurai

A location, a time, and a target.

A professional fighter pilot needs nothing else, up to a point, and Major John Mitchell met the challenge perfectly. Working backward from the time his target would be over a certain location had been paradoxically quite straightforward and tremendously complicated. In parallel with the plan he needed the men to carry it out and, equally vital, the logistics to get his fighters into the air. Mitchell's armorers sweated through the night manhandling belts of ammunition into the noses of eighteen Lightnings, and once the drop tanks arrived it was discovered that some of the underwing mounts did not fit. They had to be hand chiseled and the tanks muscled into place. If it wasn't done correctly then they wouldn't jettison, or they might come off badly and damage the rudders.

While the pilots had ironed out the mission flow, communication plan, contingencies for poor weather, airborne mechanical malfunctions, and dozens of other details, the maintenance crews worked continuously on the planes. They fixed electrical issues, replaced worn tires, repaired switches and knobs. There were literally hundreds of problems, major and minor, that had to be handled to get every P-38 possible into the air. Once airborne, literally millions of perfectly timed explosions and tens of thousands of moving pieces kept Mitchell and Barber heading northwest toward Bougainville. While this occurred, the man responsible for all the concentrated effort and risk was unaware of the difficulties he was causing.

Isoroku Yamamoto had other problems.

Since transferring his flag to the giant battleship *Musashi* in February, the harsh realities of the Pacific War and weight of command were wearing on him. "I've been ashore four times since August to visit the sick and wounded, to attend services for the dead, and so on," the admiral wrote to his friend Toshiko Furukawa, "but apart from that I've been stuck on board." He was increasingly withdrawn. His hair had gone gray, and it had been suggested by his Harvard classmate Isamu Morimura that Yamamoto's mistress Chiyoko be flown to Truk to lift his spirits.

The 17th Army's evacuation from "Starvation Island," as the Japanese called Guadalcanal, had hit him hard. The Pacific was always meant to be a naval war, and there was no Japanese amphibious assault force similar to the U.S. Marines, so the army was only meant to hold ground. Also, the Imperial Army was meant to fight a continental war against the Russians and Chinese; they were not organized, trained, or equipped for a jungle war against the Americans or Australians. Despite this, the Imperial Navy's inability to keep them supplied and safe was a tremendous failure Yamamoto could not overlook, and he now feared an Allied advance through New Guinea and the Solomons: a giant pincer that would snap shut on his great base at Rabaul.

But he had a plan.

By pulling back in the Solomons to a defensive line north of New Georgia, the admiral aimed to strengthen his air bases on Bougainville and bloodily contest every yard the Americans advanced. To halt MacArthur in the west, Yamamoto would need to reinforce Lae on New Guinea with the 51st Infantry Division. The strategy was to strike inland along the Black Cat Trail into the Owen Stanley Mountains to capture the Allied airfield at Wau. Once successful, he planned to mount an offensive against Port Moresby and Milne Bay that would recapture the Japanese initiative lost at Guadalcanal, and give the admiral one thing he desperately needed: time. He needed time to move the Imperial Army into the southwest Pacific, time to build airfields, and, most of all, time to replenish the depleted ranks of his naval aviators mauled by the Americans at Coral Sea, Midway, and the Guadalcanal campaign.

To this end, a sixteen-ship convoy labeled Operation 81 sortied from Rabaul's Simpson Harbor under the cover of darkness on February 28, 1943. Eight destroyers carrying 958 soldiers escorted eight transports with another 5,954 men of the 51st Division and 18th Army Headquarters. Sailing west through the night, the Japanese hugged New Britain's northern coast, which allowed one hundred Zeros operating in relays to cover the ships and theoretically shielded them from prying American eyes. Nevertheless, during the afternoon of March 1 as the convoy approached Cape Gloucester, it was sighted by a patrolling B-24 Liberator from the 43rd Bomb Group out of Port Moresby.

The following day both the Americans and the Royal Australian Air Force attacked the convoy, the escorting Zeros, and Lae with B-17s, B-24s, B-25s, and A-20

Bostons. Fighters were everywhere: P-38s from the 9th Fighter Squadron; 41st FS P-40s, and even P-39s from the 39th and 40th FS. Skip bombing, a technique adopted from the Royal Air Force, was used with devastating results. Just like skipping a stone, aircraft would attack just feet above the water, and the shallow angle caused the bombs to skip into the sides of ships. By March 3 all the transports had been sunk, and only four of the Japanese destroyers survived. Several thousand soldiers were rescued by submarines or destroyers, but at least three thousand perished. "Desperately needed supplies littered the Bismarck Sea . . . corpses floated in the oil, bloody waters," reports noted.

If the Imperial Army was unable to get into the fight and slow the American advance, then Yamamoto would do it from the air. His solution was *Ichi-gō Sakusen*, Operation A, which was shortened to *I-go*. To accomplish this the admiral stripped his aircraft carriers and land-based forces at Truk for the strength to derail the American advance through a series of massive aerial blows. From the 2nd and 3rd Carrier Divisions of his Third Fleet, Yamamoto deployed 96 fighters and 65 dive bombers, the combined air groups from *Shokaku, Zuikaku, Hiryo,* and *Zuiho,* to Rabaul and Ballale in the Shortland Islands. From the 11th Air Fleet he sent the 21st Air Flotilla Headquarters to Kavieng on

New Ireland, but most of the aircraft went to Rabaul. The 26th Air Flotilla at Kahili, near Buin, deployed to the southern end of Bougainville, and altogether this gave Yamamoto 346 aircraft, the largest single force mustered since his Pearl Harbor strike.

Superficially, this was an impressive number, but there were problems, including limited fuel for operations, a dislocation of the Third Fleet's carrier air groups, and a critically dwindling pool of experienced pilots. "Some of these men had behind them barely thirty days of carrier training," Commander Okumiya later wrote, "and our veteran air leaders hesitated to send the fledglings into combat against the aggressive and experienced American pilots." The 346 planes and crews represented the remaining bulk of Japan's frontline carrier aviation strength, less than it had begun the war with, after just eighteen months of combat. Japan had not effectively used the time Yamamoto gained from December 1941 until the U.S. invasion of the Solomons in August 1942, and he was aware of his own failings during this period.

Midway should have been the decisive nail in the American coffin, yet even after that failure the Imperial General Staff underestimated the Americans. The army still considered the Soviet Union its primary threat, and occupying China as a strategic necessity, though Yamamoto knew better. There were enough resources in Indochina and the Dutch East Indies to sustain the Empire, and an angry, industrialized, mobilized America was infinitely more dangerous than the landlocked Russians. The threat was in the Pacific, and that was where the Empire would live or die. The second mistake lay in not crushing the landing on the Canal. If the Imperial Army had been committed in force rather than thrown in piecemeal, then the admiral knew the island could have been retaken. With the subsequent annihilation of the only real American amphibious force in the Pacific, the admiral could have then continued south and east to cut the U.S. supply lines into Australia.

But Tokyo would not hear of it. Nor was he permitted to act.

"If army men are starving through lack of supplies, then the navy should be ashamed of itself," Yamamoto had said back in the fall of 1942. "I'll give you cover even if I have to bring the *Yamato* alongside Guadalcanal itself." He was forbidden to do so by an order from the Navy General Staff, but if the great battleships had arrived in Ironbottom Sound before the Cactus Air Force was firmly established, the fate of the 1st Marines would have been very different. As it was, the battle had been a close call; with Fletcher running and no supplies it was the raw courage of the infantrymen, and their limited artillery support, with a few Wild-cats and Airacobras that kept the American toehold on the island. This precarious position would not have withstood thousands of rounds from eighteen 18-inch guns from both battleships, intensive air attacks, and an overwhelming assault in force by the 17th Army.

Yamamoto had no intention of repeating Guadalca-nal. He knew *I-go* was a risk, but if successful it *could* buy him the time he needed. If enough American deaths were inflicted and enough confusion generated, then New Guinea and the northern Solomons could be held. Perhaps bad headlines, lengthy casualty lists, and an obviously lethal Axis would persuade Roosevelt to make a deal. If not, the admiral was perfectly willing to go down fighting for his country and his emperor. It was a gamble from an inveterate gambler; he had taken chances all his life, and was quite prepared to take an-other.

On April 1, 1943, the operation commenced with two waves of fifty-eight Zeros and Val dive bombers against the new American base in the Russell Islands, and any shipping found around Guadalcanal. At 1023 the new radar site on Banika detected the Japanese strike 125 miles up the Slot as it got airborne, formed up, and headed south. "Mainyard," as Guadalcanal was now known, was ready and six P-38s, eight Corsairs, and thirty-four Wildcats intercepted the first wave at 1100. Over the next three hours twenty-one Japanese were lost at the cost of six American aircraft. Excitable and inexperienced, many of the Japanese pilots were wildly extravagant with their claims of ships sunk and facilities destroyed. According to Radio Tokyo, all thirty-four Wildcats were shot down along with ten Lightnings and three Corsairs.

Whether Yamamoto believed all that is unknown, though he undoubtedly appreciated the morale boost it gave his pilots. What is certain is that with so much at stake the admiral decided to command the operation himself, and do it from the forward area. Commander Okumiya was explicit: "Yamamoto hoped that his personal presence in the Rabaul area would spur his instructors to bring these student pilots to a point where they could fly against the enemy with some chance of survival."

Weather closed in after the first day of Operation A, and the admiral was forced to delay his departure. Word reached him that the U.S. 11th Air Force was bombing the Aleutian Islands, and Japanese positions in Burma were under attack by American B-25s based in India. He was cheered by several letters from his mistress as well as gifts she had sent along, including real soap and a cotton kimono for Yamamoto's birthday, April 4. In his reply he wrote, "I feel I can go cheerfully now I've heard all about you. I feel happy at the chance to do something." On Saturday morning, April 3, 1943, the commander in chief of the Combined Fleet carefully climbed down the *Musashi*'s starboard ladder and stepped into his gray motor launch. From here it was a brief ride across the lagoon to the Natsushima seaplane base at Dublon, where Yamamoto and his staff boarded two huge, four-engined Kawanishi H8K flying boats. A short time later both planes lumbered into the air, circled once over *Musashi,* then headed south for the 812-mile journey to Rabaul.

Landing at Rabaul by early afternoon, the flying boat, called an "Emily" by the Allies, taxied slowly across the calm water and up the ramp of the Sulphur Creek Seaplane Base on the east side of Simpson Harbor. After being greeted by his fleet admirals, Yamamoto was driven along Mango Avenue less than a half mile into the hills and down a short, graded dirt driveway. At the end was a low white building with an elegant white entry portico flanked by two wings that angled off toward the trees. Lined with windows, the interior's high ceilings and polished wood floors kept it dark and cool. Built as the highly exclusive New Guinea Club before the war, it was now the Imperial

Navy's Southeast Area Fleet Headquarters. Admiral Jinichi Kusaka, the fleet commander, welcomed Yamamoto and gave him the former German governor's cottage that overlooked the harbor on Residency Hill.

Results from Operation A's first day were encouraging, at least as they were reported, and Yamamoto chose to accept them. Even now the Americans were striking targets at Kavieng in New Ireland and here as well, less than three hundred miles to the west on Cape Gloucester. Yamamoto did not want to be here in New Guinea, but ingrained centuries of samurai duty were impossible to ignore, and he was certain Rabaul would be the next main Allied objective. As the principal Imperial base in the region it had to be, and the admiral had no intention of losing it, but he needed time to get the army here in force.

Between the China Expeditionary Force and the Kwantung Army there were at least 620,000 idle soldiers who could be available in the South Pacific. Another four complete armies were deployed from Sumatra up to the Philippines, Formosa, and across to Burma. Equally important was the Japanese Army Air Service, and its 1,400 frontline combat aircraft. Two groups had been at Rabaul since December 1942, but what a difference they could have made four months earlier. Unlike many naval officers, Yamamoto recognized the interservice rivalry as counterproductive and remained on good terms with many army field officers, particularly Lieutenant General Hitoshi Imamura, commander of the 8th Army in Rabaul. Time. If he could buy some time, the army could be brought here, and committed as it should have been in August, in force.

Yamamoto would not allow the same scenario to occur on New Britain, and this time he had an unequivocal statement from the emperor himself. "Give enough thought to your plans so that Law and Salamaua do not become another Guadalcanal." It was plain, even to the Imperial Army, that another such failure was insupportable. With army troops, armor, and aircraft from China or Malaya, a combined operation, such as the Americans were using so successfully, could be planned. At the very least, the defenses could be shored up to the point where any Allied advance could become prohibitively costly, and if this occurred there might be room for negotiation with Washington. The possibilities were tantalizing: a withdrawal from the Axis, a separate peace with Russia, and perhaps even a rapprochement of sorts with the United States that would give them a free hand to deal with Germany

While awaiting clear weather to resume *I-go*, Yamamoto visited the hospital to chat with his sick or wounded men, and played endless games of *shogi** with Captain Yasuji Watanabe, one of his staff officers and a close friend. He also discussed strategy and operation with his admirals, watched the harbor traffic, and talked to everyone. The admiral cooked sea turtle sukiyaki, and produced a bottle of Johnnie Walker Black Label scotch for five of his former naval academy classmates who were stationed in Rabaul. Yamamoto also listened carefully to American radio broadcasts, and translated them for his officers. Through these it seemed he learned for the first time that his masterstroke at Oahu had occurred *before* the formal declaration of hostilities. Knowing his enemy as he did, the admiral now fully grasped the outrage and hatred his enemy felt over the Pearl Harbor attack.

"So we were too early, all the same," Yamamoto said to Watanabe, who later wrote of the conversation. "That's bad. I don't know which of us will get killed first, but if I die before you, I'd like you to tell the emperor that the Combined Fleet certainly did not plan things that way."

By April 7 the weather broke and *I-go* resumed. Yamamoto insisted on seeing off the big raid that day, and

---

* A strategy board game in the same category as chess.

stood near the runway in his immaculate white uniform to wave good-bye to those aircraft flying from Rabaul. In all, the raid contained nearly 200 planes, 110 of them Zeros, which were to hit shipping, convoys, and an enemy task force at Tulagi. However, reconnaissance P-38s from the 17th PRS had discovered the buildup on April 6, and the Americans were ready. Coastwatchers reported the progress of large Japanese formations down the Slot, and Mainyard scrambled thirty-six Wildcats, thirteen P-39s, nine Corsairs, and six P-40s to meet the raiders. There were also a dozen P-38s from the 12th and 339th Fighter Squadrons, including Rex Barber, who got his second and third kills of the war over Savo Island.

One hundred planes were claimed by American antiaircraft gunners and fighter pilots but the real number, born out by Japanese records, was forty lost. This was still a big number, especially given Japan's lack of replacement pilots, and the significance was not lost on the staff officers. Raids were subsequently flown on April 11 against targets in eastern New Guinea; the next day Port Moresby was attacked, and on April 14 Milne Bay was hit. American losses reported to Yamamoto were 134 aircraft shot down, a cruiser, two destroyers, and twenty-five transports sunk against forty-nine Japanese aircraft downed.* Based on these numbers and his desire to maintain high morale, the admiral reached two decisions. First, he declared *I-go* a success and terminated the operation. Second, Yamamoto announced that to conclude his tour he would make a short, one-day visit to the actual front lines in the Shortland Islands to boost spirits as he had done in Rabaul.

Virtually no one except the admiral considered this a good idea, or worth the very considerable risk. But Yamamoto was the commander in chief of the Combined Fleet, second only to the emperor in terms of prestige, so if he desired this then it would happen. The plan was straightforward: a pair of G4M1 Betty bombers from the 705th Kokutai would fly the admiral and his staff 318 miles down to the new airstrip on Ballale, then he would travel by subchaser six miles across Shortland Harbor to the Faisi-Poporang naval base. Yamamoto would visit the sick and wounded, inspire by his presence, then travel back to Ballale, where he would board the Betty for a short, twenty-one-mile up to Buin. After lunch, both bombers would depart at 1400 and fly back to Rabaul.

* American losses were actually twenty-five planes, a destroyer, a corvette, two transports, and an oil tanker.

Admiral Ozawa of the Third Fleet attempted to dissuade his chief from going, but Yamamoto politely dismissed the concerns and on April 13, utilizing the JN-25D cipher, Kusaka's staff neatly encoded times and destinations into a secret message. The format was approved, and the admiral's detailed itinerary was sent to the 11th Air Flotilla, 26th Air Flotilla, and Base Unit Number One in the Shortlands. Rear Admiral Joshima, commander of the 11th Air Flotilla units on Shortland Island, flew to Rabaul on April 17 to convince Yamamoto not to make the trip, but to no avail. "What a damn fool thing to do," Joshima remembered. "To send such a long and detailed message about the activities of the Commander in Chief so near the front."

Indeed it was.

The message was intercepted immediately by three separate, highly classified stations: FRUMEL, which was Fleet Radio Unit, Melbourne, Australia; NEGAT in Washington, D.C.; and Station HYPO, which was the Fleet Radio Unit, Pacific, or FRUPAC, on Oahu. All three stations were linked together in order to quickly exchange and compare signals information. Talented cryptanalysts and linguists like Lieutenant Commander Thomas H. Dwyer, Major Alva B. Lasswell, and Lieutenant Commander John G. Roenigk recognized the message for the opportunity it was.

Herbert O. Yardley of the Military Intelligence Service had first broken the Japanese diplomatic code back in January 1920. Office of Naval Intelligence operatives also burgled the Japanese consulate in Washington and photographed the Imperial Navy code, which was designated JN-1. By 1930, as Yamamoto was heading for the London Naval Conference, U.S. Secretary of State Henry L. Stimson cut the knees out from under American military intelligence when he was briefed on the latest code-breaking capabilities. Famously and absurdly remarking that "Gentlemen do not read each other's mail," he shut off funding for the Office of Naval Intelligence's cryptographic office.

Stimson's idiocy notwithstanding, U.S. efforts eventually resumed and by the mid-1930s technical drawings of Japan's primary cipher machine had been stolen and a workable replica constructed. This was the Type-97 Print Machine, also known as a Type-B Cipher Machine, which U.S. intelligence code-named "Purple." Subsequently, everything related to Japanese crypto systems was compartmentalized as "Magic," with only a handful of men cleared for the raw material. This did not include the White House or State Department. Lasswell, who studied Japanese in Tokyo for three years and was based in both the Philippines and Shanghai, translated the first draft.

It was cleaned up and Lasswell hand-delivered it to Commander Edwin Layton, chief intelligence officer for Admiral Nimitz.

ON 18 APRIL CINC COMBINED FLEET WILL VISIT RYZ, R____ AND RXP IN ACCORDANCE WITH THE FOLLOWING SCHEDULE:

1. DEPART RR AT 0600 INA MEDIUM ATTACK PLANE ESCORTED BY 6 FIGHTERS. ARRIVE AT RXZ AT 0800. PROCEED BY MINESWEEPER TO R___ ARRIVING 0840. (____ HAVE MINESWEEPER READY AT #1 BASE) DEPART R____ AT 0945 IN ABOVE MINESWEEPER AND ARRIVE RXZ AT 1030? (____) DEPART RXZ AT 1100? IN MEDIUM ATTACK PLANE AND ARRIVE AT RXF AT 1110. DEPART RXP AT 1400 IN MEDIUM ATTACK PLANE AND ARRIVE RR AT 1530.

The report was dropped on the Pacific Fleet commander's desk just past 0800 on April 14, 1943. Layton, a Japanese language expert himself, knew Yamamoto personally from his years in Tokyo and never hesitated. "Admiral Nimitz, it would be just as if they shot you down. There isn't anybody to replace you." Layton knew his enemy, and was aware that for the Japanese, the loss of Yamamoto would be professionally disastrous, and personally demoralizing. Chester Nimitz also knew the admiral from a 1937 trip to Emperor Hirohito's favorite game preserve, but he had higher-level concerns about ordering an attempt on his life. Assassinations were not, publicly at least, typical American solutions. Yet this was war, and no one would question killing Hitler, Mussolini, or Tojo given the chance, so Yamamoto was no different in that light.

A very real concern, for Nimitz and especially U.S. intelligence, was how to explain the sudden appearance of American fighters over Bougainville exactly as the commander in chief of the Combined Fleet happened to be descending to land. Through arrogance and carelessness the Japanese had never discovered that their codes were compromised; this advantage for Nimitz and his tactical commanders was priceless, so the overriding question was if one man's life was worth an immediate change in the enemy codes. It could take months to crack a new code, and how many American lives would that cost in the meantime? Avenging Pearl Harbor was a significant consideration, but was payback for those dead men worth more dead men?

However, another powerful motivation for vengeance also loomed in the gray areas. Rumors of Japanese atrocities had circulated from the beginning of their involvement in China but Nimitz, and other highly placed figures, had more concrete information. More than 200,000 men, women, and children had been massacred by the Imperial Army at Nanjing, and 20,000 rapes occurred. Documentation had filtered out from Chinese burial societies, Western diplomats, and reliable eyewitnesses. The Chinese, insisted Tokyo, were armed bandits and not legitimate soldiers; therefore they were not entitled to any protections. This did not, and never has, explained the civilian deaths.

There was no such doubt with Russian prisoners captured in 1938. One particularly heinous instance occurred at Lake Khasan, in the disputed border region between China and the Soviet Union. A young Russian lieutenant was wounded, captured, then tortured by the Japanese. When his body was found, a large hammer-and-sickle had been carved into his chest, and rifle cartridges hammered into his eyes. The officer's tongue was ripped out, the soles of his feet burned, and his penis cut off.

The Japanese Empire was, in fact, a signatory to the "Convention relative to the Treatment of Prisoners of War," signed in Geneva on July 27, 1929, and put into force June 19, 1931. Much has been made of the fact that the Convention was never *ratified* by the Diet; however, Japan was still legally bound by the signed and ratified obligations of the 1907 Fourth Hague Convention.* Among other clauses, this plainly states, "Prisoners of war are in the power of the hostile Government, but not of the individuals or corps who capture them. They must be humanely treated."

China aside, rumors began after the fall of Singapore on Christmas Day 1941. Atrocities were commonplace, but at 0600 soldiers of the 23rd Army burst into St. Stephen's College, which was being utilized as a field hospital. Japanese infantrymen bayoneted some seventy wounded Allied soldiers in their beds, murdered at least two doctors, and gang-raped all the nurses before killing them. Roland James Barrett, a Canadian army chaplain, later testified that "it [the hospital] was in a dreadful state. I found two men who been taken out of our room. Their bodies were badly mutilated, their ears, tongues, noses and eyes had been cut away from their faces."

Reports reached the British and Americans, who demanded explanations and that Japan honor the rules of war. During January 1942, Foreign Minister Shigenori Togo made a public declaration that his coun-

---

* Unsurprisingly, the Soviet Union also did not recognize the 1929 Geneva Convention.

try would honor the Geneva Convention, though only after it made such changes as it deemed necessary. In other words, Japan would interpret the internationally accepted rules of war, law, and civilized behavior as it wished. This began an abominable pattern of loathsome treatment that continued all through the war, and even for weeks following Japan's surrender.

Singapore fell in February 1942, and every patient in Alexandra Hospital was bayoneted, including a soldier on the operating table and his surgeon. Sixty-five army nurses from the 13th Australian General Hospital were evacuated by a ship named the *Vynor Brook* in advance of the surrender. Putting in at the island of Banka for supplies, the boat was captured by the Japanese. Divided into two groups, the men were marched away down the beach around a headland and shot. The nurses were forced to walk into the surf, and were machine gunned from behind. Captain Vivian Bullwinkel of the Australian Nursing Service recounted, "I saw the girls fall one after the other until I was hit. The bullet that hit me entered my back at about waist level and passed straight through." She passed out in the waves but was washed up on the beach, where she remained unconscious for fifteen hours, believed to be dead by the Japanese, who simply left the bodies where they lay.

By April 1943 American leaders were under no illusions concerning the vile behavior of Imperial forces, especially following Marine experiences during the Guadalcanal campaign. Captured Allied aviators in particular bore the brunt of Japanese barbarism. The survivors from two of Jimmy Doolittle's raiders were captured in China and eventually the pilots of both planes, Lieutenants Dean Hallmark and Bill Farrow, were executed along with Corporal Harold Spatz.

The average Japanese soldier or sailor was a lower-class, often rural, individual with a rudimentary education and was the product of a harsh, uncompromising military system. Inoculated with versions of Japanese nationalism and a perversion of the *bushido* code, he was too ignorant to question his instructions, and would not have done so under any circumstance. Japanese officers, by virtue of their social class and education, should have known better—and they did. Yet as one officer summarized it after the war, "we shall be the victors and will not have to answer questions." It never occurred to them that the Empire could lose, and so their conduct did not matter.

These acts, and thousands more like them, were carried out under the direct orders or with the tacit approval of commissioned officers; this included admirals and generals who were, by virtue of their positions, responsible for the conduct of their men. Rear

Admiral Kouichiro Hatakeyama, commander of the 1st Kure Special Naval Landing Force at Ambon, ordered two hundred Dutch and Australian prisoners killed because the prisoners were an inconvenience to advancing Japanese.

Lieutenant Nakagawa, who carried out the executions, later wrote: "We dug holes and killed the prisoners with swords or bayonets. It took about two hours. They were taken one by one to the spot where they were to die, and made to kneel down with a bandage over their eyes. All the corpses were buried in the holes which we had dug."

A few days before Yamamoto arrived at Rabaul a captured American pilot was led out of confinement at the Salamaua Garrison in New Guinea, given a final drink of water, and put into a truck with ten Japanese soldiers. Three officers, all wearing swords, joined them and the vehicle trundled down the coast road as the sun set over the hills. One of the Japanese soldiers who was proud to be part of it later recorded the event in his diary.

I glance at the prisoner; he had probably resigned himself to his fate. As though saying goodbye to the world, as he sits in the truck, he looks at the hills and at the sea and seems deep in thought. Now the time has come, and the prisoner is made to kneel on the back of a bomb crater filled with water. He . . . is very brave.

The unit commander has drawn his favorite sword. It glitters in the light . . . he taps the prisoner's neck lightly with the back of the blade . . . and brings it down with a sweep. Shhh . . . it must be the sound of blood spurting from the arteries. It is amazing . . . he had killed him with one stroke. The onlookers crowd forward. The head, detached from the trunk, rolls in front of it . . . the dark blood gushes out.

All is over. The head is dead white like a doll's. A superior seaman of the medical unit turns the headless body over on its back, and cuts the abdomen open with one clean stroke. Not a drop of blood comes out off the body. It is pushed down into the crater at once and buried. This will be something to remember all my life. If ever I get back alive it will make a good story to tell. . . .

Isoroku Yamamoto, as commander in chief of the Combined Fleet, was certainly aware of some of these brutal acts. Though many were perpetrated by the army, his own navy had a large part in it and he, in his unassailable position, could have had a considerable impact on such repugnant behavior. Fighting to win is one thing, but wanton acts of inhumanity against helpless enemies or civilians are another altogether. Knowledge of these incidents further served to dehumanize the Japanese in Allied eyes, and made the decision to order the admiral's death more straightforward. "To us, Admiral Yamamoto virtually was a god," Admiral Ugaki wrote in his diary. Such a man could have influenced whatever he wished.

On Rabaul, while Yamamoto was eating sea turtle and playing *shogi,* the original intercepted message was compared with those from Melbourne and Washington, and most of the unknowns were filled in. Based on previously deciphered messages, cryptoanalysts knew Rabaul was RR; RXZ was Ballale; RXP was Buin, and they then identified the missing end location as Shortland Island. There would be a total of six messages concerning Yamamoto, and Melbourne intercepted one that contained specific details for Japanese unit commanders:

SOUTHEAST AREA FLEET/CONFIDENTIAL TELEG. NO. 131755-MILITARY SECRET HA-1 CODE THE INSPECTION TOUR OF THE COMMANDER IN CHIEF TO BALLALE, SHORTLAND AND BUIN ON APRIL 18 IS SCHEDULED AS FOLLOWS:

1. 0600 DEPART RABAUL BY MEDIUM ATTACK PLANE (ESCORTED BY SIX FIGHTERS); 0800 ARRIVE BALLALE. IMMEDIATELY DEPART FOR SHORTLAND ON BOARD SUBCHASER (1ST BASE FORCE TO READY ONE BOAT), ARRIVING AT 0840. DEPART SHORTLAND 0945 ABOARD SAID SUBCHASER, ARRIVING BALLALE AT 1030 (FOR TRANSPORTATION PURPOSES, HAVE READY AN ASSAULT BOAT AT SHORTLAND AND A MOTOR LAUNCH AT BALLALE) 1100 DEPART BALLALE ON BOARD MEDIUM ATTACK PLANE, ARRIVING BUIN AT 1110. LUNCH AT 1ST BASE FORCE HEADQUARTERS (SENIOR STAFF OFFICER OF AIR FLOTILLA 26 TO BE PRESENT). 1400 DEPART BUIN ABOARD MEDIUM ATTACK PLANE; ARRIVE RABAUL AT 1540.

This latest message was relayed through Admiral Halsey to Admiral Fitch, Commander Air, South Pacific, and thence to Marc Mitscher on Guadalcanal. It was this information that led to Major John Mitchell flying sixteen P-38s off Guadalcanal on Easter Sunday morning, April 18, 1943. At 0710, as the green light flashed from Fighter Two's tower and Mitchell released his brakes, 646 miles to the northwest two Betty bombers dropped down over the mouth of Rabaul's Simpson Harbor. Angling in toward land they both touched down at Rabinjikku Airfield amid puffs of ever-present volcanic ash. Painted green on top with gray bottoms, both planes sported dark red roundels on the wings and fuselage, and if that wasn't enough, bright yellow identification stripes ran inboard along the inner wings.

Flight Warrant Officer Takeo Kotani piloted the lead Type 1 land-based attack plane, as it was officially known, and as he taxied clear the number 323 was plainly visible stenciled on his tail. Also called Lakunai, the 4,700-foot runway was Rabaul's main fighter base, and it was here that Kotani was to await the arrival of the most important man he had ever seen: Isoroku Yamamoto. The other Betty, Number 326, was flown by Flight Petty Officer Second Class Hiroshi Hayashi and it followed the first plane to the central apron and shut down. The parking area was covered with *tetsuban*, "iron plate matting" that attempted to copy American Marston matting but didn't fit together well enough for use on runways. It did, however, keep the sand and volcanic ash down in the parking or maintenance areas.

For security reasons, the pilots had only been informed of the mission the night before by Captain Yukie Konishi, commander of the 705th Kokutai. Hayashi asked why he was to wear regulation flight clothes, instead of his usual well-worn, comfortable uniform, and then Konishi told him the identity of the passengers.

Both planes were washed and cleaned during the night of April 17, and just past dawn the following morning the Bettys with their seven-man crews lifted off from their base at Vunakanau, seven miles south across Blanche Bay.

They would wait about forty minutes to depart again, but Yamamoto's punctuality was legendary and the pilots were taking no chances. Lakunai had been chosen because it spared the admiral a ten-mile drive over muddy roads down to Vunakanau, and because the escorting fighters were based here at Lakunai. Kotani and Hayashi had been briefed that two sections, or *shotai*, of three Zeros each were from the 204th Kokutai, led by Chief Petty Officer Yoshimi Hidaka. The standard navy hand signals would be used since the fighters did not carry radios, and after Yamamoto arrived the next takeoff would occur at 0600 sharp. It was a fine, clear day, perfect for flying.

Within twenty minutes three staff cars pulled up near the parked aircraft. Admirals Kusaka and Ozawa clambered from the first car to see off the commander in chief. Captain Watanabe, who had given up his seat on the plane, was also there to say farewell, though Yamamoto was expected back at Rabaul late that afternoon. The nine passengers emerged from the other two cars to see that, surprisingly, Yamamoto had forsaken his customary starched white uniform for a very plain, dark green tropical tunic. He had decided the night before that appearing on the front line in dress whites would be unseemly, and asked everyone to wear green field uniforms instead.*

In accordance with naval custom, lowest-ranking officers were first into a boat or aircraft, and the last off. Commanders Fukusaki and Toibana climbed up a ladder through the open red roundel on the left side of Betty #323, followed by Rear Admiral Takada. Isoroku Yamamoto shook hands with Ozawa, Kusaka, and Captain Watanabe, then, without knowing it, took his last living step off the planet and climbed into the waiting bomber. Vice Admiral Matome Ugaki, his chief of staff, followed four other officers into Hayashi's Betty and as those remaining stepped away the engines coughed to life.

Ground checks complete, the two bombers trundled toward the northwestern end of the runway followed by the six Zero fighters. Admiral Ozawa, commander of the Third Fleet, was not happy about the paltry es-

---

* Rear Admiral Rokuru Takada, Combined Fleet Chief Surgeon, and Captain Motoharu Kitamura, Chief Paymaster, did not get the word and were wearing whites—much to their embarrassment and Yamamoto's disgust.

cort. "If he insists on going," Ozawa complained to Ya-mamoto's staff officers several days before the flight, "six fighters is nothing like enough. Tell the chief of staff [Ugaki] that he can use as many of my planes as he likes."

It was too late now.

At precisely 0600 hours in Rabaul, as Rex Barber was sweating in his cockpit south of New Georgia and John Mitchell prepared to turn onto Leg Two, Warrant Officer Takeo Kotani released his brakes. Twin clouds of ash flared up behind the engines, and Betty #323 wobbled down the runway pointed southeast at Ma-tupi Harbor. Hayashi's bomber followed immediately, and those remaining behind watched the landing gear retract as both planes continued straight ahead over the water. Gracefully banking slightly south as they climbed, they had Mount Tavurvur off to the left and for a moment their wings were silhouetted against the green hills of New Britain.

Continuing to climb for 7,500 feet over Blanche Bay, Kotani cut across the peninsula just south of Cape Gazelle, then turned over the channel heading south-east toward Cape St. George at the tip of New Ireland. After this, they would cross the northern Solomon Sea and make the Bougainville coast near Mount Balbi be-fore continuing south toward Ballale. Kotani knew the route well, and planned to keep his passengers happy by remaining clear of the inland rough air. The bombers would fly down the shoreline until over Empress Augusta Bay, then he would slowly descend toward another prominent landmark: Moila Point. It was a beautiful morning, clear with excellent visibility, but as the plane floated across the horizon with sea and earth turning below, the shifting sunlight made it difficult to distinguish the rising sun from a setting sun.

Eleven
Vengeance

April 18, 1943: 0915
The Solomon Sea south of Bougainville

R ex felt it before he truly saw it.

Out of the corner of his eye the horizon was darker. Not all of it, just the space from *Miss Virginia*'s nose to his right wingtip. Clouds came to mind first; there were almost always clouds or squall lines, and thunderstorms sprang up frighteningly fast, but rarely in the morning. A few minutes earlier the sixteen Lightnings passed about fifteen miles south of a small group of islands—the Treasury Islands—he knew from his map, which meant John Mitchell's navigation and timing was on the nose: perfect. It also meant the last turn point was close, about five minutes away, and that the dark smudge along the horizon was no storm. It was no illusion.

It was Bougainville.

Barber, like the other pilots, had been to Bougainville before but never flown in this far south of the island, and he had never seen it from fifty feet. Last time, he remembered, had been much more difficult, and at least today they were flying in daylight. Everything is better when you can see, and like most pilots, he didn't care for night flying. Rex could do it, but it wasn't his first choice. Still, there were advantages, and several weeks earlier, in late March, he'd been up in the Shortlands on an aggressive, surprise predawn mission that almost cost him his life.

On March 28, unarmed P-38s from the 17th Photographic Squadron (Light) discovered twenty-seven floatplanes moored in the sheltered neck of water between Faisi Island and Poporang off the southern coast of Shortland. The 17th had moved to Guadalcanal's Fighter Two from Nouméa in January, and having immediate access to their photoreconnaissance had proven invaluable. There were Japanese naval facilities scattered around southern Bougainville and the Shortlands, including a seaplane base in the Tuhu Channel near the mouth of Shortland Harbor. This had been the headquarters of the Japanese Rear-Area Force, a staging zone for all the attacks against Guadalcanal, including the annoyance raids by "Washing Machine Charlie." There were really about a dozen of these open-cockpit reconnaissance biplanes, officially designated as a Mitsubishi F1M2 "Pete," and for months they had added to the misery on the Canal. There were also supposed to be a handful of floatplane fighters, the Nakajima A6M2-N "Rufe," attached to the 938 Kokutai at the same base.

A combined Army-Marine operation was planned for the next day: eight 339 FS P-38s led by Captain Tom Lanphier, and eight Corsairs from VMF-124. Taking off at 0330, the sixteen fighters planned to join up in two flights of eight, descend in darkness to a few hundred feet off the water, then head northwest up the Slot. Lanphier, with Barber flying *Diablo* as his wingman, wanted to remain west of New Georgia, out over the Solomon Sea, until he approached the Treasury Islands. This would shield the flight from Japanese units in the central Solomons and hopefully permit a surprise attack at Faisi-Poporang. Unfortunately, the Marines were unable to join up in the predawn darkness and, with one exception, all the Corsairs turned back for Guadalcanal. Lanphier and his seven P-38s orbited west of Cape Esperance as long as possible, then headed northwest on the Solomon Sea side of the Russell Islands. Rob Petit, leading the second flight of four in *Miss Virginia,* sent Lieutenant Sam Howie back to Kukum Field with a bad right engine, but gained Lieutenant Benjamin Eben Dale, the sole Corsair who made it to the rejoin point.

Lanphier got them to the Treasury Islands, then turned northeast toward Shortland, but somewhere in the overwater darkness Petit's Number Three and Four Lightnings lost sight and turned back for the Canal. By the time the sun rose the attackers were down to five P-38s and one Corsair. Crossing the Bougainville Strait, Lanphier brought the fighters into Shortland Harbor with the rising sun behind them, so they were all but invisible for a few crucial moments.

"Youth and inexperience were in control of my emotions and good fortune was at my side," Petit later wrote. "I walked my rounds into the row of float planes and saw the slashed of the strikes." The Japanese never knew what hit them, and in a matter of minutes eight floatplanes were destroyed and one left burning.*

---

* Reports vary as to the destroyed aircraft. One states they were eight Rufe fighters and the other lists five to seven Pete reconnaissance aircraft. Both had floats, and the distinction would be difficult in early morning light.

As the P-38s and lone Corsair roared out of the harbor they spotted what appeared to be a destroyer off the north coast of nearby Poporang Island. Rolling over and diving to attack, Lanphier went for the stern, Petit shot up the superstructure, and Rex attacked the bow. As they came back around for a second attack, the warship was listing and afire. Diving down over the water, with sunlight glinting on waves and antiaircraft rounds streaking past, Rex got a bit target fixated for a few seconds as he opened fire and badly misjudged his sink rate. Suddenly, with a face full of boat, he yanked back on the wheel, firewalled the throttles, and pulled away hard right. "I got too aggressive," he remembered later, and left some forty inches of his left wingtip in the ship's mast.* Barber made it back and landed fine, but *Diablo* was still not flyable three weeks later. Interestingly, the P-38 that turned back due to an engine problem landed fast, ran off the runway, and crashed. The plane, *Old Ironside*, was written off for salvage, and Lieutenant Howie re-

---

* The pilots believed the warship to be a destroyer, but it was actually a Number 28-type subchaser, which resembled a scaled-down destroyer, and patrolled inshore areas off the Shortlands. This one did not sink, and the mission report states the attack left the ship listing, which again points toward something much smaller than an Imperial Navy destroyer.

counted, "One wing was salvageable, and it was used to replace the wingtip on Rex Barber's Lightning that he sheared off during the mission."

Thinking of his last trip up here made Rex's heart beat a bit quicker, but he was too much the professional to be distracted. Leaving the propellers, throttles, and mixture controls set as they were, he glanced at the BOMB-DROP TANK box mounted on the left bulkhead near his thigh. Normal combat procedure was to keep the selector toggles up, in the ON position if one was carrying tanks or bombs, and the guarded master switch down, which powered off the whole box. Any sort of jettison situation was usually an emergency, so all a pilot had to do then was flip the MASTER outboard, which armed the system, then hit the circular RELEASE button. This was much better than inadvertently dropping a tank or, just as bad, fumbling for two switches if jumped by a Japanese pilot. He set it up this way at takeoff and of course it hadn't changed, but a pilot always checks.

Sunlight bounced off the gauges and made them hard to read, but he leaned forward and squinted anyway. Glancing at *Phoebe*, Rex then looked off the nose at Mitchell's planes about two thousand feet ahead. Riding on a carpet of gray haze, the Lightnings seemed motionless as the gray-blue waves rolled away below them. It was an illusion, of course; the waves were moving, but not nearly so quickly as he was. Reality was sixteen fighters slipping past a vengeful, vicious enemy to strike the Japanese hard where they least expected it. Reality was also the two thousand .50-caliber rounds waiting in his four Browning machine guns, and 150 shells in his 20 mm cannon.

Twisting around in the seat, Rex made out another P-38 about four football fields behind him between the tails. Major Kittel, or one of his wingmen—there was no way to tell. Everett Anglin from the 12th Fighter Squadron was leading the last four-ship, but it was invisible back there in the haze. Not that anyone would know if something had happened, since there hadn't been a word spoken in nearly two hours, nor would there be until an enemy was sighted. Facing forward, he ran an eye over the gauges again. Flying in a wing position today he had to make persistent, small changes to stay in formation, but a fairly constant 32 inches of manifold pressure kept the airspeed around 200 mph. Oil pressure and temperature were in the green. Shifting directly left across the panel, Rex noted the engine coolant and hydraulic pressure were also good.

An enemy.

Yamamoto was certainly that, and Barber hoped to have a shot at settling the score today. After Guadalcanal was secured, Rex and everyone else had taken a figurative breath; they had held on against long odds and beaten the enemy back, but there had been little time to rest. America was truly riled up, and having gained a foothold, Admiral Halsey knew that any delay in going on the offensive would benefit the Japanese. Yamamoto needed time to regroup, replenish, and fortify the islands northwest of Guadalcanal, and Halsey wasn't going to allow it. Months earlier Rex had flown in Operation CLEANSLATE, the invasion of the Russell Islands and the first offensive move up the Solomons. Since Yamamoto had already pulled the garrisons out, there was no resistance and the operation was over in a few days, but new ground was now available for air bases and even now the Seabees were finishing up a 4,200-foot crushed-coral runway on Banika.

Barber held his left wrist up so he could read his watch face against the sun's glare. 0910. Five minutes until the next turn. Flipping the map over, the pilot noted the numbers for the final leg: 020 degrees for 16 miles, and they'd hopefully pick up Motupena Point at the southwest end of Empress Augusta Bay. Eyeballing the compass, he figured that to be a 75-degree turn to the right, and they'd stay on the deck at fifty feet for five minutes, then once land was sighted, or the Betty bomber, they'd start to climb. The mist-covered smudge of the Treasury Islands was now well aft of his right rudder, and Rex knew there wouldn't be time to check fuel again in a few minutes, so he did it now. Both gauges were on the far left side of the instrument panel above the throttles, partially shielded from the sun so they were plain to see. The top one was for the forward system, the two 60-gallon reserve tanks off his shoulders. There was a bright white needle for each one, and they both read about 45 gallons. The needles for the bottom gauge looked like a single needle, straight up at 93 gallons for each main tank.

That left 276 gallons of internal fuel once he jettisoned the drop tanks. Without looking down, Rex dropped his left hand to the fuel selectors and rehearsed the procedure, which he did every time he carried drop tanks. Two clicks to the left on the top selector, then two clicks left on the bottom selector would switch the fuel feed from the drop tanks to the main tanks. Left hand straight up to the guarded ARM switch, flip it up, then punch the RELEASE button. He wouldn't be looking at the pair of lights that would illuminate as the tanks came off, but he'd instantly feel the weight fall away.

If his math was correct, he'd used about 275 gallons from the two drop tanks, and would burn maybe 50 more before reaching the Bougainville coast, which left 125 gallons of wasted fuel he'd drop into the sea. It couldn't be helped, though, because unless the situation was extreme you *never* went into a dogfight with a belly tank. Rex lost a buddy, Captain Bill Shaw, during a dogfight over Cape Esperance that way. The shackle jammed and his tank didn't release, but Shaw pressed in anyway. A Zero got in a lucky burst that blew up the tank, the P-38, and Bill Shaw.

Satisfied, he tucked the map under his leg so it wouldn't float around the cockpit, tugged his lap belt a bit tighter, and kept an eye on *Phoebe.* From the corner of his right eye he noted the dark area now stretched away north to the horizon, and what he glimpsed first was a fairly large mountain on the south end of the island. Rex remembered it from his other mission up here last month as Mount Takuan. There was a second high spot, probably another mountain, toward the center and Rex suddenly realized that if Yamamoto was on time his aircraft would be somewhere in that area. If he was on time; and if the code-breakers broke the right code; and if nothing had changed. Lots of moving parts to this mission, but that in itself was not uncommon. That's what he got paid to do. Take chances and kill things.

All the same, he fervently hoped Yamamoto was on time.

Warrant Officer Kotani was exactly one minute early, and that suited him just fine. It had taken just over twenty-four minutes to take off from Rabaul, level at the 7,500-foot cruising altitude, then fly the fifty-eight miles to Cape St. George on New Ireland's south coast. Six Zeros had followed them from Lakunai, and joined up three per side, about a thousand feet above and behind the bombers. Kotani could see them occasionally through the big canopy, hovering against the blue sky like protective spirits. In a typical tight formation, Hayashi was flying a wing's length away from the lead Betty on the left side, and a little high. In fact, the bombers were so close that Yamamoto could be seen from the second Betty.

The cockpit was bright with light, thanks to the large canopy, and the admiral was sitting calmly in the observer's seat on the right side behind the copilot. Directly behind him in the narrow, enclosed space under the dorsal was the radio operator, who, if necessary, would operate the Type 92 7.7 mm turret gun. Aft of Kotani to the left of the radioman was the navigator, who would spend the flight moving between the nose bubble, where he could see landmarks, and his folding table directly behind Kotani. Just like the radio operator, if there was trouble the navigator would scurry forward to man the 7.7 mm nose gun. The main fuselage area was behind the dorsal with blisters on each side for two waist gunners, and an additional pair of Type 92 guns. Narrow seats ran along the bulkheads aft to an elongated tail blister containing a Type 99 20 mm cannon dedicated to protecting the bomber's vulnerable six o'clock position.

Forty-five minutes after passing Cape St. George, the lead Betty passed down the coast of Buna Island, and the big air base at Buka was plainly visible off the left wing. Aiming for the nine-thousand-foot peak of Mount Balbi, Kotani made landfall near Kunau and turned southeast toward the crescent shape of Empress Augusta Bay. At this point Betty bombers and the American Lightnings were roughly pointed at each other, separated by less than one hundred miles of water, and closing toward a point in space at about 6.5 miles per minute. John Mitchell was desperately hoping the Japanese would appear, while Hayashi and Kotani were oblivious to their danger.

Rex pushed the throttles up, then cranked the wheel hard to the right as the fighters made the turn onto the last leg. He floated over *Phoebe*, passing just aft of the tail to Lanphier's right side. Besby Holmes and Ray Hines played the turn a bit farther back, then popped out on the left side. Bright, hot sunlight hit his right cheek as the P-38 rolled out heading 020 degrees for the run into the coast, which was just five minutes ahead. Mitchell had briefed a standard, four-ship spread formation on the last leg, which meant Numbers Three and Four in each flight would be to the west, or left, side.

Landfall . . . very soon. He'd been here before, but still, each time made his mouth a bit dry, and his heart beat quicker. Eyes darting around the cockpit, Rex took a last look at his fuel needles, then touched the ARMING SWITCH and made certain it was outboard in the ARM position. Dropping his hand down to the fuel selectors, he clicked the front system from DROP TANK to MAIN, then did the same for the rear system. If he never had to jettison the tanks then he could use whatever gas remained on the way home. If he did have to release them, it was now just hitting the button. Glancing up, he alternated between *Phoebe*'s wingtip and the rapidly approaching coastline.

Suddenly the haze vanished, like a window blind flying up, and the open mouth of a bay appeared off his nose. A narrow peninsula jutted like a chin into the water from the right side, and Mitchell was pointed directly at a shark-toothed bit of land on the northern side of the bay. All sixteen fighters had closed up in the last turn, and Rex could clearly see Julius Jacobson on Mitch's right wing, with Doug Canning and Delton Goerke off his left wing. The major's navigation had been flawless, and he'd picked this very distinctive point because there was no missing it. The Japanese pilots would also be flying from landmark, and the bay was a perfect reference if one was heading south to Ballale.

Poking up from the mountains left of his nose was a barren cone, a large brown peak that looked like a rotten tooth embedded in green gums. Through the canopy, on either side of his glare shield, dark hills rose from the haze, rolling up toward the mountains on the island's spine. Rough. It was rough now, as the heat from the land mixed with that over the water, and the fighter jolted hard every few seconds. A death grip on the wheel would be bad; flying tense was never a good idea, even in combat.

Especially in combat. Focusing that hard blocked everything else from a man's mind, and deep over enemy territory, with limited fuel, and a hundred Japanese fighters nearby, he needed to stay aware of everything around him as long as possible. As things heated up, Rex knew, bit by bit the less vital information would slip away. Even now Rex wasn't registering the cockpit's smell of leather, hot metal, and urine. He was leaning forward slightly, left hand on the throttles, and his eyes on *Phoebe*'s right wing, as the sixteen Lightnings roared in toward the breaking white surf around Motupena Point. Shielded by the hills, the eastern shoreline was darker blue, but farther out he now saw sunlight slanting onto the flickering waves of Empress Augusta Bay.

They were here.

Kotani had just seen the same dun-colored peak pass off his left wing, and that meant the bombers were sixty miles from the southern coast of Bougainville. Once there it was fifteen more miles over water to Ballale, but by then he needed to be low, slow, and ready to land. Up ahead the bay's curving shoreline was marred by a triangular spit of land that made a convenient visual landmark. It was time to start down. A long, slow descent so as not to make his passengers uncomfortable. He knew Yamamoto was technically a pilot, but it had probably been years since he had touched controls himself.

Smoothly pushing the MIXTURE knobs forward, the pilot then eased the throttles back a few inches, lowering the nose slightly as he did so. To the left a curving spine ran down the island to the south, and there were several more peaks visible. From the Betty's cockpit there was a magnificent view of the bay with both smooth curves meeting at the shark tooth. Away south was a peninsula, and beyond that the calm of the bay gave way to the ruffled surface of the Solomon Sea. Nudging the throttles to hold 200 mph, over the nose Kotani could see nothing between the bay and the blue haze of Bougainville's south coast. Nothing except jungle.

Bogeys . . . ten o'clock."*

The voice was calm, but Rex flinched nonetheless. He hadn't heard a voice in more than two hours and it startled him. He instantly looked up and left. Like all fighter pilots, he had superb vision and the movement registered first.

There!

A few miles inland from the northeastern shore of the bay . . . maybe ten miles distant. Perfectly silhouetted against clear blue sky above the ridgeline was a large plane. Lanphier began a slight climb, following Mitchell in front of him, and Rex automatically followed, adding power as *Phoebe* surged ahead.

---

* All radio dialogue during the Yamamoto shootdown is directly quoted from interview statements made by John Mitchell, Rex Barber, or Doug Canning.

"Roger that . . . I have him." Mitch's drawl was unmistakable.

"I've got him, too," Lanphier replied.

As the radios exploded with chatter, Rex's eyes darted between Lanphier and the contact. It wasn't a fighter . . . too big. But it was right where Mitchell had figured the admiral's plane would be. It had to be Yamamoto. It *had* to be. Picturing the geometry in his head, Mitchell knew they'd never catch the bomber by pointing right at him, so he turned to parallel; to pull lead just as you would to throw a football to a receiver, or shoot a gun at a bird. Lightnings were bobbing all around, but Rex stayed glued to *Phoebe* as Lanphier's wing dropped and he got a face full of fighter as the Lightning banked into him. Slapping the throttles back, he rolled right and pulled the wheel back hard. As the control column grazed Rex's calf, Lanphier came wings level again, pointed directly at the coast south of Motupena Point. Mitchell's calm voice broke through the radio chatter calling out *two* bombers now, not one, and Rex felt disappointment wash through him. It wasn't Yamamoto . . . they'd been briefed there would be a single Betty, but there was a pair here . . . it had to be someone else!

Then Mitch called a tally-ho on the fighters, two sections of three on either side of the bombers, several miles back and high. Just like they'd been briefed. Maybe it was Yamamoto after all.

"Okay guys, skin 'em off!"

Never looking away from Lanphier, Rex reached back to the arming switch box and jabbed the RELEASE button with his left thumb. The left wing rocked, then the right wing, so he didn't bother looking at the indicator lights. All around him tanks came tumbling off the other fighters like scales in a breeze.

"Okay Tom . . . he's your meat!"

Mitchell's nose jacked up 30 degrees, and the three other Lightnings with him soared up away from the coastline. Lanphier continued a slight climb, but the fighter lunged forward as he went to full power. Barber jammed the two MIXTURE levers full forward, then dropped his hand to the throttles and did the same. Raw power . . . the P-38 tingled with it. He could feel it through his heels, and right through his fingers on the wheel.

Blue went to green below his wings as the Lightnings crossed the coast, and Rex glanced back. A few of the trailing P-38s were visible in their climb, but most had already vanished. Mitchell would point toward Kahili, get as high as possible, then charge down into the Zeros that were sure to come.

"Roger . . . I've got him," Lanphier answered. The

radio was busy now, as others called "tally-ho," and one or two fuel checks came across. Besby Holmes also called to tell Lanphier one of his tanks would not come off, and Rex saw the other two big fighters peel away back toward the coast. Now it was just *Phoebe* and *Miss Virginia,* alone in a dangerous sky.

But they were not alone, nor was there time to think much about it. Gradually climbing between the shoreline and the bomber, Lanphier held the airspeed at 300 mph while making small left turns every few seconds. Angling in slightly toward the enemy aircraft, the two Lightnings were about seven miles off the bomber's right wing, and a little low. This had to be done perfectly.

If Lanphier turned too early, they'd end up in front of the bomber, which would see them and begin evasive action. The angles would be nearly impossible for a gunshot as well. If the P-38s attacked too soon they'd end up behind the bomber and there would be a long tail chase, which would take time the Lightnings did not have. Also, once the Americans were spotted, every Japanese fighter on the island would swarm in and Barber knew that at least six Zeros were guarding Yamamoto himself. Three-to-one odds didn't bother him a bit, but tangling with the escorts meant the bomber would likely get away and Kahili was less than twenty-five miles to the east, about four minutes of flying time for a bomber diving away at full power or, worse still, three minutes for the seventy-five Zeros coming the other way.

Flight Petty Officer Kenji Yanagiya was flying Zero #169 in the *shotai* on the right side of the bombers closest to the coast. As Number Three he was 30 degrees aft of Yoshimi's wing line and about 150 feet back on the far right side, while across his leader's tail on the left was Petty Officer 2nd Class Okazaki Yasuji. Yanagiya's position placed him farthest away from Yamamoto, and closest to any enemy coming in off the sea, which was why Yoshimi chose it. The other section of Lieutenant Morizaki Takeshi and Petty Officers Shoichi and Toyomitsu were a mile away on the northern side of the bombers.

Yanagiya and the other fighter pilots had been told any threat would come from the Solomon Sea side, not from the mountains, though no one expected any such thing to occur. Americans raided the island, but from carriers or from their bases in New Guinea. Those flying the gull-winged Corsairs or H-shaped Lightings from Guadalcanal could reach southern Bougainville, but they could not get up this far north. Not even the Americans, who often flew like crazed madmen, would be so audacious; besides that, Yanagiya and the rest of the escorts had only been told of the mission last night, so how could the Yankees know about it?

Yanagiya particularly hated the Lightnings.

Big and extremely well armored, they were faster than his Zero-sen* and carried much heavier weapons, but Yanagiya wasn't worried. He was an experienced fighter pilot, with one hundred combat missions logged since October 1942, and he was flying over friendly territory. Most of the other fighters today were the older Type 0 Model 21 fighters with Sakae-12 engines, but his plane was a newer Model 32, with a Sakae-21 engine and supercharger. There were trade-offs; it was a bit faster, but the larger engine weighed more and took up more space, which shrank his fuselage fuel tank from 26 to 16 gallons. More weight and less fuel cost the Model 32 its range, which was why most had been moved to Buka or Kahili so they could reach Guadalcanal. The wings had also been modified, and the folding mechanism removed, which made the wingspan shorter and the fighter more maneuverable at higher speeds. Despite the improvement, all the Zeros still only mounted a pair of 20 mm cannons in the wings,

---

* Pilots called it this. *Zero* for the "Model 0" and *sentōki* for "fighter plane."

and two 7.7 mm guns on the nose, though the Model 32 carried twice the shells for each cannon.

Up ahead the bombers began to descend, yet Yoshimi held his altitude, and this made sense. The big aircraft were easy to see, so there was no need to be closer than a mile or two, and by staying high the escort pilots had a magnificent view of southern Bougainville. Also, if any threats appeared, the Zeros would have the altitude advantage, which could be critical in the initial seconds of a fight, though it mattered less now against new, powerful American fighters like the Lightning and Corsair than it had a few months earlier against the Wildcats and Airacobras. He could see nothing over the bay to his right or along the coast, where shadows and movement were easier to see. Not so over land, though, especially dark-painted U.S. aircraft over a darker green jungle. His watch said just past 0730, Tokyo time, and they were due at Ballale at 0745. Not long now.

Like a water skier on a long rope, Barber was low and outside of Lanphier as the P-38 banked left and continued to climb. Looking past *Phoebe* in the direction of the turn, Rex picked up both bombers five miles away at his ten o'clock position. Incredibly, they were still descending gently. No one, Rex realized with a start, had yet spotted the Lightnings. Evenly split between the coast and the bomber's inland flight path, Rex felt the ground rising as the fighters roared over the jungle. A big, jagged ridgeline floated past the corner of his eye as Lanphier flattened his turn to stay at 1,500 feet, slightly lower than the bombers and aiming just ahead of their flight path. This was good tactics, because once the P-38s broke through the visible horizon, from the Zero's perspective, they would likely be seen. At low altitude like this over the jungle the Lightnings would be very hard to see until they got very, very close. *Phoebe*'s right wing suddenly dropped level, and Rex flicked his wrist down and right to roll out with him.

Then he saw the reason.

Lanphier was pointed in front of the enemy planes, which put the bombers at his eleven o'clock for about three miles. It was a perfect intercept. In a few seconds they'd pull a bit more lead, then play the turn to rake the planes from cockpit to tail. Rex knew his leader would take the closest Betty, the one to the south side, so he would plan on raking the other one. His eyes flickered up behind the formation and he was surprised to see the Zeros still hanging in space maybe two miles back and three thousand feet above the bombers. Left hand on the throttles, his right hand on the trembling wheel, Rex leaned forward to look around his canopy struts and keep the Japanese in sight.

Just a few more seconds . . .

Yoshimi Hidaka, leading the southern section of Zeros, saw the Lightnings first and reacted immediately. Waggling his wings, he jettisoned the belly drop tank, then simultaneously nosed over steeply and shoved the throttle up. But with no radios there was no way to communicate what he was seeing, and both his wingmen were caught off guard for a second. Yanagiya instinctively jammed the throttle forward, then dropped his left hand to the red handle on the bulkhead and yanked up hard. As his tank came off he followed Hidaka down, fumbling for the machine gun cocking levers on either side of his gun sight and staring down at the jungle off his nose. There! The unmistakable twin-boomed silhouette of a P-38 coming up through the horizon. Vapor streamed from its wingtips as the pilot pulled hard left and up into the Zeros.

At two miles Rex could see the gray belly of the nearest Betty, less than thirty seconds away, with its bright red meatball on the fuselage just behind the big clear blister. Sunlight glinted off the canopy and just the top turret, and he realized the pointed tail was also glassed in.

Twenty seconds.

Another gun station, he remembered. A 20 mm cannon. Suddenly, violently, Lanphier broke away hard to the left and Rex instinctively followed. Perfectly silhouetted against the horizon, *Phoebe*'s details were strikingly clear for an instant: the fighter's lethal guns protruding from her wasp-like nose; the point of the gondola ending at the spot where her wings met; even the edges of the landing gear doors on the bottom of her graceful booms.

Between her wings and tails the bay's blue gleam was plain, as was the ugly brown peak thirty miles to the northwest over the *Phoebe*'s nose. In the same split second, he processed the three Zeros diving at them as their belly tanks spun away in the sun, and Barber snapped back to the right toward the Bettys, just as the lead bomber abruptly dropped its nose toward the jungle. If both Lightnings went after the Zeros the bombers would escape, and the entire mission would fail. Lanphier's nose came way, way up . . . at least 45 degrees, and he disappeared aft and high as Rex roared toward the bombers just a mile away off his nose.

Fifteen seconds.

Hayashi, flying the second Betty, nosed over steeply. They were passing through 3,500 feet and, though startled, he did what a wingman does and followed his leader. Something was wrong, to be sure, but there was no way to ask. From the corners of his eyes the rising terrain to the north got bigger, and there was less blue visible from the shoreline ten miles off his right wing. All he could see in front was the lead bomber's left wingtip and lots of jungle.

Big.

The Betty was big. Rex was directly off the first bomber's right wing . . . just a little low, and much, much too fast. Slapping the throttles back, he shoved the wheel down and his butt came off the seat as the Lightning bobbed. Cranking the wheel hard right, he booted the right rudder and the fighter began to skid. It was the only way to slow down . . . except to climb and pull harder, which is exactly what he did. With the bomber filling his vision to the right, Rex darted a glance at the second Betty, yanked the wheel back . . . then cranked it hard right again with his right boot jammed against the rudder.

With its right wing low, the P-38 came screaming in about three hundred feet behind the bomber and a little high. The second Betty disappeared under his left engine as Rex thrust the throttles forward to match the bomber's airspeed. *Miss Virginia* bounced as he flicked the wheel farther right, then back left and up. Wobbling with power and prop wash, Barber rolled in 200 feet directly behind the Betty's left engine, about 1,500 feet above the jungle. Dropping the nose down, he aimed across the bomber's tail, and as the Japanese aircraft filled his gun sight Rex Barber opened fire.

"Enemy aircraft!" Petty Officer Hiroaki Tanimoto screamed. He was officially the observer, and was staring through the cockpit's clear roof as a stream of red tracers suddenly appeared. Shocked, Hayashi threw his head back and was stunned to see the pale belly of an American P-38 Lightning almost on top of his plane just right of the nose. Reacting, he shoved the throttles forward, then the yoke, and twisted it left to dive his bomber away from the enemy fighter.

POM-POM-POM-POM . . . the cannon was dull compared to the four chattering .50-caliber guns, and the Lightning's nose vibrated. Fast . . . he was still too fast, and the Betty's wings obscured the horizon, he was so close. Chopping the throttles, Rex's fighter slowed, and he released both firing buttons. His N-3 optical sight was washed out by the sun, and useless this close. He'd seen the tracers strike the right engine and it began smoking, so he nudged the rudder, aimed at the glassy cockpit area on the right side, then at one hundred feet he squeezed his right index finger and thumb together. During the three-second burst *Miss Virginia*'s four .50-caliber guns spat out 144 rounds, with another thirty shells from the 20 mm Hispano cannon. As he raked the fuselage from tail to nose, some twenty-three pounds of lead smashed into the thin-skinned bomber for each burst. Metal was cut apart, seat cushions disintegrated, and people were shredded.

The Japanese pilot steepened his dive, and Barber rammed his throttles up again as the bomber accelerated. Dipping his left wing, Rex slid left past the tail, lined up on the Betty's other engine, and sent another burst into the bomber as it leveled off over the jungle. They were on the treetops now, and he had to bob up, then drop the nose slightly each time to shoot his guns, but the Betty's right engine was pouring out thick, black smoke, which meant a gasoline fire or ruptured oil lines: or both. As Barber drifted sideways again he put another three-second burst into the fuselage from the *left* side, and the Betty staggered.

Follow plane Number One!" Admiral Ugaki yelled at Hayashi. The second bomber had made a 90-degree, spiraling left turn toward the mountains, and as the terrain rose up Hayashi reversed back to the left. He could clearly see Yamamoto's bomber at least two and a half miles off to the south, low, slow, and trailing smoke. Everyone in Hayashi's aircraft was shouting, and the gunners were frantically trying to unlimber their guns. "Follow plane Number One!" Ugaki screamed again, and Hayashi firewalled the throttles, then pulled the bomber around to the south.

Fear instantly hollowed Rex's belly, turned his mouth to sandpaper, and widened his eyes. The Betty seemed to stop in midair, and at one hundred feet Rex had a quarter of second to react as the bomber's left wing dropped at the jungle and its right wing jabbed for the Lightning's nose. Slamming the wheel up and right, *Miss Virginia* missed the Betty's right wingtip by mere feet as the bomber careened toward the trees.

Bunting over and breathing hard, Rex got light in the seat, leveled off over the flashing trees, then twisted around to look back over his left shoulder. Somehow the Japanese pilot had leveled the wings but smoke roiled behind it, and the plane was going down.

Then he saw the Zero.

Hayashi was also breathing hard as he tried to roll out, but somewhere in those wildly turning seconds he lost sight of Yamamoto's bomber under his wing. Leveled off now just over the trees, he could see the blue water off Bougainville's southern shoreline up ahead, and raced for it. Nothing else was visible except a solitary column of black smoke rising up from the dark green jungle. The entire wild fight, from the lead bomber's initial dive until now, had lasted just over two minutes.

A mile behind off Rex's tail, high, pointed straight at him, closing, and he wasn't alone; there was another one on each side. Leaning left, Barber swiveled his head from the tail to the nose. Everything ahead was a smudge, and his magnetic compass was useless, but Rex knew that if the big mountain was off his left wing then the coast was directly off his nose. So was Kahili and its fighters, so he angled a bit right to stay clear and put the sun directly in the faces of the Japanese pilots. Hopefully. With the throttles firewalled, he braced his left arm against the canopy and flew with his peripheral vision southeast toward the tip of Bougainville. The tables were turned now and he was being hunted, but he remembered the briefing about the Zero's limits at high speed. If he could just stay alive a few seconds longer his magnificent Allison engines would get him the hell out of here. Rex pulled right and put the Japanese fighters past his left tail boom. Now they'd have to turn right to line up on him, and this was hard at high speeds.

Suddenly the sunlight flickered. A shadow passed overhead, and as his head snapped up Barber's chest tightened. Out of the sun heading the opposite way came two P-38s, and Rex literally sank into the seat with relief. Glancing back again, he saw the Zeros scatter, and a single smoke trail rising from the jungle, but it was dangerous to get fixated in combat. Scanning left off his tail he saw nothing. Forward, left and high toward Kahili was also clear. Eyes darting inside the cockpit Rex squinted at his fuel needles and read 220 gallons, and at least 188 gallons were needed to get back to the Canal, best case. Not good.

Off the nose to the right was nothing but coastline with blue sky above blue water. Back inside for the engines . . . all in the green. To the right off the wing . . . another pair of P-38s! They were out over the water, "surfing," as pilots said, heading southeast down the shoreline parallel to him. Then his eye caught a flicker of movement. Something bigger than the Lightnings, but headed the same way. Rex realized what it was and grinned.

It was the second Betty bomber.

Hayashi was scared and flying all out for the coast. To get to Kahili he'd have to cut back across the south end of Bougainville, which was where all the American fighters were, so the only way to save his passengers and himself was to get out over water and run for Ballale. The Type-1 bomber wasn't rated for 300 mph, but that's what the airspeed indicator read. Below his wings the jungle was just a blur of trees, with an occasional flash of gray-green water from scores of rivers. Racing over a low rise, the terrain suddenly fell away under the nose to a thin, tan ribbon of beach, and beyond that the sea.

The bomber's wingspan was eighty-two feet and he was barely a hundred feet over the sand. Hayashi put the plane into a steep left bank, hauling back on the yoke as he did so, and muscling the aircraft around southeast. Rolling wings level with the throttles firewalled, he was paralleling the coast just over the surf line, and every second in the air was another closer to safety. At any moment Zeros from Kahili might appear to save them. Moila Point was less than ten miles away off the nose, and beyond that was Ballale. The pilot couldn't see either from this height, but he knew they were there. A few miles farther off the coast a pair of

Lightnings flying in close formation suddenly turned in toward the Betty.

Hayashi didn't see them, either.

Barber did.

He also saw the Betty, so low its propellers were throwing up spray as it raced down the coast just past the beach. Five miles off the bomber's left wing, Rex was thundering over the jungle treetops at 400 mph heading straight for Moila Point. The Zeros were gone, and his only goal now was to get off Bougainville, and head for the relative safety of the Slot; until he saw the other bomber. No one had expected two of them, so who knew which one Yamamoto was in, or if he was even here at all? This might not even be the one he'd seen in formation a few minutes earlier. It didn't matter. It was a target within killing distance and he was a fighter pilot.

Checking right about 30 degrees, Rex pictured an intercept point in front of the fleeing plane and angled in toward it. From his cockpit it looked like all four planes could converge over the protruding shoreline to the right of his nose within ninety seconds or so, and across the water was another big, dark smudge that had to be Shortland Island. As the Betty approached Moila

Point it bumped up, rolled right far enough for Rex to see belly, then leveled out again on the wave tops headed for Ballale. This instantly closed the distance between it and the other P-38s, which the Japanese pilot obviously did not see. Rex also closed to within a mile and a half as the other Lightnings attacked.

Hayashi actually thought they might make it for a few seconds, then his top turret gunner opened fire. Pulling up to gain a bit of altitude, the American fighter then half-rolled back down on the bomber with just enough height to open fire: and he did. The Lightning's nose seemed to light up like twinkling fireworks as it fired everything at the bomber. Regularly spaced lines of seawater shot up off the tail, but none hit the aircraft.

A half mile behind the charging P-38s, Rex watched the lead fighter's burst hit aft of the bomber and toss pillars of water into the air. They were firing too far out of range, and were closing much too fast . . . the bomber's sudden turn into them had spoiled the intercept, and if the lead Lightning didn't slow down he'd miss again.

Neither happened. He didn't slow down, and he didn't miss, at least not completely. Barber saw him pull up, roll away, then roll back to dive down again.

Firing as he closed, the leader "walked" a long burst up through spraying seawater into the Betty's right engine. White vapor instantly streamed beyond the bomber, then the second Lightning fired but missed completely. Both P-38s flashed past to the right then pulled away. Higher than the other Lightnings, Rex dove down himself, chopped the throttles, and slid in from the left side. As the bomber filled his gun sight he pointed the fighter's nose at the left engine and fired.

Most of the bomber's crew was already dead, and all of the gunners were. Commander Suteji Muroi, one of Yamamoto's staff officers, was sprawled over the observer's table, his head bobbing lifelessly every time the bomber jolted. Hayashi could see leaking gasoline vaporizing from holes in the right wing. He was fighting for control when Barber's five-second burst slammed more than forty pounds of high-velocity lead into the left fuselage and cockpit. Fuel tanks exploded, the left wing folded, and the Betty rolled violently left to slam into the sea at 300 mph. The last thing Hayashi saw was a windscreen full of water, and his left engine flying off across the waves.

As the stream of tracers hit the Betty it blew up in Barber's face; in the blink of an eye an expanding cloud of yellow fire and black smoke rolled over the Lightning.

Rex reacted instantly, jamming the throttles forward, yanking back on the yoke, and pulling up through the debris. It wasn't fast enough. *Miss Virginia* jolted as pieces of the bomber struck her wings and gondola. Rex's gut tightened as he bounced through the burning air, then soared up through the smoke into clear air away from the wreckage, headed straight at the northern tip of Shortland Island.

The props were still spinning but the fighter was pulling left. Nudging that throttle back, he stared hard at the RPM, OIL TEMPERATURE, and OIL PRESSURE gauges in front of his right knee, and saw they were all in the green. Sudden movement caught his right eye, and Rex rolled right, looking up just in time to see a P-38, nearly vertical, pulling his nose to bear on a Zero. A stream of red tracers spat from its nose and the Japanese fighter blew up. Something else flickered far off to his right, and he saw another P-38 trailing smoke about three miles away heading southwest out to sea.

Just then another Zero flashed past low and five hundred feet to the right of Barber's nose. Rex realized the Japanese fighter was aiming directly at the first P-38, which had fallen off from a hammerhead stall, and was heading down around Shortland Island's west coastline. Continuing to roll right, Barber dropped his nose, pulled lead, and fired a long burst. It caught the

Zero full on the unprotected fuel tanks in the left wing, the fighter exploded, and burning pieces fell into the sea. Muscling the fighter up to level flight, he halfway rolled out and rapidly scanned the sea to the south looking for the damaged P-38, which had been heading away from Mila Point toward some offshore reefs. He only saw thin black smoke in two places from the Zeros, and an oily, burning smear from the Betty when Mitchell's voice suddenly filled his headset from somewhere overhead.

"Mission accomplished. Everybody get your ass home."

Then the Lightning was gone, and Barber realized he was alone in an empty sky.

Air battles are like that. Swarming with planes, pockmarked by explosions, then nothing. Rex flipped up on his left wing, twisted around in the seat, and quartered the sky behind him; high, level, and low on both sides . . . then he saw the holes in his wing. He also saw rising dust from a bare spot on the end of Bougainville and realized that was Kahili. The dust had to be aircraft scrambling, and the only planes taking off would be Zeros looking for him. Shortland Island lay about five miles off his left wing, and Rex was tempted to cut across it, but with the Zeros nearby he knew he couldn't do it. Rolling out heading south, he sat still for a moment to feel his fighter.

Miss Virginia seemed fine and despite the holes she was flying well, though he could see the damage to his left wing and knew the intercooler was gone. Part of the engine, it removed excess heat generated by the increase in air pressure from the supercharger, and without it he had no turbo. Rex also saw he could only get 30 inches of manifold pressure out of it, and that might be a problem if there was more fighting. Not that he had the fuel for it anyway. Gradually climbing to 12,000 feet he could clearly see the Treasury Islands past his nose, and the Solomons stretching away southeast off his left wing. He'd been this far before, and knew Guadalcanal was more than three hundred miles away . . . and that was flying direct down the Slot, which he could not do. He'd have to fly down past Vella Lavella, Rendova, then cut across New Georgia and the Russells for the Canal.

Peering at the clock next to his compass, Rex was startled to see that less than ten minutes had elapsed since Mitchell's "He's your meat" call. Combat was always faster than it seemed, some type of distortion, and more fuel burned than ever figured. Fuel. Glancing at his needles, Barber's breathing quickened for a moment as he did the math. After jettisoning the drop tanks he'd had 276 gallons of internal fuel, and after the last ten minutes at full throttle there were 196 remaining now; the top gauge needles for the main tanks read 106 gallons, and the lower gauge read 90 in the reserves. Banking gently left, Rex decided to cut the far corner across Shortland and head directly for the Wilson Straight off Vella Lavella. From there he planned to pass down the southeastern edge of New Georgia, avoiding the Slot, and then on into the Canal.

Like all combat fighter pilots, Barber knew the maximum range numbers by heart because he was always short of gas. Once rolled out, he eased the manifold pressure on both engines to 27 inches, set the RPM to 2,100, and watched the airspeed needle stabilize at 220 mph. This would reduce the burn on both engines to 2.2 gallons per minute, and Guadalcanal was 90 minutes southeast, so that was . . . 198 gallons.

Two gallons more than he had.

But looking at the water, Rex could see the whitecaps pointing in the direction he was flying, so there was a tailwind and that would help. He could also save another ten gallons or so by making a long, slow descent with the power back in IDLE. Maybe it would be enough. Maybe not. But there was a strip on the Russell Islands that was forty miles closer to him than Fighter Two, so that also was possible. Forcing himself to sit back, Rex tried not to think about getting bounced by Zeros and ending up in strange jungle down there. He tried not to think about sharks, either.

Combat was always dangerous. Every single time a pilot climbed into a cockpit it was risky, and out here the odds against a man were so outrageous you just quit figuring them if you wanted to stay sane. Besides, today was worth it more than other days. Today was all about payback. Two Bettys had gone down, though there was no way of knowing if Yamamoto had even been on board one of them or if he was dead. It didn't seem possible that anyone could have survived those flaming crashes . . . at least from the first bomber that went into the jungle. But Rex Barber had survived, and as long as no Zeros appeared he felt there was a reasonable chance of making it home. The late morning sun had turned the water light blue, but the sky ahead was still clear with no storms.

At least none that he could see.

Twelve
Dominoes

In fact, Isoroku Yamamoto was quite dead.

No one knew it yet, of course, as the aircraft had not been found, and would not be for more than twenty-four hours. Five of the original 204th Kokutai Zeros, Kenji Yanagiya among them, landed at Kahili to report and refuel, while the last escort fighter made an emergency landing on Ballale with engine trouble. Yoshimi Hidaka verified that the lead Type-1 bomber crashed in the jungle west of Kahili. Cable 181109, encrypted and marked top secret, was sent to 11th Air Fleet Headquarters on April 18 by noon:

TWO RIKKO CARRYING C-IN-C, COMBINED FLEET AND HIS PARTY ENGAGED IN AERIAL COMBAT

WITH OVER 10 P-38S AT ABOUT 0740. SECOND PLANE FORCED DOWN INTO THE SEA OFF MOILA POINT . . . FIRST PLANE IN FLAMES SEEMED TO HAVE PLUNGED AT A SLIGHT ANGLE INTO THE JUNGLE ABOUT 11 MILES WEST OF RXP [BUIN]. SEARCHING UNDERWAY.

The Japanese were electrified and dismayed by the news. By noon (Tokyo time) the Southeast Area Fleet Headquarters in Rabaul was notified, and Captain Watanabe immediately tired to depart for Bougainville but was delayed by a fierce storm. Forced to remain, he and Admiral Kusaka sent Cable No. 181430 to Tokyo, which read, in part:

FROM: COMMANDER IN CHIEF SOUTHEAST AREA FLEET

"A" REPORT NO. 1

THE NO. 1 LAND-BASED ATTACK PLANE CARRYING THE C IN C . . . WAS SEEN TO DIVE AT A SHALLOW ANGLE INTO THE JUNGLE ELEVEN NAUTICAL MILES TO THE WEST OF QBV [BUIN] EMITTING FLAMES, AND NO. 2 PLANE . . . MADE AN EMERGENCY LANDING IN THE SEA TO THE SOUTH OF

MOIGA [*sic*] . . . A SEARCH AND RESCUE OPERATION IS AT PRESENT BEING ARRANGED.*

The cable went out at 1430 from Rabaul and was received at 1708 by the Tokyo Signals Unit in the Navy Ministry. Decoded within two hours it was presented to Captain Yanagisawa, a senior aide to Admiral Nagano, chief of the Naval General Staff. Very soon all the heads of the Imperial Navy, including navy minister Shimada, knew that their greatest admiral was missing. In the meantime, three survivors from the second bomber were rescued. Petty Officer Hayashi had regained consciousness to find himself floating just three hundred feet off Moila Point near the base of his bomber's left wing, which was burning. Close enough to swim for shore, the pilot noticed water sprouts leaping up all around him and realized the Japanese soldiers on the beach were shooting at him.

"Signal to them!" a voice from behind him shouted. "Signal to them!" Diving down and swimming as best he could in heavy flying gear, Hayashi crawled onto the beach and was finally recognized. Stripping off his clothes, he dove back and swam out toward the man

---

* "Moiga" is a clerical misspelling for "Moila."

who called from behind, and saw him being swept parallel along the shoreline. Recognizing Admiral Ugaki, the pilot pulled him ashore and they were given first aid by an army medic. When the plane hit, the canopy disintegrated and both men were thrown out to the left over the nose. Ugaki had sustained a compound fracture of his right arm with a severed radial artery, while Hayashi was superficially injured: a cut mouth and some bruising. A third survivor, Captain Kitamura, was picked up by a navy seaplane with "a hole in his throat" and both officers were taken to Buin for medical treatment.

Meanwhile, the Sasebo Special Naval Landing Force (SNLF) was stationed at Buin and a detachment under the command of a Lieutenant Furukawa was dispatched by 1100 to search for Yamamoto. Eighteen miles west of Kahili, along the Buin–Boku road, a Japanese army construction unit commanded by Sub-Lieutenant Mitsuyoshi Hamasuna had seen pieces of the dogfighting. They had seen a P-38 being chased by Zeros, and assumed that a column of black smoke rising from the jungle meant a dead American. However, several hours later Hamasuna received a verbally delivered message from his regimental headquarters stating, "A plane carrying top navy brass has crashed. You're to organize a search party and go to look for it. You were watching, so you'll know roughly where it crashed." Hamasuna took a sergeant with nine men and searched all afternoon, but found nothing. He returned to the village of Aku, where he was told to begin again the next morning.

On the American side the situation moved much faster, beginning with the first pilot to arrive back over Guadalcanal. Every pilot approaching the island checked in with "RECON," the fighter director, and passed his tail number, status, and any pertinent information regarding his mission. Local weather, the landing runway, and any other pertinent information was passed back. It was a terse, routine, professional procedure. But not today. Captain Tom Lanphier astonished everyone listening to RECON by announcing, on a clear, unsecure frequency:

"I got Yamamoto! I got the son-of-a-bitch! He won't dictate terms in the White House now!"

Lieutenant (j.g.) Edward C. Hutcheson was the duty officer at RECON, and was professionally and personally astounded. Not by the claim, which was unfounded and impossible to prove at the moment, but that the information was verbalized in "the clear" on a frequency the enemy could monitor. This was precisely why Major Mitchell maintained strict radio silence all the way to Empress Augusta Bay. Now, if the Japanese were listening, they would immediately wonder how the Americans knew Admiral Yamamoto was in an aircraft over Bougainville.

A 12th FS pilot, Lieutenant Joe Young, met Lanphier when the latter shut down and opened his canopy. "[H]e claimed victory over Admiral Yamamoto in no uncertain terms. His reaction was astounding to me and appeared to be irrational. He was visibly shaken, but very adamant about his victory."

"All I can remember is how upset I was when Tom Lanphier made his statement over the open mike," Lieutenant Roger Ames, who had flown the mission in the first top cover four-ship, later wrote recalling his own return to the Canal.

However, at the moment there were more important issues than Tom Lanphier and his wild talk. In pairs and alone twelve Lightnings returned to base, but four pilots were still missing: Doug Canning, Besby Holmes, Ray Hine, and Rex Barber.

It was Besby Holmes and Ray Hine who initially attacked the second Betty over Moila Point, starting an engine fire and killing most of the gunners. This Betty had guns and fired back at the attacking Lightnings, but Hine's plane was damaged *after* they pulled off and away to the southwest. This means either three of the original escort Zeros engaged the pair, or fighters did get off the ground from Kahili to engage the Americans, or both. Kenji Yanagiya has stated that he dove away from Yamamoto's bomber, found a pair of P-38s over the coast, and fired into one of them. Observing vapor or gasoline trailing from it, he did not turn back to fight, but proceeded out over the Shortlands before landing at Kahili. The Lightning in question had to be Ray Hine. In any case, Rex Barber confirmed Holmes damaged the second Betty, and after that did get a Zero.

Barber later said: "Holmes, at the point I saw him, was just coming around on a Zero . . . and he got in behind that Zero and he shot that Zero down . . . he did explode that Zero because I saw it. No question in my mind about that." Ray Hine was hit by one of these Zeros, but couldn't talk to his flight lead because Holmes's radio jack was unplugged. They got separated, and it was during these few seconds that Rex shot down a Zero boring in on Holmes. According to Barber, "He was coming up from the south, and I think that Zero was looking at this combat [Holmes] because he came on in right underneath me. . . . I rolled over on him, came right in behind him . . . very close to him . . . and I gave him a long burst and he exploded also."

When it was over and Besby Holmes got his headset plugged in, Hine was nowhere to be seen. Doug Canning eventually found and rejoined him, and both headed southeast for home. "I've got trouble, Doug," Holmes transmitted. "Not enough gas to get back to the Canal." Canning settled in off the other P-38's left wing and replied, "I'll stay with you . . . no sweat," and so he did. Holmes switched back and forth between his tanks for the next ninety minutes but finally decided there was no way he could reach Fighter Two, so the pilots let down for the Russell Islands. Crossing Pavuvu, Canning accelerated then lined up with Sunlight Field on Banika's northeastern shoreline.

Roaring in with his gear and flaps down, he startled the construction crews but they understood the emergency situation and scattered, taking the heavy equipment with them. Besby Holmes dropped the Lightning in hard on the partially finished rolled-coral runway, and "came to a skidding halt near the far end. When I opened the canopy my flying suit was dripping wet." As part of the top-cover flight, Doug Canning had enough fuel to low approach then hop the fifty-nine miles over to Fighter Two and land safely. Fortunately for Holmes, a PT boat arrived in Wernham Cove a few hours later and her skipper found out about the stranded fighter. The boat's three V-12 Packards were modified high-performance aircraft engines, so the 100-octane fuel on board could also power Holmes's Allisons. The Navy gave him 120 gallons and he was off to Guadalcanal.

Ray Hine survived the Zero attack at Moila Point, and got at least as far as the mouth of the Blanche Channel in southeastern New Georgia. Missing Aircrew Report (MACR) 609 includes a statement from Besby Holmes that he last saw Hine at 0940 (Guadalcanal Time) south of Shortland Island trailing vapor or smoke, apparently heading southeast toward the Wilson Straights off Vella Lavella, northwest of New Georgia. Around 1100, a PBY Catalina had offloaded supplies for Allied coast-watchers and took off from the Segi Bay area in New Georgia, bound for Espiritu Santo.

The pilot, Lieutenant (j.g.) Harry Metke from Navy Patrol Squadron (VP) 44, had spotted Mitchell's P-38s as they were inbound for Bougainville and heard the chatter on the radio later, so when a damaged Lightning showed up off his right wing south of New Georgia, he wasn't overly surprised. The fighter's left engine was feathered, and holes were visible in the cowling, but after Metke contacted the Army pilot on the common emergency frequency, Hine told him he had the fuel to make it back. He also asked for a compass bearing to Guadalcanal, which the Navy pilot provided. The Lightning waggled its wings, banked up gently on its one engine, and pulled away southeast for Guadalcanal. Lieutenant Ray Hine was never seen again.

But Rex Barber was.

Constantly leaning out his engine and cutting corners where he could, Rex coasted into Guadalcanal just south of Cape Esperance over the Gallego volcano. Stretching westward toward him the bloody, hard-fought island spread out off his nose, with Lunga Point thirty miles ahead. Nestled at the curve of the bay was Kukum, and south of it lay Henderson Field and Edson's Ridge. The overhead sun turned Ironbottom Sound into a sky-blue basin, its waves glistening as they rolled in toward the indigo shoreline and Doma Cove with no indication of the twisted ships, burned-out planes, and dead men who lay beneath. Right of the nose lay Mount Austen, and to the left was the crooked Matanikau, where so many Marines died. Savo Island passed directly off the solitary Lightning's left wing as Barber crossed Guadalcanal's jagged west coast and the graveyard of the Imperial 17th Army.

Barely two months earlier the Japanese survivors had been pulled aboard their destroyers at Kamimbo, Bonegi, and Segilau as the Americans closed in. It was a stark reminder that without the bayonets and bullets, and without the Cactus Air Force, there would have been no victory on the Canal and this mission today would not have been possible. Paralleling the Sound, the Lightning swept in over the runway's edge at Fighter Two. Rex Barber was the last to land. Though he didn't know at the time, April 18, 1943, would be his last combat mission over the Southwest Pacific. As he shut down the plane, he was out of gas and ammunition; there were 52 hits on his fuselage, wings, and tail section from the Zeros, which made 104 rear-to-front holes. There were streaks of paint from pieces of the second Betty on the leading edge of his left wing, along with chunks of the bomber.

By midafternoon enough information had been pieced together that one of Admiral Mitscher's staff officers, Lieutenant Commander William A. Read, crafted the first formal report detailing the mission results, and Message No. 180229 was sent to Admiral Halsey on Nouméa:

POP GOES THE WEASEL
P-38S LED BY MAJOR J. MITCHELL USAAF VISITED KAHILI AREA. ABOUT 0930L SHOT DOWN TWO BOMBERS ESCORTED BY 6 ZEROS FLYING CLOSE FORMATION. 1 OTHER BOMBER SHOT DOWN BE-LIEVED ON TEST FLIGHT. 3 ZEROS ADDED TO THE

SCORE SUMS TOTAL 6. 1 P-38 FAILED RETURN. APRIL 18 SEEMS TO BE OUR DAY.

April 18 was certainly a date the Japanese would never forget.

One year earlier, Lieutenant Colonel Jimmy Doolittle's raiders had bombed Tokyo and profoundly shocked the Japanese. Mitscher, who had been captain of the USS *Hornet,* remembered the day since he had taken Doolittle to within striking range of Japan. Now, if Yamamoto was truly dead, another deadly wound with far greater implications had been inflicted deep into the core of Japan's spirit. However, all the pilots could do was relate the destruction of the bombers, not identify those on board.

Mitscher, as an aviator, knew very well the physical, mental, and emotional costs of the mission, and wanted full credit given for the superlative airmanship, marksmanship, and courage of those concerned. Read, who would eventually retire as a vice admiral, later wrote, "I was instructed [by Mitscher] to prepare recommendations . . . for the Congressional Medal of Honor and for spot promotions."

Captain Watanabe flew out of Rabaul at dawn on Monday, April 19, with Captain Okubo, the chief medical officer of the Southeast Area Fleet. After landing on Bougainville just after 0800, both officers proceeded immediately to the makeshift hospital and visited Admiral Ugaki, who begged them to get to the crash site immediately. What if Yamamoto had survived? After all, Ugaki had lived through a similar crash. Watanabe commandeered a three-place, open cockpit, fabric-covered Type-94 Reconnaissance Seaplane and set off in search of his friend.* While this was occurring, Flight Petty Officer Hayashi was flown back to Rabaul, debriefed by naval intelligence, and sworn to secrecy.†

All morning Watanabe flew back and forth over the jungle dropping messages in net bags for anyone below looking for the crash site. Both additional search parties, Lieutenant Furukawa's SNLF detachment and the army's eleven men under Lieutenant Hamasuna, were hacking their way through the thick, buzzing jungle "untouched by ax since the beginning of history." Watanabe, frustrated by the dense canopy of trees, had his plane land just offshore, where he was taken aboard

---

* Kawanishi E7K, called an "Alf" by the Allies; very possibly from the 938 Kokutai operating from the Tuha Channel Seaplane Base on Shortland Island.
† Hiroshi Hayashi survived the war and eventually retired to the remote island of Yakushima, forty miles off the southern tip of Kyushu.

a waiting minesweeper. Sixty men had been formed into another search party, and the captain took them by boat up the twisting Wamai River into Bougainville's mangrove swamps.

By sunset on April 19 nothing had yet been found. Then one of the soldiers with Lieutenant Hamasuna smelled gasoline. Following their noses through the vines and creepers they pushed into a freshly burned clearing approximately 2.5 miles south of the Buin–Buka road, and 12.5 miles northwest of Moila Point. The Japanese officer found "the large tailfin of the wrecked Type-1 land-based attack plane . . . the massive fuselage had broken just in front of the Rising Sun mark . . . dead bodies were lying about the wreckage."

Approaching from the northeast, Hamasuna saw a large, white "323" stenciled on the tail section. The main fuselage, "a burned out hulk," was a few yards ahead off to the north side, and several hundred feet ahead, in a line east from the tail, lay the nose section. There were no wings attached to any part of the aircraft, but looking up through the thick trees it was obvious that they were torn off as the plane came down through the jungle. The left wing was nowhere in sight, but the right wing lay about fifteen feet ahead of the nose section on the right side. In the gap between the rear and forward sections the lieutenant found the bodies of two more high-ranking officers, both admirals. One man was on the ground, his dress white uniform a stark contrast against the green foliage. Flat on his back, the officer bore the gold epaulettes of a rear admiral.

Just to the left of this corpse was another man.

It was quite odd. He was still strapped firmly into his seat, but facing the tail section with his head drooping forward as though asleep. This officer wore a green uniform with ribbons on the chest, no cap, and black flying boots. As Hamasuna approached he could see the man had close-cropped gray hair and also wore epaulettes, but with three cherry blossoms. He was a *Kaigun-taishō*, a full admiral, and he was clutching a samurai sword with his white-gloved left hand, holding it upright next to his thigh.* The right hand rested on his lap, but as Hamasuna stared at the left glove again he saw the middle and index fingers tied back with thread; a full admiral who was missing two fingers. The lieutenant knew who this man was.

It was Isoroku Yamamoto.

---

* The sword was a gift from Yamamoto's elder brother Kihachi, and was made by a swordsmith named Sadayoshi Amada, who bore the same given name as the admiral's natural father, Sadayoshi Takano. Yamamoto felt the sword was a good-luck charm and would keep him safe at the front—apparently not.

The eleven men cut small trees and built a small, thatched shelter in an open area near the tail section. Yamamoto's corpse and the other ten bodies, most of them badly burned, were placed in the shelter, then covered with banyan leaves. After leaving offerings of water for the dead men, Hamasuna and his ten soldiers set off northeast for Aku, planning to return in the morning for the bodies. On the way back they discovered the exhausted Sasebo SNLF detachment and passed word of the discovery. Lieutenant Furukawa elected to camp where he was, and asked the soldiers to return at dawn to guide them to the wreck. Farther east, along the banks of the Wamai, Captain Watanabe kept searching till midnight, then collapsed in a makeshift camp until morning.

A verbal report was passed from Ako to Buin, and from there to South Eastern Area Fleet Headquarters on Rabaul. Admiral Kusaka prepared Report No. 2, and subsequently dispatched Telegram No. 181941 (TOP SECRET) to the chief of the Navy General Staff and the minister of the navy. In part it read, "It seems as if plane No. 1 made forced landing 303 degrees 9.8 nautical miles from Moira [*sic*] Point. Although three aboard plane No. 2 were soon rescued by lookout personnel and motor launch, the others seem to have been unable to escape. Arrangements being made to salvage plane, 100 meters off shore."

The next morning, April 20, the Japanese lieutenants and their men returned to the crash site to extract the bodies. While they cut their way south through the jungle, an aircraft signaled Watanabe, and he also returned downriver. Hamasuna's soldiers and Furukawa's sailors transported the corpses on stretchers to the coast, then the army detachment returned north to Ako. It was after 1600 by the time Watanabe joined Furukawa at the Wamai estuary and moved the eleven bodies aboard the No. 15 minesweeper idling offshore.* There, under an awning stretched over the bow, Captain Okubo conducted a preliminary autopsy of Yamamoto while the boat headed for Moila Point.

There were two wounds from metal fragments in the admiral's body. One piece passed through the seat and into his body through the left shoulder blade. The second entered below Yamamoto's left jawbone, traveled through his skull, and exited through the temple

---

* At 242 feet long with a draft of less than 7 feet, the W-13 class minesweeper was perfect for inshore operations. The W-15 was damaged by the USS *Tilefish* (SS-07) on March 5, 1945, in the Ryukyu Islands and later abandoned.

near his right eye. "This alone would have killed him outright," Okubo reported. After an eighteen-mile trip down the coast and around the point, the bodies were offloaded on the Kangu beach pier, placed in coffins, then taken by truck seven miles north to Buin. After sunset on April 20, in a tent outside headquarters the First Base Unit's chief medical officer, Lieutenant Commander Gisaburo Tabuchi, performed Yamamoto's official autopsy and in part his report read:

1. Almost center part of left shoulder blade, there was a wound the size of the tip of a little finger. The wound towards inside and up.

2. A shot hole at left side of lower jaw. Outlet of upper part of right eye, size fingerprint by thumb.

According to Agawa, "Yamamoto's body had wounds about the size of the tip of one little finger where a machine-gun bullet had entered at the angle of the left lower jaw and emerged at the right, and an entry wound the size of the tip of one's index finger in the center of the left shoulder blade. The latter hole went upward and to the right, but there was no exit wound."

Clearly these were fragments of Barber's .50-caliber bullets or 20 mm cannon shells, as actual rounds from either would have blown Yamamoto's chest out or taken his head off. The piece entering the admiral's left shoulder blade appears to have hit a horizontal seat support and then deflected up and into his back, which accounts for the observed angle and lack of an exit hole. Watanabe probed the wound with his finger, but the fragment was too deep to be found. The other fragment entered under the left jaw, sliced through Yamamoto's skull, and, as observed, killed him instantly.

Following the autopsy, ten cremation pits layered with brush and wood were dug on the First Base Unit farm, with one lone pit across the road for Yamamoto. Coffins were placed on top of each pile, more wood was laid over them, and then they were doused with gasoline. Fires were lit and allowed to burn through the rest of the night under a watchful guard. By midafternoon on April 21 the pits were cool enough for the remains to be extracted, and at 1500 Watanabe himself retrieved Yamamoto's ashes.* No urns were available, so they placed each man's ashes in small wooden boxes, wrapped in white cloth and labeled with a letter. The pits were refilled and a pair of papaya trees, the ad-

---

* Also, according to Agawa, the admiral's Adam's apple.

miral's favorite fruit, were planted next to Yamamoto's mound.

Watanabe, though exhausted and wracked with dengue fever, arrived back at Rabaul on the afternoon of April 22, 1943, with all eleven boxes. News of the tragic loss of their commander would have been a catastrophic blow to the Combined Fleet and the rest of the military on Rabaul, so Yamamoto's ashes were quietly conveyed to the Southeast Area Fleet Headquarters. Here, late that night, a private wake was conducted by candlelight in a dugout across from the headquarters, very close to the cottage the admiral had left only four days earlier.

On the morning of April 23, 1943, Watanabe took the ashes to Truk, and by afternoon Yamamoto had returned to his flag cabin on the battleship *Musashi* to await the long voyage back to Japan.

While the admiral made his final flight from Rabaul to Truk, Rex Barber and Tom Lanphier made one of their own for quite different reason: rest and recuperation leave. First they traveled to Nouméa, where they were met by Colonel Dean C. Strother, commander of all 13th Air Force fighters, then all three went on to Auckland, New Zealand, to enjoy clean sheets, golf, and a respite from the war. While there, and with the blessing of the U.S. Navy, the pilots were interviewed by J. Norman Lodge, senior correspondent of the Associated Press.

"He would talk about the mission," Barber recalled, "give us some fact, then ask, 'Is that about right?' He knew generally about every detail of the mission." Lodge put the story together but Strother told him it would never get past the Navy censors, and he was correct. The text *did* get to Admiral Halsey's office and he exploded, for good reason. Most of the story was typical propaganda written in bad shorthand, but several lines were not, and they froze the naval officers who read them: "we have every reason [to] believe twas *yamamoto* in one of bomber . . . as we had been tracking yamamoto right into truk and *had known where he was every minute* of those five days. . . ." (Italics added.)

Halsey ordered all copies of the story to be collected and held by naval intelligence. He forwarded the story to CINCPAC Headquarters at Pearl Harbor, and Admiral Nimitz promptly ordered an inquiry. Halsey then had the three Army pilots report to him when they returned to Nouméa.

"He just stared at us," Rex Barber recalled, still offended forty-five years later, "Then he started in on a tirade of profanity the like of which I had never heard before. He accused us of everything he could think of from being traitors to our country to being so stupid that we had no right to wear the American uniform. We should be court-martialed, reduced to privates, and jailed for even talking to Lodge about the Yamamoto mission. He asked no questions and would not give any of us the opportunity to say a word or answer his charges."

Halsey waved his hand rudely toward the door, and did not return the officers' salutes. They left, with Lanphier and Barber returning to the Canal, where they very quickly received orders back to the United States. Lanphier, through his father's connections, was given an assignment to USAAF Headquarters in Washington, while Rex was dispatched to oblivion as an instructor at Westover Field, Massachusetts. "Bull" Halsey certainly proved beyond doubt that he richly deserved his sobriquet. Aggressive and decisive, he was invaluable as a combat commander, and in the middle of a war, at his level, there was little time for niceties: but this case was an exception. These men had undertaken what many believed to be a suicide mission in order to kill an irreplaceable enemy commander. They had done so, survived, and deserved better than the shabby, unprofessional treatment meted out by Halsey.

A different man would have thought first, then reacted, by having Norman Lodge investigated and questioned immediately as to his sources. A different man would have remembered that the operation was originally a *Navy* mission, so any leaked information as to Yamamoto's itinerary had to come from the Navy, not the Army. Both pilots should have been more circumspect when interviewed, but Lodge questioned them in the presence of Colonel Strother, their overall commander, so they naturally believed his article was sanctioned by the Army's 13th Air Force, and the Navy's South Pacific Area Command. Otherwise, what was the reporter doing there?

Halsey, Nimitz, and everyone concerned were absolutely correct to be alarmed at the security lapse. The main argument against the mission had been potentially compromising the JN-25 Code and, in fact, the idea that the code was broken did occur to some Japanese officers. Admiral Jinichi Kusaka, commander of the Southeast Area Fleet at Rabaul, believed the codes had been broken by the Americans. The Fourth Division of the Navy General Staff was responsible for encryption, and Kusaka had sent them a message well *before* Yamamoto's death concerning this possibility; there was no reply. Again, Japanese hubris worked in America's favor, and the official opinion was summed up by Admiral Ugaki himself. "How could they [the Americans] possibly break the Japanese codes?" Now, however, they were sure to realize it had been done, if Lodge's story got out.

But it never did. The official Navy cover story, about a coastwatcher sighting the Betty bombers leaving Rabaul, was plausible enough, and in any event the Japanese believed the whole incident was a coincidence. Even if the code-breaking capability was compromised, and it was not, this was a risk accepted by Nimitz from the beginning, so allowing the men who flew the mission to be castigated was unworthy. Halsey was so thrilled when he heard Mitscher's news on April 18 he told Admiral Kelly Turner that "I'd hoped to lead that scoundrel up Pennsylvania Avenue in chains, with the rest of you kicking him where it would do the most good!"

Before Halsey's contemptuous, ill-mannered dismissal the admiral rifled through a sheaf of paper, lifted the pages up, and snapped, "Know what these are? These are recommendations for Mitchell, Lanphier, Barber, Holmes, and Hine to get the Medal of Honor. As far as I'm concerned, none of you deserve even the Air Medal for what you did. You ought to face a court-martial, but because of the importance of the mission, I'm reducing these citations to the Navy Cross." Not content with this, Halsey also down-

graded the decorations for every other pilot on the
mission.

Commander Read had indeed written the Medal of
Honor citations as ordered by Admiral Marc Mitscher,
and these were approved by Marine Air Group 12, then
forwarded to Halsey for endorsement. Barber's read, in
part:

FIRST LIEUTENANT REX T. BARBER, USAAF
For extraordinary achievement, outstanding courage, superb marksmanship, and conspicuous
gallantry in action as a pilot of the 339th Fighter
Squadron. On April 18, 1943, Lieutenant Barber
participated in the longest successful panned
fighter interception on record. . . . He pressed home
his attack with such fierce determination and excellent marksmanship that fragments of a bomber he
shot down were embedded in his wing. With utter
disregard for the enormous odds against him Lieutenant Barber displayed superlative gallantry and
intrepidity in action with the enemy, and at the risk
of his life above and beyond the call of duty . . . he
made a singular contribution to the cause of the
United Nations in keeping with the finest traditions
of the United States Military Service.

Admiral Mitscher enthusiastically recommended approval and forwarded his signed endorsement, which read:

> **Commander Air, Solomon Islands considers that the execution of this mission approached perfection, and that an attack of this nature, against a target of utmost importance, within a few minutes flying time of the enemy fighter base at Kahili, required the highest degree of skill and valor.**

Halsey's pettiness regarding the recommended decorations was the most disgraceful slight of all. Jimmy Doolittle had received the award for his raid on Tokyo, and Operation VENGEANCE was no less dangerous or difficult, and it certainly had larger consequences for the outcome of the Pacific War. Five pilots from the VENGEANCE mission were recommended for the Medal of Honor, and as of this writing there has been no redress of the injustice done these men, or recognition for the "skill and valor" John Mitchell and Rex Barber so richly deserve.

Life and the war went on.

For everyone except Tom Lanphier, the flight was just another combat mission. The fighter pilots did what they were trained to do, and what they were in the Pacific to do. John Mitchell later remarked, "I didn't give a damn, we did what were supposed to do. It didn't make any difference to me who shot the admiral down." Unfortunately, Lanphier did not see it that way, and once remarked to Rex Barber, "Rex, you're here because you're patriotic. Well, I'm here because I'm patriotic too, but I have another reason. I want to be President of the United States and I'm going to stake my life on a war record that will allow me the opportunity to do just that."

According to author Carroll Glines, Lanphier personally wrote the Fighter Interception Report (FIR) on the evening of April 18, thus ensuring his version of the mission was now the official one. Major John Mitchell, who planned and led the operation, was not consulted and neither was Rex Barber or any other participating pilot. This is extremely irregular, as reports are always compiled by intelligence officers based on pilot statements; the pilot never writes it himself, but in this case Lanphier did. He also acknowledged his authorship to Barber and Colonel Strother, and the report itself is extremely journalistic relative to normal combat reports, which are terse, direct, and as factual as possible. Lanphier's name appears first in the list of pilots, and his actions are prominently detailed, including "exploding the first" Zero.

Indeed, Lanphier had previously displayed a penchant for exaggeration. He had claimed sole credit for the destruction on March 28 of the "destroyer" (subchaser), which did *not* sink, and cost Barber forty inches of his left wing. While riding on a B-17 earlier in 1942, he also claimed to have shot down a Zero after seizing one of the waist guns and opening fire. This account was refuted by the crew, and there is also no record of that bomber being attacked that day, yet Lanphier's "kill" was added to his score. Then there was Lanphier's purported kill of a Zero on Christmas Eve 1942, while flying a 70th FS Airacobra, though air combat researcher Dr. Frank Olynyk has never found mention of this in the squadron's records, and claims of aerial victories are always documented.

Overall, Tom Lanphier claimed seven kills, two more than necessary to make him an ace, which is a status he desperately desired, though the USAF officially credits him with 5.5 aerial victories.* At one point this was reduced to 4.5 official kills by the Air

---

* The American Fighter Aces Association still lists Lanphier as an ace with seven aerial victories, but it is not an official body and Lanphier happened to be its first president.

Force Historical Research Agency (AFHRA), but the Zero credit for April 18 was reinstated despite Kenji Yanagiya's statement and official Japanese records to the contrary. Dr. Daniel Haulman, the chief of organizational histories at the Air Force Historical Research Agency, explains "the credit had been awarded, and we did not really have the authority to take a credit away. Our job is to keep track of the credits that were officially awarded, and not to determine whether or not they were deserved." Dr. Haulman, a distinguished author and researcher in his own right, is quite correct; however, the USAF can convene a Victory Credit Review Board to establish the credibility of past claims. Such a review for this mission is long overdue.

As for the other destroyed-Zero claims made on this mission, there were, in fact, other fighter/reconnaissance planes airborne over Bougainville on April 18, 1943. It must also be stressed that most of these aircraft did not utilize radios; they were assigned to different units, and the American method of combined joint operations simply did not exist for the Japanese so they operated independently. Frank Gibney and Roger Pineau, two eminent postwar naval historians who served as Japanese language officers during the war, interviewed one of these other pilots and recorded the conversation in a June 1949 letter.* Lieutenant Yasuo Shimizu was part of a fourteen-aircraft flight ordered to intercept and "guard" Admiral Yamamoto as he came in over Bougainville. These fourteen aircraft consisted of ten two-seaters and four three-seaters, so they were not fighters, but rather armed reconnaissance seaplanes.

The Japanese had a variety of these, but the two-seaters were likely Mitsubishi F1M2 Petes and the three-seaters either Kawanishi E7K "Alfs" or Aichi E13 Jakes. Operating from the Tuha Channel, the 958 Kokutai flew all of these aircraft, and Japanese seaplane units often utilized disparate aircraft grouped together. Shimizu and the other floatplanes did not engage anyone, but he did observe P-38s attacking the bombers. Based on his inability to engage, and the fact that the Americans never sighted his floatplanes, the fourteen aircraft had to be north of Empress Augusta Bay in the Cape Torokina area and missed the entire intercept.

However, if these aircraft were sent up, then land-

---

* After the war Gibney served as the Tokyo bureau chief for *Time*, and Pineau as the State Department's chief of Far East intelligence. Both men were talented and prolific authors.

based fighters from Kahili were also certainly airborne, or nearly so, as well. As part of Operation *I-go* the air group from the carrier *Ryuho* was at Kahili, as were the 582, 201, and 204 air groups. One report states at least 16 of these Zeros were launched as escorts, and though this is unconfirmed it is highly plausible. After all, the ground contingent at Kahili and Ballale were turned out in their dress uniforms awaiting the admiral's arrival, so dispatching additional fighter escorts is entirely in keeping with the reception of the Combined Fleet's commander in chief.

Rex Barber describes in detail how Besby Holmes shot down a Zero, and he never mentions floats, which are impossible to miss, so it had to be a land-based fighter. Holmes confirmed Zero kills for both Hine and Barber, and also says nothing about floats. We know the six escorts from Rabaul all eventually returned; this is verified by Kenji Yanagiya and by the documented deaths of the remaining five pilots later in the war.[*]

Therefore any additional Zero kills had to come from Kahili or Ballale. Lanphier's only Zero claim

---

[*] Yoshimi Hidaka, June 7, 1943; Takeshi Morizaki, June 16, 1943; Yasuji Okazaki, June 7, 1943; Toyomitsu Tsujinoue, July 1, 1943; and Shoichi Sugita, April 15, 1945.

was one of the Rabaul escorts, and this is clearly erro-
neous. He certainly could have damaged one of them
in the initial low-to-high pass, and this may have
been the one Zero that landed at Ballale with an engine issue. "As I caught my last glimpse," Lanphier
recounted, "the plane was almost on its back and
smoking." Quite possibly, but it was not destroyed.
Lanphier never mentions engaging any other fighters
and, as he was first to return to Guadalcanal, he obviously did not loiter over Bougainville.

On May 7, 1943, the battleship *Musashi* slid slowly
away from the Harushima anchorage in Truk Lagoon and turned northwest for Japan. Carrying eleven
white-wrapped boxes of ashes, she dropped anchor off
Kisarazu on the southeast edge of Tokyo Bay fourteen
days later. Isoroku Yamamoto was home.

That same day, Imperial Headquarters officially
announced to the people of Japan that, "In April this
year, Admiral Yamamoto Isoroku, commander in chief
of the Combined Fleet, met a gallant death on board
his plane in an encounter with the enemy in the course
of directing overall operations at the front line."

Just before noon two days later his ashes were transferred aboard the destroyer *Yugumo*, which bore them
ten miles across Tokyo Bay to the Yokosuka Naval

Base.* Watanabe carried them ashore and was met on the pier by Yoshimasa Yamamoto, the admiral's oldest son. They boarded a special train for the twenty-eight-mile trip, and with thousands of people lining the tracks Watanabe arrived at 1443 into Tokyo Station. More than two hundred dignitaries were on hand, including several princes, Prime Minister Hideki Tojo, and Reiko, the admiral's widow. A processional led down Uchibori Street past the Sakuradamon Gate of the Imperial Palace, then south to the Navy Club at Shiba, where the ashes would lie in state for the next fourteen days.

When the box was opened, the papaya leaves from Bougainville were still green.

Isoroku Yamamoto, now a fleet admiral, was given a state funeral on June 5, 1943. At 0850 his coffin was laid onto a black gun carriage and, as Chopin's funeral march played, solemnly wheeled through Tokyo to Hibaya Park, across the moat from the palace. Sheltered by a plain wood structure and covered with black and white curtains, the only splash of color was red roses sent by Mussolini. Following the ceremony, tens of thousands of Japanese came to pay their respects,

---

* Less than five months later the *Yugumo* was sunk by the USS *Chevalier* and USS *Selfridge* off Vella Lavella in New Guinea, less than one hundred miles from Yamamoto's death site.

and then the admiral's ashes were divided. One urn was taken to Tama cemetery in western Tokyo and interred beside those of Admiral Togo, under whose command Yamamoto lost his fingers in 1905. The second urn was taken north to the admiral's home in Nagaoka, where they were received by his seventy-eight-year-old half sister and placed in the Chokoji Zen temple.

Yamamoto's war was over, and the death knell had sounded for the Japanese Empire. His loss is impossible to quantify, though without him fighting against the Allies in the Pacific the war became somewhat more predictable. Would Yamamoto have been forced back to Japan's Inner Defensive Line as quickly as his successor, Admiral Mineichi Koga? Possibly. Would Yamamoto have exacted a much higher cost in American blood for those hard-won victories? Almost certainly. We will never know. But at the tactical, battlefield level, less blood was spilled and the path to Allied victory was made easier with the admiral dead. Perhaps the impact of his death was best summarized by Admiral Mitsumasa Yonai, the navy minister, who stated, "Yamamoto himself may have felt satisfied to die when and where he did, but he was a man whom both Japan and the navy could very ill spare."

Epilogue

The controversy over who shot down the Type 1 Attack Bomber, G4M1 Model 11, Tail #323, carrying Admiral Isoroku Yamamoto from Rabaul to Ballale on April 18, 1943, is as unnecessary as it is unfortunate. Unnecessary because the mission was accomplished; Yamamoto perished, a tremendous, unrecoverable blow was dealt to the Japanese, and vengeance exacted against the man who plunged a knife into America's back. Unfortunate because Tom Lanphier was a brave man, and in Rex Barber's words, "make no mistake, he was a good pilot."

Lanphier did turn into the oncoming Zeros, which gave Barber the opportunity to close and kill the Betty. Without this distraction, the Japanese fighters would have certainly rolled in behind the P-38s, very likely saving the bomber and Yamamoto. This should have been enough for anyone serving his country in a combat zone, but it was not enough for Lanphier. "The Yamamoto mission was a 'must' for Tom if he were to get a record that would get him national notice."

In the end, there is no controversy: spatially, geometrically, and mathematically, Tom Lanphier and *Phoebe* could not have destroyed the lead Betty bomber. The spatial geometry requires a diagram, but the math is straightforward and unequivocal. These calculations are the first of three nails in the controversy coffin. First, according to Rex Barber and Kenji Yanagiya, the P-38s were sighted late by the Japanese as they were coming up from low to high, a position from which Americans rarely attacked, and the visual pickup, or "tally," was very difficult looking down at dark aircraft over dark jungle.

By both accounts the Lightnings were within 1.5 to 2 miles from the bombers when sighted, about fifteen to twenty-five seconds away. At this point, the Zeros nosed over and jettisoned their tanks, which was a prearranged signal for Takeo Kotani in the lead bomber to dive for safety. Lanphier saw the Zeros and did the only thing he could: turned to attack.

A full military power climb for Lanphier and Barber was 280 to 300 mph, or about 440 feet per second (fps), so after Lanphier split left, Rex bored straight in at about a 90-degree angle off the lead bomber's right wing. He closed the distance, overshot, and pulled back in directly above the second Betty in twenty seconds or so. Remember that the bomber was moving forward, diving down, and accelerating from 200 mph to a methanol-injected war emergency speed of 300 mph.

Rex follows, adjusts his own throttles, closes the range, and aims during the next twenty seconds, while below his left wing the second bomber spins left and dives out of the fight. So forty seconds elapsed since the Lightings split, and in that time Lanphier had passed nose-to-nose with the Zeros, *Phoebe* going vertical in a steep climb up from 4,500 feet to 6,000 feet with the Japanese coming down in a dive. Going up bleeds off "energy," or airspeed, from the P-38, and Lanphier slows from 300 mph at the onset of his zoom to 170 mph at the top of his loop or chandelle. Here he flips over and rolls out, looking back the way he came to try to see the Zeros, or the Betty. Though he is generally going up, or into the "vertical," Lanphier is also moving horizontally across the ground. In forty seconds, with an *average* speed of 235 fps, he travels about 9,400 feet, or 1.8 miles northwest, in the opposite direction from the Betty.

During this same forty seconds, just as Rex Barber

is ready to open fire, he and the Betty have traveled 2.5 miles southeast in the other direction. So as Lanphier hangs in his straps looking down, he and Rex Barber are a *minimum* of 4.3 miles apart.* Lanphier, presumably, spots the bomber and drops his nose to chase. It takes sixteen seconds to accelerate vertically down from 170 mph to 400 mph, and in that time he would cover 3,468 feet over the ground while the Betty, now at 300 mph, covers 4,800 feet. As everyone levels off on the treetops, 56 seconds into the fight, Lanphier is a minimum of 24,036 feet (4.5 miles) northwest of Rex Barber and the Betty, who are racing southeast on a 140-degree heading for Moila Point. Lanphier has a 100 mph/147 fps speed advantage, so in a straight "tail chase" it would require 157 seconds to close within a maximum firing range of one thousand feet from the bomber.

Two minutes and 37 seconds.

But the fight has already been under way for fifty-six seconds at this point. In a 1975 videotaped interview accompanied by a sworn affidavit, Kenji Yanagiya stated, "From the time I first sighted any of the P-38s

---

* That is, 22,704 feet (4.3 miles) plus 4,800 feet bomber horizontal flight in sixteen seconds minus 3,468 feet, Lanphier's horizontal flight in sixteen seconds.

until the Admiral's airplane was down in the jungle was two minutes or less."

If, *best* case, the Betty flew on for another sixty-four seconds before crashing into the jungle, Lanphier would have only closed the distance between them to 14,256 feet, or 2.7 miles; nowhere close enough for a gunshot.* The only thing he could do was watch the Betty crash into the jungle, and Lanphier did this as he later confirmed Rex Barber's victory. Interestingly, working backward from the known crash site indicates the bomber actually flew for about sixty seconds past the point where Lanphier began his tail chase. There-fore, between the point we know Barber began and the spot where the bomber crashed it would have been mathematically impossible for Lanphier to shoot down the lead Betty bomber, the bomber confirmed to Rex Barber by Lanphier himself.

There just was not enough time.

Tom Lanphier stated, right from the beginning, that he saw Barber shoot down a Betty bomber. He wrote in the Fighter Interception Report (April 21, 1943), "He [Barber] went for one of the bombers but its maneu-

---

* The P-38 performance data were derived from Lighting pilot George T. Chandler's June 5, 1989, in-flight analysis of this interception and shootdown.

vers caused him to overshoot a little. He whipped back, however, and although pursued by Zeros, caught the bomber and destroyed it." There were only two G4M1 Type-1 attack planes over Bougainville that morning, and Barber undisputedly killed the one that carried Yamamoto. It is equally undisputed that he brought down the second plane, with assistance from Besby Holmes; there were no other Bettys airborne.

Despite numerous inconsistencies in all subsequent versions of his story, Lanphier also steadfastly maintained that he intercepted a Betty from a 90-degree angle off the bomber's right wing, not from behind. "I fired a long steady burst across the bomber's course of flight, from approximately right angles. The bomber's right engine, then its right wing burst into flame. . . ."

Yamamoto's bomber did veer about 20 degrees right of its original course, plowing into the jungle heading approximately 140 degrees, but it never turned more than that, so after the initial intercept it was geometrically impossible for Lanphier to approach the lead Betty at a right angle. The second Betty did turn, but Lanphier apparently never saw this aircraft, or if he did he never engaged it. Yanagiya plainly stated, "I first saw one P-38 *behind* the Admiral's airplane firing into it." Both Americans were behind the Betty, which never really turned, and so no one fired into Yamamoto's bomber from a right angle.

The second nail concerns the various forensic analyses of the wreckage. Again, Lanphier's statement is revealing: "Just as I moved into range of Yamamoto's bomber and its cannon, the bomber's wing tore off. The bomber plunged into the jungle. It exploded. That was the end of Isoroku Yamamoto."

This is damning on several levels. First, no American knew Yamamoto was actually aboard one of the bombers, and therefore could not possibly know which of the two he was in. Second, the bomber Tom Lanphier verified that Rex Barber shot down, the only bomber to go into the jungle, went in with both wings attached; nothing on it "tore off" and the only other Betty to go down that day went into the sea off Moila Point.

Barber's kill has been the subject of several highly credible, post-crash investigations beginning in 1972 with Dr. Charles Darby. A New Zealander and marine biologist, Darby made several crucial observations:

1) The aircraft entered the jungle approximately 40 degrees nose low, but in a *wings level* attitude. Both wings were still attached or roll control would have been impossible. The left wing was sheared off by trees

and was discovered approximately 150 feet behind the main wreckage. If the right wing had detached in flight, as claimed by Lanphier, the aircraft could not have entered the trees in a horizontal attitude, as it would have spun or cartwheeled. Also, a detached right wing would rest hundreds of feet away, yet it lies 15 feet forward of the fuselage on the right side. Finally, the right wing spars were *bent backward* along the line of the fuselage, which indicates a horizontal shearing as the plane hit the trees. In 1988 an aeronautical engineer confirmed that had the wing detached in flight, these same spars would have *bent upward* as the air flow over the still-flying Betty would have ripped the wing off vertically.

2) Both engines were found at the site, and the left engine was within fifty yards of the fuselage, near the left wing. There was scoring and damage to crumpled leading edge consistent with forward strikes against multiple objects: trees.

3) The left propeller had not been "feathered" or turned edge first into the airstream, which reduces drag and allows a longer glide if necessary. If a prop is not feathered the instantaneous drag would cause the exact situation Rex Barber encountered: the left wing dropped suddenly, and the plane veered left and slowed

drastically, which snapped the right wing up into the air as the left engine seized. No doubt Barber shot up the oil lines and oil pumps, so the pilot, either Kotani or Ohsaki, simply did not have the time to feather the propeller.

Ross Channon was an Australian working for Goodyear Rubber on Bougainville who visited the wreck in 1985 to specifically inspect the bullet and cannon holes. He reported:

> (a) [T]here are definite holes on the fuselage top forward of the tail fin . . . some of these holes are elongated and on an angle of approximately 15 degrees to the right of the fuselage centerline. This would fit with an attack from the rear and above slightly, sweeping from right to left.
>
> (b) [T]he wing I feel was torn off because of the crumpled damage on the leading edge . . . the wing is about 150 feet from the main wreckage, directly behind. Even at low altitude if the wing had been shot off it would surely be further away from the wreckage.

Terry Gwynn-Jones, an Australian author and pilot, lectured on the shootdown in 1988 at the Smithsonian Institution's National Air and Space Museum. He stated: (a) "the right wing didn't separate in flight but had separated by contact with a tall tree."

Incidentally, Lanphier claimed the Betty's gunners were viciously fighting back and despite this he managed to press in for the kill. "I was about to pass behind him [the Betty] with his guns still going which was bothering me, he just nosed into the treetops and blew up." He also stated in a postwar *New York Times* article that "[o]ut of [the bomber's] tail was a puffing a steady series of shots from the cannon lodged back there." No guns were found at the wreckage of Yamamoto's Betty by Lieutenant Hamasuna, first on the scene, or by any other team over the years. In fact, as this was an escorted transport mission, and the plane was already overweight, they apparently never loaded the four 7.7 mm machine guns and single Type 99 20 mm cannon.

Or if they did, the guns were not unlimbered and their absence at the wreck is still unexplained. The local people had no use for heavy weapons, and would not have taken them anyway as the Japanese killed anyone possessing military equipment. There was also no evidence of any return fire from Yamamoto's bomber, and the gunfire damage to *Miss Virginia* was all from the rear. There were no bullet or shellfire impact points from a forward aspect, and at one hundred feet it would have been impossible to miss the big Lightning. The second Betty did carry the standard guns, but according to Hiroshi Hayashi each weapon had only a single belt of ammunition, to save weight.

In 1991, Dr. Darby traveled to the United States and testified before a specially convened Air Force Board for Correction of Military Records concerning the Yamamoto mission. Excerpts from the transcript read:

(a) [B]y no stretch of the imagination could any large piece of the right wing have disappeared in flight.

(b) There was no evidence on any remaining wreckage of an attack from the bomber's starboard [right] beam as related in all of Lanphier's accounts.

The final nail in the controversy coffin are Yamamoto's well-documented wounds as described by Lieutenant Commander Tabuchi and Captain Okubo. Seated on the right side aft of the copilot, Yamamoto was partially shielded from three of Barber's four bursts by the radio compartment, the radio operator, and a bulkhead separating the cockpit area from the main fuselage. Rex's initial burst was fired from left to right over the bomber's tail, hitting the right wing area and starting a fire. There were eight non-self-sealing fuel tanks set between the spars of each wing: one inboard of the engine next to the fuselage, and three outboard. During his first burst Barber's .50-caliber rounds and 20 mm shells impacted the right wing area, piercing these outboard right tanks, severing fuel lines, and starting a fire. His second burst penetrated the inboard right fuel tank and went on into the cockpit area forward of Yamamoto, which very likely killed copilot Akiharu Ohsaki. The third burst was into the left engine area, followed by a fourth burst into the fuselage.

From his position one hundred feet aft and slightly below the Betty's left side, Rex simply nudged his nose a bit right when he fired this final burst. At this shallow angle, his rounds penetrated the fuselage over the wing from left to right, rear to forward. Though many of them would have remained intact, some would have impacted spars, bulkheads, and fixed equipment within the aircraft. The rounds fragmented, or spawled, and two of these flying bits of metal are what struck Yamamoto in his left shoulder blade, and under his left jawbone during Barber's final three-second burst into the fuselage from the *left* side.

Testifying in 1991, Dr. Darby stated, "There were scores of holes. But mainly just shrapnel that has broken off the aircraft; that is molten bullets [and] bits of molten airframe where it's been melted by impact from a shell. All of it is from rear to front."

It was fragments such as these that killed Yamamoto, as a hit from an intact .50-caliber round, let alone a 20 mm cannon shell, would have shredded the admiral. It is the position of the wounds that are relevant; both penetrated the admiral's body from the *left* and Lanphier, in all the variants of his story, always insisted he approached the bomber from the right. This detail never changed, so by his own admission he never fired into the aircraft from the left and could not have possibly killed the admiral, even if he had gotten within range—which he did not.

A May 25, 1988, memorandum written by Captain Roger Pineau details observations made by Dr. Steven Sohn, Captain USN, and Commander Gordon N. Wagner of the Armed Forces Institute of Pathology at Walter Reed Hospital, which in part state:

(3) Indications are that the projectiles(s) which struck Yamamoto came from below left, upward to right, back to front, perforating the mid brain, a lethal injury resulting in cadaveric spasms. Such death during high nervous stress of the attack could

have caused instant rigor mortis, and a vise-like grip on his sword which even the turbulence of the crash would not have shaken loose.

Therefore, the timing of the dogfight, the forensic analysis of damage to the wreck, and the fatal wounds sustained by Admiral Yamamoto all combine to refute Lanphier's claim. The so-called controversy has, over the past eight decades, been an unwelcome distraction from the true objective of the mission, which was to remove Yamamoto, and the success in doing so that all participants can claim. The skill and courage of all concerned should be, and are, another source of pride for all Americans. There is not now, and never was, a true controversy. The only pilot who fired on Betty #323, subsequently bringing it down over the Bougainville jungle and killing Isoroku Yamamoto, was Lieutenant Rex Theodore Barber.

On May 26, while the admiral's ashes rested in Tokyo, John Mitchell, Rex Barber, and five other pilots from the mission were ordered back to the United States for their reassignments. John Mitchell spent the next six months at Army Air Forces Headquarters, then left in December 1943 to command the newly activated 412th Fighter Group. This was a highly secretive unit involved in the operational test and evaluation of America's first jet fighter: the Bell P-59 Airacomet. During the summer of 1945, Mitch was sent to the European Theater of Operations (ETO) as a combat observer to impart his lessons learned, and study those from Europe.

After accumulating additional combat missions in the Spitfire and Hurricane, he asked for transfer back to the Pacific. Flying P-51 Mustangs now with the 15th Fighter Group, Mitchell escorted B-29s over Japan during the closing weeks of the war. On June 26, 1945, he downed his ninth Japanese fighter, a late-model Zero, over Kiso in central Japan, less than one hundred miles from Yamamoto's resting place in Nagaoka. Twenty days later he caught a pair of Kawanishi *Shiden* fighters, arguably the best dogfighting aircraft the Japanese produced, over Tsu just south of Tokyo Bay and sent them down in flames.★ Rising to command the 21st Fighter Group, Mitch flew escort missions from South Field, Iwo Jima, over Japan until the end of the war.

Rex Barber, now a captain, also could not remain on the sidelines, resting on his laurels, while the war was

---

★ Kawanishi N1K-J; called a "Rex" by the Allies, and the land-based version was fielded in 1944.

still being fought. Dislike for Westover Field quickly turned to disgust when he was thrown up against the worst type of military officer: one who missed out on combat and bitterly resented those who did not. Rebelling against the petty silliness, Rex and three other dissatisfied combat officers appropriated some surplus detonation cord, and had an impromptu fireworks show one Friday night at the Officers' Club. His commander was outraged, but could hardly discipline a man wearing the Navy Cross. On Monday morning all four veterans were standing at attention before an impotently irate lieutenant colonel who shouted, "You sons-a-bitches who wanted outa here finally get your wish! You're gone today!"

And they were.

Rex Barber joyfully left the training command and Massachusetts in late 1943 and never looked back. He was returning to combat where he belonged, flying P-38s with the 449th Fighter Squadron out of Suichwan Airfield in southeastern China. For the first few months of 1944 Rex flew close air support and escort missions, but this time his enemy were Japanese Army Air Force Ki-61 "Tonys" and Ki-43 "Oscars." Claiming three "probables," Rex, a major since April 1, flew another twenty-eight combat missions until April 29, 1944, when his luck ran out over Kiukang. As he stood on the seat to bail out, the D-ring that opened his parachute caught on the canopy and yanked him headfirst out of the cockpit. Hitting the tail, he broke his right arm at the elbow, spun around, and fractured his ankle. Clearing the burning fighter at barely four hundred feet above the ground, Rex got a half swing in the parachute then hit China; hard. Enemy units on the ground had seen the dogfight and hurried toward the crash site. Rex was under no illusions about his fate if captured, especially if the Japanese had pieced together his role in the Yamamoto mission.

Fortunately, two Chinese teenage boys had seen this as well, and got him out of the lake and into a ditch before the Japanese arrived. Coming back hours later after dark, they hid Rex for the next five weeks, treated his wounds as best they could, and slowly moved south toward Allied lines. Fifteen pounds lighter, he arrived back in American hands on June 6, 1944, as the Allies came ashore in Normandy. After being medically evacuated to the United States, Rex spent the next six months in Los Angeles undergoing multiple surgeries to repair his arm and ankle. Told he would never fly again, Barber took the news with his customary quiet good humor, then set about proving the doctors wrong.

He did just that. Rex Barber returned to flight status in 1945, when he joined the 412th Fighter Group and was briefly reunited with John Mitchell before the latter left again for the Pacific. Both men rejoiced on April 30 when Adolf Hitler shot himself in a bunker beneath the streets of Berlin as the Soviet 8th Guards Army surrounded the city. Germany surrendered on May 8, but those fighting in the Pacific expected no such capitulation from the Japanese Empire. As America tightened the noose around Japan, Imperial forces became even more reckless, ruthless, and fatalistic.

On April 1 the Americans invaded Okinawa, smallest of the Japanese Home Islands but Japanese soil nonetheless, with the U.S. Tenth Army and the III Amphibious Corps, including the 1st and 2nd Marine Divisions of Guadalcanal. Storming ashore in the largest seaborne invasion of the Pacific War, nearly 200,000 U.S. combat troops fought a vicious ninety-day battle that cost more lives than D-Day. Now less than 350 miles south of the southernmost Home Island of Kyushu, U.S. forces grimly assembled for invasion that the Joints Chiefs of Staff estimated would cost 1.2 million American casualties. Prepared to fight to the death, all Japanese on the Home Islands intended to die for their emperor, despite the forecasted loss of 5 million men, women, and children.

On August 6, 1945, three years to the day after Task Force 62 approached the Solomon Islands, a solitary aircraft lifted off at 0245 from North Field on the island of Tinian in the Northern Marianas. A B-29 Superfortress flying as "Dimples 82," under the command of Colonel Paul Tibbets, 509th Composite Group Commander, ponderously turned northwest and climbed out for the six-hour flight to Japan. At 0815 the bomber, named *Enola Gay* after Tibbets's mother, released a single ten-foot-long, 150-kiloton atomic bomb from her belly. Named "Little Boy," it detonated 1,968 feet above Hiroshima on Honshu, Japan's largest island. Shocked and disbelieving, the Japanese were still unrepentant and defiant. Three days later another Superfortress named *Bockscar* left Tinian, could not drop on its primary target of Kokura, and so dropped a second atomic bomb called "Fat Boy" over the port city of Nagasaki, on the island of Kyushu. This finally convinced the Japanese that resistance was futile, and that there was no way to combat this new weapon. Former prime minister Tojo, who, even after four years of war with the United States believed Americans were soft dilettantes obsessed with drinking and sex, maintained till the end that the "Greater East Asia War was justified and righteous."

With prevailing, ingrained attitudes like this, one must consider the cost had Rex Barber not killed Yamamoto on April 18, 1943. How much bloodier would the battles of Tarawa, Saipan, the Philippine Sea, Iwo Jima, and Okinawa have been if the man who knew America so well was alive to devise a defense? Objectively, we will never know. Subjectively, it is certain that hundreds of thousands of Americans live today because their fathers and grandfathers did *not* die in the Pacific at the hands of Isoroku Yamamoto.

Nevertheless, after the second bomb carbonized most of Nagasaki, Emperor Hirohito ordered an unconditional surrender, which took place aboard the USS *Missouri* in Tokyo Bay on September 2, 1945, not far from where Yamamoto's ashes arrived home. After a very brief thirty-minute ceremony where little was said, the eight diminutive Japanese representatives climbed back into a whaleboat and left.

World War II was over.

John Mitchell would return to combat during the Korean War in 1952, after assuming command of the famed 51st Fighter-Interceptor Wing based at Suwon. Flying the legendary F-86 Sabre from January through May 1953, Mitch downed four North Korean MiG-15 fighters, bringing his career total to fifteen enemy aircraft destroyed; a triple ace. He retired as a full colonel five years later. John William Mitchell, whose skill, discipline, and courage made Operation VEN-

GEANCE a reality, died on November 15, 1995, at the age of eighty-one. He now rests in Golden Gate National Cemetery next to his wife, Anne, on a California hilltop overlooking San Francisco Bay.

Rex Barber came home after the war and, like millions of other men, tried to pick up the bits of his former life as best he could. Some pieces fell back into place while others did not, and in 1947 he and his wife Jean divorced.* Flying was second nature now, and a true solace, so Rex remained a military pilot. It was jets now, in the 1st Fighter Group at March Field, California. Rex fell in love with the widow of Henry H. Trollope, a fellow fighter pilot who died in the Philippines, and he married Margaret Smith Trollope in late 1947. When America went to war again in Korea so did Lieutenant Colonel Rex Barber, flying missions out of Taegu, refining close air support tactics for jet fighters.

After returning from his second war in 1952, he attended LaCaze Academy in Washington, D.C., for Spanish language training, then took Margaret to Colombia, where he served as military attaché until June

---

* Richard Barber, Rex's first son, retired from the San Francisco Police Department as a shooting instructor and remains close to his brother, Rex Barber Jr., to this day.

1956. Returning to Panama City, Florida, with his six-week-old son Rex Theodore Barber Jr., the family then moved up to Myrtle Beach, South Carolina, home of the 354th Fighter-Day Wing.

Finishing the final few years of his career flying the F-100 Super Sabre, Rex was still at Myrtle Beach when his old friend Bob Petit, now also a full colonel, became the wing commander. The two men had not seen each other since that long-ago summer of 1943, when Petit loaned Barber his *Miss Virginia* for the Yamamoto mission, and both plane and pilot had changed the course of the war. On Friday nights at the Officers' Club the two veterans were often seen sitting together at a table in a dark corner. Younger pilots sang songs and flirted with local girls, but Rex and Bob were remembering those days on Guadalcanal, and the stark simplicity of combat. Lining up rows of shot glasses, both men drank toasts to each other, their beloved Lightnings, and friends who never returned from war.

By 1961 Rex had had enough; surviving 138 combat missions had garnered him the Navy Cross, two Silver Stars, and a Purple Heart, among other decorations. Just before his retirement Rex flew a Super Sabre across the country to visit his family home in Culver, Oregon. It was then that he decided that of all the places in the world he'd seen, from Fiji to New Zealand to China and everywhere in between, Oregon was where he wanted to call home for the rest of his life.

And he did.

Over the next forty years Rex and Margaret lived in Culver and Portland, finally settling on a farm near Terrebonne to bring up their own son under the wide sky and sage-scented air of the Deschutes Valley. He became a successful businessman, served in the volunteer fire department, and acquired large plots of land that his son and grandson still farm today. Rex served as a justice of the peace and from August 1969 to September 1976, was mayor of Culver. He loved his community, especially the children, and one of his greatest passions later in life was coaching Little League baseball.

Oregon loved Rex as well.

Sixty years to the day after the Yamamoto Mission, Governor Ted Kulongoski proclaimed April 18 as Rex T. Barber Day, so all Oregonians could honor one of their sons who came home from war and found peace. The barn Rex jumped from in 1928 is gone now, but several of the trees still stand around the spot, reaching skyward just as the boy did so many years ago. His house is there, though, and past it across the fields one can see the dark hills of Black Butte rising above the Crooked River Gorge. Here, close to the spot where he crossed as a boy, stands the Rex T. Barber Veterans Memorial Bridge, which replaced the old High Bridge he used as a child.*

His own son Rex Jr. is also a successful businessman and farmer who loves the land as his dad did before him. He raised his own boy, Rex Barber III, on the principles learned from his father: honor your family, be loyal to your friends, and never forget the sacrifices so many made to bequeath us all a free country. As fulfilled in life as he was successful at war, Rex Barber passed away on July 26, 2001, at the age of eighty-one. He rests now in the quiet lawn of the Redmond Memorial Cemetery, bordered by junipers and sheltered beneath the wings of a pair of P-38 Lightnings carved into his headstone. Cool breezes float down off the buttes, and against the clear sky one often catches sight of a hawk wheeling slowly overhead. It is far indeed from the battlefields of China, the South Pacific, and a remote Bougainville jungle where he changed the course of the Pacific War and all our lives today.

In the end Japan was defeated by its own culture.

Technically and militarily also, to be sure, but prior

---

* Rex also a flew a P-80 Shooting Star through the gorge and under the bridge in 1946.

to World War II, those obstacles had been overcome during the Empire's startlingly rapid transition to modernity. Imperial Japan was ambitious, resolved, and convinced of its destiny. Its fighting men were spiritually motivated, extremely tough, and tenacious. Employed effectively, in conjunction with artillery, air, and naval support, there quite likely would have been no battle for Guadalcanal in the fall of 1942. Piecemeal tactics, arrogant underestimation of their opponents, tactical inflexibility, and failure to control the air gave the Americans a toehold, a toehold from which they would not be dislodged, and this changed everything.

Yamamoto's role in this was central. Though he well understood the risk Japan was running, he failed to mass his strength at the crucial time in August 1942 and smash the Allied landing in the Solomons. This was partially due to the figurative slap across the face at Coral Sea followed by the shock and loss of four fleet carriers at Midway, but also certainly to the endemic, crippling animosity between the Imperial Army and Navy. Once cannot successfully prosecute a war against outside forces while guarding one's back from domestic intrigue, treachery, and blatant self interest. Had Emperor Hirohito been a different type of leader, this might have been avoided, but he was not. Hideki Tojo, in fact, became the de facto ruler of Japan and as an Army officer his sympathies were clear. Yamamoto was the only figure with enough power, real and inherent, to balance Tojo's fanatical traditionalism, and once the admiral was killed, Japan's fate was truly sealed.

But it had to be done.

Ethical considerations have been raised in the decades since, but these may be safely shelved. Yamamoto was a serving officer, in uniform, and engaged in a combat zone so cries of assassination ring hollow. Duty, honor, and country were the cornerstones of his life, but as the war crimes trials at Nuremberg and the Tokyo War Crimes Tribunal proved, they cannot be used to legitimize barbarity. Yamamoto knew this, and surely prosecuting a war one knows is wrong is the greatest act of barbarity. In any event, combatant enemy officers are viable targets, and the admiral would not have hesitated to attempt the same thing had the situations been reversed. It is also well to remember that the United States was in a fight to the death, a fight she did not seek, or physically initiate, and the opportunity to deliver such a blow had to be exploited.

Brave men like Rex, John, and hundreds of thousands just like them were willing to fight the Japanese Empire to the death, if necessary. These men risked their futures and their very lives for this purpose, and in so doing won the war. Their actions and sacrifices gave us a birthright free from tyranny; it's America's most enduring legacy to mankind. These men also taught the world a lesson about the United States that should never be forgotten: underestimating America may be a fatal mistake, but to attack her will always bring terrible vengeance.

In the end we all follow death's road, but to some extent how we arrive there is within our control, and this was true for Isoroku Yamamoto. How much of the world would have lived past December 1941 had he chosen a different road for himself? He was certainly a product of his upbringing, history, and training, but unlike many in Japan, Yamamoto *did* know better, and surely supporting a war one knows to be unjust is the greatest barbarity of all. In the end, how many lives on both sides were ultimately saved after 1943 because the admiral was forced down death's road on that clear April morning by Rex Barber?

The roar of engines has faded and the sky is quiet now above the Pacific. Waves cascade over beaches that were once stained with blood, and the jungles are silent. The sea has swallowed the wreckage of ships, planes, and the bodies of men, but it is quiet as well. Rex Barber and John Mitchell are also at peace, in company with the vanished millions who fought and died during the Second World War. It was a terrible conflict, to be sure, but also an enduring monument to humanity's plunging depths and soaring heights: and to the worst and best of men.

Acknowledgments

During any writing project I am always pleasantly surprised by the experts I meet during the research process who have accumulated more in-depth knowledge of their particular subjects than I could amass in a lifetime. Such expertise is a gift for a writer, and tremendously appreciated when given enthusiastically, and with a degree of professionalism that saves me from committing embarrassing errors in detail or omission.

My profound thanks go to Rex T. Barber Jr., who provided his late father's papers, maps, and photographs, and who willingly shared with me a long Oregon weekend revealing his dad's birthplace, childhood haunts, and everything else that made Rex Barber into the man he was. I owe an immeasurable debt to Phil Heathcock of the National Museum of World War II Aviation for arranging use of *White 33*, the facilities' fully flyable P-38F Lightning, and to the Erickson Museum of Madras, Oregon, for access to its flyable P-38L *Tangerine*. The irrepressible Stuart "Boot" Gordon, oldest living P-38 combat pilot, was absolutely vital in providing firsthand experience, sights and smells, and dozens of other details only a pilot would notice to ensure the cockpit recreations were historically accurate.

I wish to thank and recognize Dr. Daniel Haulman, Chief, Organizational Histories for the Air Force Historical Research Agency (AFHRA); Dr. Bill Wolf, author of the definitive work *13th Fighter Command in World War II*; Dr. John Terino, Chair, Department of Airpower, Maxwell Air Force Base; Dr. Frank Olynyk, AFHRA; Mr. Tony Wheeler, founder of Lonely Planet, aviation enthusiast, and explorer who related to me his experiences at the Yamamoto crash site; Colonel David Haulman for the introduction to his brother; Mr. Steve Blake, historian for the P-38 National Association; Justin Taylan, historian for Pacific Wrecks; Patrezia Nava, Curator of Aviation Archives, Eugene McDermott Library, University of Texas, for access to the papers of Carroll V. Glines; Chris McDougal, archivist for the National Museum of the Pacific War, Fredericksburg,

Texas, for allowing me to pore through the Nimitz Foundation's original Yamamoto Mission materials; and my old friend Guy Aceto for his inestimable assistance with rare and unusual photographs.

As always, I thank Peter Hubbard, Nick Amphlett, and the professionals at HarperCollins for their expertise in turning another rough idea of mine into a published work. I must also express my appreciation to Dr. Don Pease, Dr. Barbara Kreiger, and Professor Saul Lelchuk for their close reading of the preliminary manuscript and invaluable suggestions. Finally, no author would truly be successful without the ongoing forbearance of a patient, tolerant family, and this always merits acknowledgment.

Bibliography

Abrams, Richard. *F4U Corsair at War*. London: Ian Allen, 1977.

Adams, Michael C. C. *The Best War Ever: America and World War II*. Baltimore: Johns Hopkins University Press, 1994.

Agawa, Hiroyuki. *The Reluctant Admiral*. Tokyo: Kodansha International, 1979.

Allen, Frederick Lewis. *Only Yesterday: An Informal History of the 1920s*. New York: Harper & Brothers, 1931.

American Machinist. July 6, 1944: 16–17.

Ames, Roger J. "Yamamoto Mission." Letter to George T. Chandler, September 8, 1988.

Argyle, Christopher. *Chronology of World War II*. London: Marshall-Cavendish, 1980.

Army Battle Casualties and Nonbattle Deaths in World War II—Final Report. Washington, DC: Department of the Army, GPO, 1953.

Asprey, Robert B., and General Alexander A. Vandegrift. *Once a Marine: The Memoirs of General A. A. Vandegrift*. New York: Norton, 1964.

Astor, Gerald. *Wings of Gold: The U.S. Naval Air Campaign in World War II.* New York: Random House, 2005.

Aviation History Online Museum. http://www.aviation-history.com (accessed February–July 2019).

Barber, Colonel Rex T., interview by George Chandler. *Operation Vengeance* (September 12–13, 1987).

Barber, Colonel Rex T. "Letter to Carroll V. Glines." Carroll V. Glines, January 5, 1989.

Barber, Rex, Jr. Interview by Dan Hampton. *Life and Times of Colonel Rex Barber* (February 1–3, 2019).

———. Interview by Dan Hampton. *Life of Colonel Rex T. Barber* (November 18–22, 2018).

———. Interview by Dan Hampton. *Rex Barber's Childhood and Background* (December 20, 2018).

———. Interview by Dan Hampton. *Rex Barber's Family* (December 7, 2018).

———. Interview by Dan Hampton. *Wartime Experience of Colonel Rex T. Barber* (February 1–3, 2019).

Barber, Rex, Jr., and Rex Barber III. Interview by Dan

Hampton. *Rex Barber's Formative Years in Oregon* (January 16–17, 2019).

Barber, S. B. *Naval Aviation Combat Statistics: World War II, OPNAV-P-23V No. A129.* Washington, DC: Air Branch, Office of Naval Intelligence, 1946.

Baritz, Loren. *The Culture of the Twenties.* Indianapolis: Bobbs-Merrill, 1970.

Blom, Philipp. *Fracture: Life & Culture in the West, 1918–1938.* New York: Perseus, 2015.

Bodie, Warren M. *The Lockheed P-38 Lightning.* Hayesville, NC: Widewing, 1991.

Boyne, Walter, and Philip Handleman. *Brassey's Air Combat Reader.* London: Batsford Brassey, 1999.

Brand, Max. *Fighter Squadron at Guadalcanal.* Annapolis, MD: Naval Institute Press, 1996.

Bridman, Leonard, ed. *Jane's Fighting Aircraft of World War II.* London: Studio, 1946.

Bryson, Bill. *One Summer: America 1927.* New York: Anchor Books, 2014.

Bulwer-Lytton, Victor. "Appeal by the Chinese Government." *Report of the Commission of Enquiry. C.663.M.320. 1932. VII.* Geneva: League of Nations, October 1, 1932.

Burkman, Thomas W. *Japan and the League of Nations: Empire and World Order, 1914–1938.* Honolulu: University of Hawaii Press, 2007.

Burns, Eric. *1920: The Year That Made the Decade Roar.* New York: Pegasus Books, 2015.

Caidin, Martin. *Fork-Tailed Devil: The P38.* New York: ibooks, 1971.

Canning, Lieutenant Colonel Douglas. Interview by Bill Cox of the National Museum of the Pacfic War, October 4, 2001.

"Carriers: Airpower at Sea." http://www.sandcastlevi.com/sea/carriers (accessed May 15, 2013).

Cate, Wesley F., and James L. Craven. *The Army Air Forces in World War II,* Vol. 2. Chicago: University of Chicago Press, 1949.

Chandler, George T. "Analysis of Possibility of Lanphier Attacking the Yamamoto Bomber." Memorandum, June 5, 1989.

Channon, Ross. "Report on Yamamoto Crash Site." Arawa, Bougainville: Carroll V. Glines, December 1, 1985.

Chater, Eric. *The Chater Report.* Situation Report, Lae, Papua New Guinea: Guinea Airways Limited, 1937.

Claringbould, Michael John. *P-39/P-400 Airacobra vs A6M2/3 Zero-Sen.* Oxford: Osprey, 2018.

Clemens, Martin. *Alone on Guadalcanal.* Annapolis, MD: Naval Institute Press, 1998.

Commander, Air Solomons. "Pop Goes the Weasel." *Message No. 180229.* U.S. Navy, April 18, 1943.

Conn, Dr. Stetson. *Highlights of Mobilization, World War II, 1938–1942.* Washingon, DC: Department of the Army, 1959.

Costello, John. *The Pacific War: 1941–1945.* New York: HarperCollins, 1981.

Craven, W. F., and J. L. Cate. *The Army Air Forces in World War II. Volume Six: Men and Planes.* Washington, DC: Office of Air Force History, 1983.

Crocker, Mel. *Black Cats and Dumbos.* Crocker Media Expressions; 2 edition (August 1, 2002).

Darby, Dr. Charles. *Pacific Wrecks.* Victoria, Australia: Kookaburra Technical Publications, 1979.

———. "Transcript Docket: 91–02347." Air Force Board for Correction of Military Records. Washington, DC: USAF, October 17–18, 1991.

Davis, Burke. *Get Yamamoto.* New York: Random House, 1969.

Davis, Donald A. *Lightning Strike.* New York: St. Martin's Griffin, 2005.

Doolittle, James H., and Carroll V. Glines. *I Could Never Be So Lucky Again.* New York: Bantam Books, 2001.

Dunn, Susan. *A Blueprint for War: FDR and the Hundred Days That Mobilized America.* New Haven, CT: Yale University Press, 2018.

Everett, Susan. *The Two World Wars,* Vol. I. Bison Books, 1980.

Farago, Ladislas. *The Broken Seal.* New York: Random House, 1967.

Feldt, Eric A. *The Coastwatchers; Operation Ferdinand and the Fight for the South Pacific.* Oxford: Oxford University Press, 1946.

Fleming, Nicholas. *August 1939: The Last Days of Peace.* Pasadena, CA: Davies, 1979.

Frank Gibney, ed. *Senso: The Japanese Remember the Pacific War.* Armonk, NY: M. E. Sharpe, 1995.

Frank, Richard B. *Guadalcanal: The Definitive Account of the Landmark Battle.* New York: Random House, 1990.

Glines, Carroll V. *Attack on Yamamoto.* Atglen, PA: Schiffer, 1993.

Gordon, Stuart "Boot." Interview by Dan Hampton. *Flying the P-38 in World War II* (August 25, 2019).

———. Interview by Dan Hampton. *P-38 Operations in the South Pacific* (May 16, 2019).

———. Interview by Dan Hampton. *P-38 Systems and Procedures* (January 28, 2019).

Groom, Winston. *1942: The Year That Tried Men's Souls.* New York: Grove Press, 2005.

Grossnick, Roy A. *Dictionary of American Naval Aviation Squadrons,* Vol. 2. Washington, DC: Naval Historical Center, Department of the Navy, 1999.

Grossnick, Roy, and William J. Armstrong. *United States*

Naval Aviation, 1910–1995. Annapolis, MD: Naval Historical Center, 1997.

Gunston, Bill. *The World Encyclopaedia of Aero Engines.* Sparkford, England: Patrick Stephens, 1995.

Halsey Admiral William F., III and Lieutenant Commander J. Bryan. *Admiral Halsey's Story.* New York: McGraw-Hill, 1947.

Hampton, Dan. *Lords of the Sky.* New York: Harper-Collins, 2014.

Harrison, Mark. "Resource Mobilization for World War II: The USA, UK, USSR, and Germany, 1938–1945." *Economic History Review* 41, no. 2 (1988).

Harvey, Henry Finder, ed. *The 1940s: The Story of a Decade.* New York: Modern Library, 2014.

Hata, I., Y. Izawa, and C. Shores. *Japanese Army Fighter Aces.* London: Grub Street, 2002.

Hata, Ikuhiko, and Izawa Yasuho. *Japanese Naval Aces and Fighter Units in World War II.* Annapolis, MD: Naval Institute Press, 1975.

Hata, Ikuhiko, Yashuho Izawa, and Christopher Shores. *Japanese Army Fighter Aces, 1931–1945.* Mechanicsburg, PA: Stackpole Books, 2012.

Herman, Arthur. *Freedom's Forge: How American Business Produced Victory in World War II.* New York: Random House, 2013.

Hoffman, Jon T. *Once a Legend: "Red Mike" Edson*

of the Marine Raiders. Novato, CA: Presidio Press, 1994.

Holland, James. *The Allies Strike Back 1941–1943: The War in the West*. New York: Grove Atlantic, 2017.

———. *The Allies Strike Back: 1941–1943*. New York: Atlantic Monthly Press, 2017.

———. *The Rise of Germany 1939–1941*. London: Bantam, 2015.

Hornfischer, James D. *Neptune's Inferno*. New York: Bantam Books, 2011.

Hoyt, Edwin P. *Yamamoto: The Man Who Planned the Attack on Pearl Harbor*. Guilford, CT: Lyons Press, 2001.

Hutcheson, Edward C. "From a note left at the Nimitiz Museum reception desk." Fredericksburg, TX: Glines, note 4, p. 217, October 6, 1979.

Ienaga, Saburo. *The Pacific War, 1931–1945: A Critical Perspective on Japan's Role in World War II*. New York: Random House, 1978.

Jackson, Robert. *Fighter Pilots of World War II*. New York: Barnes & Noble, 1976.

"JN Message 006430." Japanese Navy. Honolulu: Hawaii, April 13, 1943.

Keegan, John. *The Second World War*. New York: Penguin, 1989.

Kennedy, David M. *World War II Companion*. New York: Simon & Schuster, 2007.

King, Dan. *The Last Zero Fighter*. Irvine, CA: Pacific Press, 2012.

Klingaman, William K. *The Darkest Year*. New York: St. Martin's Press, 2019.

Kyvig, David E. *Daily Life in the United States, 1920–1940*. Chicago: Ivan R. Dee, 2004.

Layton, Edwin T., Roger Pineau, and John Costello. *And I Was There: Pearl Harbor and Midway—Breaking the Secrets*. New York: William Morrow, 1985.

Leckie, Robert. *Challenge for the Pacific*. New York: Bantam Books, 1965.

———. *Helmet for My Pillow*. New York: Random House, 1957.

Liverpool, Lord Russell of. *The Knights of Bushido: A History of Japanese War Crimes During World War II*. New York: Skyhorse, 2008.

Lundstrom, John B. *The First Team and the Guadalcanal Campaign: Naval Fighter Combat from August to November 1942*. Annapolis, MD: Naval Institute Press, 2005.

Maurer, M. *Air Force Combat Units of World War II*. Washington, DC: Office of Air Force History, 1983.

Meek, Lieutenant Colonel H. B. "Marines Had Radar Too." *Marine Corps Gazette*, 1945.

Merriam, Ray, ed. *Fighter Combat Tactics in the Southwest Pacific Area*. Bennington, VT: Merriam Press, 1988.

Merrilat, Herbert Christian. *Guadalcanal Remembered*. New York: Dodd, Mead, 1982.

———. *The Island: A History of the First Marine Division on Guadalcanal, August 7–December 9, 1942*. Boston: Houghton Mifflin, 1944.

Military Analysis Division. *Air Campaigns of the Pacific War*. United States Strategic Bombing Survey. Washington, DC: U.S. Government Printing Office, 1947.

Miller, Thomas G. *The Cactus Air Force: The Story of the Handful of Fliers Who Saved Guadalcanal*. New York: Harper & Row, 1969.

Minohara, Toshihiro, and Matsato Kimura. *Tumultuous Decade: Empire, Society, and Diplomacy in 1930s Japan*. Toronto: University of Toronto Press, 2013.

Mitchell, Colonel John. Interview by George Chandler. *Operation Vengeance* (September 12–13, 1988).

———. Interview by Carroll V. Glines. *Yamamoto Mission Interview* (October 16, 1988).

Morison, Samuel Eliot. *Coral Sea, Midway and Submarine Action (History of United States Naval Opera-*

tions in World War II, vol. 4). Boston: Little, Brown, 1960.

———. *The Rising Sun in the Pacific (History of United States Naval Operations in World War II, vol. 3).* Boston: Little, Brown, 1959.

———. *The Struggle for Guadalcanal (History of United States Naval Operations in World War II, vol. 5).* Boston: Little, Brown, 1959.

Naval Analysis Division. *The Campaigns of the Pacific War.* United States Strategic Bombing Survey (Pacific). Washington, DC: U.S. Government Printing Office, 1946.

Naval History and Heritage Command. "Logistics and Support Activities, 1950–53." http://www.history. navy.mil (accessed August 2013).

———. "Telegram 131755." April 1943.

———. "Yamamoto Itinerary." IJN, April 1943.

Nelson, Craig. *The First Heroes: The Extraordinary Story of the Doolittle Raid—America's First World War II Victory.* London: Penguin Press, 2002.

Newcomb, Richard F. *Savo: The Incredible Naval Debacle off Guadalcanal.* New York: Holt, Rinehart & Winston, 1961.

Newton, Wesley P. Jr., and Calvin F. Senning. *USAF Credits for the Destruction of Enemy Aircraft, World*

War II. Study, Maxwell Air Force Base: Air Force Historical Research Agency, 1985.

New York Times. Archives. http://query.nytimes.com (accessed January–May 2019).

Nijboer, Donald. *P-38 Lightning vs. Ki-61 Tony*. Oxford: Osprey, 2010.

Nimitz, Chester, and E. B. Potter. *Sea Power*. New York: Prentice Hall, 1960.

Okrent, Daniel. *Last Call: The Rise and Fall of Prohibition*. New York: Scribner, 2010.

Okumiya, Masatake, Jiro Horikoshi, and Martin Caidin. *Zero: The Story of Japan's Air War in the Pacific—As Seen by the Enemy*. New York: J. Boylston, 1956.

O'Neill, Robert, ed. *The Pacific War: From Pearl Harbor to Okinawa*. Oxford: Osprey, 2015.

Pacific Wrecks. January 30, 2019. https://www.pacific wrecks.com/airfields/png/sulphur/index.html (accessed July 20, 2019).

Parshall, J., and A. Tully. *Shattered Sword: The Untold Story of the Battle of Midway*. Dulles, VA: Potomac Books, 2005.

Paterson, Michael. *Voices of the Code Breakers*. Barnsley, UK: Greenhill Books, 2018.

Phillips, Cabell. *The 1940s: Decade of Triumph and Turmoil*. New York: Macmillan, 1975.

"Pilot Training Manual for the P-38." *AAF Manual*

51–127–1. Washington, DC: Headquarters, Army Air Forces, August 1, 1945.

Pisano, Dominic A. *To Fill the Sky with Pilots; The Civilian Pilot Training Program, 1939–1946.* Washington, DC: Smithsonian Institution Press, 2001.

Postan, M. M. *History of the Second World War—British War Production.* London: H. M. Stationery's Office, 1952.

Potter, John Deane. *Yamamoto: The True Account of How He Plotted Pearl Harbor.* New York: Viking Press, 1967.

Prados, John. *Combined Fleet Decoded.* New York: Random House, 1995.

Rabaul Historical Society. 2016. https://www.avi.org.au /inspiring-partners/rabaul-historical-society/ (accessed August 15, 2019).

Radio Transmitter No. 13C and 13CB Supplement. Supplemental, Warren, NJ: Western Electric, 1936.

Rare and Early Newspapers. http://www.rarenewspapers .com (accessed December-March 2019).

Rearden, Jim. "Koga's Zero." *Invention & Technology,* Fall 1997: 56–63.

Reischauer, Edwin O. *Japan: Past and Present.* New York: Knopf, 1964.

Rottman, G. L. *US Marine Corps Pacific Theater of Operations.* London: Osprey, 2004.

Rottman, Gordon L. *U.S. Marine versus Japanese Infantryman.* Oxford: Osprey, 2014.

Sakai, Saburo. *Samurai.* New York: E. P. Dutton, 1957.

Sakaida, H. *Aces of the Rising Sun, 1937–1945.* London: Osprey, 2002.

Salecker, Gene E. "Cultural Clash in New Caledonia." Warfare History Network, warfarehistorynetwork. com/2019/01/21/cultural-clash-in-new-caledonia.

Schlesinger, Arthur M. *The Coming of the New Deal: 1933–1935.* New York: Houghton Mifflin, 1958.

"Selected Equipment Loss Statistics World War II (1937–1945)." http://www.taphilo.com/history/WWII/Loss-Figures-WWII (accessed May 30, 2013).

Sherrod, Robert. *History of Marine Corps Aviation in World War II.* Washington, DC: Combat Forces Press, 1952.

Sherwood, Robert E. *Roosevelt and Hopkins: An Intimate History.* New York: Grosset & Dunlap, 1950.

Short, Walter C. *Pearl Harbor Attack, Part 39.* Military After Action Report. Washington: USAAF, 1942.

Sickels, Robert. *The 1940s.* Westport, CT: Greenwood Press, 2004.

Stanaway, John. *P-38 Lightning Aces 1942–43.* Oxford: Osprey, 2014.

Stille, Mark. *USN Battleship vs IJN Battleship.* Oxford: Osprey, 2017.

————. *USN Carriers vs IJN Carriers: The Pacific 1942.* New York: Osprey, 2007.

Stillwell, Paul, ed. *Air Raid, Pearl Harbor! Recollections of a Day of Infamy.* Annapolis, MD: Naval Institute Press, 1981.

Sullivan, Mark. *Our Times, the Twenties.* New York: Scribner's, 1935.

Swanborough, Gordon, and Peter M. Bowers. *United States Navy Aircraft Since 1911.* Annapolis, MD: Naval Institute Press, 1990.

Tassava, Christopher J. *The American Economy during World War II.* [N.p.]: Backend, 2010.

Taylor, Theodore. *The Magnificent Mitscher.* Annapolis, MD: Naval Institute Press, 1991.

Toll, Ian W. *The Conquering Tide: War in the Pacific Islands, 1942–1945.* New York: Norton, 2015.

————. *Pacific Crucible: War in the Pacific, 1941–1942.* New York: Norton, 2012.

Tolland, John. *The Rising Sun: The Decline and Fall of the Japanese Empire, 1936–1945.* New York: Random House, 1970.

Tregaskis, Richard. *Guadalcanal Diary.* New York: Modern Library, 2000.

United States Census Bureau. http://www.census.gov (accessed November–May 2019).

USAAF Casualties in European, North African and Medi-

terranean *Theaters of Operations, 1942–1946.* Army Battle Casualties in World War II—Final Report. Washington, DC: Department of the Army, GPO, 1953.

USAAF. "Circular X-608." *USAAC Requirements Proposal.* Washington, DC: Headquarters, USAAC, February 1937.

U.S. Army Air Forces Statistical Digest. Washington, DC: Office of Statistical Control, 1945.

———. "K-14 Gyroscopic Gunsight." *Pilot Training Manual for the Thunderbolt P-47N.* Headquarters, Army Air Forces, September 1945.

———. "Pilot's Flight Operating Instructions for Army Models P-38D through P-38G Series." *T.O. No. 01–75F-1.* Washington, DC: USAAF, October 1, 1942.

USAF. "DD-214." *Rex Theodore Barber.* USAF, March 31, 1961.

———. "Form 11 for Colonel Rex Theodore Barber." *Officer Military Record.* USAF, March 31, 1961.

Velocci, Anthony L., Jr. "Naval Aviation: 100 Years Strong." *Aviation Week and Space Technology,* April 4, 2011: 56–80.

Walton, Francis. *The Miracle of World War II: How American Industry Made Victory Possible.* New York: Macmillan, 1956.

Watkins, T. H. *The Great Depression: America in the 1930s.* New York: Back Bay Books, 1993.

Wheelan, Joseph. *Midnight in the Pacific.* Boston: Da Capo Press, 2017.

Wible, John T. *The Yamamoto Mission: Sunday, April 18, 1943.* Fredericksburg, VA: Admiral Nimitz Foundation, 1988.

Wiener, Willard. *Two Hundred Thousand Flyers: The Story of the Civilian-AAF Pilot Training Program.* Washington, DC: Infantry Journal, 1945.

Wink, Jay. *1944: FDR and The Year That Changed History.* New York: Simon & Schuster, 2015.

Wolf, William. *13th Fighter Command in World War II: Air Combat over Guadalcanal and the Solomons.* Atglen, PA: Schiffer Military History, 2006.

"World Carrier Lists." http://www.hazegray.org/navhist /carriers/ (accessed June 5, 2013).

Wyant, William K. *Sandy Patch: A Biography of Lt. Gen. Alexander M. Patch.* New York: Praeger, 1991.

Yanagiya, Kenji, interview by the National Museum for the Pacfic War. *Interview with Kenji Yanagiya* (April 15, 1988).

Young, Edward M. *F6F Hellcat vs A6M Zero-Sen.* Oxford: Osprey, 2014.

Zimmerman, Major John L. *The Guadalcanal Campaign.* Washington, DC: Historical Branch, U.S. Marine Corps, 1949.

Notes

Prologue

3 Glancing around at the familiar switches: Gordon, 2019.

4 Dropping his right hand down: Gordon, 2019.

5 It was, Barber knew, a chance: Barber interview.

5 Nodding, Barber flipped: Gordon, 2019.

6 Rex reached to the floor: P-38G Flight Manual, 1 Oct 42 Flight Operation Instruction Chart.

7 With both engines idling normally: Gordon, 2019.

7 Quickly turning the volume down: Gordon, 2019.

8 RES position: P-38G Flight Manual, 1 Oct 42 Flight Operation Instruction Chart.

9 Finally, he flipped the gunsight on: Gordon, 2019.

15 until the white RPM needle reached 2,300: P-38G Flight Manual, 1 Oct 42 Flight Operation Instruction Chart.

Chapter One: Cauldron

28 The French also taught the Japanese: Evans and Peatie, 56–58.

29 The boy could not afford textbooks: Potter, 19.

30 Male children also took part: Potter, 20.

31 Women, tobacco, and alcohol were banned: Potter, 24.

32 "one of *Nisshin*'s own guns burst": Agawa, 2.

39 hitchhiked southwest across America: Potter, 32.

41 "Do not speak Japanese": Potter, 35.

43 the "dark valley" by historian Ian Toll: Toll, 117.

44 Lord Lytton wrote in 1932: Burkman, 165.

45 "Nobody could miss": Burkman, 194.

46 "There is no possibility of compromise": Potter, 38–39.

47 "To die for Emperor and Nation": Hoyt, 101.

49 The navy remained committed: Potter, 48.

55 There was tremendous domestic political pressure: Toll, 118.

55 The admiral, and other ranking naval officers, believed: Potter, 49.

55 a consummate gambler with a fearless nature: Agawa, 24; Potter, 85.

55 "It was the only way to save his life": Potter, 51.

Chapter Two: The Twilight

75 Thoroughly enjoying life off the farm: Rex Barber Jr. interview, 2018.

76 With its flanks exposed, Lord Gort's British Expeditionary Force: Hampton, LOS, 184–94.

76 the July 19th Naval Expansion Act: Naval History Heritage Command.

77 That summer of 1940 also saw: Conn.

77 Rex's uncle Edgar had been a U.S. Army Air Service pilot: Rex Barber Jr. interview, 2018.

78 Of these, some 10 million were initially disqualified: Klingaman, 33.

79 Rex Barber left school on September 30, 1940: Rex Barber Jr .interview, 2018.

83 President Roosevelt openly stated: *AF Magazine*.

86 "to build another Randolph Field": Wiener, viii.

86 "There's going to be war": Wiener, 8.

87 All the ground school and in-flight instruction: Wiener, 11.

87 Rex was thrilled to be accepted: Barber interview, 2018.

88 When Rex Barber arrived, Rankin Field wasn't complete: Barber documents, 2018.

90 In addition to sixty hours of flight time: Barber documents, 2018.

92 Negotiating with the Dutch: Morison, RSIP, 62.

95 In 110 minutes, 18 ships were destroyed: Tolland, RS, 235.

96 "Yesterday, December 7th, 1941": *Life*, December 8, 1941.

Chapter Three: Down but Never Out

99 Rex Barber stuck to *Phoebe*'s left wing: Mitchell interview by George Chandler.

100 Mitch had briefed an automatic change: Mitchell interview by George Chandler.

102 Japan's drive across Asia and the Pacific: Morison, 46.

104 Rev. Frederick McGuire, a missionary: George Winston War History online.

105 Another clergyman, Father Wendelin Dunker: George Winston War History online.

113 "but I suggest sir, that if you have to take": Costello, 260.

113 "Okay . . . so long people": Costello, 261.

116 "They'll come in from the northwest": Costello, 278.

123 "Call it fate, luck or what you may": Costello, 295.

125 The Japanese pilots thought they had discovered: P&T, 295–300.

126 One blew the *Hammann* in half: P&T, 383.

126 After participating in killing the helpless men: Koga's Zero.

127 For a month, Koga's body: Parsons, 35.

128 The plane also rolled left: Rearden, 56–63.

Chapter Four: Shoestring

130 Born in northwest Mississippi: Davis, 19–21.

132 Eighty-two warships slid out of the storm front: Frank, 58–59.

133 A tenacious fighter with a superb brain, Turner: Horn-fischer, 5–53.

134 Separating at Savo, the eight transports: Costello, 320–25.

137 destroyed eight Nakajima A6M2 Zero float fighters: Frank, 60.

138 Nine minutes later Lieutenant Colonel Bill Maxwell: Frank, 61–63.

140 Eighteen Zeros were airborne by 0830: Sakai, 194.

142 "The Zeros should have been able to take": Sakai, 196–97.

142 "There was a terrific man behind that stick": Sakai, 198.

142 "The after part of my fuselage was like a sieve": Lundstrom.

143 "For the first time in all my years of combat": Sakai, 201.

144 Hours later, blinded in one eye: Sakai, 201–17.

145 the pilot and his plane: Wheelan, 14.

147 The fleeing Japanese had left: Wheelan, 21–22.

147 It had also begun to be built from both ends: Frank, 126–28.

147 a treasure trove of equipment and supplies: Wheelan, 20–21.

149 In a shameful display of arrogance: Costello, 320.

149 "He's [Fletcher] left us bare ass!": Leckie, 112.

150 This cut no ice: Wheelan, 28–30.

150 At fifty-five, he was a veteran: Osprey, 63.

154 "WARNING-WARNING-STRANGE SHIPS": Leckie, 115.

Chapter Five: The American Toe

158 Turning it counterclockwise ninety degrees: Gordon interview.

159 He repeated the procedure: Gordon interview.

160 "We have gained, I believe, a toehold": Sherwood, 622.

160 a stockpile of 12 million rounds: Wheelan, 44–45.

161 Her tiny flight deck was crammed: Wheelan, 72–73.

162 Twenty-six of Smith's thirty-one fighter pilots: Miller, 21–22.

162 Here the greenest pilots of VMF-223: Sherrod, 78.

162 "Halt!" Leckie hissed: Leckie, 123, 124.

163 "Airfield Guadalcanal ready for fighters": Sherrod, 77.

163 He wanted it named after a fighting man: Wheelan, 50.

164 The destroyers also brought belted ammunition: Sherrod, 78.

166 It was a wise precaution: Clemens, 198–200.

167 an enemy he considered "effeminate": Sherrod, 78.

168 Ichiki had been a revered instructor: Leckie, 132.

169 Supremely confident: Wheelan, 61–65.

171 "That's the most beautiful sight I've ever seen": Tregaskis, 111.

173 The sky glowed pink: Clemens, 209.

175 "Here one with a backbone visible from the front": Tregaskis, 211.

175 "swarms of flies; black, circling funnels": Leckie, 74.

175 "They kept us awake, crunching": Leckie, 75.

177 "Back at the airport": Tregaskis, 131–32.

177 "Hold this course for twenty miles": D. Davis, 133.

178 "We have been defeated": Shirer, 190.

180 A radio message was sent on August 22: Ugaki, 187.

185 The landing was canceled and the remaining ships: Frank, 176–193.

186 Captain John Thompson brought in nine additional P-400s: D. Davis, 138.

187 Lieutenants Robert E. Chilson and K. W. Wyethes: *Wings at War*, ch 3.

187 Cactus Air Force pilot ran odds: Wheelan, 76–77.

187 There was also no liquor: Miller, 69–70.

188 could shoot a cow through the eye: Leckie, 124.

188 *They sent for the army to come to Tulagi*: Wyant, 50.

189 "Two Wildcats jumped on the commander's plane": Sakai, 200–202.

195 "By God, Vandegrift ": Vandy and Asprey, 147.

195 "[I]f the reinforcement requested is not made available": Frank, 214.

197 "We cannot expect to inflict heavy losses": Frank, 204.

199 a mobile SCR-270B Early Warning radar: Meek.

199 He flew back the same day for New Caledonia: Sherrod, 86.

200 "red ants and snails": Tregaskis, 179.

201 Somehow they all survived: Miller, 84.

201 Finally, later on September 11: Wheelan, 94.

203 The Raiders demolished a radio station: Frank, 221–22.

204 General Henry Harley "Hap" Arnold, bombastic chief: Wheelan, 106–7.

207 At 0530, the remnants of Major Tamura's 6th Company: Frank, 240.

208 "Then I pulled him off the wing": Buell, 126.

210 Lieutenant Brown made one more pass: Sherrod, 89.

211 Apparently, the Marines on the ridge: Frank, 240.

211 "You won't read about this in the newspapers": Spaulding.

Chapter Six: Borrowed Lives

215 This plan centered on the high-speed convoy: Frank, 287.

218 "Planes," Nimitz said: Hornfischer, 154.

219 The dive bombers immediately transmitted: Miller, 111.

222 The destroyer *Duncan*, which had: Frank, 310.

222 The destroyer *Farenholt* was also damaged: Horn, 187.

225 "apprehend and annihilate any powerful forces": Leckie, 271.

226 "Gouts of flame gushed": Leckie, 278.

228 Fighter One had been spared: Sherrod, 100; Frank, 319.

228 To emphasize the point: Frank, 322.

228 "I don't think we have a goddamn Navy": Horn, 199.

229 "I want you to pass the word along": Frank, 320–21.

229 "Jap troop transports": Crocker, *Black Cats*.

230 "Cram pulled the stick back": Leckie, 283–85.

231 "I pulled the Cat up": Crocker, *Black Cats*.

231 In any case, the *Sasago Maru*: Frank, 323.

231 "Goddamit Cram! I ought to court-martial you": Leckie, 285.

235 "We've got a war on our hands": Salecker.

235 The Americans, Montchamp whined: Salecker.

236 "A real tiger was taking over": Leckie, 293.

237 Nearly out of fuel: Brand, 102–4.

237 "Thus did the Navy suffer": Leckie, 286.

243 "Nothing moved but the crocodiles": Leckie, 304–5.

244 "You've got bayonets, haven't you?": Leckie, 315.

244 "bands of hollow-eyed men": Leckie, 317.

246 Fortunately, they were loaded: Sherrod, 143–44.

246 But all three enemy ships: Frank, 359.

247 "Already these bodies were": Leckie, 321.

247 "I couldn't have picked anything": Frank, 360.

247 The cruiser and her escorts: Sherrod, 108–9; Frank, 360–61.

248 The Zero broke in two: Sherrod, 108–9.

248 The sailors, having seen: Leckie, 321–22; Miller, 143–44.

249 Unconscious, but still alive: Frank, 359.

250 The cruiser was abandoned: Miller, 144–45.

250 One battalion of Marines: Frank, 361.

251 Total U.S. deaths for the past five days: 164th Inf Rpt Action Against Enemy, 2; 1st Mar Div Rpt, V, Int Annex N, 10; Frank, 364–65, XIV Corps, Enemy Operations, 17th Army History, 2, 7.

252 Cactus Air Force fighters claimed: Frank, 366–67.

252 Sixteen floatplanes were: Miller, 147.

254 In 1936, the U.S. Navy possessed: Bunker, 14.

254 the harbor was servicing sixty ships per day: Carter, 54.

254 This would be vital: Carter, 55.

255 Seabees, the Naval Construction Battalions: Kennedy, 330–31.

Chapter Seven: Magnificent Courage

261 Ten "Rufe" floatplane fighters: Air Force Historical Study, 85.

261 Marine Wildcats jumped the others: Miller, 178.

264 "Never before had the iron tongues": Leckie, 386.

268 Fortunately, none of the new P-38s: Sherrod, 116–17.

269 By late afternoon the Brisbane Maru: Miller, 194–97.

269 At the end of that long day: Miller, 200.

270 "[A]nd so were bunks and bulkheads glowing": Leckie, 392.

273 Washington suffered from no such limitation: Naval History and Heritage Command.

274 A shocked Kondo: Horn, 361–65.

275 "To them the men of Cactus lift their battered helmets": Halsey and Bryan, 130.

278 Of the 30,000-odd remnants: Frank, 502–20.

278 Carefully cleaned, each drum was filled: Frank, 502–20.

279 Twelve minutes after: Frank, 509.

283 Pedro del Valle, now a brigadier general: Merillat, 246.

283 Most had lost at least twenty pounds: Toll, 196.

284 Later in the war President Roosevelt: Toll, 196.

284 Sailors cried openly: Frank, 521–22.

284 Sick and walking invalids: Wheelan, 259.

285 One hit *Teruzuki*: Frank, 523–24.

286 Ironically, eight years earlier: Agawa, 24.

287 By December 1942, there were: Wheelan, 262.

Chapter Eight: At Any Cost

292 "Mitch, they want you over at the Opium Den": Glines, 28–29.

292 "Pete was a fighting fool": Taylor, xxiv.

295 "There were 15 to 20 people": Mitchell interview, 1988.

297 "There was big discussion": Mitchell interview, 1988.

298 "we would have been forty to fifty miles": Glines, 36.

299 "I want to get him in the air, sir": Mitchell interview, 1988.

299 On his way back to the operations tent: Mitchell interview, 1988.

308 From here, the JAAF initially: Hata, 37–39.

310 "I figured the odds at about a thousand to one": Mitchell interview, 1988.

314 "They were good pilots": Mitchell, 1987.

317 "We were to get that bomber": Glines, 38.

318 "The rest of us," he recalled: Glines, 37–38.

319 "I wanted to get after those Zeros": Mitchell interview, 1988.

319 "I had the utmost confidence": Mitchell interview, 1988.

319 His flight members: Mitchell interview, 1987.

320 Stooping, he tightened his boot laces: Gordon, 2018.

321 Pulling his flight helmet off its nail: Gordon, 2018.

322 Fighter pilots usually wore the seat-type parachute: Gordon, 2018.

Chapter Nine: Sharks and Dolphins

327 A bead of sweat: Gordon, 2019.

329 This appeared strange: D. Davis, 190.

331 "Seventeenth Army now requests": Toland, 477–86.

332 there were still only forty-one operational P-38s: Wolf, 97.

333 With Lieutenant Bill Daggitt as his wingman: Wolf, 97.

336 It would be different this time: Wolf, 140, picture.

338 Everything was purring: Gordon interview, 2019.

340 "sounded like an old Maytag washer": Frank, 197–98.

341 and two hours after midnight 4,935 soldiers: Frank, 588.

341 "What a sad and pitiable sight": Gibney, 132; Toll, 184–85.

341 "[T]heir beards, nails, and hair": Frank, 588.

343 From nearly 36,000 men: Frank, 595.

343 Most damaging, some 620 aircraft: Wolf, 111.

343 "Total and complete defeat of Japanese forces": Frank, 597.

345 "I suspect Hitler and Tojo": Adams, 491.

346 Ironically, the Soviet Union: *Fortune*, November 1943 and Walton, *Miracle of World War II*, 448–50.

347 "the foundation of all our hopes": Churchill, vol 5.

348 Worker strikes during the darkest days: Herman, 246.

349 U.S. Marines died on Cape Gloucester: *American Machinist*, 16–17.

349 In 1943 alone, such contemptible: Phillips, 169.

349 Nevertheless, U.S. war production: Harrison, 183–84.

349 U-boats were sinking 500,000 to 600,000 tons: Keegan, 118–19.

350 "I had lost all my optimism": Sakai, 242–43.

351 For him, the biggest difference: Caidin, 90.

354 If a Zero got behind you: Rearden, 62.

354 The P-38's top speed of 400 mph: Merriam, 52.

354 "Oh, man it was hot": Mitchell, 1987.

356 Like the back of Barber's map: Wolf, 140.

358 "I had wanted for a long time": Mitchell, 1987.

Chapter Ten: The Eight-Fingered Samurai

360 His hair had gone gray: Agawa, 337–38.

360 and it had been suggested by his Harvard classmate: Agawa, 337.

362 Eight destroyers carrying 958 soldiers: Morison, 54–56.

363 "Desperately needed supplies littered": Okumiya, 219.

364 altogether this gave Yamamoto 346 aircraft: Okumiya, 219.

364 "and our veteran air leaders hesitated": Okumiya, 220.

365 "I'll give you cover": Agawa, 328–29.

366 On April 1, 1943, the operation commenced: Wolf, 131–32.

367 "Yamamoto hoped": Okumiya, 220.

368 "I feel happy at the chance to do something": Agawa, 340–41.

368 ramp of the Sulphur Creek Seaplane Base: *Pacific Wrecks.*

369 the former German governor's cottage: Rabaul Historical Society.

370 "Give enough thought to your plans": Costello, 390.

371 "So we were too early, all the same": Agawa, 345.

372 American losses reported to Yamamoto: Okumiya, 221.

373 American losses were actually twenty-five planes: Toll, 203.

375 "Gentlemen do not read each other's mail": *Atlantic,* 2013.

375 Lasswell, who studied Japanese: Toll, 202–3.

376 "ON 18 APRIL CINC COMBINED FLEET": Transcipt of JN Message 006430, April 13, 1943; Glines, 213.

376 "There isn't anybody to replace you": Layton, 276.

378 The officer's tongue was ripped out: Russell, 235.

379 Japanese infantrymen bayoneted some: Russell, 96–98.

379 "Their bodies were badly mutilated": Russell, 98.

380 "I saw the girls fall one after the other": Russell, 102–4.

382 "We dug holes": Russell, 100–101.

382 "I glance at the prisoner": Russell, 79–81.

384 "To us, Admiral Yamamoto virtually was a god": Glines, 102.

384 "SOUTHEAST AREA FLEET/CONFIDENTIAL":
Transcript of Telegram 131755.

386 For security reasons, the pilots: Prados, 461.

388 Rear Admiral Rokuru Takada: Agawa, 349.

389 "six fighters is nothing like enough": Agawa, 346.

Chapter Eleven: Vengeance

394 "Youth and inexperience": Wolf, 124.

395 "I got too aggressive": Wolf, 125.

395 The pilots believed: *Pacific Wrecks*.

396 "One wing was salvageable": Wolf, 125.

399 Normal combat procedure: Gordon interview, 2019.

399 That left 276 gallons: Gordon interview, 2019.

400 If his math was correct: P-38G Flight Manual, 1 Oct 42
Flight Operation Instruction Chart.

403 A Zero got in a lucky burst: Wolf, 105.

404 Eyes darting around the cockpit: Gordon interview,
2019.

406 cockpit's smell of leather, hot metal, and urine: Gordon interview, 2019.

407 "Bogeys . . . ten o'clock": Canning interview, 36.

408 "Roger that . . . I have him": Mitchell interview by George
Chandler.

408 "Okay guys, skin 'em off!": Mitchell interview by George
Chandler.

408 "Okay Tom . . . he's your meat!": Mitchell interview by
George Chandler.

408 "Roger . . . I've got him": Mitchell interview by George Chandler.

410 Flight Petty Officer Kenji Yanagiya: Wible, 35.

411 Yanagiya and the rest of the escorts: Yanagiya, 12.

411 He was an experienced fighter pilot: Yanagiya, 2.

415 In the same split second: Barber sketch.

416 Hayashi, flying the second Betty: Agawa, 350.

416 Rex was directly off the first bomber's right wing: Barber drawing.

417 Dropping the nose down: Rex T. Barber interview by George Chandler.

417 "Enemy aircraft!": Ugaki Sensoruku/Agawa, 350.

417 *POM-POM-POM-POM*: Gordon interview, 2019.

418 at one hundred feet he squeezed his right: Rex T. Barber interview by George Chandler.

418 "Follow plane Number One!": Agawa, 351.

419 Bunting over and breathing hard: Rex T. Barber interview by George Chandler.

420 Nothing else was visible except: Agawa, 351.

420 The entire wild fight: Yanagiya interview.

423 Checking right about 30 degrees: Rex T. Barber interview by George Chandler.

425 Higher than the other Lightnings: Rex T. Barber interview by George Chandler.

425 one of Yamamoto's staff officers: Okumiya, 228.

425 The last thing Hayashi saw: Agawa, 351.

426 Rex reacted instantly: Rex T. Barber interview by George Chandler.

426 the Japanese fighter was aiming: Holmes interview; Glines, 74.

427 "Mission accomplished": Mitchell interview, October 16, 1988.

428 Rex also saw he could only get 30 inches: Rex T. Barber interview by George Chandler.

429 This would reduce the burn: P-38G Flight Manual, 1 Oct 42 Flight Operation Instruction Chart.

Chapter Twelve: Dominoes

431 "TWO RIKKO CARRYING": Glines, 108.

432 "THE NO. 1 LAND-BASED ATTACK PLANE": Agawa, 353.

433 Petty Officer Hayashi had regained consciousness: Agawa, 351; *Pacific Wrecks.*

433 "Signal to them!": Agawa, 353.

434 "A plane carrying top navy brass": Agawa, 357.

435 "I got Yamamoto!": Hutcheson, October 6, 1979.

436 "[H]e claimed victory": Young letter, September 11, 1988.

436 "All I can remember": Ames letter, September 8, 1988.

437 "Holmes, at the point I saw him": Rex T. Barber interview by George Chandler.

437 "He was coming up from the south": Rex T. Barber interview by George Chandler.

438 "I'll stay with you . . . no sweat": Glines, 79.

438 Besby Holmes dropped the Lightning in hard: Glines, 81.

439 The pilot, Lieutenant (j.g.) Harry Metke: Wolf, 147–48.

441 there were 52 hits: Glines, 81.

441 "POP GOES THE WEASEL": MSG 180229.

442 Read, who would eventually retire: Read, 166.

442 All morning Watanabe flew back and forth: Agawa, 356.

444 Following their noses through the vines: Agawa, 358.

444 "a burned out hulk": Hamasuna sketch.

445 He was a *Kaigun-taish* : Hamasuna; Glines, 105.

446 Admiral Kusaka prepared Report No. 2: Telegram 181941.

448 Yamamoto's official autopsy: Tabuchi, 1943.

448 The latter hole went upward: Agawa, 364.

449 the admiral's Adam's apple: Agawa, 366.

451 "He would talk about the mission": Barber interview, 1988.

451 "we have every reason [to] believe": Lodge, May 11, 1943.

451 "He just stared at us": Barber interview, 1988.

453 "How could they [the Americans]": Agawa, 369.

454 "I'd hoped to lead that scoundrel up": Halsey, 157.

454 "You ought to face a court-martial": Glines, 118.

455 "FIRST LIEUTENANT REX T. BARBER, USAAF": Citation dated April 20, 1943.

457 "I want to be President": Barber letter to Glines, January 5, 1989.

457 He also acknowledged his authorship: Glines, 114.

457 Lanphier's name appears first in the list: FIR 21, April 1943.

458 Dr. Frank Olynyk has never found: Wolf, 153; Olynyk letter, September 2019.

459 Dr. Daniel Haulman, the chief: Haulman letter, September 19, 2019.

460 Lieutenant Yasuo Shimizu was part of: Gibney/Pineau letter.

461 Yoshimi Hidaka, June 7, 1943: Wible, 46.

462 "As I caught my last glimpse": TGJ article; AFM 1985.

462 That same day, Imperial Headquarters: Agawa, 384.

Epilogue

466 This should have been enough: Barber letter, 1989.

467 coming down in a dive: Barber Jr. interview.

467 In forty seconds, with an *average* speed: Chandler letter, 1989.

468 It takes sixteen seconds: Chandler letter, 1989.

469 "down in the jungle was two minutes or less": Wolf, 157.

470 "I first saw one P-38": Wolf, 157.

472 spars would have *bent upward*: Wolf, 156.

473 No doubt Barber shot up the oil lines and oil pumps: Darby letter to AFA.

473 "[T]here are definite holes on the fuselage": Channon letter, December 15, 1985.

474 "[T]he right wing didn't separate in flight": Glines, 189–90.

474 "with his guns still going": Wolf, 153.

475 according to Hiroshi Hayashi, each weapon: Glines, 105–6.

475 In 1991, Dr. Darby traveled: Transcript of Proceedings, AFBCMR Docket: 91–02347.

475 Rex's initial burst was fired: Barber interview.

476 Rex simply nudged his nose a bit right: Barber interview.

477 Such death: Pineau letter.

480 "You sons-a-bitches who wanted outa here": Barber Jr. interview, 2019.

480 Claiming three "probables": Barber AF-11.

483 A B-29 Superfortress: Hampton, LOS, 367–70.

485 When America went to war again: Barber, AF 11.

HARPER
LARGE PRINT

We hope you enjoyed reading
our new, comfortable print size and found it
an experience you would like to repeat.

Well – you're in luck!

Harper Large Print offers the finest in
fiction and nonfiction books in this same larger
print size and paperback format. Light and easy to read,
Harper Large Print paperbacks are for the book lovers
who want to see what they are reading without strain.

For a full listing of titles and
new releases to come, please visit our website:
www.hc.com

HARPER LARGE PRINT

SEEING IS BELIEVING!